Tolkien Through Russian Eyes

Толкин Русскими Глазами

Mark T. Hooker

2003

Cormarë Series
No 5

Series Editors
Peter Buchs • Thomas Honegger • Andrew Moglestue

Edited by
Stella Hooker-Haase • Alla Khananashvili

Library of Congress Cataloging-in-Publication Data

Hooker, Mark T.
  Tolkien Through Russian Eyes / Mark T. Hooker
  Includes bibliographic references and index.
  ISBN 3-9521424-7-6
Subject headings:
Tolkien, J. R. R. (John Ronald Reuel), 1892-1973—Criticism and interpretation.
Tolkien, J. R. R. (John Ronald Reuel), 1892-1973—Translations into Russian.
Tolkien, J. R. R. (John Ronald Reuel), 1892-1973—Language.
Fantasy fiction, English—History and criticism.
Middle Earth (Imaginary place)
Translating and interpreting—Russia—History—Tolkien.
Literature, Comparative.
Literature—Translations.

All rights reserved. No portion of this book may be reproduced, by any process or technique, without the express written consent of the publisher.

First published in 2003.
Printed by LightningSource in the United Kingdom and the United States.

Acknowledgments

This book is, as its title seeks to indicate, an attempt, made by an American, to interpret the way that Tolkien's works have been received in Russia. I am, I hope, sufficiently aware of the pitfalls that await a writer who seeks to explain a foreign phenomenon. All of the topics that I have ventured to express an opinion on have had the benefit of criticism from many Russian, American and British readers, not the least of whom is the gentleman who so kindly consented to write the foreword for this book. Its errors are, of course, all my own. But I should indeed be ungrateful if I did not acknowledge the immense debt it owes, for what merit it may possess, to those readers and others who provided me with materials and answered my questions:

Natalya Grigor'eva and Vladimir Grushetskij, Aleksandr Gruzberg, his son Il'ya and his daughter Yuliya, Mariya and Valerij Kamenkovich, VAM, Maria Artamonova, Svetlana Likhacheva, Ol'ga Markova, Vladimir Popov, Tatyana Privalova (Mithrilian), Natalya Semenova, Evgeniya Smagina, Vladimir Sviridov, Dmitrij Vinokhodov, Jim Dunning and, of course, to David Doughan who, among other things, trusted me enough to lend me his only copy of the VAM *Hobbit*.

Thanks is most certainly also due to J.R.R. Tolkien himself for creating a tale so finely woven that it enchanted not only the English-speaking West, but the Russian-speaking East as well. His son Christopher similarly deserves a word of thanks for allowing me to quote his reaction to the article that became chapter 1 of this book.

Not to forget Rob Fieser, who gave me a copy of the Rakhmanova *Hobbit* for Chirstmas in 1977. This is all your fault.

Much appreciation is similarly requisite for Alla Khananashvili, whose enthusiasm, barrage of questions, insistence on 'show me,' attention to detail, and editing skills, added immeasurably to the end result of this project.

Thanks are likewise due to my wife Stella, without whose encouragement and support, not to mention fine multilingual editing skills, this project would never have seen the light of day.

:IMAGINATION:IS:GREATER:THAN:KNOWLEDGE:
:A:EINSTEIN:

Contents

Preface for the Russian Reader	7
Foreword	9
Author and Source Abbreviations	11
Russian Alphabet	13
1. A Short History of Tolkienism in Russia	15
Samizdat	17
The First Translation Boom	20
Perestroika	22
The Second Publishing Boom	24
The Adaptation of Imported Ideas	25
Tolkienism in Russia	30
Tolkianity	38
2. A Hobbit's Tale	49
Editions	53
The West is Dead. Long live God!	55
Map	69
Smaug	72
Gold	85
3. Giving up the Ring	103
Plan, Agreement and Promise	103
Bilbo's Joke	117
4. Hope Abandoned	123
5. Sam's Job: Frodo's Batman	145
6. The Temptation of Knowledge and Power	169
7. One Day in the Life of Frodo Drogovich: Stalin and Yezhov in the Shire	185
8. What's in a Name?	203
Baggins	203
Cotton	210

Crickhollow	213
Derndingle	215
Durin	218
Entmoot	219
Fallohide	224
Frogmorton	230
Gamgee	233
Goldberry	235
Hobbiton	236
Isengard	239
Lithe	241
Lune [Lhûne]	243
Michel Delving	245
Mirkwood	247
Mount Doom	251
Oliphaunt	253
Púkel-men	253
Radagast	256
Rivendell	258
Rohan	260
Sandyman	262
The Scarlet Book of Westmarch	264
Shadowfax	269
Shire	272
Town Hole	274
Treebeard	275
Variags	278
Wargs	281
And the Winner is …	284
Bibliography of Translations	291
The Lord of the Rings	291
The Hobbit	295
Hobbit Knock-offs	298
Index	299
About the Author	321
About Walking Tree Publishers	323

Preface for the Russian Reader

A number of Russians read drafts of this work while it was in progress. They made a large number of valuable suggestions and comments, but also a number of comments that made it clear that this book was not written for them. This book is the work of an English native speaker, who learned Russian as an adult. Its intended audience is not Russian native speakers, but rather English speakers who know little or no Russian. It belabors points that Russians may consider to be obvious, because these points will not be obvious to the book's intended audience. It makes short work of concepts that Russians find insufficiently elaborated upon, because to make more of them would seem like belaboring the obvious to the book's intended audience. Its explanations of morphology and grammar (be it Russian, Welsh or English) are not exhaustive, because that kind of explanation would be tedious for the intended reader. The book's point of view is that of someone on the outside looking in, writing for others on the outside.

The author belongs to the same cultural milieu as Tolkien. It is possible, that if Tolkien had himself known Russian, he would have reacted to the translations in a similar manner. Russian readers may, perhaps, find themselves in disagreement with a number of things said in this book, but they need to keep in mind that there is a large cultural gap between the English-speaking and Russian-speaking worlds, and that the author is on Tolkien's side of it. It is, therefore, not unexpected that the author's interpretation of the original texts and their translations will be from a different point of view than that of the Russian reader. If Russian readers keep that in mind, they may indeed find the book of interest.

In his evaluation of the translations, the author has tried to avoid questions of form as much as possible and to concentrate on questions of substance. This approach has raised some objections from native-Russian-speaking readers, who believe that a translation should first and foremost be literary and that accuracy should take a back seat to that. The author's decision to place substance above form is especially important in Tolkien's texts, where Tolkien's philosophical outlook can hang on the choice of but a single word. The author would have the translators follow the maxim by which doctors should work: "First do no harm."

Questions of the literary form of a text can be debated endlessly by native speakers without resolution. Discussions of the substance of a translation, on the other hand, are finite. Is a word or phrase present in both the source text and in the translation? Does the target text alter the meaning of the original? These are the questions that the author tried to answer in this volume. The author's evaluation of the translations is based primarily on their faithfulness to the original.

Whenever possible, the author points out well-crafted formulations and skillful resolutions of difficult translation problems, but to some the author's evaluation of the translations still seems very negative. That is, to a large extent, the result of the fact that a discussion of a perfect translation is uninteresting. If the translation is perfect, there is nothing to talk about. Nine perfect translations is an oxymoron. If they were all perfect, they would all be identical, and there would really only be one translation. There are, nonetheless, nine published translations of *LotR*. The author's discussion, therefore, focuses not so much on what the translators did well, as on what they did poorly, because that is a more interesting topic for discussion.

Another complaint from Russian readers who grew up in the post-Communist period is that they feel that the current volume places too much accent on the political aspects of the translations. Some members of the post-Communist generation are as vehemently apolitical as the Communists were atheistic. Soviet-era Russian readers, however, find the analysis accurate and insightful. The desire of the younger generation of Russian readers to ignore the political aspects of the translations does not mean that there is no political subtext to them. It just means that the pendulum has swung from the totally politicized atmosphere of the Soviet Union to the apolitical atmosphere of the market economy of Capitalism. A number of the translations are products of the Soviet period, and reflect the tenor of the time in which they were written.

The author's conclusion that Tolkien is still waiting on his Russian translator is not, as some have suggested, a complete dismissal of the existing Russian translations, but a warning that the published Russian translations are not perfect. There are nine of them and each is interesting in its own way, but there is still room for one more.

Foreword

Over the decades, Tolkien mania has notoriously given rise to some weird and wonderful phenomena, which older readers may recollect with greater or lesser degrees of nostalgia for their excesses. However, it turns out that the West has been relatively restrained in this field. For a truly manic brand of Tolkienism, you have to go to Russia. Russia is indeed another country. They do things differently there.

Explaining this is where Mark Hooker's book comes in. Quite apart from its obvious usefulness to specialists in Russian literature and the study of translation, it should have a definite appeal to general readers in helping them to understand certain Russian intellectual traditions, not least that of reading between the lines, even when there are no lines in the first place. Please, if you don't know Russian, don't be put off by the sight of chunks of Cyrillic - Mark Hooker carefully explains them all, and even translates them for you. What emerges is a remarkable insight into the Russian literay mind, in particular the tendency not only to adopt Western influences, but to Russify them, like Leskov's Russian craftsman Levsha putting Russian-style shoes on an English flea. And indeed, with honourable exceptions, Russians seem to know far better than the mere foreign authors what those authors actually meant. When they adopt tales of Oz, or Pinocchio, or Dr Dolittle, they adapt them to Russian ideas of what they should have been, if the Western authors had only had more insight and imagination.

The case of Tolkien, translation into Russian is perhaps the outstanding example of this tendency. Mark Hooker does an excellent job in explaining to the non-specialist the various idiosyncrasies of the many competing translations of Tolkien's fiction in Russian, with an examination of the literary / ideological / political / religious motives that have led translators to "adapt" Tolkien's texts, or even to attempt to convey as accurately as possible the author's intentions - and to be fair to the translators, it is no easy task to render works so imbued with Englishness in a language where, for example, there is no simple translation of the word "Lord", let alone "Shire" .

This book is especially for you if you are interested in attempts to narrow (or widen) cultural gaps — or indeed if you want to know what Saruman was doing in Moscow in 1936-1938. Or if you want to know who to contact about establishing a Tolkienian religion, or where the "Darned Valley" is. Or if you want to know about the Silver Crown of the Lords of Westernesse, which has the property of turning to ashes anybody unprepared to wear it (now why did Tolkien never think of that?). More seriously, looking at Tolkien through Russian eyes really will give you a different perspective on the world. And though you may sometimes be bemused, or even exasperated, you certainly won't be bored.

David Doughan
October 2003

Author and Source Abbreviations

AH	- *The Annotated Hobbit*, Boston: Houghton Mifflin, 1988.
A.xxx	- The Appendices. New York: Ballantine Books, 1965. In combination with a translator abbreviation, also identifies volume III of III, regardless of the translated title.
B H.xxx	- Bobyr' *The Hobbit* (1994)
B.xxx	- Bobyr' Повесть о кольце [Novella of the Ring] (1991)
BT:	- back translation
Dal'	- Даль, Владимир. Толковый словарь живого велико-русского языка, М/СПб: М.О. Вольфа, 1880. The classic four-volume defining dictionary of nineteenth-century Russian.
D&D	- *The Hobbit*, Forestville, CA: Eclipse Books, 1990. Dixon and Deming comic book condensation of *The Hobbit* with the David Wenzel illustrations.
F.xxx	- *The Fellowship of the Ring*. New York: Ballantine Books, 1965. In combination with a translator abbreviation, also identifies volume I of III, regardless of the translated title.
G	- Gruzberg. The print edition, edited by Zastyrets.
G&G	- Grigor'eva and Grushetskij. (1992)
G&G$_s$	- Grigor'eva and Grushetskij, the samizdat edition
G&G$_p$	- Grigor'eva and Grushetskij, the print edition
H	- *The Hobbit*. New York: Ballantine Books, 1965. In combination with a translator abbreviation, also identifies the translation, regardless of the translated title.
JRRT	- J.R.R. Tolkien.
K&K	- Kamenkovich and Karrik (1994)
Km	- Kamenkovich, *The Hobbit*. (1995)
Kr E	- Korolev, Толкин и его мир: Энциклопедия, М: ООО «Издательство АСТ»; СПб: Terra Fantastica, 2000.
Kr H	- Korolev, *The Hobbit*. (2000)
Ksk	- Kaminskaya, The translation of the D&D condensation of *The Hobbit*.
L.xxx	- J.R.R. Tolkien, *Letters*, Boston: Houghton Mifflin, 1981.
LotR	- *The Lord of the Rings*.
M	- Murav'ev without Kistyakovskij. Specifically volumes II and III of the "M&K" translation.

M:	- Moscow in the notes and Bibliography.
M&K	- Murav'ev and Kistyakovskij (1982, 1988, 1990, 1992)
OED	- *Oxford English Dictionary*
P.xxx	- Prologue. New York: Ballantine Books, 1965. In combination with a translator abbreviation, also identifies volume I of III, regardless of the translated title.
pl.	- plural
q.v.	- Latin: quod vide. See the reference given, in this book.
R H	- Rakhmanova, *The Hobbit.* (1976)
R.xxx	- *The Return of the King.* New York: Ballantine Books, 1965. In combination with a translator abbreviation, also identifies volume III of III, regardless of the translated title.
S	- *The Silmarillion.* Boston: Houghton Mifflin, 1977.
sg.	- singular
subtitles	- The Russian subtitles to the Peter Jackson movies.
T.xxx	- *The Two Towers.* New York: Ballantine Books, 1965. In combination with a translator abbreviation, also identifies volume II of III, regardless of the translated title.
TC	- *A Tolkien Compass* (Jared Lobdell ed.), New York: Ballantine Books, 1980.
T&L	- J.R.R. Tolkien. *Tree and Leaf*, London: Unwin Books, 1964.
U	- Umanskij
Ut	- Utilova, *The Hobbit.*
VAM	- Valeriya Aleksandrovna Matorina
V	- Volkovskij (2000)
Ya	- Yakhnin (2001)
БТСРЯ	- Большой толковый словарь русского языка, СПб: Норинт, 2000.
СЭС	- Советский энциклопедический словарь, М: «Советская энциклопедия», 1990.

Russian Alphabet

А а	Арагорн		Р р	Радагаст
A	Aragorn		R	Radagast
Б б	Бильбо Бэггинс		С с	Саруман
B	Bilbo Baggins		S	Saruman
В в	Валар		Т т	Толкин
V	Valar		T	Tolkien
Г г	Гандалв		У у	Урук-хай
G	Gandalf		U	Uruk-Hai
Д д	Денетор		Ф ф	Фродо Бэггинс
D	Denethor		F	Frodo Baggins
Е е	естарэ		Х х	Хоббит
E	yestarë		Kh	Hobbit
Ё ё	Хрущёв		Ц ц	царь
Yo	Khrushchyov		Ts	tsar
Ж ж	Анжелика Бэггинс	Ежов		Ч ч	Читинг
Zh	Angelica Baggins	Yezhov		Ch	Chithing
З з	Зирак-Зигиль		Ш ш	Шир
Z	Zirak-Zigil		Sh	Shire
И и	Исильдур		Щ щ	Хрущёв
I	Isildur		Shch	Khrushchyov
Й й	йавас		Ъ ъ	твёрдый знак
J	iavas			hard sign*
К к	Кхазад-Дум	фермер Коттон		Ы ы	Бэггинсы
K	Khazad-dûm	farmer Cotton		y	Baggins-y (plural)
Л л	Леголас		Ь ь	Дьюрин
L	Legolas			soft sign* Durin
М м	Мериадок (Мерри) Брендибак		Э э	Эльронд
M	Meriadoc (Merry) Brandybuck		Eh	Elrond
Н н	Нуменор		Ю ю	Юль
N	Númenor		Yu	Yule
О о	Оркрист		Я я	явиерэ
O	Orcrist		Ya	yáviérë
П п	Перегрин (Пиппин) Тук			
P	Peregrin (Pippin) Took			

* These letters are always silent. The hard sign is hardly ever used.

The Scarlet Book of Eastmarch

Chapter 1

A Short History of Tolkienism in Russia
:ᛏᛟᛚᚲᛁᛖᚾ:ᛏᚻᚱᛟᚢᚷᚻ:ᚱᚢᛋᛋᛁᚨᚾ:ᛖᛃᛖᛋ:

> The history and character of Mr. Bilbo Baggins became once again the chief topic of conversation. (F.44)

In a typescript underground there lived a Hobbit. Not in a spell-checked, crisp, laser-printed typescript fresh from the computer, but in a dog-eared, crumpled, fifth-carbon-copy typescript full of spelling mistakes, typed by hand on the back of some document that was no longer needed. It was a *samizdat* typescript, and that meant illicit, underground publishing in the Soviet Union.

After the publication of J.R.R. Tolkien's *The Lord of the Rings* (1954-55), translations followed quickly in Holland (1956-57) and Sweden (1959-61), where translated literature is widely accepted. The Polish translation (1961-63) was right on the heels of the Swedish one and ahead of the Danish (1968-70), German (1969-70), and French (1972-73) translations, but the publication of a state-sanctioned Russian translation was a long time in coming in the totalitarian Soviet Union.

The publication of the Russian translation of *The Lord of the Rings* (*LotR*) was essentially banned by the state-controlled publishing industry in the USSR until 1982, when an abridged edition of volume I—the one that is the least sensitive ideologically—was finally published. The unabridged edition of volume I by the same officially sanctioned translators did not come out for another six years. After it came out in 1988, it was followed by the translations of volumes II and III at two-year intervals in 1990 and 1992 in the wake of the Soviet collapse. Both Czechoslovakia and Bulgaria, whose ruling Communist Parties had tried to be ideologically more orthodox than Moscow, also waited until the collapse of Communism in Eastern Europe to publish Tolkien. The first published translation of *LotR* in those two countries came out in 1990-1991.

The censors found Tolkien's philosophy somewhat at odds with the official Communist Party line. The feeling was mutual. In a letter to his son Christopher, Tolkien wrote:

> My political opinions lean more and more to Anarchy (philosophically understood, meaning abolition of control not whiskered men with bombs) - or to 'unconstitutional' Monarchy. I would arrest anybody who uses the word State (in any sense other than the inanimate realm of England and its inhabitants, a thing that has neither power, rights nor mind); and after a chance of recantation, execute them if they remained obstinate! If we could get back to personal names, it would do a lot of good. Government is an abstract noun meaning the art and process of governing and it should be an offence to write it with a capital G or so as to refer to people. If people were in the habit of referring to 'King George's council, Winston and his gang', it would go a long way to clearing thought, and reducing the frightful landslide into Theyocracy. (L.63)

The last Russian Encyclopedic Dictionary (1991)[1] of the Communist era only has a terse article that characterizes *LotR* as containing "a pessimistic conception of the inexorable influence of evil on the course of historical development." That puts Tolkien directly at odds with the obligatory optimism of socialist realism, which was the only acceptable approach to literature in the Soviet Union.

The point of the Soviet dictionary article is in clear contrast with the one expressed in C.S. Lewis's article, "The Dethronement of Power."

> [T]he text itself teaches us that Sauron is eternal; the war of the Ring is only one of a thousand wars against him. Every time we shall be wise to fear his ultimate victory, after which there will be 'no more songs.' [...] Every time we win we shall know that our victory is impermanent. If we insist on asking for the moral of the story, that is its moral: a recall from facile optimism and wailing pessimism alike, to that hard, yet not quite desperate, insight into Man's unchanging predicament by which heroic ages have lived.[2]

Tolkien is a realist, who calls on the reader to rise to the occasion and meet the challenge of evil, holding out the hope to the reader that Good may win yet again, if it remains strong. That type of realism had definite political overtones in the Soviet Union.

The first published Russian translation of any of Tolkien's works was in 1969. It was an excerpt of Chapter VII of *The Hobbit* ("Queer Lodgings") in the quarterly magazine[3] *Angliya*, which was published by the British Foreign Office for distribution in the Soviet Union. *Angliya* was the British side of the Cold-War exchange of state-sponsored magazines between the UK and the USSR. The official translation of *The Hobbit*—with a few ideological adaptations—had to wait until 1976.

Samizdat

Samizdat, however, was another story. Samizdat was the opposite of the centralized Soviet-controlled publishing system. It was not a system at all, but rather a number of isolated groups of individuals who shared works of literature that were otherwise not available. The result of the isolation of the various groups was that a number of different translations of Tolkien's works began to circulate. Most often the translations were done by translators, whose imagination was captured by Tolkien's vision and who wished to share it with friends and family. They were neither paid nor encouraged to do so. In fact, they placed themselves at risk by producing the translations.

In the mid-1960s,[4] the last years of the "thaw" in Soviet literature that resulted from Khrushchev's efforts at de-Stalinization, Zinaida Anatol'evna Bobyr' produced a samizdat condensation of *LotR*. Bobyr' made a name for herself as a sanctioned translator of science fiction with the magazine Техника молодежи [Tekhnika molodezhi], where she had worked in 1943. She was one of the best among the translators who helped popularize translated science fiction in the 1950s. It was this group of translators' careful selection of only the best of the best of English-language science fiction that built the genre's popularity. Bobyr's list of credits includes Brian Aldiss, Isaac Azimov, John Gordon, Edmond Hamilton, Clifford Simak and Stanislaw Lem, whom she translated from Polish.

The version of her samizdat condensation of *LotR* that survived into print in the "publishing boom" that followed the collapse of Communism in the early 1990s is only one third as long as the original, and contains a number of embellishments to the story line. In her version, for example, in addition to the Ring of Power there is also a Silver Crown of the Lords of Westernesse, which is one of the greatest treasures brought from over the sea. "He who dares to place it upon his brow will either receive omniscience and the greatest of wisdom, or ... will be turned to ashes on the spot, if he has not sufficiently prepared for it." (B.67, U F.396) If Aragorn is capable of wearing the Silver Crown, he will prove himself worthy of marriage to Arwen and of becoming Elrond's successor. The plot thickens, because the Silver Crown is in Osgiliath, which is in the hands of the Enemy. All is not lost, however, because Sauron knows that he dare not touch the Silver Crown without the Ring. In the end, Aragorn claims the Silver Crown for his own, in a happily-ever-after fairy-tale ending. (B.472-3, U R.809)

Between 1975 and 1978,[5] Semen Ya. Umanskij, an engineer with a renaissance range of talents, edited Bobyr's condensation of *LotR*. This version survived as a manuscript in the personal library of Evgeniya Smagina, who graciously made a copy available to the author in 2003. The bound typescript likewise contained a translation of *The Hobbit*, which was, at first, thought to be a revision of Bobyr's translation. The Umanskij version of *The Hobbit*, however, shows no resemblance to the version published in 1992 by Knizhnyj Mir Publishers in Perm'. His revisions of the Bobyr' *LotR*, however, are clearly identifiable with the Bobyr' condensation of *LotR* that was published by Interprint Publishers of Moscow in 1990 as *The Story of the Ring* (Povest' o Kol'tse [Повесть о Кольце]). Although he restored many of the chapters that Bobyr' had left out, large segments of the text—including the story line of the Silver Crown—are word for word the same as in the Interprint edition.

Bobyr's condensation is almost universally dismissed as a hack job by the present generation of Russian Tolkienists, who have access to a number of full translations and even to the English original. In the context in which it first appeared, however, it was a daring effort at making Tolkien available—albeit in condensed form—to the Russian reading public, despite the unreceptive political climate of the Soviet, state-controlled publishing industry.

In about 1975, Aleksandr A. Gruzberg produced a complete samizdat translation. Gruzberg, a linguist by profession, was secretly also a very active samizdat science fiction translator, sometimes published under the pen-name of D. Arsen'ev. His list of credits includes Poul Anderson, Isaac Azimov, Edgar Rice Burroughs, A. Norton and Perry Rhodan.

Gruzberg discovered Tolkien in the Library of Foreign Literature in Moscow. He ordered a microfilm copy of the three volumes from the library. This service was very inexpensive, especially when compared to buying real English-language books, which were hard to find in any event. The first version of his translation was written out entirely by hand. A number of other respondents also reported writing out *LotR* by hand; some more than once. Typewriters were deficit luxuries and computers were undreamed of at that time. It took Gruzberg about a year to complete his translation. His daughter Yuliya—now Yuliya Batalina—translated the poems.

His translation of *LotR* circulated in the same way that his other samizdat science fiction translations did. The manuscripts were typed in six copies—copying machines were also controlled items—and sent off to Leningrad (now Saint Petersburg). From there, they circulated throughout the country. Gruzberg notes that "most of the translations [circulating in samizdat] were, by the way, terribly poor. They were so illiterately done that it is hard to believe. The translators not only didn't know English, but didn't even have the most elementary knowledge of the history or culture of the country. But undemanding readers [...] just swallowed it all."[6]

Participation in the illicit publishing industry was not without its dangers. The head of the samizdat ring that Gruzberg supplied with translations was named Klimov. "They say that he had some problems with the KGB—how could you expect otherwise, doing this kind of thing—but he managed to worm his way out of them and kept his business going," said Gruzberg. Gruzberg himself had a close call with the authorities because of his samizdat activities. "You could be fired and prosecuted for that kind of thing. I was lucky. I had a close call once, when they found one of my translations at the home of an acquaintance of mine, whom they were accusing of distributing samizdat. They came out to see me, but only warned me that I should not do things like this any more. That was in 1981, I think, and for a long time after that incident, I stopped doing translations."

"The appearance of an author in samizdat was almost inevitably accompanied by fundamental changes in the author's life. A person could lose the chance to work in his or her specialty (or the opportunity to continue his or her education), their earnings potential was limited in general, and administrative measures could be applied. And that is in the best case. In a word, one bid farewell to his past life and started to live like a dissident par excellence. You had to have some very serious reasons to dare to do that. And, by the way, it also meant spoiling the lives of your family, relatives, friends and colleagues," said Evgeniya Smagina, one of the first to read the Bobyr' samizdat condensation.[7]

Reading a samizdat typescript of *LotR* had a special feeling to it. It was something to read alone, where no one else could see you reading it. While reading it—to a certain extent—you literally shared the dangers of the fellowship. The mere possession of this book was a criminal offense, though hardly anyone was prosecuted for this alone. The ideas contained in the book made a special impression on the reader, because the reader was taking a risk to learn what they were. If they were not special, anyone could read it. Evgeniya Smagina said: "reading uncensored, free speech gave you a feeling of freedom, a breath of fresh air (which made up for the literary imperfections of many of these texts). Besides that, there was a certain pride in yourself, a sense of your own courage, a euphoria from having performed a free, unsanctioned act, which must be hard to comprehend for a person who has lived their whole life under conditions of freedom of speech and the press."[8]

The samizdat copy of a book was only on loan to you for three to four days and people stayed up all night and ignored their jobs and classes to read it. One informant memorized the text of *LotR* and became the book, bringing life to the fiction that was Ray Bradbury's *Fahrenheit 451*. This is the way that books like Pasternak's *Doctor Zhivago*, Solzhenitsyn's *Archipelago GULAG* and the Strugatskijs'[9] *Ugly Swans* and *Tale of the Troika* first reached the Soviet reading public.

The First Translation Boom

In 1982, an abridged translation of volume I of the three was officially published by the Children's Literature (Детская литература) Publishing House in Moscow. This translation was done by Vladimir Sergeevich Murav'ev and Andrej Andreevich Kistyakovskij (M&K), who had first read Tolkien in the early 1970s and were enthralled by him. They wanted to use *LotR* as a "rather long, militant manifesto" for "the revolt of the prisoners of the GULAG," said C.S.-Lewis-scholar, and friend of the translators, Professor N.L. Trauberg.[10]

The abridged translation was an immediate best seller. The initial print run of 100,000 copies sold out, and in 1983 Children's Literature Publishing House took the unusual step for a planned-economy publishing house of printing two more runs totaling 300,000 copies. So unusual was this step that one Russian scholar, who seemed to come from the "show-me" state of Missouri rather than Moscow, had to see the registration numbers for each print run before she was convinced.[11] These extra copies, too, rapidly sold out and before long the book was not even available in libraries, as the copies were stolen from the shelves.[12]

The publication of the abridged M&K translation of volume I came at a politically inopportune time, at the height of the Cold War. On 8 June 1982, Ronald Reagan made his famous "Evil Empire" speech in which some Tolkien scholars—both East and West—see clear allusions to Gandalf's speeches at the Council of Elrond in Chapter II of Book II and at the council in Aragorn's tents in Chapter IX of Book V. In his article[13] "Eurasian Tendencies in Domestic Fantasy Literature," Anatolij Moshnitskij directly credits Reagan's "quote" from Tolkien in the "Evil Empire" speech for stopping the publication of the next two volumes of the M&K translation of the three.

Speaking before the British House of Commons—a venue strongly suggestive of the Council of Elrond—Reagan said: "If history teaches anything, it teaches that self-delusion in the face of unpleasant facts is folly. [...] Let us offer hope. Let us tell the world that a new age is not only possible, but probable." [14]

Speaking at the Council of Elrond, Gandalf said: "It is wisdom to recognize necessity, when all other courses have been weighed, though as folly it may appear to those who cling to false hope." (F.352) In the council in Aragorn's tents, Gandalf holds out the hope of a new age that Reagan turned into a probability: "We must walk open-eyed into that trap, with courage, but small hope for ourselves. For, my lords, it may well prove that we ourselves shall perish utterly in a black battle far from the living lands; so that even if Barad-dûr be thrown down, we shall not live to see a new age. But this, I deem, is our duty. And better so than to perish nonetheless — as we surely shall, if we sit here — and know as we die that no new age shall be." (R.191)

When, after the publication of the M&K abridged translation of volume I, it became apparent that publication of volumes II and III would be some time in coming, other unofficial translators stepped in to meet the demand for translations of volumes II and III, resulting in a "translation boom" for *LotR*. One key characteristic of the "boom" translations is that, since they were picking up where M&K left off, they maintained the names and, to some extent, the style of M&K's volume I.

In the Ukraine, Alina Nemirova came forward. Valeriya Aleksandrovna Matorina, a technical translator, who signs her translations "VAM," which is not only her initials, but also the Russian word meaning *for you*, implying, as she herself notes, that her translation is *a gift for you*, did a translation. N. Estel'—the Tolkien pseudonym for Nadezhda Chertkova—whose translation of *The Silmarillion* has been widely reprinted, was a member of the cohort of the boom as well. In August of 1989, A.I. Alekhin brought out his translation of volumes II and III—done from Skibniewska's Polish translation[15] as books on tape. In the 1990s, Irina Zabelina, whose translations of Tolkien's minor works like "Leaf by Niggle" and "Farmer Giles of Ham", have been published, also did a translation of *LotR* that has yet to be published. The most widely circulated samizdat translation, the one that found its way onto the web, was the one by Natalya Grigor'eva and Vladimir Grushetskij (G&G), which is peppered with phrases, sentences and paragraphs that are word for word the same as the Bobyr' condensation. The date on the Umanskij manuscript, clearly shows that the Bobyr' version came first.[16] On the web, their translation of volumes II and III was often combined with Gruzberg's translation of volume I to form a complete digital set of the three volumes.

Perestroika

In a paper[17] presented at the "Star Bridge-99 Festival," Alina Nemirova—one of the translators of *LotR*—examines Tolkien as a literary and social phenomenon. Nemirova notes that Tolkien's works are most resonant with people in the same social class that Tolkien occupied in England, the middle-class "working intelligentsia," which includes people like teachers, doctors, engineers and scientists. Those members of Tolkien's cohort of the British middle class, she notes, who had assimilated the unshakable foundations of the Victorian era, were the ones who "suffered the most mental distress at the onset of the frightening new age" of the twentieth century. They were also the ones who possessed the pleasant traits of "humanity, a rich spiritual life, and a tendency to creativity," all traits readily identifiable with Tolkien.

Nemirova attributes part of Tolkien's popularity in Russia to the fact that his writings were shaped by the period in which he lived; the crucial transitional period from the Victorian era of the nineteenth century to the harsh realities of the twentieth century, the break-point for which was not the year 1900, but rather World War I, in which Tolkien fought. She feels that the resulting mind-set is what makes Tolkien's works so resonant for modern-day readers from the xUSSR, who have lived through a social transition at the change of the millennium no less harsh than the one that befell Tolkien's generation as they crossed from the nineteenth to the twentieth century. For the readers from the xUSSR, the transition-point was the event that put the 'X' in the xUSSR: Perestroika and the collapse of Communism.

The translation boom would have been impossible without Perestroika, which reined in the literary strong arm of the State, the Main Directorate for Literary and Publishing Affairs [Главлит (Glavlit)]. Glavlit had been established in 1922 to centralize censorship of the press and theatrical arts. Its function was to prohibit the publication and distribution of works containing propaganda against the power of the Soviets, divulging military secrets, inciting public opinion, inciting nationalistic or religious fanaticism or having a pornographic character. It was a political organization and its character changed to match the political ebb and flow of the times; strong under Stalin, relaxed under Khrushchev, tightened again under Brezhnev. Beginning in 1986, Glavlit slowly lost its powers. In 1990, it was reorganized as the Main Directorate for the Protection of Government Secrets in the Press [ГУОТ (GUOT)] to accent its role in protecting state secrets. As Perestroika took hold, the younger generation felt less and less intimidated. As the power of the Glavlit waned, samizdat lost its impact. The younger generation no longer viewed typescript books as samizdat, but as simply "unpublished manuscripts". The change in attitude meant a wider circulation for unofficial views, which sped the process of political change in the Soviet Union. It was under Perestroika that the second, unabridged edition of the M&K translation of volume I was first published in 1988.

In October 1991, the Glavlit, now GUOT, was finally disbanded, and the publishing boom began. The state-controlled publishing system changed into a market-driven entity almost overnight. Samizdat moved from a bound typescript with six carbon copies to a computer typeset book with thousands of copies. Translations of Tolkien, who is popularly known in Russia as "The Professor," were no exception. The full translation of *LotR* came out in 1988, 1990 and 1992. The last two volumes were Murav'ev's translation without Kistyakovskij. Kistyakovskij had died in 1987, before all three volumes could be completed. Bobyr's 'adaptation' was published as a single-volume in 1990. The VAM translation came out in 1991, as did the first edition of the full G&G.

The Second Publishing Boom

Not quite ten years later, there was a second publishing boom. The end of the old millennium and the start of the new saw a burst of new activity. In 1999, a retelling of *LotR* for children by Leonid Yakhnin came on stage. The second revised edition of the full G&G came out in 2000. The M&K translation was widely reprinted. The Gruzberg translation finally was published on CD-ROM. The Kamenkovich and Karrik (K&K) translation, first published in 1994, was republished. A new translation done by V. Volkovskij appeared in print. And that was just in the year 2000. As "movie fever" hit Russia, M&K, G&G, K&K and Yakhnin were all reprinted in 2001. The Gruzberg CD-ROM was also re-issued. In 2002, the Nemirova and Gruzberg translations finally reached print, and everything else was republished. In 2003, the revised VAM finally arrived in bookstores. A search for "Tolkien" at a well-stocked on-line Russian bookstore[18] in early 2003 returned 105 titles. By the summer, the number of hits had climbed to 162.

The second publishing boom was accompanied by a "read-Tolkien-in-the-original" boom. It was typified by a Russian Tolkienist limerick that goes like this:

> Although I am old and gray of head,
> And free of the stresses that others all dread,
> I would learn English and only because,
> The professor in it wove a marvelous clause.

This boom manifested itself in the appearance of an English-language edition[19] of *The Hobbit* by Presto Publishers in 2000, and an English-language edition of *LotR* published in 2002/3 by Rolf Publishing.[20] Both were accompanied by vocabulary notes and commentary.

The result of the years of 'exile' in samizdat, and the two publishing booms is that there is not just one published translation of Tolkien's works in Russia as is common in other countries. There are numerous contemporary published translations competing with each other for the reader's attention. There are eleven different translations of "Leaf by Niggle"; ten translations of *LotR*; nine translations of *The Hobbit* and six translations of *The Silmarillion*. Each translator has a slightly different approach to the text. Each translation has a slightly different interpretation of Tolkien. Each translator has a different story to tell. Most of the existing translations are only Tolkienesque, they are not really Tolkienian. They have been adapted to the Russian mental climate. As Vladimir Sviridov, one of the leading members of the Tolkien Text Translation Group (TTT) aptly noted, "translating Tolkien was and is primarily a method of self-expression, and only secondarily a method of earning money or becoming famous." The goal of this book is to point out the differences between the translations and the original.

The Adaptation of Imported Ideas

The adaptation of imported of ideas is not a new phenomenon in Russia. The Marxist revolution was imported. Marx would have been surprised at the result. Tolkien would undoubtedly have had the same reaction to what has happened to his ideas in Russia. In his characterization of the Russian mental legacy, P.Ya. Chaadaev[21] said that: "The deepest trait of our historical nature is the lack of spontaneity in our social development. Look carefully, and you will see that each important fact of our history has been imposed upon us, that almost every new idea is an imported idea." [22] Those new ideas are not taken over lock, stock, and barrel, however, but are adapted to the Russian mental climate, as it were. Diderot (1713-1784) once remarked to the Russian Empress Catherine II, "Ideas transplanted from Paris to St. Petersburg take on a different shade." [23]

Bobyr's embellishment of her samizdat condensation of *LotR* with the Silver Crown of Westernesse is a good example of what can happen to ideas when they are imported to Russia. Other examples can easily be found in the classics of children's literature. The retelling of *Le Aventure di Pinocchio* by Carlo Collodi (1826-1890) done by Aleksej N. Tolstoj (1883-1945) ends, not with Pinocchio earning the right to become a real boy, but with Buratino finding a home for himself among other living puppets like himself.

One of Tolkien's more recent translators, Mariya Kamenkovich, offers a good insight into some of the reasons for this in an interview in the newspaper Смена [Smena].[24] She says that:

> A specific perception of Tolkien has come about in Russia that has no analog in the West. It can best be compared to the boy of whom everyone has read in Dostoevskij, who, having been given a star map one evening, returns it the next morning with his own notes on it. And the relationship to Tolkien is not without pretentiousness and a sense of superiority. It's only an Englishman. What could he write. We're the ones who know what life is. In addition, young readers get the desire to "debunk" Tolkien, to bring him down to their own level. A favorite situation at the [role-playing] games is to find Galadriel sitting at the camp fire, drying her socks. This relationship, incidentally, comes from the translations in which the Elves quite often sound like crude teenagers when they talk. This is pure Soviet heritage: the rejection of aristocratism. And, no matter how much we have tried to disown that time, its spirit is still alive. That is why, in the majority of the translations, the relationship between Frodo and Sam is buddy-buddy, while in the original, it is the relationship between a master and a servant. That is why we simply need Tolkien today, if we really want to cure our predilection for simplification. He is a medicine that needs to be given a spoonful at a time.

Natalya Semenova, a Tolkien scholar, relates that, in response to her criticisms of the M&K translation, readers at times say: "Yes, you're right, but what they wrote is a cool story." From the explanations that follow, it is sometimes clear that they mean "it's a lot better than Tolkien," she says.[25]

Writing Tolkienesque poems, parodies and stories that offer a distinctly Russian look at life is indeed quite popular in Russia. In an interview he gave to the magazine MK-Bul'var (МК-Бульвар),[26] one of the more prominent—some Russian Tolkienists would say infamous—Russian Tolkienesque writers, Nik Perumov, offers an excellent example of what Kamenkovich was talking about, when she said: " It's only an Englishman. What could he write. We're the ones who know what life is." Perumov is known in Russia as the man who finished what Tolkien had begun to write. (Человек, который дописал Толкина.) His novel *Ring of Darkness* (Кольцо тьмы) picks up 300 years after the end of the Third Age.[27] It caused quite a stir in Russian Tolkienist circles. Perumov says that his novel is a reaction to Tolkien's depiction of World War II.

> It is 1945. The war in Europe is ending. Russian soldiers are storming Berlin, Americans are quavering at the Rhine, the Germans on the Eastern front are fighting to the death. In quiet, peaceful England, Mr.

Tolkien is sitting in Oxford, writing *The Lord of the Rings*. No matter how much the Professor disavows the fact that *The Lord* is not an allegory, that it does not have anything to do with the war, [his assertion] strained and strained and gave way. After the war, in order to depict Evil going into battle under a red flag [the banner that the Russians followed into Berlin], you have to hate it [the flag] very much. Because at that time, it was more than just a symbol, very much more than just a combat banner, than even the country's flag, it was the Banner of Victory. That is just one of the many, many reasons [that I decided to finish what Tolkien had started].

Tolkien's treatment of the red banner that Perumov so strenuously objects to is found in Chapter IV of volume III ("The Siege of Gondor"), where "the lines of fire became flowing torrents, file upon file of Orcs bearing flames, and wild Southron men with red banners, shouting with harsh tongues, surging up, overtaking the retreat." (R.113)

Red Banner (Красное знамя) is indeed a loaded term in the Soviet context. It was the symbol of the Revolution. *The Order of Red Banner* was a military decoration, which was paralleled on the civilian side by *the Order of the Red Banner of Labor*. This symbol of the Revolution also became the national flag of the USSR. The Soviet equivalent of the Iwo Jima Memorial is the painting of the raising of the Red Flag over the Reichstag in Berlin in 1945. While it is common practice for a translator to avoid loaded terms in the target language to prevent the reader from jumping to the wrong conclusions, none of the translators flinched from the use of *red banner* in this sentence, even though they had made such changes in other places. *The Red Book of Westmarch* [q.v.], for example, became *the Scarlet Book of Westmarch* and *Durin* [q.v.] became Дьюрин [D'yurin].

While Perumov could blame Tolkien for the use of the *red banner* in "The Siege of Gondor", he had only the translators to blame in Chapter VI of volume III ("The Battle of Pelennor Fields"). There, the chieftain of the Haradrim "was filled with a red wrath and shouted aloud, and displaying his standard, black serpent upon scarlet," he attacked. (R.139) There are subtle differences between *standard* and *banner*, and between *scarlet* and *red*; enough to break the connection with the Red Banner of Soviet fame. A number of the translators, however, were not loath to ignore them in favor of something more (anti-)Soviet. The condensed Bobyr' (Umanskij) retelling had left out the red banner in Chapter IV (B.365, U R.708), but in Chapter VI, her chieftain of the Haradrim "raised a banner with a black snake on a red field." (знамя с черным змеем на красном поле) and attacked.) (B.389, U R.728) G&G's version is word for word the same. (G&G R.113) VAM and the post-Soviet (1994-95) academic translation by K&K had strikingly similar formulations. Their chieftain of the Haradrim unfurled a banner with a Black Snake on a *blood-red field* (на кроваво-красном поле). (VAM R.124; K&K R.150) That particular color combination will prompt the older Soviet reader to think of the time in Soviet history, when millions died in what Sergej P. Melgounov termed *The Red Terror*[28] of the post-Revolutionary period. The new (2000) Volkovskij translation avoided a color altogether here. Murav'ev missed the opportunity for another political statement and made it a *scarlet banner*, in step with Tolkien. In his earlier versions, Gruzberg, who made no efforts at political editorializing, also had a *scarlet banner*. The CD-ROM edition (2000) of Gruzberg's translation, edited by E. Yu. Aleksandrova, even managed to avoid the loaded word *banner*, returning to Tolkien's apolitical *scarlet standard* (штандарт).

Perumov is a young writer, born after World War II. His comments typify a truism of Sovietology: for many Russians, young and old, World War II only ended yesterday. He, however, is not typical of most young Russian Tolkienists, who describe themselves as apolitical, eschewing any political interpretation of Tolkien's original texts. Russian readers' perceptions of Tolkien are, nevertheless, greatly influenced by the Russian mentality, which—as familiar as it may seem to Westerners—can still be full of surprises.

Tolkien would not have been entirely oblivious to the significance of the color of the Flag. The anthem of the British Labour Party, traditionally sung at every party conference is *The Red Flag*, in which the refrain is (**emphasis** added):

> Then raise the **scarlet standard** high
> Beneath its fold we'll live and die
> Though cowards flinch and traitors sneer
> We'll keep the red flag flying here

The song was so much a part of British working-class culture that British children were often surprised to discover that the tune to which it is sung was much better known outside the United Kingdom as *Oh, Tannenbaum*, or *Oh, Christmas Tree*. The lyrics were written in 1889 by Jim Connell (1852-1929), a prominent figure in the British Labor Movement. He took his inspiration from the London dock strike, which was taking place at that time, and from the activities of the Irish Land League, the Paris Commune, the Russian nihilists and the Chicago anarchists. The song quickly spread throughout the International Labor Movement. In the wake of the Cold War and the fall of Communism, the present Labour Party Prime Minister, Tony Blair, has turned away from the song, which is more in the spirit of the Paris Commune than of modern European Social Democracy.

Perumov may have been right that there was a political association behind Tolkien's choice of color for the flag of the enemy. He was probably wrong, however, in associating it exclusively with the Russians and the Red Banner of Victory of World War II. For Tolkien, the image, undoubtedly had older origins.

Another prominent, and equally controversial Russian Tolkienesque author is known as Nienna. Her pen-name is taken from Tolkien's Queen of the Valar, one of the Aratar. Her province is mourning and suffering, seeking not endless grief, but rather pity, hope and the steadfastness of spirit. The Russian Nienna's book is entitled *The Black Book of Arda* (Черная книга Арды [Chernaya kniga Ardy]).[29] It begins with the premise that accepted history is written by the victors and turns accepted history around. This is the history of Middle-earth from the point of view of the vanquished. It is a chronicle written not from Iluvatar's point of view, but from Melkor's. Niennism has a substantial following in Russia.

Irina Shrejner examined Russian perceptions of *The Black Book of Arda* in her presentation ("The Phenomenon of Niennism")[30] at a Round Table discussion entitled "Professor Tolkien and his Heritage" held on 22 April 2000 at the Russian State University for the Humanities in Moscow. Nienna's approach to Tolkien offers a much greater breadth "than traditional Tolkienism does for writing your own apocrypha. Within the framework of Tolkienism, there is nothing to continue or to rewrite. Tolkien's books stand out by the astounding characteristic of English literature: they are *finished*. Perfect. Completely balanced internally." In addition, it is particularly attractive to Russians to consider the idea that the other side might be right. Shrejner sees a possible source for this in a feeling many members of twentieth-century society have: "the complete lack of any personal possibility of influencing events and processes, not just occurring within the surrounding world, but forming the surrounding world. Perhaps, it is worthwhile to look for one of the foundations of [Russian] Tolkienism as a whole in this, but Niennism once again offers a wider scope as a point of view, supposing that the minority and not the majority is right."

The formulation of her statement is very politically charged in the post-Soviet era. The victory of the gerrymandered majority (the literal meaning of the Russian loanword *Bolshevik*) over the minority (the literal meaning of the Russian loanword *Menshevik*) in the wake of the Russian Revolution of 1917 laid the foundation for Lenin's rise to power and the establishment of the Communist State.

Shrejner concludes her presentation with the statement that *The Black Book of Arda* is a very liberal book, "precisely because liberalism names individual freedom one of the most basic and primary values, placing perhaps only this one restriction upon it: 'personal freedom is limited only by the freedom of another person'." This maxim, applied to *The Black Book of Arda*, is what attracts people to it and makes them Niennists. It makes it a book "about the human right to have the freedom to be oneself."

Tolkienism in Russia

The official publication of the abridged translation of volume I (1982) by M&K and the supplementary samizdat translations of volumes II and III (mid-1980s) gave rise to the first wave of Tolkienism. Before that, the number of Russian Tolkienists had hardly been enough to constitute a ripple. The inconsistencies between the official, M&K translation of volume I and the samizdat continuations sent many of the readers of the first wave of Tolkienism scurrying in search of hard-to-find copies of the English-language original. Microfilm copies from the Library of Foreign Literature in Moscow, where Vladimir Murav'ev worked, were one relatively accessible source. The ability to read English, however, was a factor that restricted this cohort of Tolkienists essentially to intellectuals in the humanities.

What they found when they read the original was surprising for them. In his essay[31] on Tolkien translation, Sergej Smirnov elegantly notes that:

> "the original turned out to be a completely different book. So different that later I did not give my son either the M&K or the G&G translations to read. After several months of wandering around the shelves of our home library, these editions [M&K and G&G] could not find themselves a home, even next to Volkov's *The Wizard of the Emerald City*, Chukovskij's *Ajbolit* or Tolstoj's *Buratino*, which seem more honest to me now, inasmuch as they did not try to conceal their "variations on a theme" behind the names of the authors of the originals."

The Wizard of the Emerald City (Волшебник изумрудного города) by Aleksandr Volkov is based on *The Wizard of Oz* by Frank L. Baum (1856-1919). *Ajbolit* (Айболит), which literally means "Ouch! It hurts!," by Kornej Chukovskij (1882-1969) is based on *Dr. Dolittle* by Hugh Lofting (1886-1947). *The Golden Key, or the Adventures of Buratino* (Золотой ключик, или Приключения Буратино) by Aleksej Tolstoj (1883-1945) is based on *Le Aventure di Pinocchio* by Carlo Collodi (1826-1890). All three are classics of Russian children's literature, identified more with their Russian, than with their original authors.

The Russian adaptation of Tolkien's works and philosophy has a significant impact on what is called "Tolkienism" in Russia, as the Russians try to fill the philosophical vacuum left by the collapse of Communism. This is compounded by the fact that, as K.V. Asmolov succinctly explains in his article[32] on the history of Tolkienism in Russia, Tolkien is quite often read "out of context".

> The fact of the matter is that our admirers of Tolkien, in contrast to those, who study his legacy in the West, do not imagine the dimensions of the underwater part of the iceberg, on top of which his works rest. This is the mythological legacy of England and its neighbors, on the basis of which Tolkien created his own myths, and certain moments from Tolkien's own biography, without a knowledge of which it is very difficult to correctly place the accents. Europeans study Tolkien's legacy just like we study the legacy of Pushkin [the Russian equivalent of Shakespeare], knowing and feeling the roots; tying the life of the author to the era in which he wrote; trying to understand the motives of his actions. While here—partially from ignorance, partially from a lack of desire to search—reality is replaced by personal, artificial and imaginary constructions within which reality is turned into what the authors of these constructions want to see.

In a collection of notes[33] that he had made for the day that he would write his memoirs about the history of Tolkienism in Russia, Vladimir Popov, formerly one of the webmasters of the prominent Russian Tolkienist web site *Arda out in the Sticks,*[34] describes the ideological vacuum that was beginning to form in the Soviet Union in the period that the first officially published translation of *LotR* appeared on the scene in 1982. Things were still far from the critical state that they would reach in post-Soviet Russia, when "not only all political, nationalist, and other such ideals for the masses were compromised, but also those who proclaimed or defended those ideals." His metaphor for the dissatisfaction and disobedience in the Soviet Union of that time frame is not Orwell's *1984*, but rather *Alice in Wonderland*.

In this initial stage of the early 1980s, he says, it was not the broad masses, but the intelligentsia who had absolutely no faith in any of the slogans that were being so loudly proclaimed. He likens the intellectual climate of this time to a variant of the old saw about workers under Communism: 'They pretend that they are paying us, and we pretend that we are working.' When recrafted to describe the intelligentsia, it becomes: "They pretend to be telling us about socialism, and we pretend to be listening."

According to Popov, Tolkien offered an alternative guide to the morality that was taught in *The Moral Code of a Builder of Communism*, the little booklet handed out to all its members by the Comsomol [The Communist Youth League] in order to shape the character of the new Soviet man and woman. Tolkien was "the ABCs of faith, but of faith in the bright and intelligent, not in some high abstraction that had been compromised by the history of its application. And, perhaps, most importantly, Tolkien was not being forced on you, nor was it urging you on to something. Maybe the keyword to describe *LotR* is that it is a book about individual choice."

Individual choice was antithema to the Soviet moral code that taught that the collective is more important than the individual. In the political climate of the 1980s, this was heady stuff.

Perestroika and the subsequent collapse of the Soviet, State monopoly on the publishing industry set the stage for the second wave of Russian Tolkienism. In the "publishing boom" that followed Perestroika, freedom of the press tried to fill the suppressed demand for "forbidden-fruit" books like Tolkien, Norton, Fleming, Clancy, Solzhenitsyn, Pasternak and the Strugatskijs. Pirated editions—no rights paid to the copyright holder and no royalties to the translator—abounded.

This period saw four Russian versions of *LotR* come on the market. The single-volume heavily abridged translation by Zinaida Anatol'evna Bobyr' came out in 1990. The VAM translation came out in 1991. The full M&K (1988, 1990 and 1992) and full G&G (1991) translations, however, quickly became leading contenders for the title of the interpreter of Tolkien's works for the Russian reading public.

Feelings run high in Russia about which translation is the best. One Russian personal web page, on which the page-owner lists his favorite books, posts a WARNING to readers. "Do not under any circumstances read the Murav'ev translation (the bookstores have been flooded with them), and especially not the 'retelling for children' (the compiler of which is a certain L. **Yakhnin**). That is harmful not only to your mental and physical (you will be beat up, if you quote [from them]) health, but also to that of those around you."[35]

In the run-up to the release of Peter Jackson's movie version of *LotR* in 2001, a Russian web site conducted a straw poll[36] of who should be entrusted with the translation of the movie. Of the 264 responses to the poll, 20.8% felt that Murav'ev should be entrusted with the translation (Kistyakovskij died in 1987), and 19.3% wanted G&G to be given the job. The poll did not mention VAM, Gruzberg, Volkovskij or K&K as possible candidates for the job. Most of the responses (44.5%), however, were a none-of-the-above choice. These respondents felt that members of the elite of Tolkien fandom should be involved in the translation. That was indeed the final outcome. The movie subtitles were done by a team of Russian Tolkienists.[37] The pollsters were not without a sense of humor. One of the choices was to "threaten the studio with a terrorist attack" in the event that the translation was bad. This answer was chosen by 5.6% of the respondents.

The first translation boom widened the intellectual base of Russian Tolkienism, and greatly increased its numbers. The expanded ranks of Tolkienists gave Russian Tolkienism, which had previously been primarily intellectual and scholarly, a fandom. Tolkien scholars continued to look at Tolkien's works as myth, examining them from a historical, philological perspective. Tolkien fans, however, were younger—high school and college students—who were not well-read in Northern and Western European culture. Their knowledge of English—if any—was poor and they were forced, as it were, to take the word of Tolkien's translators and Tolkien scholars at face value, because they could not read Tolkien in the original. In his article[38] on the history of Tolkienism in Russia, K.V. Asmolov says that *Tolkienism* is really a misnomer for many of the new wave of Tolkienists.

> The majority of the new representatives of the movement, to which the name *Tolkienism* can already only be applied in inverted commas, can be compared mentally to American teenagers who are trying out all the delights of pop culture. This type of nonconformist can be found both at the role-playing games in the Neskuchnyj Sad Gardens and on the Arbat[[39]], only in the Neskuchnyj Sad Gardens, instead of roller-blades, they have wooden swords. The mass media lumps them together with punkers, ravers and hippies. The number of those among them who know Tolkien by other than hearsay is disastrously small.

In his notes on the history of Tolkienism in Russia, Vladimir Popov says that the Tolkienist movement in twenty-first century Russia can be viewed as four mainstreams, defined by their philosophical approach to Tolkien: the Christians, the Northerners, the "alternativists," and the aphilosophicals.[40]

Popov's aphilosopicals are those who do not look for an underlying philosophical foundation in Tolkien's works. They just like *LotR* because it is a good book, and there are quite a few people like that, he notes.

The slogan of the "alternativists" of Popov's system of classification is "The Professor was wrong!" They reject Tolkien's philosophy and try to recreate their own vision of Middle-earth. The leading proponents of this branch of Russian Tolkienism are Nienna with her *The Black Book of Arda* (Черная книга Арды [Chernaya kniga Ardy]), and Nik Perumov, (in)famous as the man who completed Tolkien. Popov feels that the alternativist "phenomenon is more characteristic of the state of thinking in modern Russia, than it is of any actual premise in Tolkien's texts."

The Christians in Popov's system are those who focus their attention on Tolkien's own Christianity—specifically Catholicism—and on the Christian elements in his Legendarium. Vladimir Sviridov, of the TTT, has coined the term *Tolkianity* to describe this particular brand of Christianity.

The Northerners are those who take heed of the elements of the Nordic Sagas that are so richly sprinkled about Tolkien's text. This group is taken with the Northern theory of Courage, which led the Nordic heroes and gods to fight without hope of victory at the coming of Ragnarok. (q.v. **Hope Abandoned**)

In the vernacular, the increasingly visible wave of Tolkienists has begun to be referred to as the толкинутые [tolkinutye, pl.]. This neologism is possible because Tolkien's name is similar to a real Russian word, which means *to push, to shove* (толкнуть [tolknut']), which as a past passive participle is written толкнутый [tolknutyj]. The usage of толкинутый [tolkinutyj] is analogous with the usage of the past passive participle of тронуть [tronut'] in the frequent collocation *touched in the head* (тронутый умом [tronutyj umom]), which in the vernacular is often reduced to just тронутый [tronutyj].[41] Literally толкинутый [tolkinutyj] might be read as *touched [in the head] by Tolkien*, or clinically as *Mythomania Tolkienensis*.

In an article[42] from the early 1990s, which appeared in the newspaper Комсомольская правда [Komsomolskaya pravda], S. Kirillova—very much tongue in cheek—described the four stages of *Mythomania Tolkienensis* as the affliction has developed in Russia. Subjects in the first stage are contagious. They want to expose as many others as possible to Tolkien's works. Subjects in the second stage are characterized by the belief that "everything that The Professor wrote in his books is true, and I have seen it with my own eyes."

This is one of the new ideas that accompanied the appearance of a mass fandom in the wake of the first translation boom. Some Russian Tolkienists came to see Middle-earth as a brave new world, engendered by Tolkien the "visionary" (визионер), who had not created Middle-earth in his imagination, but who had rather somehow been able to see and describe a parallel world that actually exists.[43]

In Kirillova's third stage, the subject's perspective changes, and starts to become more self-centered. Subjects in this stage are characterized by the belief that "I have seen everything that The Professor wrote about in his books with my own eyes and it's not that way at all!" In the fourth and final stage of Kirillova's hierarchical description, subjects exhibit megalomaniacal, homicidal tendencies, threatening to kill others whose perceptions of Tolkien's works do not coincide with theirs. In this stage subjects believe that "Only I know what really happened in Tolkien's novels! The other толкинутые [tolkinutye, pl.] are liars!" While the article is humorous in its approach, its description of the underlying reality is very much on target. Russian discussions of Tolkien have a tendency to quickly take on a strident air of the sort of philosophical debate in search of "the truth" that Russian intellectuals are infamous for.

During his visit to Russia in the early 1990s, the science fiction writer Bruce Sterling came into contact with these new Russian Tolkienists. In an article in *Wired* magazine, he summed up the movement as: "a unique Russian contribution to counterculture are the 'System hippies,' J.R.R. Tolkien fanatics who espouse a kind of Russian-blood-and-Russian-soil-Green-back-to-nature mystic ideology, like a New Age hybrid of Rasputin and a Hobbit."[44] He cannot have been too much off base with his description. It was prominently quoted on a well-known Russian Tolkien site.[45]

The Tolkienists of this boom period had a sense of being initiates into something inaccessible to the vast majority. Tolkien was the symbol of another world that was not open to everybody. This can be seen in the vast array of Tolkienesque poetry and lyrics that was, and still is being produced.

In the ode[46] "To a Girl, Buying *The Lord of the Rings* at a Book Stand," the speaker tries to talk the girl out of buying the books, by explaining all the consequences of her action. These scriptures, he expounds, are worse than hash for such an innocent young soul as she. She will be "touched [in the head] by Tolkien" (толкинешься) and start to seek her own kind. Then Heaven help her, she'll take on a strange name, sew herself a costume, learn to speak Elvish, make herself a wooden sword. Before she knows it, she'll be off to take part in the "Hobbit Games" [role-playing games somewhat like those put on by the Society for Creative Anachronism], where she'll run through the woods with a bow and arrow, fight Orcs, dance strange dances and sing "Oh, Elbereth" into the night. As if this were not enough, when she is eighteen, she will fall in love with another Tolkien-fool, who will buy her flowers, read her poems and timidly kiss her hand, almost as if this were the chivalrous Middle Ages and not the go-to-bed-on-the-first-date here and now. They will, of course, get married, but instead of going to the beach on vacation as others do, they will go off to the games, to the heat and the mud. Her friends, her teachers, her parents, the parents of her friends will all think it's a craze. At first they'll laugh quietly about it, but then they will be more direct. Some will call her an escapist, others a "nut."

The tone begins to change at this point. The speaker's final argument is not so much an argument against becoming a Tolkienist, as it is for. He asks: Isn't that too high a price to pay for the light of stars, a magic rhyme, for a world that seems a dream? The girl, who only takes silent part in the conversation, agrees to pay the price, and the ode works its way to the punch line at the end. The speaker has only been trying to assuage his conscience. He tried to talk her out of it, but since he could not, he invites her to join the club. Meetings are once a week on Thursdays. The final line is the punch line: "Man, this is the fifth time I've been at this stand." The ode is essentially a recruiting poster in rhyme, a manifestation of Kirillova's first stage of *Mythomania Tolkienensis*. The description of the life of a Russian Tolkienist contained in the ode is, nonetheless, quite accurate.

The feeling of belonging and the illicit excitement of an underground movement were not the only forces at work in the early Russian Tolkienist movement. It was also the revolutionary feeling that things could be different, which M&K first felt when they read Tolkien. In his article[47] on the history of role-playing games, Vladislav Goncharov expresses it as:

> In order to understand why *The Lord of the Rings* became a "cult book," it is necessary to recall some of the theoretical work done by Tolkien himself, specifically his essay "On Fairy-Stories." It is there that he talks directly about the creation of Secondary Worlds and escapism. "Not the flight of the soldier from the field of battle, but the

flight of the prisoner from the hateful prison." Having acknowledged his dislike for modern mechanized civilization, for progress, which primarily gave birth to bombs and machine guns, likewise, for especially "science fiction," Tolkien took the next step. He wove together the best images from the epics of the world, creating his own "Secondary World." An absolutely fairy-tale world, subject to completely different laws, but one that simultaneously attracts, hypnotizes and subjects one to its will.

Goncharov's "quote" from "On Fairy-Stories" is a further example of Russian adaptation of imported ideas. Tolkien did not say anything about "the hateful prison." In the original it says: "They are confusing [...] the Escape of the Prisoner with the Flight of the Deserter." (T&L.54)

Having escaped from the "prison" of obligatory State atheism, when the Soviet Union collapsed, Russian society began actively seeking new sets of spiritual values to fill the vacuum. The Christian-like doctrine of Tolkienism has attracted a substantial following, and has become a significant social phenomenon in Russia. This should hardly be surprising, as the present social climate of Russia shows a number of parallels with the social climate of England in the 1930s, when Tolkien was working on his Legendarium.

In his book *The Will to Believe*, Richard Johnstone examines the effect on the work of novelists of the 1930s produced by the change from the "largely mythical but nevertheless potently remembered world of order and purpose"[48] of Edwardian society to the tumultuous post-war world of modernity, before we learned to number the world wars. The post-war modern world was one of uncertainty and change. Johnstone saw "an increasingly mechanized and standardized 'post-war' society [which] seemed to deny the value and function of the individual, and writers," who sought "to reassert the strength and purpose of the individual through the medium of belief."[49] Catholicism and Marxism are the two beliefs that Johnstone identifies as the cures of choice for the problems of the generation of writers that he is describing.

Tolkien, however, was not of the generation that Johnstone describes in his book. Tolkien had fought in the war, while Johnstone's authors had not. Nevertheless, Tolkien exhibits a number of traits similar to Johnstone's novelists. Johnstone's description of Edwardian society as "largely mythical but nevertheless potently remembered" has a strangely resonant ring to it in the context of Tolkien's Legendarium. Johnstone's quote of Christopher Isherwood on the "connection between the worlds of the public school and the Icelandic sagas" sounds almost insightful when applied to Tolkien. "The saga-world is a schoolboy world, with its feuds, its practical jokes, its dark threats conveyed in puns and riddles and understatements."[50]

Tolkien also clearly rejected the mechanization and standardization of society, for the Hobbits, like Tolkien, "do not and did not understand or like machines more complicated than a forge-bellows, a water-mill, or a handloom." (F.19) But while he was a devout Catholic, clearly disinclined to Marxism, Tolkien found a third path that asked his readers for a "suspension of disbelief" instead of directing them to one of the two dominant beliefs of the time.

Tolkianity

There are a number of Russians who, having read Tolkien, converted to Catholicism. As is generally the rule, converts are more zealous than cradle-Catholics, and in late October 2002 on a discussion forum on the prominent Russian Tolkienist web site *Arda out in the Sticks*,[51] one of them opened the question of the beatification of J.R.R. Tolkien as a prelude to canonization in recognition for all the converts that Tolkien had won to Christianity. The discussion that followed was in earnest and touched on the details of canon law that govern canonization. Saint John of Oxford?[52]

In his foreword[53] to the Russian edition of C.S. Lewis's *Out of the Silent Planet* and *Perelandra*, Ya. Krotov offers an insightful explanation of what makes Tolkienism so popular, by comparing Lewis's and Tolkien's narrative approaches to the topic of God. He sees Lewis's approach as a "photo-positive" and Tolkien's as a "photo-negative." The photo-positive approach defines God in terms of what he is. The photo-negative approach defines God in terms of what he is not.

> The approach of "photo-negative theology" chosen by Tolkien is not only more attractive (though in the absence of talent this approach can be both tiresome and hackneyed). It does not frighten one away with the necessity of thinking, looking for hidden meaning, because the meaning has been purposely and completely expunged. Tolkien truly entertains without being didactic, something that Lewis could not avoid. Tolkien's approach is more advantageous theologically, because by not saying anything positive about God, Tolkien avoids the risk of making an error. A theologian could make a large number of critical

comments about Lewis's trilogy. [...] But there is nothing to accuse Tolkien of, because he did not say anything at all. As is known, however, a vacuum bonds two hemispheres together better than any bands or chains.

Tolkien's approach is more attractive not only for its seeming ease. It strikes right to the heart of a world, which is clothed in an armor of coquettish, religious chastity, which fears every word about God, which has already had its patience eaten away by repeats of the name of Christ, which is inclined to shut its ears, when listening to any sermon, consciously considering it to be trite. Our world is not one of many civilizations, but is civilization, which has been Christian for centuries, which has had "more than it can stomach" of Christianity (tasteless, of course, because there is no Christ in it). Therefore, in our culture, a direct or even allegorical conversation on similar topics often frightens away the audience before it begins.

Tolkien has certainly not been frightening the audience away in Russia. Krotov's explanation could easily be taken as the corollary to Johnstone's explanation of why Catholicism emerged victorious from this clash of beliefs in 1930s England. Religious beliefs, said Johnstone, "more easily allowed scepticism and faith to coexist. Once adopted, the religious belief could be left almost out of sight, occasionally making its presence felt, but for the most part remaining in the background, a safety net against despair. Political beliefs on the other hand claimed the foreground, limiting the novelists' options in ways that eventually defeated them."[54]

In Russia today, now that Marxism has been discredited by the failure of the Soviet social experiment, it is Market Capitalism and Religion that the younger generation is examining in search of something to believe in. Johnstone's description of the ferment of English society of the 1930s, derived from numerous autobiographies and reminiscences, could equally well be applied to Russia in the post-Soviet period of the 1990s. Johnstone's description of a "movement from certainty to uncertainty, from order to chaos, a movement which the individual feels powerless to check"[55] sounds very much like Irina Shrejner's description of modern-day Russia in her presentation "The Phenomenon of Niennism," where she sees Niennism as a response to "the complete lack of any personal possibility of influencing events and processes, not just occurring within the surrounding world, but forming the surrounding world."

A closer look at the Round Table discussion ("Professor Tolkien and his Heritage") at which Shrejner spoke, offers an insight into the scope and breadth of the Russian search of Tolkien's writings for something to believe in. In his opening remarks, Petr Chistyakov, the event's organizer, characterized Russian Tolkienism as "a phenomenon that is unusually multifaceted, multidimensional, with its own complex internal structure." The wide range of talks presented at this event confirms his assessment.

Mariya Shtejnman's comparison of Tolkien and C.S. Lewis in her presentation ("The Prose of Tolkien and Lewis: The Formal Similarities and Different Themes"), points to a growing popularity gap between the two. While Lewis is more philosophical, theological and didactic, Tolkien created his own myth. Entering Tolkien's "secondary creation" of another world has become the goal of many Russian young people, and this side of the Russian phenomenon of Tolkienism is being described as "neo-paganism". Shtejnman feels Tolkien would have been very much surprised to hear himself referred to as a "neo-paganist", and insightfully notes that it is more a fact of Tolkien's name being associated with the current young people's movement than his philosophy.

This point of view is unintentionally supported by Petr Chistyakov and Mikhail A. Sivertsev who, in their presentations, discuss the seemingly paradoxical phenomenon of Russian 'Tolkienists" who have not read Tolkien. This is a reflection of what Asmolov and Kamenkovich were talking about. It is Tolkien being adapted to the Russian mental climate.

In his presentation ("Tolkien's Works: Sacred Texts or Pseudo-Historical Chronicles?"), Petr Chistyakov examines the significance of Tolkien's "pseudo-historical chronicles" in Russian Tolkienism. Initially, Russian Tolkienism grew out of Tolkien's texts. The texts are a link between two places: the world of the quasi-historical past and the present. Russian Tolkienism, however, has grown much larger than the texts. Chistyakov asserts that contemporary experience has shown that it is possible to be a Tolkienist without having read Tolkien. "This seemingly paradoxical situation is explained by the fact that Tolkien's reality is much broader than the text, and many of its aspects remain outside the framework of the narrative." This means that Tolkien's world and his text are not synonymous, and that it is possible to immerse oneself in Tolkien's world, bypassing the text. The texts, nevertheless, retain their status as sacred texts for a movement that is beginning to function independently, without direct connection to the texts.

In her rebuttal to Chistyakov's presentation, Ekaterina Kinn pointedly noted that, while there are people who do believe that Tolkien's texts are sacred, they are but a small minority. Drawing a comparison between the modern-day phenomenon of Tolkienism and the past phenomenon of Soviet Communism, she says that to this day, there are also "people, who religiously believe in the history of the CPSU [Communist Party of the Soviet Union]," but that does not make it true.

Dmitrij Gromov supports Kinn's view in his presentation ("Tolkienism as a Return to Mythological Consciousness"), in which he examines whether Tolkien's mythology—defined as "a specific perception of the world"—is, or can become a religion. While he notes that "without a doubt mythological consciousness is religious," he adds that the majority of the people associated with Tolkienism do not perceive it as a form of world view, but rather as a game, referring to the popularity of the 'Hobbit Games".

Vladimir Sviridov, a member of the TTT and attendee at the conference, said that the religious content of Tolkien's works is not especially significant for the "tolkinutye" (pl.). While members of the project team are both Christians and Atheists, and even religious non-Christians, religion is not an issue in the work of the project to bring Tolkien's texts to the Russian-speaking world, continues Sviridov. The project's charter, he points out, specifically forbids team members from undertaking any religious or atheistic activities in the name of the project.[56]

In her own presentation ("Parallel Story Lines in *The Silmarillion* and *The Lord of the Rings* as a Reflection of Christianity and the 'Northern theory of Courage'"), Ekaterina Kinn comments on the tendency of analyses of Tolkien to focus on only one aspect of Tolkien's mythology. They either demonstrate its resemblance to Christian or Christianized mythology or its resemblance to European pagan mythology. She finds that Tolkien needs to be compared to Tolkien, examining the development of individual story lines in his Legendarium, pointing to an article by Irina Emel'yanova as a good example. This article traces the development of the story line of Finrod. She views the history of this story line as "a pivotal moment, connecting the ethics and models of behavior of pagan Northern theory of Courage and of Christianity. It is the breakdown of the barrier between the two ethics." Christianity creeps into Tolkien's pre-Christian world through the actions of the heroes. The pagan hero dies, dooming all around him, because he acts according to the pagan mythological stereotype, while the true hero acts counter to this stereotype and becomes a savior. "The evangelization of this story line is what Tolkien was talking about in his lecture 'On Fairy-Stories'; we can see the Gospels in every fairy tale. This is how the duality of mythology is realized and how it becomes intertwined."

Mikhail A. Sivertsev begins his presentation ("Tolkienism as an Element of Neo-Religiosity") with a provocative question to which he gives his own provocative reply. "Do the prerequisites exist for the development of a Tolkienian Church, not just the concept, but an organization with all the appropriate attributes?" He lists a minimum of four characteristics necessary for that to happen, which had already been touched on during the course of the Round Table. The first is the presence of a sacred text. The second is the potential of constructing a sacred history. The third is the presence of Tolkienists, who have not read Tolkien. The fourth is the continuing discussion of who is a Tolkienist. All of these are characteristics of existing religions. He concludes with the assertion that the appearance of "a strong Tolkienian Church" within the next hundred years is indeed a possibility.

There was a strong negative audience reaction to Sivertsev's presentation, which the next speaker, Aleksandra Barkova ("The History and Meaning of the Culture of Tolkienism" and "Tolkienist Thinking"), attributed to modern Russians' concept of "The Church" with its associations of State control and hierarchical structures built up during the Soviet period. She noted that throughout its history, the Tolkienist movement has strived to avoid these kinds of structures. "The idea of introducing membership cards for some Tolkienist Club runs contrary to the essence of Russian Tolkienism." The key difference between Tolkienism as it has taken shape on the territory of the former Soviet Union and as it has taken shape in America lies in "the questioning of Tolkien's system of values." This is "to a considerable extent, the core of the Russian Tolkienist movement." This does not mean that Russian Tolkienists completely reject all of Tolkien's values. "We love Aragorn, especially the ladies, we deeply respect Frodo, but at the same time we cannot forgive the Valar for the loss of Numenor and many other things." Melkorianism, rebellion, is the quintessence of Russian Tolkienism. The Russian Tolkienist movement grew out of "opposition to Soviet ideology," which forms one of the two component parts of the movement; the first being Tolkien's works themselves. This opposition to governmental structures, in turn, led to the questioning of Tolkien's values. "We all remember the 'Ainulindale', we all remember the prescriptiveness of the 'themes given out' by Iluvatar." Russian Tolkienism is anti-establishmentarian.

In her presentation ("On the Connections of Tolkienistics with Religious Systems: An Attempt at Polemics"), Irina Shrejner makes a plea not to be too quick to classify Tolkienism as a religion. She cites an article in the recent issue of *Professional*, the official journal of the Russian Ministry of the Interior [the police], entitled "Religious Cults of Evil as a Source of Crime," to support her fears of potential police intervention. Her fears center around a quote she makes from the article. "Ecumenicalism, eclecticism, and vague formulations in spiritual-moral space, as well as assertions that there are ALLEGEDLY a number of truths, are beneficial only for concealing criminal activity and destructiveness..." Her fears reflect the Soviet experience, and are not without foundation in post-Communist Russia.

Before beginning her examination of "Tolkienism and Magic", Natal'ya Filimonova provides a definition of Tolkienism as it exists in Moscow. It is a liminal sociocultural phenomenon, like the hippies, "uniting fans of fantasy with a common or similar world view supposing the presence of a Secondary World (a term taken from Tolkien's essay "On Fairy-Stories") based on the model of Tolkien's Middle-earth (*The Silmarillion*, *The Lord of the Rings*, *The Hobbit*), who are striving to recreate elements of the Secondary World in reality (i.e. role-playing games). [...] It appeared in the crisis period of the late eighties and early nineties, and, it is, perhaps, for this reason that the value system of Tolkienism runs counter not only to Communist ideology, but also to those values that are now developing in Russian society. Like any liminal system (the hippies, punkers), Tolkienism is anti-authoritarian. You could say that Tolkienism is a continuation of a search for values that could be called common to all mankind. That is, first and foremost, the search for spirituality, for an understanding that the spiritual has precedence over the material, the search for love (true love and not what they preach nowadays), harmony with nature, good and mercy (good and mercy not in the Christian sense, but nevertheless ...)." The key to understanding the relationship of magic to Tolkienism is "the belief in the actual existence of a Secondary World," which is the basis of her definition of Tolkienism.

In the question and answer session that follows, she is forced to admit, however, that there are many Tolkienists, who do not practice magic, and that this definition cannot be applied to all Tolkienists. This reinforces Kinn's and Gromov's objections to painting all "Tolkienists" with the same brush, and only serves to highlight the diversity of Russian Tolkienism.

Anna Sal'nikova ("Tolkienism and the Contemporary Rebirth of Paganism in Russia") criticizes recent articles in the press, comparing

Tolkienism to neo-paganism, as superficial. While she admits that there are a number of characteristics common to both groups, the key difference is the military-like regimentation of the neo-pagan groups, which she sees as completely alien to Tolkienism. Both the neo-paganists and Tolkienists are trying to reconstruct a sort of lost "Golden Age". In the case of Tolkienism, "the basis for this reconstruction is found in the quasi-historical chronicles created by professor Tolkien in the fifties." Tolkien's works talk about a primordial age "in which the human race coexisted with tribes of other anthropomorphic and intelligent beings, and there was a place in the world for miracles and magic." Regaining this lost age offers a chance to be cleansed of the ills of the present. "Tolkienists sometimes seek out their personal place in Tolkienian reality by identifying themselves with a specific persona, sometimes using their own images, identifying in this way, the true essence of themselves."

In her presentation ("The Phenomenon of Neo-Religiosity: 'Finding Oneself' in Tolkienism"), Kseniya Yartseva touches on that very topic. She discusses the effect of the rite of taking on the name and persona of a character from Tolkien's works. "Tolkienists' concepts of the world and the events occurring in it are different, but identifying oneself with some concrete personality from the world created (or described) by Tolkien is a distinguishing characteristic of the world view of every Tolkienist." She feels this identification helps the individual to discover a new "me," which exists in the parallel Tolkienian reality and supplements the "me" of this reality. This makes it possible for an individual to exist both within the bounds of the reality created by Tolkien's Secondary World and within the bounds of the twenty-first century, which enables the Tolkienist to return to the primordial state of the original, complete individual that is described in a number of mythological world views of the duality of the individual.

Dmitrij Vinokhodov identifies three approaches to the study of Tolkien's texts in his presentation ("Approaches to the Study of Tolkien's Texts"): philological, canonical-historiographic and historical. Vinokhodov feels that the philological approach is the most realistic, because it attempts to understand Tolkien's works as works of literature connected to objective reality by their origins in the epic cycles of the peoples of Northern and Western Europe, Catholic religious concepts and English literary tradition. The two other approaches treat Tolkien's works as real quasi-historical documents, miraculously preserved through the ages, which describe events of the distant past. The difference between them is the categorization of the texts. The canonical-historiographic approach deals with the inconsistencies in Tolkien's texts by "canonizing" some and rejecting others. The historical approach regards all of Tolkien's texts as authentic. It does not regard the inconsistencies as troublesome errors made by the author, which have to be identified and eliminated, but examines them and attempts to explain their meaning.

While Vinokhodov's approach to the study of Tolkien is a good one in an English-speaking environment, it leaves aside the problem of the study of Tolkien for the monoglot Russian speaker, who has to contend with the numerous competing translations of Tolkien's works. Given that Russian Tolkianity is so far along the way to becoming a religion, or at least a philosophy, more attention should be paid to producing a "canonical" Russian translation than to identifying "canonical" texts.

In a private letter to David Doughan, Christopher Tolkien said:

[T]he deliberations at the Russian State University for the Humanities in Moscow last April introduce a new dimension, or colonizes new territory, in my atlas of Tolkienia: and it is very much less depressing than reading correspondence about the "creation" in America of a Lord of the Rings breakfast cereal. But these Russian thoughts on sacred texts, or on a "Tolkienism" that exists independently of any knowledge of what he wrote (because "Tolkienian reality is broader than the text"), float at a level above my critical capacity. I can however suggest some (admittedly well-known) words of the new prophet that might be carved on the portal of the Tolkienist temple or cathedral when it is built: "I begin to feel that I am shut up in a madhouse" (letter to his publishers, 12 September 1965).

Christopher Tolkien's comment is more on the mark in Russia than he probably imagined. Russia is, after all, the land in which a fan of Tolkien's works is referred to as a *Mythomaniac Tolkienensis* [толкинутый (tolkinutyj)].

Notes:

1. Большой энциклопедический словарь, М: Советская энциклопедия, 1991, т. 2, стр. 480.
2. *A Reader's Companion to The Hobbit and The Lord of the Rings*, NY.: Quality Paperback Book Club, 1995, p. 41.
3. Англия: Журнал о сегодняшней жизни в Великобритании.
4. An unpublished interview with Evgeniya Smagina, eMail Tue, 19 Dec. 2000 11:30:50 +0300 (MSK).
5. The dates are taken from the title page of the manuscript.
6. An unpublished interview with A.A. Gruzberg.
7. Smagina, eMail.
8. Smagina, eMail.
9. Arkadij and Boris Strugatskij are co-authors of a number of science fiction novels critical of the Soviet state, that were not permitted to be officially published in the Soviet Union. These novels were published in tamizdat (outside the Soviet Union) and samizdat.
10. Pre-publication copy of Круглый стол: «Профессор Толкин и его наследие», 22 апреля 2000 года, РГГУ. стр. 5. These materials were subsequently published in *Palantir*, No. 25-27, 2003.
11. eMail Fri, 15 Dec. 2000 00:55:25 +0300 (MSK).
12. Алексей Киякин, В начале было слово …(памяти кондуктора под вагоном) <http://www.kulichki.com/tolkien//arhiv/ugolok/posadnik.html>. Also, eMail 16 Dec. 2000 02:46:52 +0300 (MSK).
13. Анатолий Мошницкий, Евразийские тенденции в отечественной литературе жанра фэнтэзи, <http://arctogaia.krasu.ru/works/moshnitsky1.shtm>.
14. <http://www.luminet.net/~tgort/empire.htm>.
15. Skibniewska, Maria, Władca Pierścieni, Warsaw: Czytelnik Publishers, Vol. 1 (Wyprawa), 1961; Vol. 2 (Dwie wieże), 1962; Vol. 3 (Powrót króla), 1963.
16. This issue is discussed in some detail in: Nataliya Semenova. „К вопросу о генезисе русских переводов «Властелина Колец» Дж.Р.Р. Толкина", in *Palantir*, No. 37, 2003, pp. 20-34.
17. „Творчество Толкиена как литературный и социальный феномен", Доклад на фестивале „Звездный мост-99" 8 октября 1999 г., секция „Фантастика и просветительская традиция на рубеже тысячелетий". <http://www.kulichki.com/tolkien/arhiv/manuscr/nemirova.shtml>
18. <http://www.ozon.ru>.
19. J.R.R. Tolkien. *The Hobbit, or There and Back Again*, M: Presto Publishers, 2000. Text abridged and adapted by S.N. Cherkhanova. Illustrations M.I. Sukharev.

20. J.R.R. Tolkien. *The Lord of the Rings*, M: Rolf Publishers, 2002-03. In the "Let's read in the original" series.
21. Petr Yakovlevich Chaadaev (1794-1856) was the first Western-style Russian philosopher. Chaadaev spent six years in Western Europe where he met such famous thinkers as Lamennais and Schelling. In the nineteenth century, his *Philosophical Letters* touched off the battle between the Slavophiles and the Westerners.
22. Quoted in: Marthe Blinoff, *Life and Thought in Old Russia*, Clearfield, PA: The Pennsylvania State University Press, 1961, p. 179.
23. Quoted in: Stuart Ramsay Tompkins, *The Russian Mind: From Peter the Great Through the Enlightenment*, Norman, OK: University of Oklahoma Press, 1953, p. 230.
24. Интервью с переводчицей М. Каменкович. газета „Смена", 1.06.95 <http://www.fbit.ru/elinor/jrrt/intervi.htm>.
25. eMail 11 Dec. 2000 23:18:40 +0300 (MSK).
26. Малинина, Юлия, „Я не плясал на трупе Толкиена", МК-Бульвар, 10-16 июля 2000 г., стр. 42-47.
27. Ник Перумов, Кольцо тьмы: 1) Эльфийский клинок, 2) Черное копье, 3) Адамант Хенны, СПб: Терра—Азбука, 1996.
28. Sergey Petrovich Melgounov (1879-1956), *The Red Terror in Russia: 1918-1923*, London, Toronto: Dent, 1925.
29. Ниэннах (Васильева, Н.Э.), Иллет (Некрасова, Н.В.), Черная книга Арды: Крылья черного ветра, М: ДИАС лтд, 1995; М: ЭКСМО-Пресс, 2000. Черная книга Арды: Исповедь стража, М: ЭКСМО-Пресс, 2000.
30. Pre-publication copy of Круглый стол: «Профессор Толкин и его наследие», 22 апреля 2000 года, РГГУ. стр. 45-47. These materials were subsequently published in *Palantir*, No. 25-27, 2003.
31. Сергей Смирнов. J.R.R. — как жертва «национального» перевода, <http://uralstalker.ekaterinburg.com/2000/02/0002-10.html>.
32. К.В. Асмолов. О Толкине, толкинизме и толкинутых: заметки историка-наблюдателя, 1997, <http://www.kulichki.com/tolkien/arhiv/fandom/makavity.shtml>.
33. <http://www.kulichki.com/tolkien/forum/showthread.php?s=&threadid=547>, <http://www.kulichki.com/tolkien/forum/showthread.php?s=&threadid=548>, <http://www.kulichki.com/tolkien/forum/showthread.php?s=&threadid=549>.
34. <http://www.kulichki.com/tolkien/index.html>.
35. <http://ivbespalov.chat.ru/library.htm>, 23 January, 2002.
36. <http://fan.theonering.net/~henneth-annun/cgi-bin/kompoll/poll_ssi.cgi>.
37. The subtitles team is listed in the bibliography under "Subtitles."
38. Асмолов, 1997.

39. This is the same Arbat Street that was made famous in the Arbat Trilogy by Anatolij N. Rybakov (1911-1999): 1) Дети Арбата, 2) Страх: тридцать пятый и другие годы 3) Прах и пепел.
40. <http://www.kulichki.com/tolkien/forum/showthread.php?s=&threadid=549>.
41. БТСРЯ, стр. 1347.1.
42. С. Кириллова, „Наши студенты уже на четвертой стадии толкиенутости", Комсомольская правда, 27.11.93.
43. Асмолов, 1997.
44. Bruce Sterling, "Compost of Empire," *Wired*, Issue 2.04, April 1994.
45. Quoted at the Russian Tolkienist site Eglador <http://kulichki.rambler.com/tolkien/ambar/eglador/welcome.html>.
46. By Elrin (Эльрин), the Tolkienish pseudonym for Marina Avdonina. <http://www.kulichki.com/tolkien/kaminzal/txt1ah/elrin7.html>.
47. Болезнь, симптом, лекарство, <http://www-koi.sf.amc.ru/esli/rubr/publ/es499gon.htm>.
48. R. Johnstone, *The Will to Believe: Novelists of the 1930s*, Oxford University Press, 1982, p. 1.
49. Johnstone, p. 3.
50. "Some Notes on Auden's Early Poetry" (1937) *Exhumations*, p. 19, quoted in Johnstone, p. 11.
51. <http://www.webboard.ru/mes.php?id=4835970&fs=0&ord=0&board=8571&lst=&arhv=yes>.
52. Those who find the creation of a religious movement based on the writings of a modern author completely out in left field, are invited to read more about Tolstoyanism, a religious movement based on the teachings of the Russian novelist count Leo Tolstoy (1828-1910), the author of *War and Peace* and *Anna Karenina*. *"Tolstoyanism"* became a moral force throughout the world, and was an influence on Mahatma Gandhi.
53. <http://kulichki.rambler.com/moshkow/LEWISCL/aboutlewis.txt>.
54. Johnstone, p. 137-38.
55. Johnstone, p. 1.
56. eMail: Monday, 4 February 2002 03:04:44 +0300.

Chapter 2

A Hobbit's Tale
⸪ᛏᛔᛚᚴᛁᛖᚾ⸪ᛏᚻᚱᛟᚢᚷᚻ⸪ᚱᚢᛋᛋᛁᚨᚾ⸪ᛖᚣᛖᛋ⸪

> Then the prophecies of the old songs have turned out to be true, **after a fashion**!
> Bilbo Baggins (H.286, **emphasis** added)

The Russian reader can choose from nine complete Russian translations of *The Hobbit*, each of them different from the others, and from the original in its own way. Six of them are from translators (marked with an asterisk *) who likewise translated *LotR*.

1. Anonymous
2. Zinaida A. Bobyr'*
3. Aleksandr A. Gruzberg*
4. Mariya Kamenkovich*
5. Kirill Korolev
6. Valeriya A. Matorina, a.k.a "VAM" *
7. Nataliya Rakhmanova
8. Semen Umanskij*
9. Leonid Yakhnin*

The *LotR* translators need no special introduction, as they are discussed at length in other parts of the present volume. The exclusively Hobbit translators, however, do.

The Anonymous samizdat translation comes from the World Wide Web. It reads well, and, if it were the only version, it would be a worthy effort. In comparison to the other versions, however, it lacks the sparkle to make it stand out.

The Korolev translation published by Terra Fantastica Publishing, is part of a complete set of Tolkien's collected works in Russian. Its characteristic feature, unfortunately, is its changes to the original. In Chapter V ("Riddles in the Dark"), for example, the narrator's description of the creatures living under the mountains is changed to omit the harmless, lost fish and concentrates on the more sinister inhabitants. Korolev's narrator says:

> Ходили слухи, что в горных подземельях обитают диковинные существа, чьи предки затаились во мраке невесть сколько лет назад, когда им опротивел солнечный свет. Отчасти эти слухи были справедливы: даже в пещерах, обжитых гоблинами, встречались такие твари, о существовании которых не подозревали и сами гоблины (вообще-то эти самые твари обитали в подземельях от начала времени —гоблины всего-навсего бесцеремонно захватили их пещеры, а потом соединили проходами). (Kr H.90)

BT: There were rumors that the mountain underworld was populated by strange beings, whose forefathers hid themselves in the dark untold years ago, when the light of day became abhorrent to them. In part, these rumors were justified: even in the caves inhabited by the goblins, creatures could be found, the existence of which the goblins themselves did not suspect (in general, these creatures had populated the underworld since the beginning of time—the goblins, by and large, unceremoniously seized their caves and afterwards connected them with passages).

JRRT (lacunae **highlighted**): There are strange things living **in the pools and lakes in the hearts of** mountains: **fish whose fathers swam in, goodness only knows how many years ago, and never swam out again, while their eyes grew bigger and bigger and bigger from trying to see in the blackness; also there are other things more slimy than fish.** Even in the **tunnels and** caves the goblins **have made for themselves** there are other things living unbeknown to them that have sneaked in from outside to lie up in the dark. Some of the caves, too, go back in their beginnings to ages before the goblins, who only widened them and joined them up with passages, **and the original owners are still there in odd corners, slinking and nosing about**. (H.78-79)

Rakhmanova's was the first officially published complete translation and is also the most widely available. The first edition of her translation came out in 1976 while the publishing industry was still under State control in the Soviet Union, and it reflects its heritage. Her translation is the most readable, and continues to be reprinted. It was recently included in a Russian compendium[1] of the best fairy tales of the twentieth century, where it is kept company by Lewis Carroll's *Alice in Wonderland*, James Barry's *Peter Pan*, Rudyard Kipling's *Mowgli* and *Rikki-tikki-tavi*, Evgenij Shvarts's, *Cinderella* (Золушка [Zolushka]) and *The Dragon* (Дракон [Drakon]), Yurij Olesha's, *The Three Fat Men* (Три толстяка [Tri tolstyaka]), Antoine de Saint Exupery's *The Little Prince*, P.L. Travers's *Mary Poppins*, Astrid Lindgren's *Karlson on the Roof* and Yurij Koval's *The Silver Fox Napoleon III* (Недопёсок Наполеон III [Nedopyesok Napoleon III]).

The honor for the first published excerpt of *The Hobbit* in Russian, however, goes to Англия [Angliya][2] magazine, which, in 1969, published an unattributed translation of a part of Chapter VII ("Queer Lodgings"), in which Bilbo and the Dwarves visit Beorn. *Angliya* magazine was a product of the Cold War. It was published in Russian by the British government for distribution in the Soviet Union as a source of positive information about life in the United Kingdom to counter the normally negative reporting on England in the Soviet, State-controlled press. In exchange for permitting the distribution of *Angliya* in the Soviet Union, the Soviets could distribute their own English-language propaganda magazine in the U.K. While distribution of *Angliya* was essentially restricted to Moscow and Leningrad, where the British diplomatic legations were located, *Angliya* was to some extent successful in spreading British ideas.

There are two editions of the Bobyr' *Hobbit*. Version A was published in 1991 by Molodaya Gvardiya Publishers in Moscow. Version B was copyrighted in 1992 by Knizhnyj Mir Publishers in Perm'. Version B was edited by Yuliya Batalina, Gruzberg's daughter, who played a double role in the project. She was not only the editor, but also the proofreader, working under the pen-name of A. Romanova. She was joined by her husband, Aleksej Batalin, who took on the role of technical editor. The version B edition of the Bobyr' *Hobbit* was originally conceived as a companion volume to accompany Knizhnyj Mir's edition of Gruzberg's translation of *LotR*, and consequently, the names were all changed to match those in Gruzberg's *LotR*. Other than the names, the differences between the two versions are mostly minor editorial changes. Even though the Knizhnyj Mir team considered Rakhmanova's translation better, they settled on Bobyr's translation because there was a problem with obtaining the rights to the Rakhmanova. In the end, the plan to publish Gruzberg's *LotR* at Knizhnyj Mir fell through, but the Bobyr' *Hobbit* nevertheless made it into publication in 1994. Gruzberg's own translation of *The Hobbit* was done later. The Umanskij translation of

The Hobbit, which was originally thought to be version C of the Bobyr' *Hobbit* edited by Umanskij, has never been published.

In addition to the nine full translations, there is a Russian translation of the English-language comic-book abridgement of *The Hobbit*, done by Charles Dixon and Sean Deming (D&D) with the David Wenzel illustrations.[3] The illustrations, to some extent, make up for the abridgement, which left out some, but not all of the translation challenges discussed in the present volume. This translation was done by Lyudmila Kaminskaya.

There are also three comic-book editions of *The Hobbit*, which compress the story into 60, 12 and 16 pages respectively:

1. the N. Utilova edition, published by *Avlad* in 1992, illustrated by R. Ramazanov, A. Shevtsov and R. Azizov,
2. the S. Sedov edition, published by *Belyj gorod* in 1999, illustrated by E. Uzdennikova,
3. the Lev Yakovlev edition, published by *Egmont Rossia* in 2001, illustrated by Elena Volod'kina.

The texts of the comic-book editions are so abbreviated that none of the philosophical issues of translating Tolkien's work would seem to come into play in them. While a picture is normally said to be worth a thousand words, the cover illustrations on these three volumes all have one detail that makes them all immediately recognizable as Russian, and that detail boils down to one word: *feet*. Tolkien said that the Hobbits seldom wore shoes, "because their feet grow natural leathery soles and thick warm brown hair." (H.16) In the Russian translations, the word most often used for *feet* in this sentence was ноги [nogi]. This is a word that does not distinguish between *foot* and *leg*. It means both together. All three of the comic books show Bilbo in three-quarter length pants, with thick hair covering both his feet and as much of his legs as can be seen. The effect is to make Bilbo look like his bottom half is a bear.

The translators whom the Russian reading public have to thank for this are Rakhmanova (the author of the first and most-often republished version), Gruzberg, Umanskij, VAM, Kamenkovich and Yakhnin. Sedov was the only comic-book editor to include this phrase and he used the word ноги [nogi] as well. The other translators worked their way around this problem by using one or the other of the two Russian words that correspond to the English word *foot*: ступня [stupnya] or стопа [stopa]. It is not hard to guess that the illustrators did not read Anonymous, Bobyr', Kaminskaya or Korolev.

Tolkien repeated the explanation of why Hobbits infrequently wore shoes in *LotR*. (F.20) Of the ten *LotR* translators, five—Gruzberg, VAM, G&G, Nemirova, Umanskij and Yakhnin—used the word ноги [nogi]. Yakhnin used the diminutive form ножки [nozhki], which makes the Hobbits seem small and cute. (Ya F.8) G&G hedged their bet a little, and included a parenthetical after ноги [nogi] that said "especially lower down" (книзу в особенности), which was not a bad work-around for this problem. (G&G F.10) M&K, Volkovskij and Gruzberg's CD-ROM editor, Aleksandrova, all used ступня [stupnya]. Bobyr' omitted this detail, and K&K had a none-of-the-above solution. Their narrator said that "a thick, curly fur, like that on their heads, grew on their ankles" (на щиколотках у них, равно как и на голове, росла густая вьющая шерстка). (K&K F.19)

The word *feet* can hardly be considered a complex philosophical concept, but its treatment in the Russian translations of *The Hobbit* and *LotR* is a good example of the myriad challenges that the translators faced in trying to bring Tolkien to the Russian reading public. Bridging the cultural gap is harder than it looks.

Editions

Tolkien produced three editions of *The Hobbit*. The changes that distinguish each of these editions are not simply cosmetic, but are changes to the characters and plot, prompted, in part, by a need to make the story lines of *The Hobbit* and *LotR* agree. The changes to Gollum's character, for example, are studied in Bonniejean Christiansen's article in *A Tolkien Compass*.[4] Each of the changes to the text is carefully detailed in Douglas A. Anderson's *The Annotated Hobbit*.[5] Two of the Russian translations were done from the second edition, while the rest were done from the third.

The third edition (1966) of *The Hobbit* can be distinguished from the first (1937) and the second (1951) by the line in Chapter III ("A Short Rest"), which in the first and second editions reads: "One afternoon they forded a river …" In the third edition, it reads: "One morning they forded a river …" In the Bobyr', Umanskij and Gruzberg translations, the party crosses the river in the afternoon. (B H_{1994}.55; U H.39; G H.47) In the Rakhmanova, VAM, Kamenkovich, Korolev, Yakhnin and Anonymous translations the river crossing took place in the morning, indicating that these translations were done from the third edition. Neither the D&D, nor any of the comic books contains this sentence.

The second edition (1951) incorporates changes to Chapter V ("Riddles in the Dark"), in which Bilbo 'wins' the Ring from Gollum in a riddling contest. The second edition can be distinguished from the first (1937) by the line in Chapter V that in the first edition reads: "before the goblins came, and he was cut off from his friends far under under [sic] the mountains." In the second edition, this line became: "before he lost all his friends and was driven away, alone, and crept down, down, into the dark under the mountains." In the Bobyr', Umanskij and Gruzberg translations, Gollum lost all his friends, which points to the second edition rather than the first as the source text for them. (B H_{1994}.89; U H.55; G H.73) While the parallel English text in the Gruzberg/Aleksandrova CD-ROM is from the third edition, no effort was made to make the Russian text—from the second edition—match.

The West is Dead. Long live God!

> But there's no accounting for East and
> West, as we say in Bree
> Barliman Butterbur (F.214)

The pages of *The Hobbit* tell the tale of the adventures and battles that took place on the eve of the War of the Ring, which marked the end of the Third Age on Middle-earth. The pages of the first official Russian translation of *The Hobbit* not only tell that tale, but also the tale of another war that is closer to our own time: the Cold War. The tale of the Cold War, however, is so skillfully woven into the text, that—like Lunar Letters—it can only be read in a certain light. To read the tale of the Cold War you have to read the Rakhmanova translation side by side with Tolkien's original text or with one of the post-Soviet editions. The Russians love to play games like this. Reading between the lines is practically every Russian intellectual's favorite sport.

The jargon of the Cold War pitted "the West" against "the East." Since Russian readers are infamous for reading things into a text, even when they are not there, every mention of the word *west*, where it could have been (mis)construed as the political West of the Cold War—the enemy of the political East, the Soviet Union—was expurgated from the text of the first official Russian edition of *The Hobbit*. Rakhmanova, however, did not just cave-in to the censors, but rather skillfully played a game of hide-and-seek with them. While references to *west* were relegated to the dust bin of history with efficient dispatch, every exclamation of surprise or amazement based on one of Tolkien's empty euphemisms for God was translated non-euphemistically. "Good gracious me!" (H.19) became "Dear God!" (Боже милостивый!). Tolkien was a religious writer, but the word *God* does not make an appearance in *The Hobbit*. In Rakhmanova's version, on the other hand, God is alive and well in the speech of the book's characters. The effect of this change is to subtly move God into the foreground, while in Tolkien's version God is very much in the background. Since the Soviet state did its best to suppress religion in word and in deed, this was a subtly powerful statement on Rakhmanova's part.

Some Russians of the post-Communist generation continue to maintain that there are no traces of the Cold War in the Rakhmanova translation. They assert that the words *East* and *West* are both in their places and that the text was not embellished with the word *God*. When given the cites for the first (1976) edition, they usually counter that these problems were fixed in later editions. For those Russian readers, cites to the 2002 edition of the Rakhmanova translation are included as well.

In Chapter III ("A Short Rest"), in the scene in which Elrond examines the swords found in the trolls' lair, he says that they were made by "the High Elves of the West, my kin." (H.61) Rakhmanova's version left out the reference to *the West*, and the *High Elves* became the "elves of old."

> Мечи старинные, работы древних великих эльфов, с которыми я в родстве. (R H_{1976}.51, H_{2002}.41)
> BT: The swords are ancient, the work of the great Elves of old, to whom I am related.

This deletion is possibly the result of the influence of the Soviet inferiority complex about military technology; they copied the printed circuit boards for American sonar buoys right down to the copyright notice and boasted that their technology was the best. For a censor sensitive to this issue, the fact that the swords, which so impressed Elrond, were made in the West would be a sensitive one. It would have the potential of being (mis)read as a reference to the superiority of Western military technology, and, as such, would have to go.

All the other translators, except Gruzberg, Umanskij and Bobyr', left the word *West* right where it should have been. Kamenkovich even included an endnote explaining who the "High Elves of the West" were:

> High Elves—elves belonging to the elven tribes at the dawn of the history of Middle-earth, who, answering the call of the Valar, sailed off to Valinor (the place of residence of the Valar), but later returned to Middle-earth for various reasons. (K&K F.633)

The reason that there is no mention of *the West* in Gruzberg's, Umanksij's and Bobyr's renditions is that they were working from the second edition, in which the swords belonged, not to the "High Elves of the West, my kin" (H.61), but to "the Elves that are now called Gnomes." (AH.324) In earlier works in Tolkien's Legendarium, the name *Gnome* was used for the Noldor—those who know—playing on the meaning of the word *gnome*, which is *maxim* or *aphorism*. For the Russian translators, the word *Gnomes* was a major problem, because in Russian, гном [gnom] is also the translation for *Dwarf* in the context of folklore. The standard translation of *Snow White and the Seven Dwarves* is Белоснежка и семь гномов [Belosnezhka i sem' gnomov], and гном [gnom] is the word used for the *Dwarves* by all the translators, except in the Bobyr/Umanskij *LotR* and the Umanskij *Hobbit*. There, the Dwarves are called карлики [karliki (pl.)]. The decision to use гном [gnom] as the translation of *Dwarf* will, however, be a problem that will come back to roost as future translators tackle other, earlier works from Tolkien's Legendarium, and have to deal with Tolkien's use of the name *Gnome* to refer to the Noldor. Gruzberg and Bobyr' solved this problem, essentially as Tolkien instructed (L.318), by leaving out the end of the phrase: "that are now called Gnomes." Gruzberg's version reads:

> Это древние мечи, очень древние, и принадлежали они эльфам.
> (G H.54-55)
> BT: These are old swords, very old, and they belonged to Elves.

The CD-ROM edition of Gruzberg reads the same. Bobyr's version reads:

> Это древние, очень древние мечи ельфов (B H_{1994}.63)
> BT: These are old, very old swords of the Elves.

Umanskij was the only translator to use *Gnomes* at this point.

> Это старинные, очень старинные мечи тех эльфов, которых теперь называются Гномами. (U H.43)
> BT: These are old, very old swords of those Elves, who are now called the Gnomes.

His use of карлики [karliki (pl.)] as the translation of *Dwarves* dovetails perfectly with this.

In Chapter VIII ("Flies and Spiders"), the narrator's explanation of who the Wood-elves were is also deprived of its association with *the West*. In the original, the Wood-elves "differed from the High Elves of the West, and were more dangerous and less wise. For most of them (together with their scattered relations in the hills and mountains) were descended from the ancient tribes that never went to Faerie in the West." (H.164) For the sake of consistency with the segment above, if for no other reason, the reference to "the High Elves of the West" in this segment had to be changed, and Faerie, obviously, could not be located in the West. Its description in this segment makes it sound like the source of culture and learning, because the elven tribes that never went there were "more dangerous and less wise." At the height of the Cold War, that statement could easily have been interpreted as a comment on the Soviets, who were ever sensitive to comments about their level of cultural refinement and were constantly at odds with Western history's interpretation of who invented what when.

For example, while no mention was made of Aleksandr F. Mozhajskij (1825-1890) in the 1929 edition of the *Great Soviet Encyclopedia*, the 1949 edition pointedly underscores that Mozhajskij built the first airplane, 21 years before the Wright brothers made their first flight in 1903.[6] The same edition of the *Great Soviet Encyclopedia* proudly points to Aleksandr S. Popov (1859-1905/06) as the inventor of the radio.[7] The tone of these assertions had changed by the time that the *Soviet Encyclopedic Dictionary* of 1990 came out. There, the article on Mozhajskij only says that he was granted a patent on his flying machine in 1881, making no mention of the Wright brothers,[8] while the article on the Wright brothers credits them with making the world's first flight.[9] The article on Popov quietly calls him "one of the pioneers of putting electromagnetic waves to practical use," [10] with no direct comparison to the dates of Marconi's inventions.

The same sense of inferiority toward America (The West) can also be seen in a political joke that made the rounds during the Cold War.

> At a mass meeting:
> Political commentator: "Our goal is to catch up to and overtake America in every area!"
> Voice from the crowd: "And where is America now?"
> Political commentator: "America is on the brink of political, economic and moral collapse."

The joke was funny because the commentator's lines were clichés from Soviet political propaganda of the Cold War taken slightly out of context. Normally they would never be seen so close together. Therefore, from the point of view of a Soviet censor—brought up to believe that Mozhajskij built the first airplane and Popov the first radio, and inculcated with slogans that urged the Soviets to overtake America (The West)—Faerie could certainly not be in the West. Indeed, both references to *the West* in Rakhmanova's text are gone.

Они были не так мудры, как высшие эльфы, но тоже умели искусно колдовать и были более коварны. Ведь, большинство из них, в том числе их родственники с гор и холмов, происходили от древних племен, не посещавших славного Волшебного царства. (R H$_{1976}$.141, H$_{2002}$.107)

BT: They were not as wise as the high Elves, but they also knew how to skillfully practice magic and were more treacherous, because most of them, including their kin folk from the mountains and hills, were descended from the ancient tribes that had not visited the glorious Magic kingdom.

JRRT: They differed from the High Elves of the West, and were more dangerous and less wise. For most of them (together with their scattered relations in the hills and mountains) were descended from the ancient tribes that never went to Faerie in the West. (H.164)

Yakhnin also called it the Magic kingdom (Волшебное царство), but omitted "in the West." (Ya H.203) He did, however, have *West* where it belonged in the appellation of the High Elves.

None of the other translators had trouble with the location of Faerie. Anonymous said that Faerie was a "Wondrous Western Land" (Дивный Западный Край). Umanskij called Faerie the homeland of the ancient tribes, in the West (от древнего племени, родиной которого была страна Фэйрие, что на Западе). (U H.111) In the Bobyr' version, the Wood-elves had never been in the "distant homeland of the Elves—in the West" (далекая родина эльфов —на Западе). (B H$_{1994}$.193) VAM termed Faerie a "magical land beyond the edge [of the world] in the West" (волшебная страна на Заокраинном Западе). (VAM H$_{1990}$.137, H$_{2000}$.208) Gruzberg called Faerie "the magic kingdom in the west" (волшебное царство на западе). (G H.160) Korolev termed Faerie "the miraculous land that lies in the utter west" (чудесная страна, что лежит на крайнем западе). (Kr H.191) Kamenkovich located it "on the Elven Side, which is in the West" (в Эльфийской Стороне, что лежит на Западе), repeating her endnote about who the High Elves were. (Km H.168)

Even though the D&D abridged edition included the passage intact, Kaminskaya's translation of it seriously rearranged it, and deleted the reference to Faerie. Her version said:

Лесные эльфы не так мудры, как высшие эльфы из западных стран, а потому они опаснее. Большинство из них (так же, как и их родня, разбросанная среди гор и холмов) происходит от древних племен. (Ksk H.80)

BT: The Wood-elves are not as wise as the high Elves from the western countries, and they are, therefore, more dangerous. The majority of them (as well as their kin scattered about the mountains and hills) are descended from the ancient tribes.

Kaminskaya's rendition is a much more explicit statement than Tolkien's that less wisdom makes one more dangerous. It is also a much sharper comparison of the West and the East. It would never have been approved by the Soviet thought police.

Equally bad, if not worse, from the point of view of a Soviet censor is the description of the West in Thorin Oakenshield's farewell dialog with Bilbo. There, Thorin calls Bilbo a "child of the kindly West." (H.273) In the Soviet jargon of the Cold War, America and The West were always imperialist aggressors, so how could any politically correct Soviet censor possibly allow the West to be called *kindly* in *The Hobbit*? If Yakhnin had done his translation in the Soviet period, he would have passed muster for the censor. He omitted the entire phrase. (Ya H.342) Rakhmanova's 'censored' version called Bilbo a "child of a benevolent country" (родился в доброжелательном краю, R H_{1976}.240, H_{2002}.176), ignoring its geographic location. Of the other translators only Gruzberg and Umanskij joined Rakhmanova in choosing an adjective that reflects the opposition of *Good* and *Evil*. In their versions, Bilbo was "a child of the good west." (дитя доброго запада) (G H.271; U H.180) Theirs is the most correct rendition.

Most of the other translators chose adjectives that make the West sound like a kindly old grandmother. The majority vote in this category went to *gentle, tender* (ласковый, VAM H_{1990}.228, H_{2000}.348; B H.331; Km H.292), while the one dissenting vote went to: *delicate, effeminate* (изнеженный, Anonymous). Neither of these descriptions would have bothered any Soviet censor nearly as much as having the West be *benevolent* or *good*, and the East, by implication, be *mean* or *evil*. Kaminskaya made a none-of-the-above choice for an archaic word for *hospitable* (странноприимный, Ksk H.127), making the West a nice place to visit. Korolev, too, took a completely different tack. He made Bilbo a child of the *bright* west (светлый, Kr H.327), which prompts the modern reader to think of the light of the Two Trees of Valinor. At the same time, for Soviet readers, *bright* echoes the cliché for Soviet heaven, the "bright future" (светлое будущее) promised by Communism.[11]

In Chapter IV ("Over Hill and Under Hill"), the metaphor used by Tolkien's narrator to describe "thunder and lightning in the mountains at night" is also too politically sensitive for a politically correct Soviet book:

> More terrible still are thunder and lightning in the mountains at night, when storms come up from East and West and make war. (H.65)

For the Soviet censor, this metaphor implies the unthinkable terror of the Cold War turning hot and has to be removed. In Rakhmanova's text the storms come out of nowhere, while the other translators—less Yakhnin—all included their points of origin.

> Всякий знает, как страшно бушуют гром и молнии в горах, ночью, когда две грозы идут войной друг на друга. (R H_{1976}.55, H_{2002}.44)
> BT: Everyone knows how terrifyingly thunder and lightning rage in the mountains at night when two storms wage war on one another.

Yakhnin would have, once again, had no trouble passing review by a Soviet censor. His elegantly turned description of the storm at night in the mountains contained no mention of *East* or *West*.

> Но еще ужаснее ночная гроза в горах. Сверкание и грохот. Злобный вой и свист встречных ветров, скрутившихся в смертельной схватке. (Ya H.75)
> BT: But more terrible still is a night-time storm in the mountains. Flashing and rumbling. The malicious howl and whistle of winds meeting, twisted up together in a deadly fight.

Two of the translators—VAM and Anonymous—followed Tolkien's lead and capitalized *West* and *East*. In Russian, which has no articles (a, the), the effect of capitalization is to make it much easier to read *West* and *East* in their political sense of "The West" and "The East." In VAM's version, it was "a real heavenly war between East and West." (настоящая небесная война между Востоком и Западом) (VAM H_{1990}.52, H_{2000}.77) The addition of *heavenly* mitigates the impact a little, but this direct formulation is very easy to read with political overtones. Tolkien's formulation was much more indirect and subtle. The Anonymous version softpedaled the issue of war and peace even more by substituting "meet in single combat" (сходятся в единоборстве) for *make war*. This is a duel, a battle of champions with historical overtones. While this formulation could be read with a political subtext, it is not the Cold War turning hot. It is more like a summit meeting.

All the rest of the translators used lower case for *east* and *west*, which considerably lessens the tendency of the Russian reader to look for a political subtext between the lines. Kamenkovich's typically verbose, but correct version reads:

> [...] двигаясь навстречу друг другу с востока и запада, изрыгая громы и молнии, две грозы сошлись на страшную битву, да еще ночью! (Km H.63)
>
> BT: Moving toward one another from the west and the east, belching thunder and lightning, two storms converged for a terrible battle, and at night no less!

All of the translators who avoided capitalizing the *West* and *East*, also avoided the use of the word *war* (война). Korolev, like Kamenkovich, substituted the word *battle* (битва). In Korolev's version:

> [...] сходятся в битве стремительные вихри с запада и с востока! (Kr H.74)
>
> BT: rushing whirlwinds from the west and east come together in battle.

Even Gruzberg avoided the use of the word *war*. His formulation is closer stylistically to Tolkien's, and can be understood both literally and figuratively. While its first meaning is *an engagement on the field of battle*, its second is *an engagement on a sport field*. The standard desk-top defining dictionary offers the example of "soccer teams engaging one another" (Сражаются футбольные команды).[12]

> Но еще ужаснее гром и молнии в горах ночью, когда встречаются и начинают сражаться ветры с запада и востока.
>
> BT: But even more terrifying are thunder and lightning in the mountains at night, when winds from the west and the east meet and begin to engage one another.

Chernyak, Gruzberg's print editor, gave a martial air to this segment, replacing Gruzberg's ambiguity with the unambiguous phrase *enter into battle*. His version reads:

Но еще ужаснее гром и молнии в горах ночью, когда встречаются и вступают в битву ветры с запада и востока. (G H.58)

BT: But even more terrifying are thunder and lightning in the mountains at night, when winds from the west and the east meet and enter into battle.

Umanskij took essentially the same approach as Gruzberg. The only difference was that he used the noun derivative of Gruzberg's verb. His rendition reads:

Но еще ужаснее гром и молния ночью в горах, когда с востока и запада приходят ураганы и начинают сражение между собой. (U H.45)

BT: But even more terrifying are thunder and lightning in the mountains at night, when hurricanes come from the west and the east and start an engagement.

Bobyr' took yet another tack that is subtly closer to the original and could be read politically without evoking an image of the unthinkable Cold War turning hot. In her version:

Но еще ужаснее бывает гром и молния ночью в горах, когда сталкиваются и воюют между собой бури с востока и с запада. (В H_{1991}.44)

BT: But still more terrifying are thunder and lightning at night in the mountains, when storms from the east and the west collide and wage war with one another.

Batalina has a subtle one-letter, unintentional change in Bobyr's text that removed *wage war* from her version of the text.[13] In her version the storms "howl." The Russian verbs *to wage war* and *to howl* are differentiated by only one letter in the third-person plural. *To wage war* is воевать/воюют [voevat'/voyuyut]. *To howl* is выть/воют [vyt'/voyut]. This is the first of the two deviations between the two versions of Bobyr' considered in the present volume. (q.v. **Mirkwood**)

Но еще ужаснее бывает гром и молния ночью в горах, когда воют и сталкиваются между собой бури с востока и с запада. (В H_{1994}.69)

BT: But still more terrifying are thunder and lightning at night in the mountains, when storms from the east and the west howl and collide with one another.

While the thought of the unthinkable war was too much for them as well, these translators did preserve Tolkien's "East and West." D&D's abridged version condensed the passage so much that it would have been quite acceptable to the Soviet censors. D&D left out the sentence with "East and West" and "make war," choosing instead to use a sentence just before it.

All was well, until one day they met a thunderstorm—more than a thunderstorm, a thunder-battle. (D&D H.29; JRRT H.65)

Kaminskaya missed even the military subtleties of this abridgement, changing the *thunder-battle* into a *hurricane*:

Все было хорошо, пока однажды не началась буря. Да что там буря — ураган! (Ksk H.29)
BT: All was well, until one day a storm started. No, more than a storm, it was a hurricane!

This is essentially the same approach that Umanskij took in the segment about the storms from East and West making war, that was discussed above.

This formulation finds a certain resonance in Korolev's translation, which was published seven years later:

Началась буря — да какая там буря, самый что ни на есть настоящий ураган. (Kr H.74)
BT: A windstorm started — No, more than a windstorm, it was a real, honest to goodness hurricane.

None of the other translators turned the *thunder-battle* into a *hurricane*. Anonymous, Umanskij and Yakhnin used two weather synonyms (*thunderstorm* [гроза] and *windstorm* [буря]), but the comparison is equally flat. Yakhnin was also elegantly pacifistic, addressing his young readers directly with a question so as to make them feel more involved in the story.

Да что там гроза! Настоящая буря. Вы знаете, что такое буря, сметающая все на своем пути, или шторм на море, когда встречаются две разъяренные стихии? (Ya H.75)

BT: No, more than a thunderstorm! A real windstorm. Do you know what a storm is, sweeping everything from its path, or a gale at sea, when two enraged natural elements meet?

Kamenkovich also took a pacifist approach to *thunder-battle*, changing *thunderstorm* into a *gigantic thunderstorm* with a suffix that is added to make things huge in Russian. This is the same suffix that Volkovskij used to turn *stride* into *gigantic stride* in his description of the strides taken by the giant tree-men seen on the North Moors: шажище [shazhishche].

Gruzberg was right on target with his *thunder battle* (no dash is needed because the adjective *thunder* in Russian has a different morphological form from the noun *thunder*: громовая битва). Gruzberg's print editor, Chernyak, however, retreated from Gruzberg's well-formulated position and reduced Tolkien's *thunder-battle* to the same pedestrian *thunderstorm-windstorm* opposition that Anonymous and Yakhnin had used. (G H.58)

Rakhmanova had the most evocative, elegant image:

Казалось, гремит гром не грозовой, а пушечный. (R H_{1976}.55, H_{2002}.44)
BT: It seemed that the thunder was not that of a storm, but of cannon.

Bobyr' made it a *heavenly battle*. (небесная битва) (B H_{1994}.69) VAM repeated *heavenly* and combined it with the word *engagement* (небесное сражение, VAM H_{1990}.52, H_{1990}.76), the same root that Gruzberg and Umanskij used for their formulations of *make war*.

In Chapter XVI ("A Thief in the Night"), Bilbo wishes that he "was back in the West in my own home, where folk are more reasonable." (H.256) While Bilbo is talking about Thorin Oakenshield and not "the East," the comparison between The West and The East would have been practically inevitable in the Soviet reading climate. The obvious corollary to this would be that the folk in the East are unreasonable. Korolev was the only translator to remove *the West* from this segment. Even Rakhmanova's censors let it through. To give the censors their due, however, without the amplification of all the other repeats of *West* that had already been expurgated, the impact of this passage would have been minimal. Besides that, in Rakhmanova's version, the word *west* was written with a lower case letter, reducing the impact even further. Rakhmanova's version simply reads:

[…] домой, на запад, там жители гораздо благоразумнее.
R H₁₉₇₆.224, H₂₀₀₂.165)
BT: at home, in the west, the inhabitants are much more reasonable there.

Korolev not only threw out *the West*, but also *reasonability*:

Я всем этим уже сыт по горло и с радостью вернулся бы восвояси — там куда как спокойнее и уютнее. Загвоздка только в сокровищах. Мне кое-что из них причитается — если быть точным, одна четырнадцатая от общей доли. (Kr H.307)
BT: I am already fed up with this up to here and would happily go back home—where it is more peaceful and more comfortable. The only catch is the treasure. I'm due some of it—one fourteenth of the common share to be exact.
JRRT (lacunae **highlighted**): Personally I am tired of the whole affair. I wish I was back **in the West** in **my own** home, where **folk are more reasonable**. But I have an interest in this matter—one fourteenth share, to be precise, […] (H.256)

When *the East* was accompanied by negative modifiers in Tolkien's text, it met the same fate at the hands of Rakhmanova's Soviet censors as *the West* did with positive modifiers. It was disappeared. In Chapter XIV ("Fire and Water"), the narrator explains that "the men of the lake-town Esgaroth were mostly indoors, for the breeze was from the black East and chill […]" (H.234) In the context of *LotR*, the word *black* has a number of negative connotations: the black arts (T.363), the black breath (F.236, R.171), the Black Country (Mordor), the Black Gate (Morannon), the Black Horsemen (Nazgul), the Black Land (Mordor), the Black Master (Sauron), the Black One (Sauron), the Black Riders (Nazgul), the Black Speech, the Black Years .(F.81, F.333) Tolkien undoubtedly had this meaning in mind.

Anonymous made *the East* sound like Mirkwood with his/her "a piercing wind blew from the gloomy east" (с мрачного востока дул пронизывающий ветер). Kamenkovich has the breeze blowing "from the darkened east" (с потемневшего востока, Km H.247) These are both good efforts, but are much more understated than Tolkien's *black East*. In the Rakhmanova translation, the direction from which the breeze came was expurgated, and the adjective that had belonged to it now described the sky.

> Жители Озёрного города Эсгарота сидели по домам, испугавшись сильнейшего ветра и промозглого воздуха (R H_{1976}.202, H_{1976}.151)
> BT: The inhabitants of the Lake-town Esgaroth sat at home, frightened by the very strong wind and the dank sky.

Most of the other translators follow Rakhmanova's lead and interpret *black* as the color of the sky and not as the color of *the East*. VAM said: "it was overcast and a cold wind blew from the east." (было пасмурно и с востока дул холодный ветер) (VAM, H_{1990}.195, H_{1990}.297) Gruzberg, Bobyr' and Korolev deprived *the East* of its modifier. Bobyr's rendition has the people of Esgaroth staying at home because "the east wind was very cold" (восточный ветер был очень холодным, B H_{1994}.281), without saying anything about *the East* being black. Yakhnin's narrator also talks of a "cold east wind" (холодный восточный ветер) (Ya H.293) Gruzberg's version says that the residents of Esgaroth stayed home "because a cold east wind was blowing." (потому что дул холодный восточный ветер) (G H.231). Korolev had them stay at home because "a cold wind was blowing from the east." (с востока задувал холодный ветер) (Kr H.279) The coincidence of both Gruzberg and Bobyr' leaving off the modifier for *the East* suggests a difference between the second edition, which Gruzberg and Bobyr' used, and the third edition, which all the other translators used. That, however, is not the case. Tolkien did not make any revisions to Chapter XIV ("Fire and Water").[14] This is confirmed by Umanskij, who was likewise working from the second edition. He had both *the East* and its adjective in their places. His narrator said:

> Люди озерного города Эсгарота большей частью сидели дома, так как с темного востока дул холодный ветер (U H.156)
> BT: Most of the people of the Lake-town Esgaroth sat at home, because a cold wind was blowing from the dark east.

The changes to the description of *the East* as *black* deprive the passage of its connection with *LotR* and reduce it to a mere weather report, while it should be a commentary on the land from whence the breeze came.

No discussion of the geopolitical implications of the expurgation of *East* and *West* from Rakhmanova's text to eliminate the possibility that they would be (mis)read as political fault lines rather than as simple compass points would be complete without a look at the map that accompanied her text. The map in the 1976 first edition—often reprinted—was redrawn by

Mikhail Belomlinskij whose illustrations are considered by many Russians to be the classic ones for *The Hobbit*. The compass rose on Belomlinskij's map has North at the top, as is customary in modern maps. Tolkien's original map, however, had East at the top, as is customary in Dwarf maps. Belomlinskij's shift in the compass rose produces a political shift in the geographic layout of events that would warm a Soviet censor's heart. According to Belomlinskij's map, Bilbo and Company traveled north and not east. On Belomlinskij's map, Hobbiton is in the lower left corner (southwest) and the Lonely Mountain in the upper right corner (north-east). (See the diagram on page 69.) It has been argued that the shift is just a mistake, brought about by Tolkien's use of the Dwarvish convention for the placement of the compass rose. While this is possible, the evidence of the expurgation of *West* and *East* from Rakhmanova's text, suggests that the censors would not have been adverse to having the compass rose shifted for political reasons. If that was the case, however, the joke was on them when the Armenian translation with the Belomlinskij illustrations, including, of course, the map with the shifted compass rose was printed in Yerevan in 1984.[15] In Armenia, the political fault lines of that period did not run East and West, but North (the Soviet Union) and South (Armenia). Belomlinskij's map lines up perfectly with them for the political game of read-between-the-lines Armenian style.

All the while that the word *West* was being purged from the Russian text, Rakhmanova was busily writing the name of God into it. All the empty euphemisms for God that Tolkien used for exclamations of surprise became explicit references to God. Tolkien's exclamations of:

"Good gracious me!" (H.19), "Dear me!" (H.19), "Good gracious heavens" (H.118), "Good heavens!" (H.96,125), "Good Gracious!" (H.200), "Bless me!" (H.284), "goodness only knows" (H.78), "heaven knows" (H.118), "goodness knows" (H.77, 174)

became

"Dear God" (Боже милостивый, R H_{1976}.10, 104, 111, 172, 250; H_{2002}.10, 79, 84, 129, 184), "My God!" (Бог мой!, R H_{1976}.10; H_{2002}.10), "Merciful God" (Боже милосердный!, R H_{1976}.84; H_{2002}.65), "god knows" (бог знает, R H_{1976}.65; H_{2002}.51), "god only knows" (бог весть [archaic], R H_{1976}.66, 81; H_{2002}.52, 63), "only god knows" (один бог знает, R H_{1976}.103; H_{2002}.79) "perhaps god knows" (а то бог знает, R H_{1976}.150; H_{2002}.113),

Iron Hills   The
                                         Lonely Mountain

            Esgaroth
                                                    Dale

            Long Lake

    Palace of
   the Elvenking

                    M i r k w o o d

                         Carrock   Beorn's Home

         The Misty Mountains

             The Last   The Wild
           Homely Home
                                          N
                                       W ← ○ → E
                                          ↓
         Hobbiton   S

Belomlinskij's map

in Rakhmanova's translation. There was no necessity for Rakhmanova to consistently use set expressions that made God explicit, where he was not explicitly present in the original. The other translators found plenty of viable alternatives. Anonymous and Gruzberg used set expressions with God in their translations of the phrases "goodness only knows," "heaven knows," and "goodness knows," but they did not use set expressions with God consistently as Rakhmanova did.

Rakhmanova did not limit herself to making Tolkien's empty euphemisms explicit, she also wrote God into the text at other places without the justification of a euphemism. In Chapter V ("Riddles in the Dark"), in the narrator's description of Bilbo's leap in the dark over Gollum's head, Rakhmanova's version says:

> Для человека такой прыжок был бы не бог весть как труден, но ведь это был ещё и прыжок в неизвестность. (R H_{1976}.81, H_{2002}.63)
> BT: Not even god knows how difficult a leap like that would have been for a man, but it was also a leap into the unknown.

Tolkien's original had said: "No great leap for a man, but a leap in the dark." (H.93) Only Anonymous joins Rakhmanova in bringing God into the picture here with: "Not even god knows what kind of leap that was" (Не бог весть какой это был прыжок).

In Chapter XVI ("A Thief in the Night"), where Bilbo and Bombur are talking of Thorin, Rakhmanova has Bombur say:

> Упаси бог, чтобы я осуждал Торина, да растёт его борода беспредельно." (R H_{1976}.222, H_{2002}.164)
> BT: God forbid that I should criticize Thorin, may his beard grow limitlessly.

Tolkien's Bombur says nothing about God in his comment about Thorin. Tolkien's version was: "Not that I venture to disagree with Thorin, may his beard grow ever longer." (H.254) Additionally, in the same chapter, where the narrator is describing Bilbo's return after having delivered the Arkenstone of Thrain to Bard and the Elvenking, when Bilbo returns to the rope to climb back up it, Rakhmanova's narrator says: "The rope, thank god, was hanging where he [Bilbo] had left it." (Верёвка, слава богу, висела там, где он её оставил,) (R H_{1976}.226, H_{2002}.167) Tolkien's narrator says nothing about God or being thankful to him. In the original, the narrator says: "[…]

but it was well before midnight when he [Bilbo] clambered up the rope again—it was still where he had left it." (H.258) None of the other translators felt compelled to insert *God* into the text at these places.

Rakhmanova was a skilled translator with a good sense of the use of language. She could have easily avoided the use of set expressions containing *God*, if she had wanted to. It was no problem for the other translators. At the time that she did her translation, *God* was a sensitive word to Soviet editors and censors. It was never spelled with a capital "G", unless it began a sentence. The quotes from 1976 Rakhmanova above are a good example of that. In the 2002 edition of Rakhmanova, *God* has been capitalized in all of them.

Lyudmila Yu. Braude, a well-respected Russian translator of Scandinavian literature, tells a story[16] from the Soviet period, of religious Russian authors and translators who, not having any other way of expressing themselves religiously in writing, went to the trouble of formulating sentences so that the word *God* would be the first word in the sentence and would be capitalized. The censors would then go to the trouble of rearranging the sentences so that the word *God* would be in the middle and not be capitalized: *god*. In that climate, it would have been asking for trouble to use set expressions containing *God*, yet Rakhmanova did. The path of least resistance would be to use other set expressions that conveyed the same idea without *God*. The renditions of the other translators—who had no censor to play hide-and-seek with—are none the worse for it. The key to Rakhmanova's success with this tactic is that, with a translation and a censor who does not read English, it is easy enough to justify the use of expressions with the word *God*. The argument is "that is what it says in the original". Given her skill as a translator and a wordsmith, Rakhmanova's consistent use of set expressions containing the word *God* as translations for Tolkien's empty euphemisms, and for her renditions of sentences in which there were no empty euphemisms in the original, shows that she did it on purpose and that she had an agenda to pursue.

Smaug

> The small smoke-breathing figure
> became suddenly aware of them.
> (T.206)

Tolkien says that the name *Smaug* is a "pseudonym—the past tense of the primitive Germanic verb *Smugan*, to squeeze through a hole: a low philological jest," (L.31) referring to the passage in which the company is looking at the map of the Mountain, and Gandalf explains that Smaug could not possibly have used the hidden passage to the lower halls, "because it is too small."

> 'Five feet high the door and three may walk abreast' say the runes, but Smaug could not creep into a hole that size, not even when he was a young dragon, certainly not after devouring so many of the Dwarves and men of Dale." (H.32)

In the first edition it said: "devouring so many maidens of the valley." (AH.323) The change above was not introduced until 1966, for the third edition.

Tolkien's explanation of the origin of the name must be regarded as authoritative, but before I read Tolkien's letter I had developed a different derivation of the name on strictly linguistic grounds, which only goes to point out that derivational studies of Tolkien's names and words are more of an art than a science.

My linguistic etymology was based on the Proto-Indo-European root for *smoke* *smeug(h)-/smeuqh-. *Smaug* (Smoke) would be a particularly picturesque name for a fire-breathing dragon. In Old Lithuanian *smoke* is *smáugiu*; in Teutonic it is **smauk*. In Middle-high German it is *smouch* and in old Dutch it is *smooc*. An excursion into the Slavonic languages, of which Russian is a member, adds an even more interesting twist to an etymological study of the name. In Old Church Slavonic смокъ (smok" [the silent vowel Ъ is transliterated in English as a quote mark "]) is the word for *dragon*, and in Old Czech it is *smok*. In modern Polish the word for *dragon* still is *smok*, which is pronounced almost exactly like the English word *smoke*. For a reader with a background in historical linguistics, the Polish translation almost makes you feel like you are seeing double. (**Emphasis** added.)

> **Smoki**, jak wiadomo, kradną złoto i klejnoty ludziom, elfom i krasnoludom, gdziekolwiek się da; [...] Szczególnie chciwy, silny i zły był gad imieniem **Smaug**. (p. 23)
> BT: Dragons, as everyone knows, steal gold and jewels from Men, Elves and Dwarves, wherever they can. [...] Especially greedy, strong and evil was the reptile named Smaug.

All the translators—except Anonymous, Bobyr', Umanskij and Kamenkovich—rendered the name *Smaug* as Смог (Smog), which is pronounced with a long 'O' so that it almost sounds like *smoke*. (I personally think that they missed a good bet by not using смокъ [smok"].) Anonymous, Bobyr', Umanskij and Kamenkovich used a letter-for-letter transliteration: Смауг (Smaug), which would be pronounced approximately like it is in English. When Christopher Tolkien reads the name *Smaug*, he pronounces it [smowg].[17]

The difference between the two versions is the same as the difference between the two versions of the Russian spelling of Tolkien's name: Толкин [Tolkin: pronounced tolkeen] and Толкиен [Tolkien: pronounced tolki-yen]. Tolkien is transliterated as Толкин (Tolkin) in the Rakhmanova, Gruzberg, Bobyr', Umanskij, VAM, Korolev, Kamenkovich and G&G translations. This captures the sound of his name pretty well. M&K, Yakhnin and the unknown editors of Gruzberg-A and -B, as well as Kaminskaya, Utilova and Yakovlev, however, transliterate it as Толкиен (Tolkien), which reflects its English spelling instead of its sound. The editors of the 2002 Eksmo/Terra Fantastica edition of Korolev's translation added their support to this spelling as well, as did the editors of the 2001 edition of the Gruzberg CD-ROM. The Russian spelling of Tolkien's name is usually an indication of which translation the writer read first or prefers. Feelings run so high on this point that in the 2000 EKSMO-Press edition of *The Hobbit*, which has Толкиен (Tolkien) on the cover, the editors felt obliged to footnote the spelling of Tolkien's name as Толкин (Tolkin) in the introduction to "Durin's Folk," which immediately follows VAM's translation of *The Hobbit*. They explained that "this is how the translator thinks that the author's name should be spelled,"[18] distancing themselves from this spelling and directing any possible displeasure on the part of the reader at seeing the name spelled thusly at the translator.

Tolkien's Smaug, the dragon of the Ered Mithrin, was "a most specially greedy, strong and wicked" dragon. (H.35) The majority vote for the translation of these three adjectives went to *greedy*, *strong* and *wicked* (жадный, сильный и злобный). (G H.26; U H.25) There were, however, some interesting variations on *wicked*. Kaminskaya's Smaug was *evil* (злой). (Ksk H.11) Rakhmanova's was *repulsive*. (отвратительный) (R H_{1976}.26, H_{2002}.23) VAM's was *treacherous* (коварный, VAM H_{1990}. 28, H_{2000}. 38), the same adjective that Rakhmanova had used to describe the "dangerous" Wood-elves. Korolev kept her company. (Kr H.36) Kamenkovich's verbose rendition turned *wicked* into *ferocious* (свирепый, Km H.29), and Yakhnin followed her lead. (Ya H.35) Anonymous, Bobyr' and Yakhnin gave the adjective string an unnecessarily bookish air with their choice of *avaricious* (алчный) as the translation of *greedy*. Bobyr' and Yakhnin were the only dissenting vote for the translation of *strong*. Bobyr's rendition made Smaug *powerful* (могучий, B H_{1994}.29), which can have figurative meaning as well, and could readily refer to both Smaug's physical strength and the power of dragon-spell (H.214) and dragon-talk (H.215) that Tolkien introduced later in the story. Yakhnin had no reference to Smaug's strength at all. Yakhnin's third adjective was *vile*. (гнусный) (Ya H.35) Korolev also left out *strong*. In addition to that, he misread *a most* as *the most*, and his Smaug was "the most wicked among them, the most treacherous and greedy." (Самого злобного среди них, самого коварного и жадного звали Смогом) (Kr H.36) This greatly elevates Smaug in stature, while pointing clearly to a flaw in Korolev's grasp of English. The other translators all got the translation of *a most* right.

These variations each produce a subtle shift in the image of Smaug in the reader's mind, but on the whole, Smaug remains a negative character, as are Tolkien's dragons in general. Thorin's description of them is compact, yet full of interesting insights.

> Dragons steal gold and jewels, you know, from Men and Elves and Dwarves, wherever they can find them; and they guard their plunder as long as they live (which is practically forever, unless they are killed), and never enjoy a brass ring of it. Indeed they hardly know a good bit of work from a bad, though they usually have a good notion of the current market value; and they can't make a thing for themselves, not even mend a little loose scale of their armor. (H.35)

The translators were all relatively successful with the first sentence in Thorin's description, except for the last phrase: "and never enjoy a brass ring of it." Part of the problem with translating this phrase is that the most direct Russian translation of "enjoy a brass ring of it" has some serious sexual overtones to it. The use of the diminutive of the noun *ring* (колечко [kolechko]) in the context of the verb *to enjoy* (насладиться [nasladit'sya]) suggests a physical act akin to the one that you would be told to perform on a flying doughnut, if you stepped on a drunk's toes in an Army barracks. The style marker for the Russian phrase is, however, a bit less coarse. It is no wonder, therefore, that all the translators bent over backwards to avoid producing that combination. Korolev left it out. Three of them—Gruzberg, VAM and Rakhmanova—built their translations around the verb *to use*. Gruzberg's was the best in this respect, because it kept the brass ring, while the others abandoned it: "and never even use a little brass ring of it." (и никогда даже медным колечком не попользуются) (G H.26)

Bobyr' had a similar ." (и никогда не тратят ни медного колечка из нее) (B H$_{1994}$.29) Anonymous said that "they do not give up even a brass ring." (они не поступятся ни медным колечком) All of these variants are later shown to be quite true when Bilbo steals "a great two-handled cup" from the hoard. "Dragons may not have much real use for all their wealth, but they know it to an ounce as a rule, especially after long possession; and Smaug was no exception." (H.207) None of these renditions, however, was the point that Tolkien was trying to make.

This phrase is the set-up for the first part of the sentence that follows: "Indeed they hardly know a good bit of work from a bad, though they usually have a good notion of the current market value." This context makes it clear that when Thorin says "enjoy," he is talking about the esthetic pleasure of seeing a finely crafted chalice or plate, a quite Dwarvish point of view. Only Umanskij and Kamenkovich got it right. Kamenkovich's version was verbosely elegant: they are "not capable of understanding all their [the stolen things'] priceless beauty." (не способные понять всей их бесценной красоты) (Km H.29) Umanskij's was more to the point: "they do not know how to really enjoy their treasures." (они не умеют по-настоящему наслаждаться своими сокровищами) (U H.25) Yakhnin had yet another idea. His Thorin said that dragons are only interested in gold and jewels, and were not interested in some old brass ring, "no matter how finely it was crafted." (а на какое-нибудь медное колечко, будь оно выковано самым чудесным мастером, и внимания не обращали, Ya H.35)

Unfortunately, Kamenkovich's success with this phrase was marred by her handling of the second part of the next sentence: "though they usually have a good notion of the current market value." She used the wrong register for the narrator's text. Her version was a colloquial: "although they well know what someth'n costs" (хотя прекрасно знают, что почем). The phrase falls flat in comparison to Gruzberg's "although they usually have a good idea as to the current market value" (хотя обычно имеют неплохое представление о текущей рыночной стоимости). There were only minor stylistic changes in the Chernyak edition of Gruzberg. (G H.26)

All the other translators—except Rakhmanova, Korolev and Yakhnin—have satisfactory renditions of *market value* along these lines, but none are nearly as pleasing to a native speaker of English as Gruzberg's. Rakhmanova and Korolev drop both phrases completely. Yakhnin reworks them, introducing subtle changes to the story.

Korolev's retelling of this passage shows that he is a great storyteller. It is full of interesting images, but is missing all of Tolkien's more philosophical comments.

> Ведь драконы — большие охотники до чужих сокровищ, им бы каждый день кого-нибудь грабить, эльфов, людей, гномов — все одно. И ведь тащат без разбору, что под лапу подвернется, и доспех изукрашенный, и кувшины медные, лишь бы захапать. А сами ничего толком не умеют — ни даже прореху крохотную в собственной чешуе залатать; правда, цену добыче ведают. Поживу они сгребают в кучу, залегают на ней и стерегут ее до конца своих дней. Век же драконий, знаете ли, еще как долог: коли дракона прежде не убьют, он всех переживет … (Kr H.35-36)

BT (embellishments **highlighted**): Dragons are, **after all, great lovers of other people's treasures. They would like to rob someone every day**, Elves, Men, Dwarves, **it doesn't matter who. And, you know, they take unselectively, whatever winds up under their paws; finely decorated armor and copper pitchers, so long as they can grab it.** They themselves can't do anything—not even gild a tiny little tear in their own scales; true, they do know the value of their plunder. **They gather up all their loot in a pile, lie on top of it and guard it to the end of their days. Dragon's years are, perhaps you know, very long indeed:** unless you kill a dragon beforehand, they outlive everybody …

JRRT (Lacunae **highlighted**): Dragons steal gold and jewels, you know, from Men and Elves and Dwarves, wherever they can find them; and they guard their plunder as long as they live (which is practically forever, unless they are killed), **and never enjoy a brass ring of it. Indeed they hardly know a good bit of work from a bad,** though they **usually** have a **good** notion of the **current market** value;

and they can't make a thing for themselves, not even mend a little loose scale of their armor. (H.35)

The parts of Rakhmanova's terse version of this passage that are there, at least sound more like the original:

> Драконы, как известно, воруют золото и драгоценности у людей, у эльфов, у гномов — где и когда только могут — и стерегут свою добычу до конца жизни (а живут драконы практически вечно, если только их не убьют), но никогда не попользуются даже самым дешёвым колечком. Сами они сделать неспособны ровно ничего, даже не могут укрепить какую-нибудь разболтавшуюся чешуйку в своей броне. (R H_{1976}.26, H_{2002}.23)[19]

> BT: Dragons, as you know, steal gold and valuables from Men, Elves and Dwarves—where and whenever they can—and guard their loot to the end of their lives (and dragons live practically eternally, unless someone kills them), but never use even the cheapest little ring. They themselves are incapable of doing absolutely anything, they cannot even tighten some scale or other in their armor that has gotten loose.

The kind of abridgement seen in Rakhmanova's text can be expected in D&D, but it feels very much out of place in the most widely available—some would say the standard—Russian translation of *The Hobbit*. While D&D did shorten this passage, Kaminskaya shortened their shortened version even more, and embellished it as well.

> D&D: Dragons steal gold and jewels wherever they can find them; and they guard their plunder as long as they live (which is practically forever), and never enjoy it at all. (D&D H.11)

> Kaminskaya: Драконы ведь отовсюду похищают золото и драгоценности, стерегут добычу до самой смерти — а они, считай, бессмертны, — и все им мало. (Ksk H.11)

> BT: Dragons, after all, steal gold and valuables from all over, guard their plunder until their very death—and they, you could say, are immortal—and all of it is not enough for them.

Her change makes dragons seem greedier still, but without the follow-up line to specify what enjoyment means, this particular deviation from the original abridgement is of little consequence for the reader.

Yakhnin does not let the original get in the way of his showing his skill as a storyteller. His formulation of the last phrase of this passage, where he says that the dragons "knew the price of gold very well," refocuses the dragons' greed specifically on gold, excluding the other things in the trove. Tolkien's description was all-inclusive. Yakhnin's version fits well with Tolkien's view of gold as the root of all evil, but it is Yakhnin's story, not Tolkien's.

> Они [драконы] стали налетать и грабить всех без разбору — людей, эльфов, гномов. Добычу они утаскивали в свои логова и стерегли пуще собственной жизни, а живет дракон вечно, если его не убить. Зарились драконы только на золото и драгоценные камни, а на какое-нибудь медное колечко, будь оно выковано самым чудесным мастером, и внимания не обращали. Эти невежды никогда не умели отличить отменную работу от простой подделки, зато цену золота знали прекрасно. (Ya H.35)

BT: They [the dragons] started raiding and robbing everyone indiscriminately—Men, Elves, Dwarves. They dragged their loot off to their lairs and guarded it better than their own lives, and a dragon lives forever, unless you kill him. Dragons only hankered after gold and precious stones, and paid no attention to some brass ring or other, even if it was forged by the most marvelous craftsman. These ignoramuses could never distinguish a piece of excellent work from a simple copy, but they knew the price of gold very well.

The final part of the passage—"not even mend a little loose scale of their armor"—is important to the story line, because it hints at a weakness that will be Smaug's undoing: the unprotected spot on his soft underbelly where Bard's arrow will find its mark. (H.237) Though their formulations varied, all the translators—except Kaminskaya, VAM and Korolev—had quite acceptable renditions of it. This phrase was missing in D&D, and, therefore, is also not in Kaminskaya. VAM interpreted armor as a suit of ringed mail armor, like the coat of mithril mail that Bilbo received from the Dwarves as the first payment of his reward. (H.228) Her version reads:

> Они ничего не умеют делать сами, даже сломанное кольчужное колечко не починят. (VAM H_{1990}.28; H_{2002}.38)

BT: They do not know how to do anything themselves, they won't even repair a broken mail ring.

In Korolev's version, it is not a loose scale, but a scale with a "tiny little tear" (прореха крохотная, Kr H.36) in it, which is hardly suggestive of an opening that an arrow could penetrate.

With the narrator's commentary on Bilbo's conversation with Smaug, Tolkien again provides some interesting insights into dragon-lore. The narrator praises the way that Bilbo fields Smaug's questions as being:

> the way to talk to dragons, if you don't want to reveal your proper name (which is wise), and don't want to infuriate them by a flat refusal (which is also very wise). No dragon can resist the fascination of riddling talk and of wasting time trying to understand it. (H.213)

In *LotR*, Tolkien took a much closer look at the power of proper or real names. Fortunately, almost all the translators—Anonymous, VAM, Gruzberg, Rakhmanova, Umanskij and Kamenkovich—used *real name* (настоящее имя) here, as had been the case with the best translations of this term in the *LotR*. The rest of the passage is handled competently by all the translators, but none of the renditions were nearly as elegant as Rakhmanova's:

> Разговаривать с драконами нужно именно так, когда не хочешь раскрыть своё настоящее имя (что весьма благоразумно) и не хочешь разозлить их прямым отказом (что тоже весьма благоразумно). Никакой дракон не устоит перед соблазном поговорить загадками и потратить время на их разгадывание. (R H$_{1976}$.184, H$_{2002}$.137)
>
> BT: This is exactly how you need to talk to dragons when you don't want to reveal your proper name (which is very wise) and don't want to anger them with a direct refusal (which is also very wise). No dragon can resist the temptation of talking in riddles and wasting time on their solution.

Kamenkovich included a very insightful endnote with this passage. It says that Bilbo's conversation with Smaug is reminiscent of the conversation in the *Elder Edda* between Sigurd and the dragon Fafnir, whom Sigurd had wounded. Sigurd, like Bilbo, wisely does not reveal his true name to the dragon, because he knows, unlike Bilbo, that the dragon can use his name to put a dragon's curse on him. (Km H.343)

As Bilbo's conversation with Smaug continues across the next several pages, Tolkien slowly builds up his view of dragon-lore touching briefly on dragon-spell and dragon-talk.

Bilbo was now beginning to feel really uncomfortable. Whenever Smaug's roving eye, seeking for him in the shadows, flashed across him, he trembled, and an unaccountable desire seized hold of him to rush out and reveal himself and tell all the truth to Smaug. In fact he was in grievous danger of coming under the dragon-spell. (H.214)

This passage clearly demonstrates the power that dragons have to compel others to do their bidding. In this passage, the main problem for the translators was the phrase *unaccountable desire*. D&D did not bother with this segment at all. Yakhnin glossed over it, simplifying it to "poor [old Bilbo] wanted to" (бедняге так и хотелось) for his young readers. (Ya H.268) Rakhmanova, Kamenkovich and VAM tried to stay in step with Tolkien and used the most literal Russian translation of *unaccountable desire*. (безотчётное желание) (R H_{1976}.185, H_{2002}.138; Km H.225; VAM H_{1990}.179, H_{2000}.271) Korolev, Anonymous, Gruzberg, Umanskij and Bobyr' all came up with other adjectives to qualify Bilbo's desire "to rush out and reveal himself and tell the truth to Smaug." Korolev called it *an almost insurmountable desire*. (почти неодолимое желание) (Kr H.255) Anonymous said that it was an *unrestrainable desire* (безудержное желание). Gruzberg called it an *almost irresistible desire*. (почти непреодолимое желание) (G H.211) Umanskij's narrator said that it was an *inexplicable desire*. (необъяснимое желание) (U H.143) Bobyr's version was that it was an *incomprehensible desire*. (непонятное желание) (B H_{1994}.255) Gruzberg's, Bobyr's and Umanskij's versions are the least out of step with the original. Korolev's and Anonymous are quite expressive, but are too strong. Bilbo was indeed able to resist.

In the next passage, however, Tolkien shows that Bilbo was not entirely immune to Smaug's power of suggestion, and "a nasty suspicion began to grow" in Bilbo's mind:

had the Dwarves forgotten this important point too, or were they laughing in their sleeves at him all the time? That is the effect that dragon-talk has on the inexperienced. Bilbo of course ought to have been on his guard; but Smaug had rather an overwhelming personality. (H.215)

Smaug's "overwhelming personality" seemed to be an almost overwhelming problem for the translators. A large part of the problem is the word *personality*. Stalin was **the** overwhelming personality of the Soviet period from 1922, when he took on the leadership of the Party after Lenin's death, until his own death in 1953, and this period of Stalinist terror is known in Russian as the *personality cult* (культ личности). This term was coined by Party Chairman Khrushchev in his secret speech condemning Stalin at the XX Party Congress in February 1956. Because of this, the Russian word *personality* (личность) is a very loaded word in the context of negative characters like Smaug. Most of the translators avoided using it in this passage. Bobyr's rendition, which originally circulated in samizdat and would not, therefore, have had to worry about the Soviet censors, reads:

Смог был в состоянии подавить своей личностью кого угодно. (В H$_{1994}$.256)
BT: Smaug was capable of overwhelming anyone at all with his personality.

Her use of the word *personality* here would have made this segment too potentially political to be approved by the Soviet thought police. The Kamenkovich post-Soviet version, done at a time that the term *personality cult* was no longer burned into every Soviet intellectual's consciousness, and the word *personality* had been rehabilitated, reads:

Смауг просто подавил его своей личностью. (Km H.226)
BT: Smaug simply overwhelmed him [Bilbo] with his personality.

For the modern, post-Soviet Russian reader, this rendition is quite acceptable, although, perhaps, a bit too free. In her post-Communist revision of her translation (2000), VAM changed her rather bland rendition of "Smaug overwhelmed him [Bilbo]" (Смог подавлял его, VAM, H$_{1990}$.179) to include *personality* as well. In this edition, her narrator said: "Smaug's personality overwhelmed him [Bilbo]." (Смог как личность подавлял его) (H$_{2000}$.273)

Anonymous and D&D (ergo Kaminskaya) skirted the issue of personality altogether. D&D skirted it by leaving out the phrase completely. Anonymous said that: "Smaug turned out to be much stronger than he [Bilbo]." (Смауг оказался гораздо сильнее его) This rendition is too vague and calls out for an explanation of how Smaug overpowered or overwhelmed Bilbo. This is the same problem that existed with VAM's original version, which she corrected by adding *personality*. Yakhnin found an easy way out by changing *Smaug* to *Smaug's magical powers* (да слишком уж сильны были колдовские чары Смога), which gives the phrase the non-physical context that it needs. (Ya H.269)

Umanskij's version demonstrates a fatal weakness of some of his translations. They can be almost right, but not quite.

> Таков вот эффект от разговора дракона с неопытным слушателем. Бильбо, конечно, не забывал, с кем имеет дело, но аргументы Смауга казались неотразимыми. (U H.144)
>
> BT: That is the effect of a dragon talking with an unexperienced listener. Bilbo, of course, did not forget whom he was dealing with, but Smaug's arguments seemed incontrovertible.
>
> JRRT: That is the effect that dragon-talk has on the inexperienced. Bilbo of course ought to have been on his guard; but Smaug had rather an overwhelming personality. (H.215)

Tolkien's Bilbo should have been on his guard, while Umanskij's Bilbo was on his guard. Tolkien's Smaug was an overwhelming personality, but the arguments advanced by Umanskij's Smaug were incontrovertible.

Rakhmanova's translation, however, came out in 1976, in the Brezhnev period, during which Stalin was returned to favor, after the country's brief flirtation with destalinization under Khrushchev. In that period, the censor would have been very much aware of the political sensitivity of the word *personality*, and it is inconceivable that any translation of *overwhelming personality* that included the Russian word *personality* (личность) would have been approved by the thought police at that time. Rakhmanova demonstrates her skill as a wordsmith with a good feel for the language in her rendition of this term. Her version of *overwhelming personality* does not include the Russian word *personality* (личность), but it nevertheless contains a politically charged word from Khrushchev's Secret Speech at the XX Party Congress in February 1956.

> Конечно, Бильбо следовало бы остеречься, но уж очень деспотичной натурой был Смог. (R H_{1976}.186, H_{2002}.139)
>
> BT: Of course, Bilbo should have been more careful, but Smaug had a very, very despotic nature.

In his Secret Speech condemning Stalin, Khrushchev denies that Stalin was a "mindless despot" (безумный деспот).[20] He would not have made such a denial, if that epithet was not being widely bandied about. Khrushchev's goal was to discredit Stalin, but not to the point that it would discredit the system. Khrushchev needed the system to stay in power. A scant two pages later, in the context of calling on the delegates to help him eliminate the consequences of Stalin's personality cult (культ личности), Khrushchev asks the Congress to "fight against the autocracy (произвол) of individual persons, misusing their power," which is, in essence, the definition of despotism.[21] Khrushchev was trying to have his cake and eat it too. The final result was a return to collective rule, which made life safer for senior Communist Party members, but left the dictatorship of the proletariat in place.

Soviet-era Russian readers familiar with the Secret Speech would have no trouble in seeing a hidden reference to Stalin in the description "had a very, very despotic nature," whether Rakhmanova intended it that way or not. In 1921, before Stalin came to political prominence, Kornej Chukovskij wrote a children's story in rhyme about a cockroach terrorizing the animal kingdom: "The Big Bad Cockroach" (Тараканище).[22] For a whole generation of Russians in the post-Stalinist period, who did not know when it was first written, this story was read with delight as a parody of Stalin. The identification of the cockroach as Stalin hinged on a single word—mustache, a Stalin trademark characteristic—but that is the way that the game of hide-and-seek with the censors was played.

With her undeniable linguistic skill and feel for the language, however, Rakhmanova could have certainly found other, less politically charged ways of saying *overwhelming personality*. A number of the other translators less literarily skilled than Rakhmanova found viable ways of doing so. Rakhmanova's skill at playing hide-and-seek with the censor has already been demonstrated in the exchange of *God* for *West/East*, so without any justification in the original text for her choice of the adjective *despotic*, this choice was clearly a conscious decision, made for the effect that it would have on the Soviet reader.

Gruzberg had the best translation of this phrase. It avoided the political booby traps of the word *personality* (личность), while preserving the meaning of the original.

> но уж очень подавляла натура Смога. (G H.212)
> BT: but Smaug's nature was very, very overwhelming.

He used the same noun—*nature* (натура [natura])—that Rakhmanova used for this phrase, but instead of combining it with the adjective *despotic*, he combined it with the verb, which, in various forms, got the majority vote as the translation of *overwhelming*: подавить. With so many other viable choices to render the meaning of this phrase, Rakhmanova's careful attention to linguistic detail, and her exchange of *God* for *the West*, Rakhmanova's choice of the adjective *despotic* was certainly a conscious decision made for the effect that it would have on the Soviet reader. She might well have preferred to have the combination *despotic personality*, but that would never have made it past the censors in the Brezhnev period, during which Stalin was returned to favor, after the country's brief flirtation with destalinization under Khrushchev. The first edition of her translation of *The Hobbit* came out in 1976.

Korolev's retelling of the passage deftly skirts the political issues of the word *personality*, and in rearranging it, shifts the focus of the passage to the strength of Bilbo's character.

> У него зародилось ужасное подозрение — а что, если гномы и вправду замыслили обмануть его и все время втихомолку посмеивались над простаком Торбинсом? Нет, этого не может быть! Гномы — друзья, настоящие друзья!
> Как видите, драконьи чары начинали действовать. И то сказать, редко кому удается против них устоять.
> — Золото — не главное, — проговорил хоббит. (Kr H.256)

BT: A terrible suspicion was born in him—and what if the Dwarves were really planning to deceive him and all this time had been quietly laughing at the simpleton Torbins? No, that was impossible! The Dwarves were friends, real friends!
As you see, the dragon-spell had begun to work. And to tell the truth, it is rare for someone to be able to resist it.
"Gold is not the main thing," said the Hobbit.

JRRT: Now a nasty suspicion began to grow in his mind—had the Dwarves forgotten this important point too, or were they laughing in their sleeves at him all the time? That is the effect that dragon-talk has on the inexperienced. Bilbo of course ought to have been on his guard; but Smaug had rather an overwhelming personality.
"I tell you," he said, in an effort to remain loyal to his friends and to keep his end up, "that gold was only an afterthought with us. […] (H.215)

Korolev's version is a nice tale, but it is not Tolkien. It is a different story altogether that concentrates on different issues and points of philosophical interest.

Gold

> To Sam he gave a little bag of gold ...
> Almost the last drop of the Smaug vintage. ... May come in useful, if you think of getting married, Sam.
> Bilbo Baggins (R.328)

Gold is the root of all evil in *The Hobbit*. It was what brought Smaug the dragon into the story. Smaug "was a most specially greedy, strong and wicked" dragon, (H.35) who flew out of the north and laid waste to the domain of the King under the Mountain, stealing the Dwarves' treasure and the wealth of the nearby Dale. A part of Tolkien's story describes "the power that gold has upon which a dragon has long brooded," (H.250) and the effect that it has on Dwarves, Men, Elves and Hobbits. Gold is at the root of the troubles between the Dwarf Thorin Oakenshield on the one side and Bard, heir of Girion of Dale, and the Elvenking on the other. On his deathbed, however, Thorin Oakenshield recognizes the evil side of gold and wishes that more of his people could be like Bilbo, whose head was "more clear of the bewitchment" of gold than were the heads of the Dwarves. (H.228) Tolkien returns briefly to this topic in *LotR* with Galadriel's wish for Gimli as the fellowship leaves Lórien. Her wish is that Gimli's "hands shall flow with gold" but that "gold shall have no dominion" over him. (F.487) This wish completes the redemption of the Dwarves that was begun by Thorin on his deathbed and brings Tolkien's story of gold to an end, for gold has no part to play in *LotR*. *LotR* is the story of power.

Tolkien contrasts the attitude of the Dwarves to that of Beorn. While the Dwarves "spoke most of gold and silver and jewels and the making of things by smith-craft," "Beorn did not appear to care for such things: there were no things of gold or silver in his hall, and few save the knives were made of metal at all." (H.127) With only a few minor variations, the translators were all in agreement on this passage and all rendered it very well, though Umanskij did have an interesting embellishment. His narrator said that with the exception of "some knives and an ax," few items in Beorn's home were made of metal. (U H.86)

Even the abridged D&D version managed to save the contrast of gold and silver, but it did leave out Beorn's dislike of the products of industry: metal objects.

> When dinner was over the Dwarves began to tell tales of their own, of gold and silver and smith-craft, but Beorn paid little heed to them—he did not appear to care for such things. (D&D H.66)

Kaminskaya's rendition of the D&D text gave an interesting interpretation to "tales of their own, of gold and silver and smith-craft." Her version said that the Dwarves "turned to their pet topic and talked of treasure and of goldsmiths." (гномы сели на своего конька —разговорились о сокровищах, о золотых дел мастерах) (Ksk H.66) This would be out of place in an unabridged version, because it is belaboring the obvious, which Tolkien never did. His text was the epitome of layered understatement. In an abridged version, however, a little exaggeration is needed now and then.

In Chapter XIII ("Not at Home"), Bilbo leads the company to the treasure, and, as they revel in the treasure trove, Tolkien contrasts the effect of the power of the gold and riches on Bilbo to its effect on the Dwarves.

> All the same Mr. Baggins kept his head more clear of the bewitchment of the hoard than the Dwarves did. Long before the Dwarves were tired of examining the treasures, he became wary of it and sat down on the floor; and he began to wonder nervously what the end of it all would be. "I would give a good many of these precious goblets," he thought, "for a drink of something cheering out of one of Beorn's wooden bowls!" (H.228-229)

There are two key elements in the first sentence. One is the word *bewitchment*. It communicates the idea of the captivating power of the hoard. This is Tolkien's repeated thesis. The second element is *Bilbo kept his head more clear*. This is a positive statement that makes Bilbo an active participant in the process. He was affected by the bewitchment of the hoard, too, but was able to keep his wits about him. Almost all the translations of this passage are the worse for not giving Bilbo his due for actively keeping his head clear of the bewitchment of the hoard. The most common construction used by the translators was *did not lose his head* (не потерял голову). Rakhmanova's version was the best, because she added a phrase that makes Bilbo the active participant in the process that he deserves to be. Her narrator said:

> Мистер Бэггинс в отличие от гномов не потерял головы при виде богатств и устоял перед их чарами. (R H.197)
>
> BT: Mister Baggins, in contrast to the Dwarves, did not lose his head at the sight of the riches and resisted their charms.

Umanskij also had a good rendition of this sentence in the proper voice. His narrator said: "All the same Mr. Baggins gave in less to the bewitchment of the trove than the Dwarves" (Все же мистер Бэггинс меньше поддался очарованию клада, чем карлики, U H.152) Its compact elegance makes it a worthy equal to Rakhmanova's.

The renditions of the other translators who used *charms* (чары)—Bobyr' and VAM—were less successful because the constructions they used made Bilbo less of an active participant in the process of keeping his head clear of the charms of the hoard of treasure. Their formulations say that the charms of the hoard had less effect on him, which is true, but Bilbo is no longer the active participant that he is in the original and in Rakhmanova.

Bobyr': Однако голова у Бильбо была яснее, чем у прочих, и чары сокровищ действовали на него меньше. (B H_{1994}.273)
BT: However, Mister Baggins' head was clearer than the others, and the charms of the treasure had less effect on him.

VAM: У господина Торбинса от сокровищ не так кружилась голова, как у остальных. Их чары на него не действовали. (VAM H_{1990}.190, H_{1990}.290)
BT: The treasures did not make Mister Baggins' head spin like it did the rest. Their charms did not work on him.

Yakhnin has an excellent translation of *bewitched* (зачарован), but his formulation, unfortunately, also deprives Bilbo of an active role in the process of resisting the enchantment of the hoard.

В отличие от гномов Бильбо не был зачарован несметными сокровищами дракона. (Ya H.285)
BT: In contrast to the Dwarves Bilbo was not bewitched by the countless treasures of the dragon.

Gruzberg had a less enchanting, though serviceable formulation along the same line that made the treasure the active subject of the sentence instead of Bilbo.

И тем не менее сокровище не затуманило мистеру Бэггинсу голову, как гномам. (G H.224)
BT: Nevertheless, the treasure did not cloud mister Baggins' mind like it did those of the Dwarves.

Anonymous has a workable, though unbewitching version that follows the same train of thought.

> И все же почтенный Торбинс менее всех потерял голову при виде груды сокровищ.
> BT: Still, at the sight of the pile of treasure, the honorable Baggins lost his head least of all.

Kamenkovich used the same underlying construction as Anonymous, but took a wrong turn when she got to the adverb. Her narrator says that Bilbo "did not lose his head at all at the sight of all the gold." (отнюдь не потерял головы при виде золота, Km H.240) Bilbo was affected by the power of the hoard, but he kept his head more clear.

Korolev skirted the issue altogether and omitted the first sentence in this passage entirely. (Kr H.272)

The second sentence in this passage makes the abstract statement of the first concrete, and the majority of the translators dealt with it without much trouble. "Long before the Dwarves were tired of examining the treasures, he [Bilbo] became wary of it and sat down on the floor; and he began to wonder nervously what the end of it all would be." Korolev and VAM left out the adverb *nervously*, which the other translators easily handled with the word *anxiously* (тревожно). In Tolkien's finely crafted text, any lacunae make the translation a poor reflection of the original. While nervousness may be Bilbo's natural state during his adventure, that is no reason to leave it out of the translation.

Yakhnin not only left out *nervously*, but all of Bilbo's concerns as well.

> Он [Бильбо] уселся прямо на пол и, пока гномы лихорадочно копались в драгоценностях, перебирал в памяти прежние приключения. (Ya H.285)
> BT: He [Bilbo] sat right on the floor, and, while the Dwarves were feverishly digging through the valuables, turned over the earlier adventures in his mind.

Rakhmanova's version was rather more terse. She chopped the sentence—and the paragraph—off at the end of the first phrase:

Гномы всё ещё рылись в сокровищнице, но Бильбо прискучило это занятие. [New paragraph] (R H.197)

BT: The Dwarves were still digging in the treasure trove, but Bilbo became bored with this.

JRRT (lacunae highlighted): Long before the Dwarves were tired of examining the treasures, he became wary of it **and sat down on the floor; and he began to wonder nervously what the end of it all would be**. (H.228)

The third sentence in the passage, Bilbo's aside to himself, is carefully wrought to place an even finer point on Bilbo's attitude towards gold and treasure. "I would give a good many of these precious goblets,' he thought, 'for a drink of something cheering out of one of Beorn's wooden bowls!" (H.229) His rejection of the *precious goblets*, which were most likely made of gold or silver and encrusted with jewels, and his preference for "something cheering out of one of Beorn's wooden bowls" puts Bilbo firmly in Beorn's camp with regard to the gold, prompting the reader to recall that in Beorn's hall few things "save the knives were made of metal at all." (H.127) Rakhmanova's rendition of this passage is disappointing because the second and third sentences are missing from it. It is understakable in an abridged version like D&D, but in the otherwise excellent Rakhmanova translation lacunae like this stand out quite starkly.

The contrast of *precious goblet* and *wooden bowl* are key to the success of this sentence. Bobyr's version of the comparison was right on target: "precious cups" (драгоценные кубки) and "wooden bowl" (деревянная чаша). Kamenkovich had an acceptable version, comparing "golden cups" (золотые кубки) to a "wooden bowl" (деревянная чаша), and embellishing the quantity that Bilbo was prepared to exchange: "this entire pile of golden cups" (всю эту груду золотых кубков). Yakhnin's rendition was almost exactly the same as Kamenkovich's. It was just a little more terse. His Bilbo was ready to exchange "all these golden cups" (все эти золотые кубки). Gruzberg's version was slightly less satisfying because he compared "priceless cups" (бесценные кубки) to a "wooden cup" (деревянный кубок). For the full effect, the names of the vessels need to be different. Umanskij had suitably different names for the vessels, but his adjective in front of *goblets* was far from satisfying. His Bilbo was prepared to exchange "a goodly part of these beautiful goblets in order to be able to drink something refreshing from one of Beorn's wooden bowls." ("Я отдал бы добрую часть этих прекрасных бокалов",— подумал он, — "за то, чтобы выпить чего-нибудь ободряющего из деревянных чаш Беорна!") (U H.152-153) VAM had an even less pleasing version because she dropped the adjective in front of *cups*. Her Bilbo simply said: "I would give a lot of these cups ..." (Я бы много этих кубков отдал ...). (VAM H_{1990}.190, H_{1990}.290)

The Anonymous version abandoned the comparison of *goblets* and *bowls*, but nevertheless produced an evocative image, very much in the tone of Tolkien's views on gold.

> «Честное слово, — думал он, — я отдал бы половину всей этой золоченой чепухи за глоточек чего-нибудь бодрящего из Беорнова деревянного кубка!»
> BT: "On my word," he thought, "I would give half of all this gilded nonsense for a sip of something invigorating from a wooden cup of Beorn's.

Korolev kept the *goblets* and *bowls*, but left out what they were made of. When combined with his omission of the first sentence, this completely robs Tolkien's passage of its power.

> Какой толк ото всех этих кубков, ведь они пустые, —подумалось ему. —Эх, глотнуть бы сейчас из Беорновой чаши! (Kr H.272)
> BT: "What use are all these cups, they are empty after all," he thought to himself. "Oh, to gulp something from one of Beorn's bowls now!"

The addition of the phrase "they are empty after all" reduces Bilbo's comment to one of practicality, whereas Tolkien had meant it as a philosophical comment. Following Korolev's practical introduction, the desire for something to drink from one of Beorn's bowls is left without its *raison d'être*. There is no explanation of why it would be good to drink something from one of Beorn's bowls, other than that it tasted good and Bilbo was thirsty.

Smaug and the Dwarves are not alone in their love of gold and treasure as Tolkien shows in Chapter XIV ("Fire and Water"), in which the Elvenking learns of Smaug's death and decides to seek a share of the treasure for himself.

> "That will be the last we shall hear of Thorin Oakenshield, I fear," said the king. "He would have done better to have remained my guest. It is an ill wind, all the same," he added, "that blows no one any

good." For he too had not forgotten the legend of the wealth of Thror. (H.241)

The quoted dialog in which the king presumes that Thorin Oakenshield is dead was not a problem for the translators, but the speaker's identification at the end of the first sentence was. Rakhmanova, Kamenkovich, Korolev, and Yakhnin felt compelled to make the reference to "the king" more specific as if some confusion could result, if there were no amplification to denote which king it was. Rakhmanova and Yakhnin specified that it was the "king of the Wood-elves" (король лесных эльфов) (R H.210; Ya H.303), while Kamenkovich and Korolev specified that it was the "king of the Elves." (король эльфов) (Km H.255; Kr H.289) Their caution at this point was not entirely without justification, because VAM interpreted the speaker reference to mean "the new leader of the orcs." (новый Главарь орков) (VAM H_{1990}.202) Apparently she could not believe that the Elvenking would do such a thing. She had forgotten that the Wood-elves "were more dangerous and less wise." (H.164) She corrected this error in a subsequent, revised edition published by Eksmo publishers in 2000. (VAM H_{2000}.348)

Rakhmanova and Yakhnin alone of all the translators felt the need to eliminate the sarcasm of the second sentence. "He would have done better to have remained my guest." Their rendition changed *guest* to *prisoner* (пленник). VAM also felt uncomfortable with this sentence and added a laugh—"ha-ha-ha" (ха-ха-ха)—at the end to make sure the reader got the point. All the other translators found varied, but quite satisfactory formulations for this sentence.

The translators divided into two camps for the third sentence, with its proverbial "an ill wind, all the same, […] that blows no one any good." There were those translators who used a Russian proverb and those who provided a word-for-word translation. The Russian proverb that the English-Russian dictionary[23] gives as a translation of "it is an ill wind that blows nobody good" is more commonly translated into English as "every cloud has a silver lining" (нет худа без добра). This proverb was the one used by VAM (H.202), Kamenkovich (H.255) and Korolev (H.289). The Anonymous, Yakhnin, Gruzberg, Umanskij and Rakhmanova formulations were all simple paraphrases of the original. Rakhmanova's is, perhaps, the best for its "as they say," which gives it a certain proverbial air.

Rakhmanova: Но, как говорится, и самый дурной ветер приносит добрую весть. (R H.210)

BT: Well, as they say, even the worst wind brings good news.

Anonymous: Впрочем, даже худой ветер иногда приносит добро!

BT: Anyway, even an ill wind sometimes brings good!

Gruzberg: Но даже дурной ветер способен принести добрую новость. (G H.238)

BT: But even an ill wind is capable of bringing good news.

Yakhnin: Но и плохой ветер приносит иногда хорошие вести. (Ya H.303)

BT: But even a bad wind sometimes brings good news.

Umanskij: Но все-таки нет такого дурного ветра, который не принес бы чего-нибудь полезного. (U H.161)

BT: But nevertheless there is no wind so ill that it does not bring something useful.

Bobyr's translation stood out as the only one that found no good in the news carried by the wind. Her version said:

Но все же эта весть — злой ветер, и он не принесет добра никому. (B H_{1994}.291)

BT: But still this news is an evil wind, and it will not bring good to anyone.

She is right as far as the story line goes, but it puts a whole new face on the Elvenking. It makes him much wiser than the surrounding context would imply.

For Tolkien's thoughts on the wisdom of the High Elves concerning gold, the reader has to go to *LotR*, where they can be found in Chapter 8 of Book II ("Farewell to Lórien"), in the scene in which Galadriel bestows a gift on Gimli as the fellowship leaves Lórien. When Gimli at first refuses a gift, saying that the sight of the Lady of the Galadrim and her gentle words were enough for him, Galadriel insists that he ask for a gift, and he asks for a single strand of her hair. She grants his request with these words:

"These words shall go with the gift," she said. [...] "Gimli, son of Gloin, that your hands shall flow with gold, and yet over you gold shall have no dominion." (F.487)

Yakhnin, true to fashion for the terse retelling he was forging, left this segment out. (Ya F. 303) Bobyr' likewise had a small, but significant hole in her translation at this point. She omits the astonishment of the Elves at Gimli's bold request, and the Lady's complimentary reaction and question. Her Gimli says:

> Если вы приказываете, — сказал Гимли, низко кланяясь, — то я посмею попросить у вас только прядь ваших волос, которые настолько же прекраснее золота, насколько звезды прекраснее всяких алмазов. Я сохраню их на память о ваших добрых словах при нашей первой встрече. И если я вернусь в свои родные пещеры, то велю заключить ваш подарок в нетленный хрусталь, дабы он был залогом дружбы между Горами и Лесом до конца времени. (B.120-121)

BT: 'If you insist,' said Gimli, bowing low, 'then I dare to ask you only for a lock of your hair, which is as much more beautiful than gold, as the stars are more beautiful than diamonds. I will preserve it as a remembrance of your kind words at our first meeting. And, if I return to my native caves, then I will command that it be set in imperishable crystal, to be a pledge of friendship between the Mountains and the Forest to the end of time.'

JRRT: 'There is nothing, Lady Galadriel,' said Gimli, bowing low and stammering. 'Nothing, unless it might be – unless it is permitted to ask, nay, to name a single strand of your hair, which surpasses the gold of the earth as the stars surpass the gems of the mine. I do not ask for such a gift. But you commanded me to name my desire.'

The Elves stirred and murmured with astonishment, and Celeborn gazed at the Dwarf in wonder, but the Lady smiled. 'It is said that the skill of the Dwarves is in their hands rather than in their tongues ' she said; 'yet that is not true of Gimli. For none have ever made to me a request so bold and yet so courteous. And how shall I refuse, since I commanded him to speak? But tell me, what would you do with such a gift? '

'Treasure it, Lady,' he answered, 'in memory of your words to me at our first meeting. And if ever I return to the smithies of my home, it shall be set in imperishable crystal to be an heirloom of my house, and a pledge of good will between the Mountain and the Wood until the end of days.' (F.487)

Umanskij did not restore any of the missing lines, but left this segment exactly as it was. (U F.444)

Though their formulations varied greatly, all the other translators got the idea right. Gruzberg's is the best, because it is closest to the original, preserving the repeat of the word "gold," while the other translators used a pronoun the second time.

> — Пусть слова мои пойдут вместе с подарком, — сказала она. — […] Гимли, сын Глойна, пусть ваши руки будут полны золотом, но золото не будет иметь над вами власти. (Gruzberg-C)
> BT: "Let these words of mine go with the gift," she said […] "Gimli, son of Gloin, may your hands be full of gold, but gold will not have power over you."

Galadriel's wish is in essence the full redemption of the Dwarves from the power that gold has on Dwarvish hearts that was begun in *The Hobbit*. In Chapter XVIII ("The Return Journey"), in which Thorin makes his deathbed peace with Bilbo, Tolkien shows that Thorin has had a change of heart, when he has Thorin say:

> If more of us valued food and cheer and song above hoarded gold, it would be a merrier world. (H.273)

Tolkien changed this line for the second edition (1951). In the first edition it reads: "If more men ..." (AH.328) This is a serious change, because *men* is much more restrictive than *us*. *Us* can include Men and Dwarves and Hobbits. Tolkien's new version makes Thorin's comment broader in scope. Some of the translators made it more restrictive. VAM's Thorin felt that it was restricted to "my fellow-tribesmen." (моих соплеменников) VAM $H_{1990}.228$, $H_{2000}.348$) Kamenkovich's Thorin felt that it only need apply to Dwarves. (Km H.292) Yakhnin had the same thought, but his rendition was more verbose. His Thorin said: "if Dwarves, like you Hobbits." (Ya H.342) Rakhmanova's and Kaminskaya's Thorins both said it was "the likes of us." (наш брат) (R H.240; Ksk H.127) Gruzberg's Thorin thought that "we also" (мы тоже) should value food and cheer and song above hoarded gold, which compares Dwarves to Hobbits. (G H.271) The Thorin in Anonymous got it almost right with "some of us" (кое-кто из нас). Bobyr's, Umanskij's and Korolev's Thorins overshot the mark with "the majority of us" (большинство из нас, B $H_{1994}.331$; U H.180) and "all of us." (все мы) (Kr H.327)

The second part of this 'if-then' clause was almost a clean sweep, with the majority vote for *merrier* going to the Russian word веселее.

Korolev and Yakhnin cast the dissenting votes. Korolev's Thorin said that the world would be "much more pleasant" (гораздо приятнее, Kr H.327), and Yakhnin's said that the world would be "a lot brighter and happier." (намного светлее и радостнее) (Ya H.342) Anonymous, however, decided that "the world would be a better place" (мир бы был лучше), and he or she was quite right philosophically, just not linguistically.

Another passage from that same dialog provides an insight into the value of gold and silver in the afterlife of the Dwarves. As Thorin bids farewell to Bilbo, he says:

> I go now to the halls of waiting to sit beside my fathers, until the world is renewed. Since I leave now all gold and silver, and go where it is of little worth, I wish to part in friendship from you, and I would take back my words and deeds at the Gate. (H.272)

The first sentence in Thorin's reconciliation dialog with Bilbo says where Thorin will go in death and how long he will remain there. It is a very compact philosophical treatise on the afterlife of Dwarves in which any distortion of Tolkien's carefully chosen words will have a major impact on the philosophical construct that Tolkien wants to place before the reader.

Yakhnin's view of the afterlife to which Thorin goes is the most out of step with Tolkien. His Thorin is going to "the land of silence" (в страну молчания), where he will wait with his ancestors for the world to be renewed. (Ya H.341) The concept is frighteningly chilling, and entirely Yakhnin's. Tolkien's halls of waiting are most likely modeled on Valhalla (Val + Höll): the Hall of fallen heroes in Odin's palace from Scandinavian myth. This is where fallen heroes feast with the gods while waiting for Ragnarok. It is hard to imagine a silent Viking feast.

Umanskij caught the sense of grandeur of Valhalla in his rendition of *the halls of waiting* as *the Far Palaces* (Далекие Дворцы), but that title seems like it belongs in another story. (U H.180)

The majority vote for the translation of the word *halls* went to the archaic word чертог [chertog]. Anonymous, Rakhmanova, Kamenkovich, and Kaminskaya all used this word, which is a grand, luxuriously furnished room in a wealthy house. The Tsar's *Chertog* (Царский чертог) was the hall in which the Tsars were coronated in the Uspenskij Cathedral in Moscow. *Chertog* is also the word used in the *Soviet Encyclopedic Dictionary*[24] in the definition of *Valhalla*.

Korolev chose another grandiose word for *Hall* (палата [palata]), but given the context, чертог [chertog] is better. VAM and Gruzberg used the modern, straightforward translation of *hall*: зал (zal). Bobyr' was the odd woman out with her rendition of *hall* as обитель [obitel']: an archaic word which means *abode*, or *monastery*. This is the same word that Anonymous and Korolev (*The Hobbit*), and that M&K, Kamenkovich and Volkovskij (*LotR*) use for *The Last Homely House*. (H.60, F.296) Bobyr's own translation for *The Last Homely House* in *The Hobbit*, however, was *the last sanctuary* (последнее убежище B H_{1994}.62, U H.42), which is correct in the context of the story, but which lacks the reserved understatement of Tolkien's name. The paragraph in *LotR* with *The Last Homely House* is missing in both Bobyr' and Umanskij. (B.47, U F.358)

In modern usage, the English word *hall* has lost much of the grandeur that it once had. The *Oxford American Dictionary* defines it as: "a large room or building for meetings, meals, concerts, etc." This is the sense that VAM and Gruzberg capture exactly in their translation of *halls* as залы [zaly, pl.]. (G H.270; VAM H_{1990}.228, H_{2000}.348) A common word collocation in Russian, however, creates problems for the use of the word *zaly*. Зал ожидания (zal ozhidaniya)—Gruzberg's rendition—is a passenger waiting room at train stations (they still have passenger trains in Russia) and at airplane terminals. That association will evoke a rather prosaic image in the mind of the Russian reader, and should, therefore, be avoided.

VAM tries to avoid this interference by adding a qualifier to *halls*. Her version of "halls of waiting" is "Halls of Long Waiting" (Залы Долгого Ожидания) written with all capitals, as if it were a title. Anonymous, however, has the most interesting variant of the modifier of the word *halls*. He calls them the "halls of timelessness" (чертоги безвременья), which has a more satisfying feeling to it than VAM's version. Not only does it use *chertog* instead of *zal*, but a long wait can be boring, while waiting in a timeless space can make a thousand years or ten thousand seem like but an instant. I would rather wait in the "halls of timelessness" than in the "Halls of Long Waiting."

None of the alternate words for *hall* is as satisfying as the image evoked by the use of the word чертог [chertog], with its associations of royal, heavenly grandeur. For the Russian reader, it preserves the association with Valhalla much more certainly and clearly than Tolkien's formulation ever could for those English readers who have not recently read the

Scandinavian Myths, and have forgotten that halls are the dwellings of the gods, as is illustrated by the quote below from *The Norse Myths*.[25]

> The other gods have halls too. The first is called Ydalir, dales where yews grow, and Ull lives there. The second is called Alfheim, where the light Elves live. The gods gave that place to Freyr when he cut his first tooth. The third is called Valaskjalf, Hall of the Slain; one god built it for himself, and with their own hands the others thatched it with silver. The fourth is Sokkvabekk, the sinking floor—it is lapped on all sides by cool murmuring water and there, every day, Odin and Saga drink joyfully from gold goblets.
> The fifth is Gladsheim, home of gladness, and Valhalla stands near by, vast and gold-bright. [...] Valhalla itself has five hundred and forty doors, and when the time comes to fight against Fenrir, eight hundred warriors will march out of each door, shoulder to shoulder. [...] The twelfth is Vidi where Vidar lives, a land of long grass and saplings.

The Nordic Sagas are entirely in step with Thorin's description of the halls of waiting, which Thorin describes as a place "where it [gold and silver] is of little worth." The short quote from *The Norse Myths* above contains two references to gold and silver: the roof of Valaskjalf—Hall of the Slain—is thatched with silver, and Odin and Saga drink from gold goblets. The uses to which the gold and silver are put are very commonplace ones. Silver must indeed be almost worthless, if the roof of a great hall could be thatched with it. While the onion domes of Russian cathedrals were, in fact, sometimes covered in gold leaf, it is not a suitable comparison for the worth of silver as a roofing material on the halls of the gods. On earth, this is an act of conspicuous consumption, a great financial sacrifice to win the favor of the gods, and to show that those on earth are worthy of their favor. In the Halls of the gods, who have no need of artifices to impress anyone, worth is defined in other terms.

The phrase "where it [gold and silver] is of little worth" was a troublesome one for the translators. The English word *worth* has an ambiguity that is hard to replicate in a single word in Russian. The *Oxford American Dictionary* defines *worth* as: "value, merit, usefulness." Umanskij had the best solution. His Thorin says that gold and silver "have no worth." (всё это ничего не стоит) (U H.180) The verb in this phrase has the right sort of ambiguity. It can be used in sentences that define concrete relations of price, like 'This book costs $10' (Эта книга стоит 10 долларов). It can also be used figuratively in sentences like 'It is not worth the effort' (Это не стоит усилий).

Gruzberg and Anonymous came the next closest, while the others wandered further afield. Gruzberg's version is the best of the two. He uses a colloquialism that is normally translated as *use*, or *benefit* or *good*. The *Oxford Russian Dictionary* example—"no good will come of this" (из этого не будет проку)[26]—is very close to Gruzberg's rendition: "where there is little good of it" (где от него мало проку). While his use of a colloquialism is slightly out of step with Thorin's stylized speech, getting the thought behind the words right was more important. Anonymous gave the phrase an interesting philosophical turn by rendering it as (**emphasis** added): "gold and silver are of no consequence **to me** there" (золото и серебро мне там ни к чему), making their worth a personal instead of a general assessment, but still capturing the ambiguity of the English word *worth*. Korolev eliminated that problem by using the same formulation, but without "to me" (там оно ни к чему).

Four of the translators—Rakhmanova, Kamenkovich, Kaminskaya and VAM—decided that *value* was the quality of *worth* that Tolkien had in mind in the context of Dwarves and gold and silver. This is a readily defensible choice, and for the most part conveys the idea of *worth* in this context quite well. All their translations were some variant of the Russian word for *value* цена [tsena]. Rakhmanova's rendition was the most elegant: "it is little valued." (оно мало ценится) (R H$_{1976}$.240) Kamenkovich and Kaminskaya both had an equally interesting formulation along the same lines: "they [gold and silver] are not of value." (они не в цене) (Km H.292; Ksk, H.127) VAM's rendition was a less satisfactory: "it has no value" (оно не имеет ценности) (VAM H$_{1990}$.228), because it is more unequivocal than Tolkien's formulation, which does grant gold and silver some small value, like that of the material used to thatch a roof.

Bobyr', however, decided that *usefulness* was the quality of *worth* that Tolkien had in mind for the afterlife of the Dwarves. This approach produces a major philosophical shift in the meaning of the sentence. The choice between *value* and *usefulness* points to different underlying assumptions on the part of the author. In choosing for *value*, Rakhmanova, Kamenkovich, Kaminskaya and VAM put the accent on money and capital, while also permitting a figurative interpretation to match Thorin's comment about dragons not enjoying any of the fine things in their hoard. In choosing for *usefulness*, Bobyr' put the accent on utilitarianism and practicality, which, in some respects, is the same choice that Gruzberg, VAM and Rakhmanova made when translating *enjoy* with *use* in Thorin's comment about dragons not enjoying any of the fine things in their hoard. (H.35) The distinction is a very Marxist, materialistic one: things have value because they are useful, not for any reason that is intrinsic to the thing itself. In other words, it is a very Soviet distinction. Bobyr's version, like VAM's, was categorical. It reads: "where they are useless." (где они бесполезны) (B H_{1994}.331) Yakhnin kept her company. He said: "gold and silver are not needed." (золото и серебро не нужно) (Ya H.341)

Thorin's stay in "the halls of waiting" will not be forever. He will only remain there "until the world is renewed." Most of the translators had no problem with this phrase, rendering it with the Russian verb *to renew* (обновиться [obnovit'sya], Km H.292; B H.331; G H.270), or the verbal noun *renewal* (обновление [obnovlenie], Anonymous). Korolev offered an interesting alternative with *reborn*. (возродится [vozroditsya]) (Kr H.327) Umanskij had essentially the same formulation with his "until the world be born anew" (пока мир не родится заново [poka mir ne roditsya zanovo], U H.180) In the context of Tolkien and the Norse Myths, the phrase "until the world is renewed" evokes the image of Ragnarok, when the gods and the fallen heroes in Valhalla will rush forth into the final battle with Fenrir and the forces of evil, which will end in the destruction and renewal of the world.

> The earth will sink into the sea. The earth will rise again out of the water, fair and green.[27]

Rakhmanova took a different approach to *renewal*. The world of her version was going to "change for the better." (изменится к лучшему) (R H.239) Kaminskaya took the same tack but with a different verbal prefix: "changes for the better." (переменится к лучшему) (Ksk H.127) VAM's rendition is the least satisfactory of the three, because, while it also voted for change, it did not specify what kind. Using the same verb as Kaminskaya, her version simply reads: "changes." (переменится) (VAM H.228) Yakhnin could not make up his mind and took one from column A and one from column B. His Thorin would remain in the Halls of Silence until "everything was renewed and changed." (все обновится и переменится) (Ya H.341) Change can be for better or for worse and that is why Rakhmanova and Kaminskaya specified which kind of change it would be. While it could be effectively argued that the end of the world at Ragnarok and its rebirth are a change, change is not the word that Tolkien used. The hope that the renewed world will be better is certainly implicit in the reader's mind when looking at this phrase, but it is not explicitly stated in Tolkien's formulation.

This passage is the only one reviewed for the present work that is also in Utilova. The uniqueness of Rakhmanova's translation of the phrase "until the world is renewed" makes it easy to demonstrate that hers was the source text for Utilova's condensed version. Utilova's reads:

> Прощай, добрый вор. Я ухожу из того мира к моим предкам до той поры, пока мир изменится к лучшему. (Ut H.59)
> BT: Farewell, good thief. I leave this world to go to my ancestors, until the world changes for the better.

Compare Rakhmanova (**emphasis** added):

> —— Прощай, добрый вор, —— сказал он. —— Я ухожу в чертоги ожидания к моим праотцам до той поры, когда мир изменится к лучшему. (R H.239)
> BT: "**Farewell, good thief**," he said. "**I leave** to join my forefathers in the halls of waiting, **until the world changes for the better**."

Utilova's use of the Rakhmanova translation as the basis for her condensation only strengthens Rakhmanova's hold on the title of the standard Russian translation of *The Hobbit*. Rakhmanova's translation, however, really does need 'to be brought up to date' to rid itself of its Cold War heritage and its unfortunate lacunae.

Notes:

1. Сказки века-2 (серия «Итоги века. Взгляд из России»), Составитель Ролан Антонович Быков, М: Полифакт, 1999.
2. Англия: журнал о сегодняшней жизни в Великобритании began quarterly publication in 1962.
3. J.R.R. Tolkien. *The Hobbit: or There and Back Again* Adapted by Charles Dixon with Sean Deming, illustrated by David Wenzel), Forrestville, CA/New York: Eclipse Books, New York: Ballantine Books, 1990.
4. Lobdell, Jared, ed. *A Tolkien Compass*, New York: Ballantine Books, 1980, pp. 9-28.
5. Anderson, Douglas A. *The Annotated Hobbit*, Boston: Houghton Mifflin, 1988, ppg. 321-328. In the second edition (2002), these notes are integrated into the body of the book.
6. Большая советская энциклопедия, 1949, т. 1, "Авиация", стр. 92-93.
7. Ibid., т. 35, стр. 542.
8. СЭС, 1990, стр. 831.
9. Ibid., стр. 1110.
10. Ibid., стр. 1051.
11. В.М. Мокиенко, Т.Г. Никитина. Толковый словарь языка Совдепии, СПб: Фолио-Пресс, 1998, стр. 69.
12. Ожегов/Шведова, стр. 759.
13. Confirmed in an eMail to Alla Khananashvili.
14. Anderson, p. 327.
15. Hobit: Kam Gnaln ou Galû, Sovetakan Grogh, Yerevan - 1984. Emma Makaryan (trans.).
16. Thanks to Natal'ya Prokhorova, who heard the story firsthand from Braude.
17. Jane Morgan. "Pronunciation for: *The Lord of the Rings*. Unbound folio. These pronunciations were taken from a tape prepared by Christopher Tolkien on 8/10/80.
18. Джон Р.Р. Толкиен. Хоббит, или туда и обратно, М: ЭКСМО-Пресс, 2000, стр. 367.
19. In the 2002 edition, the word *practically* (практически) was replaced with the word *actually* (фактически).
20. Хрущев, Н.С., Речь Хрущева на закрытом заседании XX съезда КПСС (24-25 февраля 1956 г.) [Khrushchev's Speech at the Closed Session of the XX Congress of the CPSU (24-25 February 1956)]. Munich, изд. «Голос народа», 1956, стр. 54.
21. Хрущев, Н.С., стр. 56.
22. Чуковский, Корней. Тараканище [The Big Bad Cockroach], Saint Petersburg, изд. «Радуга», 1923 (first published edition).

23. *New English-Russian Dictionary*, in two volumes, I.R. Galperin, ed., M: Soviet Encyclopedia Publishing House, 1972.
24. СЭС, стр. 192.
25. *The Norse Myths* (Introduced and retold by Kevin Crossley-Holland), New York, Pantheon Books, 1980, pp. 61-62.
26. *Oxford Russian Dictionary*, (Wheeler and Unbegaun eds.), Oxford, Oxford University Press, 1995, p. 422.
27. *The Norse Myths*, p. 175.

Chapter 3

Giving up the Ring
Plan, Agreement And Promise
:TOLKIEN:THROUGH:RUSSIAN:EYES:

> Freedom without ideals does much more harm than good.
> Arturo Graf (1848-1913)
> Italian author, cultural historian, philologist[1]

While Tolkien's description of Bilbo's decision to give up the Ring—played as two conversations between Bilbo and Gandalf—is short, it is, nevertheless, loaded with information. It provides the reader with key elements of each character's persona. Tolkien's character development in this episode is a layered evolutionary structure built on the words *plan*, *agreement*, *promise*. In this type of structure the context stays the same, but the key word changes. In each of the three segments of the conversation, the context is the Ring. Gandalf is encouraging Bilbo to give it up, increasing the moral pressure on Bilbo at each stage.

In the first segment, Gandalf asks Bilbo if he means to go on with his [Bilbo's] plan. Tolkien's Gandalf repeats the word *plan* three times, making it practically impossible for the reader to miss the point that Bilbo is following a plan, and that Gandalf knows what the plan is. (**Emphasis** added.)

> "You mean to go on with your **plan** then?"
> "I do. I made up my mind months ago, and I haven't changed it."
> "Very well. It is no good saying any more. Stick to your **plan**—your whole **plan**, mind—and I hope that it will turn out for the best, for you, and for all of us." (F.49)

As the conversation between Gandalf and Bilbo resumes later in the story, Tolkien shows that Gandalf has a much larger place in the process of the creation of Bilbo's plan. Tolkien's Gandalf reminds Bilbo that Bilbo had "agreed" to leave the Ring to Frodo. That clearly implies that Gandalf had asked Bilbo to do so. It takes two to make an agreement. In reminding Bilbo of his agreement, Tolkien's Gandalf is slowly stepping up the moral pressure on Bilbo to stick to the plan. (**Emphasis** added.)

> "I am leaving everything to him, of course, except a few oddments. I hope he will be happy, when he gets used to being on his own. It's time he was his own master now."
> "Everything?" said Gandalf. "The ring as well? You **agreed** to that, you remember." (F.59)

In the closing segment of his layered evolutionary structure, Tolkien has Gandalf urge Bilbo to do as he had "promised," reconfirming Gandalf's role in the making of the plan, because a promise has to be made to somebody. Since Gandalf knows about it and is holding Bilbo accountable for it, it must have been made to him.

> "Now, now, my dear Hobbit!" said Gandalf. "All your long life we have been friends, and you owe me something. Come! Do as you **promised**: give it up!" (F.60)

The changes introduced by some of the translations caused significant shifts in both Bilbo's and Gandalf's character. The major differences are who knew what when.

Bobyr' condensed the whole first chapter into a single paragraph, which left Gandalf out of the picture altogether. Her version said:

> With the help of the Ring Bilbo lived a number of years yet. He did not use it often and did not know all its power, but he could feel its effect upon him. Unknown to him, it had begun to turn him into a ghost. Feeling that something strange and unpleasant was happening to him (but not attributing it to the Ring), Bilbo decided to leave his homeland and to go tramping. And that is what he did. He left his home and all his property, including the Ring, to a young relative, his adopted son named Frodo. (B.9)

Umanskij put the first chapter back in.

The initial element in Tolkien's structure—*plan*—fell afoul of two things. The first was the universal admonition of language arts teachers everywhere not to repeat yourself. This doomed Tolkien's 3 repeats of *plan* within the space of 32 words to certain editorial oblivion. Of the translators, only G&G replicated Tolkien's series of repeats.

The second problem for *plan* was that in Russian it carries a number of infamous political associations. It is connected with the grand Soviet five-year plans, that were often filled only on paper. Jokes about plan production targets were legion. The satirical magazine Крокодил [Krokodil]—roughly equivalent to *Punch*—once ran a cartoon on its cover showing a fantastically huge chandelier hanging from a ceiling beam that was obviously bowed under the weight of this monstrosity. The caption read: Who cares if no one will buy it? It meets, even exceeds, the plan production target in one fell swoop. The point was that it did not matter if the factory produced anything useful or not. Only the plan target was important, no matter how ridiculously it was formulated. In the case of the chandelier on the cover of *Krokodil*, weight was the implied plan target. Tolkien's *plan*, therefore, was replaced by various unsatisfactory circumlocutions, except in Gruzberg's (Aleksandrova's), Umanskij's and Nemirova's versions.

While Gruzberg does use *plan* in his rendition of the first segment of the conversation between Bilbo and Gandalf, *plan* is missing two of its three repeats, even in the C version. The circumlocution for Tolkien's first use of *plan* in Gruzberg-A weakens the impact of Tolkien's structure. Gruzberg-A starts the conversation off on a different foot, with Gandalf asking Bilbo if he wants to leave. The same thought is implied in the question that Tolkien's Gandalf asks, but Tolkien's question is broader in its implications. Both Gandalfs know that Bilbo is planning to leave and are asking if Bilbo is going to stick to his plan. The problem is that Gruzberg's reader does not know that there is a plan until the next time that Gandalf speaks, and Tolkien's reader does not know that Bilbo's plan involves leaving the Shire until much later in the story. Tolkien's reader remains in suspense, while Gruzberg telegraphs Bilbo's intention to the reader long before Tolkien intended.

— Ты хочешь уйти?
— Да. Я задумал это давно, и теперь мой замысел окреп.
— Хорошо. Больше говорить не будем. Укрепляйся в своем плане, и так будет лучше и для тебя, и для всех нас. (Gruzberg-A)
BT: "You want to leave?"
      "Yes. I thought this up a long time ago, and now my idea has firmed up.

"Good. We won't talk about that any more. Stick firm to your plan and it will be better for you and for the rest of us."

Aleksandrova cleans up a number of the problems with this segment in her revision of Gruzberg's text for publication on CD-ROM. Even though she cannot bring herself to use the word *plan* three times in the segment, she restores the idea of a plan to its rightful place in the lead question with the formulation "You decided to take the idea through to the end?". This avoids the political implications of *plan*, and restores the suspense inherent in Tolkien's formulation. She keeps *plan* in the same place that Gruzberg had it, with only minor stylistic changes.

    — Так ты решил довести задуманное до конца?
    — Да. Я давно решился и с тех пор не передумал.
    — Отлично. Больше ни слова об этом: ни к чему. Не отступай от своего плана — *ни в чем* не отступай — и, надеюсь, все закончится хорошо и для тебя, и для всех нас.
BT: "So you decided to take the idea through to the end?"
    "Yes. I decided long ago, and have not changed my mind since then.
    "Excellent. Not another word about that is necessary. Do not deviate from your plan — do not deviate *in any way* — and, I hope, that everything will end well both for you and for the rest of us."

Nemirova has a similar approach. She begins with "So, you really intend to …" This maintains the suspense for the reader, because it leaves the question of what Bilbo intends to do up in the air. Her single use of *plan* is essentially the same as Gruzberg/Aleksandrova.

    — Значит, ты действительно собираешься …
    — Да. Я решился уже несколько месяцев назад и не передумал.
    — Отлично! Тогда не стоит больше и говорить об этом. Держись только плана, не отступай ни в чем, и все обернется к лучшему и для тебя, и для нас всех. (N F.35)
BT: "So, you really intend to …"
    "Yes, I decided several months ago and have not changed my mind."
    "Excellent! Then there is nothing more to talk about. Stick right to the plan, don't deviate in any way, and everything will turn out

better for you and for all of us."

Umanskij begins well with two repeats of the word *plan*, but falters on the third, not only by leaving it out, but by a change in the word order of the phrase that produces a significant semantic shift.

> — Следовательно, вы продолжаете настаивать на вашем плане?
> — Да. Я пришел к этому решению много месяцев назад и не изменю его.
> — Хорошо. Не будем больше говорить об этом. Держитесь вашего плана, — целиком вашего, заметьте, — и я надеюсь, что для вас — и для всех нас — все кончится к лучшему. (U F.208)
> BT: "Therefore, you continue to insist upon your plan?"
> "Yes. I made this decision months ago and I won't change it."
> "Good. We won't talk about that any more. Stick to your plan, wholly yours, mind you, and I hope that for you and for all of us, everything will turn out better."

Umanksij's formulation puts the accent on *YOUR whole plan* (i.e. not someone else's) rather than on *your WHOLE plan* (i.e. not just parts of it). If he had just left out the word *your* along with the word *plan*, his construction would have worked. This point will come back to haunt Umanskij later in the present chapter when the question of whose plan it really is is discussed.

Yakhnin has a particularly interesting, unique approach to the question of Bilbo's plan. Bilbo has one, but does not know that Gandalf knows about it. Yakhnin's Gandalf opens the conversation with: "That's a nice garden you've got there, Bilbo. It's probably sad to have to leave it?" Bilbo's reaction is one of surprise: "Leave it? How did you know?" Yakhnin's Gandalf only smiled in reply. (Ya F.16-17) This rendition of the dialog is full of implications. It leaves Gandalf out of the planning stage for giving up the Ring, while making him seem all-knowing and mysterious. It completely changes the relationship between Gandalf and Bilbo, from trusting friends who share in the making of a complex decision, to a small Hobbit acquainted with a busybody of a wizard.

In M&K's rendition of this episode, Bilbo is presented as a much stronger character than he is in the original. This difference is in very sharp contrast to Tolkien's presentation of Gandalf as the determined force behind the decision to leave the Ring to Frodo. M&K disturb the balance of strength of character between the two so that it contradicts the defining characteristic of Tolkien's heroes given by Dr. N.L. Trauberg, a Russian specialist on C.S. Lewis.

> It is not the important, triumphant, conquering characters who become their [Tolkien and C.S. Lewis] heroes; it is the funny and unheroic persona who becomes the hero. Most importantly, it is whether the hero's concern is for himself or for others.[2]

While Tolkien's Gandalf asks Bilbo if he meant to go through with his plan, M&K's Gandalf asks Bilbo if: "You're going to do what you said, then?" (Значит, как сказал, так и сделаешь?). (M&K, F_{1982}.14; F_{1988}.57) In isolation, there is hardly any difference in the formulation of the two questions, but the answers following them place them in a context where the difference in meaning becomes significant. Tolkien's answer shows that Bilbo decided "months ago" to go through with the plan, but Tolkien qualifies the decision as one still subject to change, by having Bilbo add that he hasn't changed his mind: "I do. I made up my mind months ago, and I haven't changed it." (F.49) The possibility of changing his decision is a reflection of the internal struggle that Bilbo is having about giving up the Ring, and an indication that freedom of choice plays in Tolkien's Weltanschauung. M&K, on the other hand, springboard from their use of "do what you [Bilbo] said" to an answer that is unequivocal in its resolve to go forward: "Of course. I never go back on my word" (Конечно. Я от своего слова никогда не отступаюсь). (M&K, F_{1982}.14; F_{1988}.57)

With this formulation M&K put the cart before the horse. They telegraph the punch to the Russian reader that Tolkien will deliver to the English reader later on, and much more subtly. In M&K's version, Bilbo's *word* [of honor], which he never goes back on, is clearly a reference to Bilbo's promise, which Tolkien will not introduce for another 11 pages. By moving the promise forward to this point M&K set the whole structure of *plan*, *agreement* and *promise* on its head and redefine Bilbo's character.

Volkovskij makes the same philosophical detour that M&K made. His Gandalf begins the conversation by asking if Bilbo has changed his mind. This makes it clear that Gandalf knows what Bilbo plans to do, but Bilbo's answer is full of firm resolve, essentially rejecting any chance of a change of plans, eliminating all reflection of the internal struggle that is going on inside Bilbo about giving up the Ring. The result is to move Gandalf to the sidelines, while Bilbo steps to center stage as the determined force behind the course of events about to unfold.

> — Выходит, ты не передумал?
> — Нет. Да и с чего бы? Коли уж решил, надо действовать.
> — Что ж, хватит об этом. Надеюсь, все пойдет так, как ты задумал, и сложится удачно для тебя и для всех нас. (V F.44)

BT: "So, you haven't changed your mind?"

"No. And why should I? Since I've already decided, I need to take action."

"Well, that's enough of that. I hope that everything will go the way you planned it, and will work out successfully for you and for all of us."

G&G's Gandalf does not ask Bilbo about his plan, but about his decision. "That means that you're going to do what you decided after all?" (Значит, все-таки будешь делать, как решил?) (G&G F.35) The difference between *plan* and *decision* is very slight, and does not significantly change the impact on the reader. It can be simply viewed as another reflection of the translators' aversion to the word *plan*. While the other translators avoided repeats, G&G go Tolkien one better by accenting *decided/make up your mind* [both based on the same root in Russian: решил(ся)] with four repeats so that the reader cannot possibly miss it. (**Emphasis** added.)

> — Значит, все-таки будешь делать, как решил?
> — Решил-то я давно, а вот решился, пожалуй, только сейчас.
> — Ну и ладно. Раз решил — делай. Только уж делай, как задумал, глядишь, еще и обойдется все, и для тебя, и для других тоже. (G&G F.35, G&G$_{2002}$, 211)

BT: "That means that you're going to do what you **decided** nevertheless?"

"I **decided** long ago, but it's perhaps only just now that I **made up my mind**."

"Very well. Since you've **decided**, do it! Only do it the way you planned. Before you know it, everything will still turn out right, both for you and for others as well."

G&G's "it's perhaps only just now that I made up my mind" elegantly preserves Tolkien's indication of Bilbo's internal struggle about giving up the Ring. It shows this as the culminating moment in a process that has been going on for a long time.

VAM's formulation of the lead question in Gandalf's and Bilbo's dialog is a question aimed at someone who has made a decision that the questioner does not agree with. Her Gandalf asks: "You are standing your ground nevertheless?" (Все-таки стоишь на своем?). He would not ask this question, if he agreed with the decision. As Tolkien makes clear in his version of the dialog, Gandalf had a large part in the making of the plan, and was taking pains to make sure that it was carried out. VAM's Gandalf is still trying to influence a decision he does not agree with.

K&K skillfully replicate Tolkien's layered evolutionary structure of *plan, agreement,* and *promise* with *plan* (замысел) (K&K F.50), *agreement* (уговор) (K&K F.62) and *promise* (обещание) (K&K F.64), but not without a certain verbosity. Tolkien's *your plan* becomes "your plan of long standing." Tolkien's "You agreed to that" is captured in a Russian proverb, which literally means "an agreement is more valued than money" (Уговор дороже денег!). Tolkien's "Do as you promised" is transformed into a very un-Russian calque of the English proverb "a promise is a promise" (Обещание есть обещание).

In the first segment of the dialog, Tolkien highlights Bilbo's freedom of choice in carrying out the plan, by having Gandalf caution Bilbo to stick to the whole—with emphasis added—plan, thereby implying that less than 100% adherence to the plan is still an option: "Stick to your plan—your whole plan, mind—and I hope it will turn out for the best, for you, and for all of us." (F.49) This reinforces the fact that Bilbo still has freedom of choice in the matter. The translators who glossed over this admonition, glossed over the issue of freedom of choice.

Gruzberg-A left it out altogether, but Aleksandrova put it back in for the CD-ROM. VAM's rendition of "whole plan" is better than Aleksandrova's because it is a positive construction, while Aleksandrova's is a negative one.

VAM:
— Отлично. Значит, нечего и болтать. Делай, что задумал, — только учти, делай все до конца! — и, как мне кажется, всем будет лучше и тебе, и нам. (VAM F_{2003}.230)

BT: "Fine. That means that there is nothing to talk about. Do what you planned, only mind, all the way to the end! And, as it seems to me, it will be better for everyone, both you and us."

Aleksandrova:
— Отлично. Больше ни слова об этом: ни к чему. Не отступай

от своего плана — *ни в чем не отступай* — и, надеюсь, все закончится хорошо и для тебя, и для всех нас.

BT: "Excellent. Not another word about that is necessary. Do not deviate from your plan — do not deviate *in any way* — and, I hope, that everything will end well both for you and for the rest of us."

Nemirova had an acceptable variant, and Volkovskij and G&G had workable renditions, all, however, the worse for not including Tolkien's repeats of *plan*.

Yakhnin's Bilbo has nothing but free choice, and apparently very little doubt about the correctness of his decision. He will miss his home and his garden, but he is determined to go through with his decision to leave. Yakhnin's version of the dialog is much more verbose than Tolkien's and covers some interesting new ground.

"That's a nice garden you've got there, Bilbo," said Gandalf quietly. "It's probably sad to have to leave it?"
"Leave it? How did you know?" said the Hobbit in surprise.
The wizard only smiled.
"Yes, sighed Bilbo, I am tired. I dream of resting. I love Hobbitaniya very much, and will miss my home and my garden, but I've made up my mind and will not back down.
"Then there's nothing to talk about," nodded Gandalf, and added mysteriously, "Maybe that's for the best." (Ya. F.16-17)

The source of Yakhnin's embellishments to the dialog can be found in the original, only they occur ten pages later in the scene in which Bilbo and Gandalf say goodbye. (F.59) This type of compression is typical for Yakhnin's retelling. *Agreement* and *promise* likewise fall victim to his condensation of Tolkien's tale.

M&K leave out Tolkien's emphasis on the "whole plan" altogether. Had they included it, it would have cast doubt on Bilbo's character, by implying that he might not always keep his word entirely. In their version Gandalf replies: "As long as you've made up your mind. Do everything the way it was thought up." [Решил так решил — сделай все по-задуманному]. (M&K F_{1982}.14; F_{1988}.57) Without the extra emphasis offered by Tolkien's repeat in the original, it fails to sufficiently prompt the reader to think about freedom of choice. It is more of a prompt to be precise.

While K&K's renditions of the three elements of Tolkien's layered structure maintain Gandalf's key role in the formulation of Bilbo's plan, their rendition of Gandalf's admonition to Bilbo to stick to his "whole plan" does Bilbo an injustice. Their Gandalf tells Bilbo: "In that case, carry out your decision, only don't chicken out!" [В таком случае выполняй свое решение — только смотри не струсь!]. It is beneath Gandalf's dignity to accuse Bilbo of a lack of courage. He knows Bilbo better than that. K&K's formulation has too much of the air of school-yard bravado and *I double dare you* in it.

The issue is not one of courage, but of willpower. Tolkien's formulation keeps the reader's attention focused on Bilbo's freedom of choice. Bilbo has agreed to the plan, but can change his mind. Gandalf's role is to offer Bilbo the support and encouragement of a wise advisor, not to egg him on to something foolish like a stupid boy on a playground. This role is confirmed when the conversation between Gandalf and Bilbo is resumed after Bilbo's grand disappearance and Bilbo admits that "I expect you [Gandalf] know best, as usual." (F.58)

K&K's rendition of this part of the conversation sends it on a subtle philosophical detour. Instead of saying "I expect that you know best," they have Bilbo say: "But you probably knew what you were doing. As always." (Впрочем, ты, наверное, знал, что делаешь. Как и всегда.) (K&K F.61) This changes the focus ever so slightly. The actions that K&K's Gandalf takes are well-thought-out, conscious decisions, reminiscent of the classic English definition of a gentleman: someone who never insults anyone unintentionally. Tolkien's Bilbo, however, is focusing on Gandalf's wisdom in comparison to others, in particular himself, and Gandalf is wiser. Though their formulations varied, none of the other translators—except, of course, Yakhnin and Bobyr', who left it out—had any trouble with "I expect you [Gandalf] know best, as usual." (F.58)

In the remaining two segments of Tolkien's triptych (*plan*, *agreement*, *promise*), Gruzberg and Umanskij stick more closely to Tolkien's version of the story than do the other translators, as can be seen in Gruzberg's rendition of the segments with *agreement* and *promise*. (**Emphasis** added.)

> — Я все оставляю ему, за исключением, конечно, нескольких мелочей. Надеюсь, он будет счастлив, когда привыкнет все это считать своим. С этого времени он сам себе хозяин.
> — Все? — спросил Гэндалвф — И кольцо? Вспомни, ты на это согласился. (G F.56)

BT: "I am leaving everything to him, with the exception, of course,

Giving up the Ring

of a few small things. I hope that he will be happy when he gets used to considering all this his own. From that time, he's his own master."

"Everything?" asked Gandalf. "And the ring, too? You **agreed** to that, remember?"

> — Ну, ну, мой дорогой хоббит, — сказал Гандалв. — Всю твою долгую жизнь мы были друзьями, и ты задолжал мне кое-что. Выполняй свое обещание — отдай кольцо! (G F.58)
> BT: "Come now, my dear Hobbit!" said Gandalf. "All your long life we have been friends, and you owe me something. Fulfill your **promise**, give up the ring!."

Though she does make some changes, Aleksandrova leaves the key elements of *agreement* as they were. Her rendition of the promise is altered, but without a serious shift in meaning. Instead of "Do as you promised!", her Gandalf says: "Keep your word!". The slight stylistic changes in her formulations make the text more elegant. (**Emphasis** added.)

> — Ну, ну, мой дорогой хоббит, — сказал Гандальв. — Всю твою долгую жизнь мы дружили, и ты кое-чем мне обязан. Ну же! Сдержи слово — отдай кольцо!
> BT: "Come now, my dear Hobbit!" said Gandalf. "All your long life we have been friends, and you owe me something. **Keep your word**, give up the ring!."

Umanskij has some very lucid moments, but the quality of his text is uneven. While he got the *agreement* and *promise* part of the text right, he was out in left field with his translation of *now, now* as *right away* (teper' zhe [теперь же]). Gruzberg was right. It should have been *Nu, nu* (Ну, ну).

> — Оставляете все, вы говорите? — спросил Ганнальф. — А как насчет кольца? Вы согласились расстаться с ним, помните? (U F.215)
> BT: "You left everything, you say?" asked Gandalf. "What about the ring? You agreed to part with it, remember?"

> — Теперь же, теперь же, мой дорогой коротыш! — сказал Гандальф. — Всю вашу долгую жизнь мы были друзьями, и вы кое-чем мне обязаны. Уходите! И сделайте, как обещали: оставьте эту вещь! (U F.216)
> BT: "Right away, right away, my dear shortnik!" said Gandalf. "All

your long life we have been friends, and you owe me something. Leave! And do as you promised: leave this thing!"

Nemirova completely misses the boat for the middle panel of the triptych (*agreement*), but does make it on board for the third (*promise*). Her Gandalf prompts Bilbo that this is what he wanted (Ведь ты этого и хотел!), instead of reminding him of his agreement to the plan. (N F.44) That formulation could just as easily refer to a decision that Gandalf did not agree with, as in 'this is what you wanted, and now you are stuck with it.' Her formulation shows that Gandalf was aware of the decision, but does not indicate that he had any role in making it. When it comes time for her Gandalf to hold Bilbo to his promise, she uses Gruzberg's formulation. (N F.45)

With a formulation much like Nemirova's, G&G also miss the boat for the *agreement* between Bilbo and Gandalf, placing Gandalf on the sidelines of the decision. Their Gandalf reminds Bilbo that that was what he wanted [Ты ведь так хотел? (G&G F.44, G&G$_{2002}$, 218)]. Nemirova's and G&G's renditions make Bilbo a much stronger character than he is in the original. G&G manage *promise* in the continuation of the conversation well enough, but without the base of the layered, evolutionary structure of *plan*, *agreement* and *promise* to support it, the effort is wasted. (G&G F.46, G&G$_{2002}$, 220)

Volkovskij misses the agreement step as well. His Bilbo and Gandalf have discussed the Ring, but there was no agreement. He also makes Gandalf more threatening here than Tolkien does. Tolkien saves that for the final step, the promise. For Volkovskij's reader, the change in Gandalf's attitude is not justified, given Bilbo's positive stance in the plan stage.

— *Все*, говоришь, оставил? — с нажимом спросил Гэндальф.
— И кольцо тоже? Помнишь, мы о том толковали? (V F.55)
BT: "You left *everything*, you said," asked Gandalf emphatically. "And the ring as well. Remember we discussed that?"

In the third stage of Tolkien's structure, Volkovskij finally comes through with the promise that Tolkien has been building to, but, since he missed the build-up, it comes as a complete surprise to his reader.

— А ну полегче, любезный хоббит, — сказал Гэндальф. — Как никак, мы с тобой долго были друзьями, и ты мне кое-чем обязан. Так что выполняй-ка обещанное. Оставь кольцо! (V F.56)

BT: "Easy there, my dear Hobbit," said Gandalf. "One way or another, you and I have long been friends, and you are obliged to me for a thing or two. So do what you promised. Leave the ring!"

M&K likewise miss the beat on *agreement*. Their Gandalf simply reminds Bilbo that that is what he [Bilbo] decided. This, too, leaves Gandalf out of the decision process. He knows what was decided, but cannot hold Bilbo accountable for it.

— Все оставил? — спросил Гэндальф. — И Кольцо тоже? У тебя ведь так было решено, помнишь? (M&K F_{1982}.20; F_{1988}.65)
BT: "Everything?" asked Gandalf. "And the Ring as well? After all, that's what you made up your mind to do, remember?"

As the conversation continues, the Russian reader is hardly surprised when M&K's Gandalf tells Bilbo to "do as you promised" (Делай, как обещано), because M&K began with *word* [of honor] instead of with *plan*. For the English reader the promise is the culmination of Tolkien's layered, evolutionary structure: *plan*, *agreement*, *promise*, each becoming more insistent. For the Russian reader the structure is: *word* [of honor], *plan*, *promise*. This shifts the accent from Bilbo's freedom of choice to whether he keeps his word or not.

— Легче, легче, любезный хоббит! — проговорил Гэндальф. — Всю твою жизнь мы были друзьями, припомни-ка. Ну-ну! Делай, как обещано: выкладывай Кольцо! (M&K F_{1982}.21; F_{1988}.67)
BT: "Easy, easy, my dear Hobbit," said Gandalf. "We have been friends all your life, remember. Come on! Do as you promised. Give up the Ring!"

Another small, but interesting stumbling block for the translators in this segment is the subtle hint about the effect of the Ring on Bilbo, which made him seem to possess "perpetual youth." (F.43) Tolkien's Gandalf says: "All your long life we have been friends." Three of the translators missed this cue. Two (Bobyr' and Yakhnin) left it out altogether. Gruzberg, Aleksandrova, Nemirova, Umanskij and VAM got it right. M&K's Gandalf said: "We have been friends all your life." G&G's and Volkovskij's declared: "You and I have long been friends," while K&K's Gandalf ventured: "This is not the first day we have known each other." These statements are all true, but this is not the point that Tolkien was trying to make. It is only one word, and many a casual reader will not even notice it, but leaving it out, or repositioning it makes Tolkien's work shallower and less full of detail. Strangely enough, it is precisely those translators whose renditions are widely dismissed for a lack of literariness who got it right.

Bilbo's Joke

> A joke's a very serious thing.
> Charles Churchill (1731-1764),
> *The Ghost*, book III, line 1386

Throughout the episode of Bilbo's struggle to give up the Ring, Tolkien keeps referring to Bilbo's *joke*. (**Emphasis** added.)

"I mean to enjoy myself on Thursday and have my little **joke**." (F.49)

"And would spoil my **joke**." (F.57)

"It would quite spoil the **joke**." (F.61)

It is not until Gandalf's conversation with Frodo at the end of the chapter, that Tolkien capitalizes on the set-up to underscore the difficulty of Bilbo's decision.

> "I wish—I mean, I hoped until this evening that it was only a **joke**," said Frodo. "But I knew in my heart that he really meant to go. He always used to **joke** about serious things. I wish I had come back sooner, just to see him off." (F.63)

Because Bilbo always joked about serious things, this had been a serious matter indeed and not, as it would at first seem from all the talk about his joke, something to be laughed at. He was giving up the Ring, and leaving the Shire for good.

There were a number of excellent translations of Frodo's characterization of Bilbo as always joking about serious things, but these well-crafted renditions were often marred by missteps in the build-up to the punch line. Almost all of the translators included *joke* on the first rung of the ladder. The obvious exception was Bobyr', who compressed the whole first chapter to a single paragraph. Not all of the translators, however, managed to replicate each of the other two rungs of the ladder. Rung number two is missing in Nemirova and K&K, rung three in Gruzberg, Umanskij and M&K. In these translations, the incomplete build-up diminishes the impact of an otherwise well-done punch line.

Aleksandrova made a slight detour in preparing Gruzberg for publication on the CD-ROM when she replaced Gruzberg's *joke* [шутка (shutka)] with *practical joke* [розыгрыш (rozygrysh)]. While this interpretation is not incorrect in as far as the text goes, it breaks the connection between the build-up and the punch line in the conversation between Frodo and Gandalf. She left *joke* [шутка (shutka)] in the punch line.

Gruzberg himself made a slight detour on his way to the punch line, which itself was very well done. On rung two of the build-up, Bilbo is admonishing Gandalf for the startling flash that accompanied his disappearance. He felt that it spoiled his joke. Gruzberg's Bilbo, on the other hand, does not reproach Gandalf—be it ever so slightly—the way Tolkien's did. The remark that Gruzberg's Bilbo makes to Gandalf is more of a compliment than a complaint.

   — Это еще улучшило мою шутку. Вы интересный старый хлопотун, — засмеялся Бильбо. (G F.55)
   BT: "That just made my joke better. You are an interesting old busybody," laughed Bilbo."

Aleksandrova restores the reproach, but her use of *practical joke* (розыгрыш [rozygrysh]) instead of *joke* (шутка [shutka]) makes things worse instead of better.

   — И испортить мой розыгрыш. Ах, несносный старик! — засмеялся Бильбо.
   BT: "And ruin my practical joke. Oh, you intolerable old man!" laughed Bilbo.

  M&K missed rung three of Tolkien's build-up to the punch line that would underscore the difficulty of Bilbo's decision in a conversation between Frodo and Gandalf. While that weakens the impact of Frodo's punch line on the Russian reader, the punch line lost even more in translation. In their version, M&K use *serious* as an adverb, which tells the reader how Bilbo carried out his jokes: seriously (всерьез). Tolkien's formulation uses *serious* as an adjective. Bilbo always used to joke about serious things, which explains why Bilbo kept going on and on about his joke as he talked with Gandalf and struggled to make up his mind to leave. It was a serious matter, which, as Tolkien's Frodo notes, was what Bilbo always joked about. M&K's Frodo says: "He always was serious about his jokes." (Он всегда шутил всерьез.)

(M&K, F_{1982}.23; F_{1988}.69) M&K's translation is an elegant literary work of art, but it is not quite Tolkien.

Umanskij had a particularly interesting punch line that has both of Frodo's repeats of the word *joke*. The image that Umanskij's description invokes is intriguing, and his interpretation of Tolkien's elaborate formulation is not that far afield.

> — Я хотел ... вернее, я надеялся до нынешнего вечера, что все это было только шуткой, — сказал Фродо. — Но сердцем я чувствовал, что он действительно собирается уйти. Он всегда шуткой маскировал серьезные намерения. Мне жаль, что я не успел попрощаться с ним. (U F.218)
>
> BT: "I wanted ... I mean, I had hoped up to this evening that it was all only a joke," said Frodo. "But in my heart I felt that he really meant to go. He always camouflaged serious intentions with a joke. I am sorry that I did not get to say goodbye to him."

While Yakhnin had rungs one and two of the build-up, he left out rung three and the punch line. The story takes an entirely different turn in his rendition of the conversation between Frodo and Gandalf after Bilbo has left. Yakhnin's Frodo says nothing about Bilbo's joke, but rather that he really envies Bilbo. Yakhnin's Gandalf tells Frodo not to worry. "Perhaps you will get your share of distant travels and unusual adventures." (Ya. F.25-26) This foreshadowing—which is missing in the original—aids Yakhnin in compressing the story and robs it of its depth. In the original, Frodo does say that he would have liked to go off tramping in the wilderness with Bilbo, but Gandalf does not hint at what may happen in the future. (F.69)

G&G had no trouble with the first three rungs of the ladder in the build-up to the punch line, but failed to capitalize on them by leaving the punch line out of the closing conversation between Frodo and Gandalf altogether. (**Lacunae** highlighted)

> — Ушел? — спросил Фродо.
> — Да, — ответил Гэндальф, — все-таки ушел.
> — Я думал, ну, то есть надеялся до самого сегодняшнего вечера, что это только шутка, — вымолвил Фродо. — А в душе-то знал: уйдет он. Вот, хотел пораньше вернуться, застать его. (G&G F.48)
>
> BT: "Has he gone?" asked Frodo.
> "Yes," answered Gandalf, "he left after all."
> "I thought, well, I hoped right up until this evening, that it was

just a joke," said Frodo. But in my heart, I knew he would go. I really wanted to come back earlier and catch him."

JRRT: "Has he gone?" he [Frodo] asked."

"Yes," answered Gandalf, "he has gone at last."

"I wish—I mean, I hoped until this evening that it was only a joke," said Frodo. "But I knew in my heart that he really meant to go. **He always used to joke about serious things.** I wish I had come back sooner, just to see him off." (F.63)

Lacunae like this are the major failing of G&G's translation. It was not restored in their revised edition that did make some other significant changes. (G&G$_{2002}$, 222)

On the third rung of the ladder, Gruzberg momentarily loses sight of the trail and skips two lines. He omits Bilbo's joke, and also omits Gandalf's reply, which—in Tolkien's version—serves to reinforce Gandalf's role in helping Bilbo to decide to give away the Ring. (**Lacunae** highlighted)

— В конце концов я и прием устроил для этого же: чтобы раздать подарки и вместе с ними легче расстаться с кольцом. Это оказалось не так легко. Итак, кольцо вместе со всем остальным переходит к Фродо. — Он глубоко вздохнул. — А теперь я и в самом деле должен идти, иначе меня кто-нибудь увидит. (Gruzberg-C)

BT: "After all, I arranged this reception to give away presents, and together with them more easily part with the ring. But it did not turn out to be quite that easy. So, the ring goes to Frodo together with all the rest, then." He sighed deeply. "And now, I really have to go, otherwise, somebody might see me."

JRRT: "After all that's what this party business was all about, really: to give away lots of birthday presents, and somehow make it easier to give it away at that same time. It hasn't made it any easier in the end, **but it would be a pity to waste all my preparations. It would quite spoil the joke."**

"Indeed it would take away the only point I ever saw in the affair," said Gandalf.

"Very well," said Bilbo, "it goes to Frodo with all the rest." He drew a deep breath. "And now I really must be starting, or somebody else will catch me. ..." (F.61)

This kind of mistake is atypical of Gruzberg's normal close attention to detail, but as he admitted, he sometimes skipped lines when he did not understand what Tolkien meant. Aleksandrova put back the two missing lines and stuck to her choice of *practical joke* [розыгрыш (rozygrysh)] as the translation for Bilbo's *joke*. Zastyrets, Gruzberg's book editor, only made slight cosmetic changes to this segment, without restoring the joke. (G F.59)

Umanskij has a wonderful punch line, but has an even larger gap in his text than Gruzberg. He leaves out the whole paragraph about the reason for the party being to give presents away.

> Некоторое время коротыш стоял в нерешительности, потом перевел дыхание. — Хорошо, — сказал он с усилием. — Я так и сделаю. — Затем пожал плечами и немного печально улыбнулся. — Дарить так дарить. Оно достанется Фродо вместе со всем прочим. — Бильбо глубоко вздохнул. — А теперь я действительно должен тронуться в путь, иначе кто-нибудь еще задержит меня. (U F.217)

BT: The shortnik stood for a minute undecided, and then sighed. "All right," he said with an effort. "That's what I'll do." Then he shrugged his shoulders and smiled somewhat ruefully. "Giving presents is giving presents. It goes to Frodo along with all the rest." Bilbo drew a deep breath. And now I really must get on my way, or somebody else will catch me."

In an otherwise excellent replication of Tolkien's build-up and punch line, Volkovskij adds an embellishment that introduces a sinister element of foreboding that Tolkien will not introduce for sometime yet. At the third step in the ladder, Volkovskij adds an extra repeat of the word *joke*, as his Gandalf makes a dire warning. This gives the conversation a much more serious turn than did Tolkien at this point, who was matching the lighthearted air of Bilbo's joke. Bilbo is explaining that the idea behind the party was to give away lots of presents, so as to make it easier to give away the Ring as well, and if he does not go through with giving the Ring to Frodo, it would waste all his preparations, and "it would quite spoil the joke." Tolkien's Gandalf replies: "Indeed it would take away the only point I ever saw in the affair." (F.61) Volkovskij's Gandalf, however, says: "If you can't make up your mind, you will not only spoil your joke, but everything will go to rack and ruin." (Коли не решишься, так не только шутку испортишь, все прахом пойдет.) (V F.57)

VAM, too, added an extra repeat of *joke* to her quite serviceable replication of the build-up and punch line. It came at the second rung of the ladder. The result is to make her version sound somewhat less obtuse than Tolkien's. Tolkien's Bilbo tells Gandalf that Gandalf probably knows best as usual, to which Gandalf replies: "I do—when I know anything. But I don't feel too sure about this whole affair [Bilbo's Grand Disappearance]." (F.58) VAM's Gandalf says: "Of course," answered the wizard. "When I know anything at all, I know best. I haven't comprehended everything yet, but I don't like your joke very much." [Безусловно, — ответил маг. — Когда хоть что-то видно, то видней. Я еще не все понял, но не очень-то мне нравится твоя шутка.] (VAM. F.47) This is one of VAM's claims to fame. Her version is much less difficult to read because she tries to make Tolkien's points explicit instead of implicit.

In general, Gruzberg's and Nemirova's translations followed the doctors' dictum of 'first do no harm,' which made them the most satisfactory philosophically, but both lack the elegant turn of phrase necessary for literariness. Literary kudos go to M&K, G&G and K&K. M&K and G&G lose points, however, for philosophical deviations and K&K for verbosity. Umanskij was simply too inconsistent. Overall for this segment, K&K is the best.

Notes:

1. Жемчужины мысли, 3-е изд., Минск: «Беларусь», 1991, стр.45.
2. Сказки старой Англии [Fairy Tales of Old England], M: Master Publishing House, 1992, p. 208.

Chapter 4

Hope Abandoned
ᛏᛟᛚᚴᛁᛖᚾ ᛏᚺᚱᛟᚢᚷᚺ ᚱᚢᛋᛋᛁᚪᚾ ᛖᛁᛖᛋ

> Abandon all hope, ye who enter here.
> Dante (1265-1321)
> *The Inferno*, canto 3.

Hope—a key tenet of Christianity—plays a central role in Tolkien's story. It is a major structural element in his world view. "I am a Christian (which can be deduced from my stories)," said Tolkien in a letter to a reader. (L.288) The whole of Frodo's quest is built on hope. Tolkien makes this clear in Chapter 8 of Book II of *The Fellowship of the Ring*, in a conversation between Galadriel and Gimli, in which Galadriel says:

> I do not foretell, for all foretelling is now vain: on the one hand lies darkness, and on the other only hope. But if hope should not fail, then I say to you, Gimli son of Glóin, that your hands shall flow with gold, and yet over you gold shall have no dominion. (F.487)

Not all the translators, however, seemed to be aware of this, and many of them had problems with the word *hope* in their translations. The changes that they made to episodes containing *hope* made significant changes to the way that Tolkien's philosophy will be perceived by the Russian reader. M&K's Galadriel abandons *hope* all together:

> — Я ничего не хочу предрекать, ибо на Средиземье надвигается Тьма и мы не знаем, что ждет нас в будущем. Но если Тьме суждено развеяться, ты сумеешь добыть немало золота — однако не станешь его рабом. (M&K F_{1982}.300; F_{1988}.463)

BT: "I do not want to foretell anything, because Darkness is advancing on Middle-earth and we do not know what awaits us in the future. But if the Darkness is destined to dissipate, you [Gimli] will manage to obtain a lot of gold, however, you will not become its slave."

Not only does M&K's version not contain either of the two uses of *hope* in the original, its use of the word *destined* in Tolkien's 'if-then' clause gives their view of the future a flavor of fatalism. M&K maintain this viewpoint throughout the text, which is one of the things that makes their version of the story very typically Russian.

Bobyr's condensed version also abandons *hope* altogether, leaving only the wish for golden riches behind.

> — Пусть ваши руки струятся золотом, — сказала она, — и пусть над вами золото не имеет власти. (B.121, U F.444)
> BT: "May your hands stream with gold," she said, "and may gold not have any power over you."

While these formulations preserve Tolkien's redemption of the Dwarves from the evil power of gold, their lack of *hope* leaves Tolkien's greater message impoverished. In Yakhnin's version, both *hope* and the redemption of the Dwarves have been abandoned. (Ya F.303)

The other translators all have the word *hope* in its place in Galadriel's wish for Gimli, but not all of them are equally elegant. Gruzberg's attracted my attention, because it is closest to the original.

> — Я не предсказываю, потому что любые предсказания теперь напрасны; на одной ладони лежит Тьма, на другой — лишь надежда. Но если надежда не обманет, то я скажу вам, Гимли, сын Глойна: что ваши руки наполнятся золотом, но золото не будет иметь над вами власти. (Gruzberg-C)
> BT: "I do not foretell, for any foretellings are now vain: on the one hand lies darkness, and on the other only hope. But if hope does not deceive, then I say to you, Gimli son of Glóin, that your hands will be filled with gold, but gold will have no power over you."

Nemirova has a very elegant rendition of the two repeats of *hope*, but it falls flat because her translation of *vain* echoes the root of the word *hope*. She says that predictions are ненадежны [nenadezhny], using a word made up of a negation (не- [ne-]) plus the short adjective form of *hope* (надежны [nadezhny]). The most common translation of ненадежны [nenadezhny] is *unreliable*, which is logically correct, but the interference created by the echo of the root of the word *hope* destroys the effect of the following, well-executed formulation.

> — Я не стану пророчествовать, предсказания ныне ненадежны, ибо с одной стороны у нас тьма, а с другой — только надежда. Но если надежда не подведет, ... (N F.441)
> BT: "I will not begin to prophesize, foretellings are something that you cannot have faith in these days, for on the one hand we have darkness, and on the other only hope. But if hope should not let us down, ..."

Nemirova's 'if-then' clause was deftly executed, something that a number of the other translators could have done better.

Even though VAM's version does have *hope*, it nevertheless has some of the same feel as M&K's, because of the way she constructed her 'if-then' clause:

> — [...] с одной стороны на нас надвигается Тьма, а с другой — мы вооружены только надеждой. Но если надежде суждено сбыться, [...] (VAM F.430)
> BT: "[...] on the one hand Darkness is advancing upon us, on the other we are armed only with hope. But if hope is destined to come true, [...]"

Her version of the 'if-then' clause—just like M&K's—is based on the word for *fate* (судьба > суждено [sud'ba > suzhdeno]).

Volkovskij follows VAM's lead. His version begins well enough, but it has essentially the same 'if-then' clause as VAM and M&K have. His version says: "if our hopes are destined to be justified" (если нашим надеждам суждено оправдаться.) (V F.519)

K&K have the best rendition of the 'if-then' clause, but it, unfortunately, takes a philosophical detour, because of their embellishment of *only hope*.

> — [...] по одну сторону — тьма, по другую — единственная надежда. Но если надежда наша оправдается, [...] (K&K F.552)
> BT: "[...] on the one hand darkness, on the other only one hope. But if our hope is justified, [...]"

Their embellishment of *only hope* as *only one hope* is supported by the story line. Destroying the Ring is the only hope of success. The embellishment, however, makes the hope specific, robbing Galadriel's statement of its universality, and reducing it in stature from a philosophy to a mere statement of fact. None of the other translators who preserved *hope* had trouble with the formulation of this part of the clause.

G&G have a particularly elegant—though somewhat verbose—formulation of this segment that replaces the standard dictionary translation[1] of *on the one hand ... on the other hand* that was used by a number of the translators with a formulation that evokes an image of the scales of justice weighing whether good or evil shall prevail in the future.

> — Я не предсказываю, — молвила она, — ибо напрасны предсказания в наши дни, когда на одной чаше весов лежит Тьма, а на другой — лишь надежда. Но если наша надежда не обманчива, я скажу тебе, Гимли, сын Глоина: золото будет само течь тебе в руки, но над сердцем твоим власти не будет иметь никогда. (G&G F.444)

BT: "I will not foretell," she spoke, "for foretellings are in vain in our time, when on the one side of the scales lies Darkness and on the other only hope. But if our hope is not deceptive, I say to you, Gimli son of Glóin: gold will flow into your hands of its own accord, but it will never have power over your heart."

Hope is introduced—seemingly insignificantly—early in the story in the conversation between Gandalf and Bilbo about giving up the Ring, when Gandalf says: "Stick to your plan—your whole plan, mind—and I hope it will turn out for the best, for you, and for all of us." (F.49) Gandalf, like Galadriel, cannot foretell the outcome of their actions. He can only hope that what they are about to do is the right choice.

Only K&K, Aleksandrova and Volkovskij used the word *hope* in this line of Gandalf's conversation with Bilbo. Abandoning *hope* in Gandalf's answer weakens Tolkien's layered structure of *hope*, and changes the philosophical outlook of the story. Leaving out *hope* here weakens its role and makes Gandalf seem more sure of himself than he is.

Gruzberg's Gandalf is certain of the outcome. He says (**emphasis** added): "it **will** be for the best for you and for all of us" (это будет к лучшему для тебя и для всех нас). There are small stylistic differences in the print version, but it remains equally 'hopeless.' (G F.46) Aleksandrova cleans up this passage and puts *hope* back in its place. Her Gandalf says:

"and I hope that everything will finish well both for you and for all of us" (и, надеюсь, все закончится хорошо и для тебя, и для всех нас). Nemirova's Gandalf sounds essentially like Gruzberg's. He says: "it will turn out better, both for you and for all of us" (и все обернется к лучшему и для тебя, и для всех нас). (N F.35)

M&K's Gandalf is both certain and uncertain at the same time. He says "it will be better for you, and maybe not only for you" (тебе же будет лучше, а может, и не только тебе). (M&K F_{1982}.14; F_{1988}.57) This implies that Gandalf can foretell Bilbo's future clearly, but he cannot see the future of others clearly. The result is a logical blur in their rendition that is not present in Tolkien's. There is another subtle shift in M&K's formulation as well. It has to do with whom Bilbo's decision will affect. M&K's formulation of "and maybe not only for you" could mean one person (or Hobbit), or ten, or a thousand. It is not as encompassing as Tolkien's definition of who will be affected—*all of us*—which ties not only Gandalf's fate to the action that Bilbo may or may not take, but, to a certain extent, the reader's fate as well, because the reader's initial subconscious impulse is to feel included in any group defined by the word *us*.

G&G joined M&K in replacing *us* with *others*, and circumlocuted their way around *hope* with a common expression reminiscent of a conversation in which an adult is trying to convince a child to do something: "before you know it":

    — Только уж делай, как задумал, глядишь, еще и обойдется все, и для тебя, и для других тоже. (G&G F.35)
BT: "Only do it the way you planned. Before you know it, everything will still turn out right, both for you and for others as well."

VAM's rendition also abandons *hope*, but conveys a sense of uncertainty about the outcome of Bilbo's actions with the formulation "it seems to me":

    — Делай, что задумал, — только учти, делай все до конца!
    — и, как мне кажется, всем будет лучше и тебе, и нам.
BT: "Do what you planned, only mind, all the way to the end! And, as it seems to me, it will be better for everyone, both for you and for us." (VAM F.39)

Her description of the group of those affected by Bilbo's decision is much better than M&K's and G&G's.

Yakhnin has an equally vague formulation that abandons both hope and all comment about those who will be affected by Bilbo's decision. His Gandalf says "mysteriously" that "maybe it will be for the best" [и загадочно добавил: — Может, это и к лучшему.].(Ya F.17)

At the council of Elrond, Tolkien takes the decision to give up the Ring to a higher level. Here it is not simply the struggle of a single Hobbit to give up the Ring, but the struggle of the whole of Middle-earth. The debate between Gandalf and Erestor is key to understanding Tolkien's view of *hope* and *foretelling*. Erestor calls the plan to destroy the ring "the path of despair. Of folly I would say, if the long wisdom of Elrond did not forbid me." Gandalf's response rejects the premise of Erestor's argument:

> "Despair, or folly?" said Gandalf. "It is not despair, for despair is only for those who see the end beyond all doubt. We do not. It is wisdom to recognize necessity, when all other courses have been weighed, though as folly it may appear to those who cling to false hope [...]" (F.352)

The use of *despair* as a bookend to *hope* frames this as a religious argument, because in that context, hope and despair are antonyms. In its article on hope, *The Encyclopedia of Religion* defines hope as the obverse of despair, and says that despair sets in "where all possibilities seem closed off." [2]

Gandalf's assertion that they do not see the end beyond all doubt is echoed in Galadriel's view of foretelling, "for all foretelling is now vain." The world is changing: "on the one hand lies darkness, and on the other only hope." (F.487) Gandalf's rejection of the *false hope* of those who think that they could use the Ring, implies the existence of true hope. In religious arguments, hope is doomed to fail when it becomes excessive and crosses the threshold into desire. Tolkien sees that this would quickly be the case with the Ring, and that they cannot hope to wield its power.

K&K find themselves on the other side of a philosophical fault line with their rendition of "see the end beyond all doubt." K&K's Gandalf counters Erestor's argument with:

> — Так безнадежность или безумие? — переспросил Гэндальф. — О безнадежности речи нет: отчаиваются и теряют надежду только те, чей конец уже предрешен. А наш — нет.
> BT: "So it is hopelessness or insanity," rejoined Gandalf. "We are

not talking about hopelessness: only those whose end is already predetermined lose hope and despair. Our [end] is not [predetermined]. (K&K F.403)

The philosophical fault line that divides K&K and Tolkien is the difference between predestination and foreseeing. Tolkien does not entirely reject the possibility of foretelling. Galadriel's statement that (**emphasis** added) "for all foretelling is **now** vain," implies that at other times foretelling is possible and useful. Tolkien had made this point explicit earlier in the conversation between Galadriel and Frodo, when Galadriel says: "I will not give you counsel, saying do this, or do that. For not in doing or contriving, nor in choosing between this course and another, can I avail; but only in knowing what was and is, and in part also what shall be." (F.462)

Gandalf, too, does not entirely dismiss their ability to project future outcomes, only the certainty that they can assign to the outcome that they foresee. "It is not despair, for despair is for those who see the end **beyond all doubt**. We do not." (F.352, **emphasis** added) While predestination is an end that is beyond all doubt, it is not what Tolkien is talking about. For Tolkien the future can change, based on the choices that they make.

For Tolkien's Gandalf the decision to be taken is an intellectual exercise to be resolved by the application of wisdom, not the fates: "It is wisdom to recognize necessity, when all other courses have been weighed, though as folly it may appear to those who cling to false hope." (F.352) K&K begin their version of this line with an embellished Socratic formulation of the definition of true wisdom, and *necessity* takes a holiday.

> — В чем истинная мудрость?* В том, чтобы, взвесив все возможные пути, выбрать среди них единственный. Может быть, тем, кто тешит себя ложными надеждами, это и впрямь покажется безумием. (K&K F.403)
>
> BT: "What is true wisdom?* It is, having weighed all the courses of action, picking the only one among them. Perhaps to those who harbor false hopes this indeed seems like insanity."

Their embellishment of the definition of wisdom is not only the addition of the word *true*, which is a loaded word in any Russian philosophical discussion, but also by the addition of a lengthy endnote '*' (K&K F.685), which supports their use of *predestination* in Gandalf's lines above. They view *true wisdom* as synonymous with "the Northern theory of Courage" about which Tolkien wrote in *The Monsters and The Critics*,[1] concluding that "it is necessary to fight to the end, even if victory cannot be counted upon, fight, knowing that the higher powers are fighting on your side and that they too may suffer a defeat (поражение) in the end." (K&K F.685)

In their endnote, K&K support their interpretation of "true wisdom" with two quotes from Tolkien's essay, in which Tolkien says that the author of *Beowulf* "and his hearers were thinking of the *eormengrund*, the great earth, ringed with *garsecg*, the shoreless sea, beneath the sky's inaccessible roof; whereon, as in a little circle of light about their halls, men with courage as their stay went forward to that battle with the hostile world and the offspring of the dark which ends for all, even the kings and champions, in defeat. That even this 'geography,' once held as a material fact, could now be classed as a mere folk-tale affects its value very little. It transcends astronomy. Not that astronomy has done anything to make the island seem more secure or the outer seas less formidable."[3] "… Northern Courage: the theory of Courage, which is the great contribution of early Northern literature. … I refer rather to the central position the creed of unyielding will holds in the North. … The Northern Gods,' Ker said, 'have an exultant extravagance in their warfare which makes them more like Titans than Olympians; *only they are on the right side, though it is not the side that wins. The winning side is Chaos and Unreason*' … '*but the gods, who are defeated, think that defeat no refutation.*'[4] And in their war men are their chosen allies, able, when heroic, to share in this 'absolute resistance, perfect because without hope.'"[5]

The key difference between the philosophies of *Beowulf* and *LotR* is the last word in K&K's quote from Tolkien's essay: *hope*. Beowulf has what Tolkien calls "the old dogma; despair of the event, combined with faith in the value of doomed resistance."[6] The victory of Christianity over paganism displaced fate as an independent or supreme force in the universe, and introduced hope. Tolkien's Gandalf rejects despair—the handmaiden of fate—and embraces hope. "It is not despair, for despair is for those who see the end beyond all doubt. We do not. It is wisdom to recognize necessity, when all other courses have been weighed, though as folly it may appear to those who cling to false hope." (F.352) Gandalf has hope; not the false hope that they could use the Ring, but Galadriel's hope that they can prevail over the darkness; (F.487) Elrond's hope that they may succeed if they take "a hard road, a road unforeseen." (F.350) K&K have read too much into *LotR* from the old dogma of *Beowulf*, where predetermination was a given in the form of Ragnarok.

M&K make essentially the same—very Russian—interpretation of the debate. In his very verbose argument, M&K's Erestor, too, sees the end of the path that Gandalf proposes beyond all doubt: defeat for them all.

> — Элронд мудр, мы все это знаем, и единственную дорогу, ведущую к победе, никто не назовет дорогой безрассудства... но вместе с тем она неодолима, и нас неминуемо ждет поражение. (M&K F_{1982}.201; F_{1988}.333)
> BT: "Elrond is wise, we all know that, and no one would name the only path that leads to victory the path of folly ... but at the same time it is impassable and defeat inexorably awaits us."

This, too, is the philosophy of Ragnarok, which dooms the gods to defeat at the hands of the forces of evil, after which the world will be renewed. Tolkien does not speak of defeat at all, and that is a major departure from the philosophy of the Norse tales that Tolkien obviously drew on in his story, but reconfigured to suit his own ends.

M&K's text, in general, is much more full of doom and gloom than Tolkien's. In Chapter 8 of Book IV ("The Stairs of Cirith Ungol"), for example, the narrator describes what Frodo, Sam and Gollum "expected would be their last meal before they went down into the Nameless Land, maybe the last meal they would ever eat together." (T.406) While all the other translators manage to capture the idea behind "maybe the last meal that they would ever eat together," M&K turn it into "maybe even the last meal of their lives." (может, и последнюю [трапезу] в жизни) (M&K T.378)

The response that Tolkien's Gandalf makes to Erestor rejects the predetermination of Ragnarok. His is a logical argument based on their inability to clearly foresee the future, but yet founded on hope. It is followed by a statement that softly echoes Engels' dictum that freedom is the recognition of necessity, which should be familiar to the university-educated Soviet reader—like M&K—for whom courses in Marxism-Leninism were compulsory. "It is wisdom to recognize necessity, when all other courses have been weighed." (F.352)

M&K's Gandalf instead responds to Erestor with an argument couched in terms of courage and bravery:

> — Поражение неминуемо ждет лишь того, кто отчаялся заранее,— возразил Гэндальф. — Признать неизбежность опасного пути, когда все другие дороги отрезаны,— это и есть истинная мудрость. (M&K F_{1982}.201; F_{1988}.333)
>
> BT: "Defeat inexorably awaits only those who have given themselves over to despair beforehand," countered Gandalf. "To recognize the necessity of a dangerous course of action, when all other paths have been cut off, that is true wisdom."

For M&K's Gandalf there is no other choice. He is between a rock and a hard place. This was the choice of Russian troops in the punishment battalions [штрафбат (shtrafbat)] of World War II. They could make a frontal assault on heavily fortified German positions where the probability of death was very high, or they could be shot where they stood. For them the choice was constrained by the definition of the problem. For Tolkien's Gandalf the problem is not defined in those terms. He is defining the problem, and is proactive. M&K's Gandalf is accepting the constraints of the situation as the definition of the problem, and is reactive. M&K's Gandalf is a fatalist. There is no other choice, therefore we must bravely do as the fates decree. Tolkien's Gandalf believes he has the freedom of action to affect the course of events. The philosophical gap between them is a very wide one.

Volkovskij keeps M&K company with his verbose formulation of this segment by defining the problem in terms of *victory* and *defeat*. Framing the situation in these military terms tips the story over into the realm of adventure—swords and sorcery—which Tolkien was studiously avoiding at this point. For the Russian reader, Volkovskij's text has a certain taste of the literature of World War II.

> — Путь в Мордор — это тропа отчаяния! Да что там, лишь ведомая всем мудрость Элронда не позволяет мне сказать — тропа безумия!
>
> — По-твоему выходит — отчаяние или безумие? — возвысил голос Гэндальф. — Но так ли это? Отчаяние — удел тех, кто уже потерпел поражение или не видит возможности победы. Но мы не побеждены, и знаем, что нам следует делать. Рассмотреть все возможности и выбрать из них единственно осуществимую, сколь бы ни была она опасна, — не безумие, а мудрость. Безумным такое решение может показаться лишь тем, кто обольщается ложными надеждами. (V F.374)

BT: "The road to Mordor is the path of despair! No, hardly, only the well-know wisdom of Elrond prevents me from saying: the path of insanity!"

"So you see it as despair or insanity?" said Gandalf raising his voice. "But is that the case? Despair is the lot of those who have already suffered defeat or see no possibility of victory. But we are not defeated, and know what we have to do. To examine all the possibilities and chose from them the single one that is doable, no matter how dangerous, is not insanity, but wisdom. This decision may seem like insanity only to those laboring under the delusion of false hope."

JRRT: "That is the path of despair. Of folly I would say, if the long wisdom of Elrond did not forbid me."

"Despair, or folly?" said Gandalf. "It is not despair, for despair is only for those who see the end beyond all doubt. We do not. It is wisdom to recognize necessity, when all other courses have been weighed, though as folly it may appear to those who cling to false hope." (F.352)

Despite his militaristic approach to the situation, Volkovskij's treatment of hope is right on target.

Yakhnin, likewise, set the scene in military tones, but completely eliminated *Erestor*, *despair*, *folly* and *hope* in his recasting of Gandalf's summation at council.

— Не знаю, что случится с миром в далеком будущем, — медленно проговорил он, — но мы, живущие сегодня, должны избавить Средиземье от угрозы замогильного Мрака и всепоглощающей Тьмы. Да, дорога в Мордор смертельно опасна, и все же это единственный путь к победе. (Ya F.205)

BT: "I do not know what will happen to the world in the distant future," he [Gandalf] said slowly, "but we, who live today, must rid Middle-earth of the threat of the sepulchral Darkness and all-consuming Shadow. Yes, the road to Mordor is deathly perilous, but yet it is the only path to victory."

The scene is painted with chilling skill, displaying Yaknin's skill as a story-teller, but it retains little of Tolkien's philosophical argumentation.

Despite its literary failings, Gruzberg's rendition of the debate between Gandalf and Erestor is the best. It has none of these philosophical divergences.

> — Это путь отчаяния. Или безумия, сказал бы я, если бы не мудрость Эльронда.
> — Отчаяние или безумие? — спросил Гандалв. — Это не отчаяние: отчаиваются лишь те, кто видит свой неизбежный конец. Мы не отчаиваемся. Мудрость заключается в том, чтобы признать необходимость, когда взвешены все другие пути. Хотя тем, кто лелеет лживую надежду, эта мудрость может показаться безумием.

BT: "That is the path of despair … Or insanity, would say I, were it not for Elrond's wisdom."

"Despair or insanity?" said Gandalf. It is not despair: only those despair, who see their inescapable end. We do not despair. It is wisdom to recognize necessity, when all other paths have been weighed, however, to those, who cherish false hope, that wisdom may seem to be insanity."

Aleksandrova's CD-ROM version and the book version edited by Arkadij Zastyrets (G F.358) made only slight stylistic changes, which did not affect the meaning of the passage.

Nemirova sparkles with her elegant rendition of this passage that suffers little from her embellishments.

> — Этот замысел отчаянный, я даже назвал бы его безумным, если бы не помнил о копившейся веками мудрости Элронда!
> — Отчаянный, безумный? — повторил Гэндальф. — Нет, об отчаянии стоит говорить, лишь когда приходит несомненный конец всему. Но этого пока не случилось. Мудрость заключается в том, чтобы распознать необходимое, когда все прочие средства отпали, сколь безумно ни выглядело бы оно в глазах тех, кто тешится ложными надеждами. (N F.316)

BT: "That is a desperate idea, I would even call it foolish, did I not recall the wisdom of Elrond built up over the ages."

"Desperate, foolish?" repeated Gandalf. No, one should only talk of despair when the undoubted end of everything approaches. But that has not happened yet. Wisdom is to recognize necessity, when all other means have fallen by the wayside, no matter how foolish it may seem in the eyes of those who harbor false hopes."

G&G's version is a slightly verbose paraphrase, but it, too, is very close to Tolkien's original idea.

— Первый же шаг к Ородруину — шаг отчаяния. Я бы даже осмелился назвать это глупостью, и только известная всем мудрость правителя Элронда останавливает меня.

— Значит, ты считаешь — отчаяние или глупость? — усмехнулся Гэндальф. — Но отчаяние существует для того, кто увидел несомненный крах своих устремлений. Где он? Мы взвесили все пути, мы увидели всего лишь несомненную необходимость одного из них и выбираем его — это мудрость. Глупостью она может показаться обольщающемуся ложными надеждами. (G&G F.321)

BT: "The first step to Orodruin is a step of despair. I would even dare to call it folly, were it not that the wisdom of Lord Elrond, of which all are aware, stops me."

"You consider it, therefore, despair or folly?" laughed Gandalf. "But despair exists for those, who have seen the undoubted failure of their efforts. Where is it [failure]? We have weighed all the paths. We have only seen the undoubted necessity of one of them and we choose it. That is wisdom. It may seem folly to those who labor under the delusion of false hope."

Bobyr's version is on an equally even—though terse—philosophic keel as far as predetermination and the ability to foresee the future is concerned. Its primary fault is the omission of *hope*, which is what turns Bobyr's version from a philosophical discourse with religious overtones into an adventure story that would have been acceptable to the Soviet censors.

— Мне кажется, это путь отчаяния; я сказал бы даже — безумия, если бы мудрость Эльронда не останавливала меня.

— Отчаяния? — повторил Гандальф. — Отчаяние — это удел тех, кто видит впереди несомненную гибель. Мы ее не видим. Когда все возможности взвешены, то примирение с необходимостью — это мудрость, хотя со стороны оно может показаться безумием. (B.62)

BT: "It seems to me that this is the path of despair; I would even say insanity, if the wisdom of Elrond did not stop me."

"Despair?" repeated Gandalf. "Despair is the lot of those who see before them doubtless downfall. We cannot see it. When all possibilities have been weighed, reconciling oneself to necessity is wisdom, though, from the side it may seem like folly."

Umanskij restored the *hope* that Bobyr' had omitted.

— Это путь отчаяния. Я сказал бы — путь безумия, если бы глубокая мудрость Эльронда не удерживала меня.
— Отчаяние или безумие? — сказал Гандальф. — Это [не]⁷ отчаяние, потому что отчаиваются только те, кто види[т за] всеми трудностями лишь печальный конец. Мудро — сог[лаша]ться с необходимостью, когда все другие возможности [уже] взвешены, хотя это и может показаться безумным тем, [кто] цепляется за ложную надежду. (U F.391)

BT: "That is the path of despair. I would say that path of insanity, if the deep wisdom of Elrond did not restrain me."

"Despair or insanity?" said Gandalf. It is not despair, because only those despair who see but a sorrowful end beyond all the difficulties. It is wise to [come to terms] with necessity when all other possibilities have been weighed, though this may seem insanity to those who grasp at false hope."

Despite its semantic lapses, Bobyr's is a much more elegant formulation.

While *hope* was absent in VAM's rendition of Gandalf's conversation with Bilbo, it showed up unexpectedly an extra time in VAM's version of Gandalf's debate with Erestor. Even though the translation of the debate may be a bit free, it nevertheless conveys the idea behind the words well enough and the addition of *hope* at the beginning makes an interesting bookend for *hope*'s reoccurrence at the end, better focusing the reader's attention on the importance of *hope*. (**Emphasis** added.)

— Это путь без надежды. Если бы меня не сдерживала вера в мудрость Элронда, я бы сказал, что это отчаянное безрассудство!
— Отчаяние или безрассудство? — сказал Гэндальф. — Это не отчаяние, ибо отчаиваются те, кто видит поражение и неизбежный конец. Мы его пока не видим. Понимание неизбежности риска, когда рассмотрены все возможные пути, — есть проявление мудрости. Безрассудством это может показаться тем, кто тешит себя ложными надеждами. (VAM F.308-9)

BT: "That is a path without **hope**. If I were not restrained by a belief in the wisdom of Elrond, I would say that it is desperate folly!"

"Despair or folly?" said Gandalf. "It is not despair, for those despair who see defeat and an inevitable end. We do not see this as yet. Understanding the necessity of risk, when all possible paths have been examined is a sign of wisdom. It may seem folly to those who comfort themselves with false **hope**."

Her embellishment of *necessity* as "the necessity of risk" is also quite in keeping with the story line, making implicit what Tolkien had left implied, and making the story more accessible to Russian readers.

Tolkien hints that "the Northern theory of Courage" is still a part of the world view of the Dwarves in Elrond's dialog with the messenger of King Dáin II of the Dwarves at the Council of Elrond. Elrond says:

> You will hear today all that you need in order to understand the purposes of the Enemy. There is naught that you can do, other than to resist, with hope or without it. But you do not stand alone. (F.317)

Resistance without hope is "the Northern theory of Courage," which shares a common literary ancestry with the Dwarves. Most of Tolkien's Dwarf names—including Dáin—are from the *Eddas*. It is not, however, an exclusively Northern philosophy. It is rather a pre-Christian one. The *Iliad* (written circa 800 B.C.E.) says that "Like strength is felt from hope and from despair." [8] In contrast, Goethe (1749-1832), who stands on the other side of the pagan-Christian divide, says "In all things it is better to hope than to despair." Tolkien's contrast of "with hope or without it," underscores the differentiation of the pagan Northern theory of Courage from Christian hope, which is what Tolkien was trying to convey.

Bobyr' abandons *hope* completely, robbing Elrond's statement of any philosophical import.

> — Вы можете только защищаться — больше ничего. (B.55, U F.369)
> BT: "You can only defend yourselves — nothing more."

Umanskij left this segment unaltered.

Yakhnin avoids any hint of philosophizing by eliminating this segment entirely.

Gruzberg (Aleksandrova, Zastyrets), VAM and G&G all correctly conveyed the idea behind "resist, with hope or without it," while the other translators introduced new ideas into the equation. Gruzberg's version was best because it was the most literal:

> — Вам ничего не остается делать, кроме как сопротивляться — с надеждой на победу или без нее. (G F.322)

BT: "There is nothing left for you to do except resist, with hope of victory or without it.

G&G's version has a certain verbose eloquence that does little to change Tolkien's underlying philosophy.

> — Но выхода нет, и не только у гномов. С надеждой или без нее, вам придется противостоять Темной Стране. (G&G F.289)

BT: "But there is no way out, and not only for the Dwarves. With hope or without it, you will have to resist the Dark Country.

VAM's verbose circumlocution, however, took a philosophical detour. Her Elrond tells the Dwarf that:

> — Единственное, что вы сможете сделать, — это сопротивляться до последнего, пока есть надежда, и даже если ее не станет. (VAM F_{1990}.275, F_{2003}.428)

BT: "The only thing that you can do is to resist to the last, while there is hope and even if it [hope] ceases to exist.

In VAM's version, the starting point is hope, and resistance should continue even if hope should vanish. Tolkien's Elrond, on the other hand, offers two possible starting points: resistance based on hope and doomed resistance without hope, i.e. the Northern theory of Courage.

The other translators abandon the contrast of "with hope or without it," which makes Elrond's statement one-dimensional. Nemirova's Elrond hints at the contrast, but the hint falls far short of the power of Tolkien's statement:

> — Вам остается только сопротивляться — пусть даже без всякой надежды. (N F.282)

BT: "There is nothing left for you but to resist, even should there be no hope at all."

K&K follow the same line of reasoning. Their Elrond says that the hope that they have is weak. While this may be true, it eliminates the choice that Tolkien's Elrond presents to the Dwarves.

— Гномам остается только стоять насмерть и надеяться на лучшее, хотя надежда эта будет слабой. (K&K F.362)
BT: "All that is left to the Dwarves is to stand to the death and hope for the best, although that hope will be weak."

It also introduces a more dire note to Elrond's advice, before Tolkien was ready to do so. M&K's version is, as always, full of doom and gloom.

— Ты поймешь, что у вас нет иного выхода, кроме битвы с Врагом не на жизнь, а на смерть — даже без надежды победить в этой битве. (M&K F_{1982}.172; F_{1988}.297)
BT: "You understand that you have no other way out than battle with the Enemy not for life but to the death, even without hope of victory in that battle."

M&K's version abandons the hope of victory, and makes "the Northern theory of Courage" explicit and applies it to all, while Tolkien had only implied it for the Dwarves. Battling with the Enemy to the death of all at the end of the world with no hope of victory is the definition of the Northern theory of Courage. It is very much alive and well in M&K's version of *LotR*.

Volkovskij, as is often the case, follows M&K's lead in this segment. His Elrond, too, tells the Dwarves that they have to fight "even without hope of victory" (даже без надежды на победу) (V F.333), in line with his—and M&K's—definition of the problem in terms of *victory* or *defeat*.

Acceptance of one's fate is the clue to the endurance of the Russian people in the face of all the adversity that has come their way. The Russian predilection for fatalism and predestination is reflected in P.Ya. Chaadaev's[9] characterization of the Russian mental legacy. "The deepest trait of our historical nature is the lack of spontaneity in our social development. Look carefully, and you will see that each important fact of our history has been imposed upon us, that almost every new idea is an imported idea."[10] This passivity was reinforced by the accent that the Eastern Orthodox Church of Byzantium places on acceptance of earthly suffering as a key to heavenly redemption. This was the version of Christianity that the Russians 'imported.' This outlook on life balances despair with resignation and submission.

Chaadaev views this choice as a mistake. "While the structure of modern civilization was arising from the struggle between the energetic barbarity of Northern peoples and the lofty idea of religion, what were we doing? Driven by a fatal destiny, we turned to wretched Byzantium, object of those peoples' profound scorn, for the moral code that was to educate us. [...] The eminent qualities with which religion had endowed modern nations and which, in the eyes of sane reason, raised them as high above the ancients as these rise above the Hottentots and Lapps, the new forces with which it had enriched human intelligence, the manners which, through submission to a disarmed authority, had become mild as earlier they had been harsh: none of this had emerged among us. [...] What bright lights had then already emerged in Europe from the seeming darkness that had covered it! [...] and by turning back to pagan antiquity, the Christian world had rediscovered the form of beauty that it still lacked. Estranged by our schism, nothing reached us of what happened in Europe." [11]

The philosophical divide between the Church of Byzantium and the Church of Rome can be seen on the map of Europe as the alphabetic divide that marks which Church got there first. The Church of Byzantium brought Cyrillic letters and the Church of Rome Latin letters. The Russians, the Belorussians, the Ukrainians, the Bulgarians and the Serbs use Cyrillic letters. The Poles, the Czechs and the Slovaks use Latin letters.

Chaadaev was right that Russia is an importer of ideas that come and go: Paganism was replaced by the import of Byzantine Christianity, which was replaced by the import of Communism, which has since been replaced by the import of Market Capitalism. What he left out was the fact that the imports are always adapted to the Russian soil in which they must grow. As Diderot (1713-1784) once remarked to the Russian Empress Catherine II, "Ideas transplanted from Paris to St. Petersburg take on a different shade." [12] M&K's translation is a good example of that. Fatalism, doom and gloom are the shade that they add to Tolkien. Those have always been defining characteristics of Russian literature.

M&K are the representatives of the old order. The other translators and their less manipulated versions represent the new order, importing more new ideas from abroad. If any Christian writer has rediscovered the beauty of pagan antiquity, it is Tolkien, and the new translators are bridging Chaadaev's schism that kept the ideas of Europe out of Russia.

It is clear that those ideas are getting through. In his foreword[13] to the Russian edition of C.S. Lewis's *Out of the Silent Planet* and *Perelandra*, Ya. Krotov summarizes the role of hope in *LotR*:

> [A]t first glance, the secondary World of Middle-earth that he [Tolkien] created in the fantastic trilogy, *The Lord of the Rings*, seems close to the world of paganism, to the world of novels about knights. But both the pagans and the knights were certainly not either areligious nor irreligious. The pagans even had a great many gods, and the knights could pay homage to Christ, to Perun[14], to Odin, to Allah, to Fortuna, or, in the worst case, to their own strength. Tolkien's heroes refrain from calling on God, Luck or their own strength, even when everything is pushing them in that direction. Their world is entirely devoid of those religious realities, which fill the world view of the pagans or the heroic epics. His heroes are filled to overflowing with hope, but that hope rests on an absolutely unnamed, unmarked space, on emptiness. And—it stands! This vast emptiness, unnamed through an absolute stroke of genius, is God, more than that, it is the God of the Bible, the God of [C.S.] Lewis, of the Church.

In the Chapter "The White Rider," Gandalf is resurrected in a scene recalling Christ's Transfiguration on Mount Tabor. (Matthew 17:1-9, Mark 9:2-9 and Luke 9:28-36) The three remaining members of the Fellowship—Aragorn, Legolas and Gimli—can find "no words to say" as they are caught "between wonder, joy and fear." (T.125) Aragorn's statement, when he regains the presence of mind to speak, echoes the Catholic Catechism on the meaning of the resurrection. There, Christ's cry from the cross is seen as a prayer for all mankind, which the Father answers "beyond all hope" by raising his Son. (2606) Tolkien's Aragorn echoes this in his statement: "Beyond all hope you return to us in our need!" (T.125) The context that surrounds this use of *hope* in Aragorn's statement is so strongly—consciously or subconsciously—Christian that the translators who abandon hope at this juncture are depriving the reader of a key point in Tolkien's underlying philosophy.

Not surprisingly, Yakhnin is one of the ones who abandons *hope* here. (Ya T.82) Surprisingly, however, it is Nemirova and not Bobyr' who joins him in abandoning *hope*. She left out the entire sentence. (N T.98) Bobyr' obviously recognized the key nature of this scene and has a rather literal rendition of Aragorn's statement that misses the Biblical style register and sense of the passage. (B.161, U T.517) Gruzberg (G T.116) and VAM (VAM T_{2003}.667) likewise got the words right and the style wrong. G&G and Volkovskij have an almost equally gloomy view of event, because their

Gandalf has returned "when we were beginning to lose hope" (когда мы уже стали терять надежду). (V T.142; G&G T.89)

K&K got both the words and the style right. Their Aragorn says that Gandalf has returned паче всякого чаяния. (K&K T.130) They put the icing on the cake with their endnote, in which they point to the parallels between the Biblical story of the Transfiguration of Christ on Mount Tabor before the three Apostles and Gandalf's resurrection and appearance to the three members of the Fellowship. (K&K T.506)

M&K's variant of the key statement—*beyond all hope*—reflects the close linguistic relationship between *hope* and *despair* in Russian. Their Aragorn says that Gandalf has "returned to us in our hour of despair!" (M&K T.110) The word they use for *despair* is отчаяние [otchayanie]. The word that K&K used for *hope* is чаяние [chayanie]. The difference in the two is the prefix от- [ot-], which means *a departure from*. The Russian verb *to walk*, for example, is ходить [khodit']. Adding the prefix от- [ot-] to this root verb changes its meaning to *to leave* (отходить [otkhodit']). The Russian word for *despair*, therefore, is literally *the departure of hope*.

M&K's use of the word *despair* (отчаяние [otchayanie]) returns the reader to the Counsel of Elrond and the debate between Gandalf and Erestor, in which Erestor calls the plan to destroy the ring "the path of despair. Of folly I would say, if the long wisdom of Elrond did not forbid me." (F.352) While *hope* and *despair* form the bookends of a religious argument, Tolkien's use of *beyond all hope* is not a synonym for *despair*. In the context that Tolkien has created in this segment, it carries the same meaning as it does in the Catholic Catechism. It is a synonym for the improbable, for something that is so unlikely that it could not be hoped for, for the resurrection of Gandalf from the dead. In this context, *beyond all hope* is not a description of the lack of hope or of the despair of the three remaining members of the fellowship, but of their surprise at seeing Gandalf return from the dead, which is something that no one could logically have hoped for. By introducing despair into the scene, M&K come back to the definition of *despair* from the debate at the Council of Elrond, which in M&K's terms leads inexorably to defeat. (M&K F_{1982}.201; F_{1988}.333) The echo of *despair* from the debate creates a resonance of doom and gloom that is not a part of Tolkien's picture, but which does fit nicely with M&K's view of the world.

Notes:

1. Большой Англо-русский словарь, И.Р. Гальперин (ред.), М: издательство «Советская Энциклопедия», 1972, стр. 627.
2. *The Encyclopedia of Religion*, Mircea Eliade (ed.), New York: Macmillan, 1987, vol. 6, p. 461.
3. J.R.R. Tolkien, *The Monsters and The Critics and Other Essays*, Christopher Tolkien (ed.), Boston: Houghton Mifflin, 1984.
4. *The Monsters and The Critics*, p. 18. Quoted in K&K, F.685.
5. *The Dark Ages*, p. 57. Quoted in *The Monsters and The Critics*, pp. 20-21.
6. *The Monsters and The Critics*, pp. 20-21. Quoted in K&K, F.685.
7. *The Monsters and The Critics*, p. 23.
8. The edge of the page is missing at this point. Words and letters assumed to have been on the missing edge are enclosed in square brackets [].
9. The Pope translation (1715), book XV, line 852.
10. Petr Yakovlevich Chaadaev (1794-1856) was the first Russian philosopher. Chaadaev spent six years in Western Europe where he met such famous thinkers as Lamennais and Schelling. In the nineteenth century, his *Philosophical Letters* touched off the battle between the Slavophiles and the Westerners.
11. Quoted in: Marthe Blinoff, *Life and Thought in Old Russia*, Clearfield, PA: The Pennsylvania State University Press, 1961, p. 179.
12. Quoted in: Blinoff, p. 175.
13. Quoted in: Stuart Ramsay Tompkins, *The Russian Mind: From Peter the Great Through the Enlightenment*, Norman, OK: University of Oklahoma Press, 1953, p. 230.
14. <http://kulichki.rambler.ru/moshkow/LEWISCL/aboutlewis.txt>.
15. The god of Thunder of the pagan Slavs.

: SAMWISE : SON : OF : HAMFAST :

Chapter 5

Sam's Job: Frodo's Batman
:TOLKIEN:THROUGH:RUSSIAN:EYES:

> But be not afraid of greatness:
> Some men are born great,
> Some achieve greatness,
> And some have greatness thrust upon them.
> William Shakespeare,
> *Twelfth Night* (1601), Act II, Scene 5.

While *LotR* was not published until the early 1950s, it is nevertheless to some extent a product, not of World War II, but of the six months during which Tolkien fought with the 11th Lancashire Fusiliers during World War I, before trench fever took him back to England. Tolkien wrote that Sam was "a reflection of the English soldier, of the privates and batmen [an officer's valet] I knew in the 1914 war, and recognized as so far superior to myself."[1]

The most likely association with the word *batman* for the modern reader is probably to Batman and Robin of film and comic book fame. Tolkien, however, had another image in mind. Before World War II, when officers were indeed gentlemen, in the British sense of the word, having a soldier-servant was the accepted order of the day. The word *batman* comes, not from cricket bats, as some have suggested, but from the French word *bât*, which means *pack saddle*. A batman was, therefore, the man who took care of the luggage carried on the pack-horse or pack-mule. In time, the word came also to mean an officer's valet.

The literature of World War I recounts many examples of the loyalty and devotion of army batmen to the officers they cared for.[2] Theirs are the characteristics that Tolkien gives to Sam. "He did not think of himself as heroic or even brave, or in any way admirable—except in his service and loyalty to his master," wrote Tolkien in a letter to a reader. (L.329)

Tolkien clearly establishes the relationship between Frodo and Sam as "master" and "servant" by spreading those two terms throughout the text to describe them. Gruzberg, M&K, K&K, VAM and Yakhnin were successful in replicating Tolkien's markers for this relationship. The other translators had some difficulties with them from time to time, weakening the relationship that Tolkien built up with a profuse number of repeats. Bobyr' remolded their relationship altogether, making Sam and Frodo just "friends." When he edited Bobyr', Umanskij did restore some of Tolkien's *master-servant* markers, but by no means all of them.

In the scene in which Bilbo and Frodo stay up late, talking on the eve of the Council, Sam sticks his head in the door to hint that it is time for Frodo to go to sleep, because he has a big day tomorrow. Bilbo gets the hint immediately and says: "I guess you mean that it is time your master went to bed." (F.313) Yakhnin went Tolkien one better here, throwing an extra *servant* (слуга [sluga]) and *master* (хозяин [khozyain]) into his version of the scene. (Ya F.181-2) Bobyr' and M&K both left out *master* in their versions of this scene (B.52, M&K F_{1982}.169, F_{1988}.292), but Umanskij restored it to his edition of Bobyr'. (U. F.367)

At the feast in Rivendell, where Sam begs to be allowed "to wait on his master," (F.300) M&K swapped *servant* for *master* with no ill effect. Their narrator said that the Elves had to argue with Sam to convince him that he was not a servant, but an honored guest, when he wanted to wait on Frodo at table. [он не слуга, а почетный гость — он хотел прислуживать Фродо за столом] (M&K F_{1982}.161, F_{1988}.279) Bobyr's narrator glossed over this marker as well. He said that, "looking around the table, [Frodo] could see all his friends near Gandalf." (Оглядывая стол, он увидел поблизости от Гандальфа всех своих друзей.) (B.49, U F.360) While Umanskij did not restore this missing episode, he did restore a *Mr. Frodo* that Bobyr' had excised a page earlier. (B. 48, U F.359)

Servant, however, did not fare as well with the translators in the scene following the breaking of the Fellowship, where Aragorn puzzles with the question of where Frodo has gone, and comes to the conclusion that: "Frodo has gone by boat, and his servant has gone with him." (T.25) In this segment, only Gruzberg, M&K and K&K had *servant* in its place. (M&K T.16, K&K T.21) VAM had a close equivalent that hints at Sam's duties as batman, using a word taken from the time when knighthood was in flower. Her Aragorn said that Frodo had left and his squire (оруженосец [oruzhenosets]) had gone with him. (VAM T.17) The others all left *servant* out, preferring instead to say *Sam* at this point. (B.148, U T.469, N T.12, Ya T.10, G&G T.18, G&G$_{2002}$ 548, V T.18)

There are an exceptionally large number of markers for Frodo's and Sam's master-servant relationship in the episode in which Frodo and Sam meet Faramir. When Sam steps forward to defend his master from Faramir's insinuations, Faramir puts Sam firmly in his place with "Do not speak before your master, whose wit is greater than yours." (T.346) Most of the translators had no problem replicating the put down. (N T.284, M&K T.322, K&K T.380, VAM T.309) Yakhnin skipped over this particular line, but had more than enough uses of *master* sprinkled around the surrounding text to make up for it. Bobyr' (Umanskij), G&G and Volkovskij all substituted the word *friend* (друг [drug]) for *master* in this line. (G&G T.258, G&G$_{2002}$ 727, V T.424) Bobyr's formulation was the most elegant. Her Faramir said: "That's enough! Do not talk like that in front of your friend, who is, of course, smarter than you." (Довольно! Не говорите так в присутствии вашего друга, который, конечно, умнее вас.) (B.207, U T.561)

As the episode with Faramir closes, Tolkien has two repeats of *servant* in close proximity to *master*. The narrator begins with: "Another bed was set beside [Frodo] for his servant." (T.368) In the dialog between Sam and Faramir that follows, Faramir calls Sam "a pert servant," and Sam refers to Frodo as "my master." The translators' line-up remained essentially unchanged. Gruzberg, M&K, K&K and VAM stayed in step with Tolkien. (M&K T.342-3, K&K T.404-5, VAM T.330) The others did not.

Yakhnin omitted this segment entirely. (Ya T.256) Volkovskij let the two uses of *servant* fall through the cracks, but did keep the use of *master*. (V T.455-6) Nemirova turned in a mixed performance with *master* in its place, but with only one of the two uses of *servant*. Her narrator said that another bed was set up "for Sam." (постель для Сэма) (N T.302)

Bobyr' again avoided all the markers. Her narrator said that "another bed had been prepared next to it for [Frodo's] companion." (Другая постель, рядом, была приготовлена для его спутника.) The retort that her Faramir made to Sam was "you're a sly one, Samwise." (Вы хитрец, Сэмвиз.) Sam's reference to Frodo was not to *my master*, but to "my friend." (мой друг) (B.221-2, U T.573) This segment is one of the many in which G&G's formulation matches Bobyr's word for word, pointing to G&G's use of Bobyr' as a crib for their translation. (G&G T.277-8, G&G$_{2002}$ 741) The probability that Bobyr' and G&G created the same formulation of this segment independently is very low. Of the 7 other translations, not one used the combination *companion* [спутник (sputnik)], *sly one* [хитрец (khitrets)] and *my friend* [мой друг (moj drug)] for the three markers in this segment. Another example of the same kind of similarity will follow below.

Sam was not born to greatness, but had greatness thrust upon him. His participation in the quest to destroy the Ring was a "punishment" for eavesdropping on Frodo and Gandalf, when they were planning Frodo's departure.

> "Get up, Sam!" said Gandalf. "I have thought of something better than that. Something to shut your mouth, and punish you properly for listening. You shall go away with Mr. Frodo!" (F.98)

M&K, however, avoid the use of the word *punishment*. Instead, their Gandalf has thought of something "even more terrifying" than being turned into a spotted toad in a garden full of grass-snakes. (F.98)

> — Встань, Сэм! — велел Гэндальф. — Я придумал кое-что пострашнее: ни о чем ты не проболтаешься и впредь будешь знать, как подслушивать. Ты пойдешь с Фродо! (M&K F_{1982}.47; F_{1988}.102)
>
> BT: "Get up, Sam!" commanded Gandalf. "I have thought of something even more terrifying: you won't blab about anything and in the future, you'll know better than to listen [to other people's conversations]. You're going with Frodo!"

Yakhnin has essentially the same formulation, showing the influence of M&K on his retelling. None of the other translators said anything about *terrifying*. Yakhnin's Gandalf says: "There is a punishment even more terrifying." (Есть наказание пострашнее.) (Ya F.42-3) By making Gandalf's punishment something "even more terrifying," M&K and Yakhnin telegraph the punch to the Russian reader that Tolkien will deliver to the English-speaking reader much more slowly and much more subtly. Tolkien's Gandalf does not say what kind of punishment Sam will receive. A reader with no foreknowledge of the tale could suppose that the punishment would be having to leave the Shire (uncommon for Hobbits), or exhausting, or uncomfortable, or even terrifying, but because Tolkien does not say what it is, the reader—and Sam—are not immediately scared off by it. Sam's reaction to this "punishment" is one of enthusiasm. He is happy to go, because he will get to see "Elves and all! Hooray!" (F.98) It is only later—much like the British soldiers who went off to World War I full of enthusiasm—that Sam will find out how terrifying his quest is. "And we shouldn't be here at all, if we'd known more about it before we started," says Sam to Frodo. (T.407)

All of the other translators had *punishment* (наказание) in its place and none of them had any problem with "I have thought of something better." Almost all of them had exactly the same correct formulation: Я придумал кое-что получше. Nemirova was the only hold-out. She combined *punishment* with *something better*, to produce a serviceable: "I've thought of a better punishment for you." (Я придумал тебе наказание почище.) (N F.83)

Tolkien repeats the plot line of Sam listening to things he should not have listened to later in the episode at the Council of Elrond. In that episode, Sam is again caught listening where he should not have been. This time, however, there is a slight difference. Sam has taken up his new job of serving and protecting Frodo. Elrond's pronouncement that Sam will accompany Frodo, therefore, is not a punishment, as was Gandalf's, but an evaluation of Sam's performance in his new role as Frodo's batman.

> "You [Sam] at least shall go with him [Frodo]. It is hardly possible to separate you from him, even when he is summoned to a secret council and you are not." (F.355)

From this point on Sam becomes Frodo's "ever-present companion," to borrow a line from *Biography of a Batman*[3] by Lieutenant Colonel Graham Seton Hutchison (1890-1946), the author of a number of books on World War I. As Frodo and Sam discuss leaving Lórien to get on with their quest, Tolkien shows Sam in the role of counselor, another of the duties that Hutchison attributed to his batman Peter McLintock.[4] Sam's part of the dialog conveys a sense of reluctance to proceed, combined with a feeling of 'let's get this over with.'

> "You're right," said Sam. [...] I don't want to leave. All the same, I'm beginning to feel that if we've got to go on, then we'd best get it over.
> *"It's the job that's never started as takes longest to finish*, as my old gaffer used to say. And I don't reckon that these folk can do much more to help us, magic or no." (F.467)

All the translators—except Bobyr' (Umanskij) and Volkovskij—convey the sense of the dialog well enough. Volkovskij's verbose rendition introduces an element of fear that is not implicit in the original.

> —Вы правы, сударь, — кивнул Сэм. […] уходить мне отсюда неохота, но чует мое сердце, что пора. Лучше уж не тянуть, да отрезать. А что боязно, так на сей счет мой Старбень так говаривал: «Глаза боятся, руки делают». Наше ведь с вами, сударь, дело, за нас никто не сделает. Эльфы здешние с нами не пойдут, так что от ворожбы ихней, будь она хоть самой расчудесной, нам помощи мало.
> BT: (**Emphasis** added) "You are right, sir," nodded Sam. […] I don't want to be leaving here, but my heart feels that it is time. It's better not to drag it out, but to cut it short. **And what you're afraid of**, well, what my old gaffer used to say about that was: '**The eyes are afraid**, but the hands do.' **After all, nobody's going to do our job for us, sir. These here Elves will not go with us**, so them's sorcery, **be it even the most absolutely marvelous**, will be of little use to us. (V F.497)

Bobyr' (Umanskij) just left this episode out. (B.116, U F.440) The other translators are more true to the original. Tolkien's proverb—*It's the job that's never started as takes longest to finish*—is well treated by all of them.

Job is a key word in the story, and Tolkien repeats it again and again to help define Sam's character and explain his motivation. His job as Frodo's batman is to serve and protect his charge. The problem for the translators in dealing with Tolkien's use of the word *job* is in finding the correct Russian word to convey the meaning that Tolkien wanted in this context. The *Merriam-Webster Dictionary* defines *job* as:

> **job** \jäb\ **n**. 1: a piece of work 2: something that has to be done: DUTY 3: a regular remunerative position — **jobless** *adj*.[5]

The second meaning from this definition—*duty*—comes clearly to the fore in Chapter 1 of Book VI, at the Tower of Cirith Ungol, in which Sam "turned quickly and ran back up the stairs":

> "Wrong again, I expect," he sighed. "But it's my job to go right up to the top first, whatever happens afterwards." (R.224)

An earlier segment from the same chapter in exactly the same context—but with the word *duty* in the place that the word *job* occupies in the segment above—clearly shows that Tolkien intended for *job* to be understood as *duty*. His role model for Sam, was, after all, the privates and batmen that he had known in World War I. In the context of soldiers at war, a sense of duty is one of the primary motivations for sane men to stand steadfast in harm's way. This is a defining trait of Sam's character.

> He [Sam] no longer had any doubt about his duty: he must rescue his master or perish in the attempt. (R.211)

The primary difference in the two sentences is the voice in which they are written. The first sentence, the one with the word *job*, is in Sam's voice, which is notable for its conversational tone. The second sentence, the one with the word *duty*, is in the narrator's voice, which is bookish.

Gruzberg's *job/duty* pair was right on target. His Sam said that "it is my job to go up to the top." (мое дело идти наверх) Gruzberg's narrator matched that with: "he no longer doubted what his duty was." (Он больше не сомневался в своем долге)

K&K's rendition of the narrator's sentence from the *job/duty* pair was elegantly complete, and untypically compact. *Duty* and *master* were both in their appointed places. (K&K R.231) While their rendition of Sam's speech to himself as he ran up the stairs has *job* where it is supposed to be, it does, however, make a slight detour when it comes to "whatever happens afterwards":

> — Наверное, я опять сделал что-то не так, — вздохнул он про себя. — Но мое дело — попасть на верхушку, а там будь что будет! (K&K R.246)
>
> BT: "I probably did something the wrong way again," he sighed to himself. "But it is my job to get to the summit, and there what happens happens."

While the second meaning of а там [a tam] listed in the *Great Russian Defining Dictionary*[6] is *and then*, the first meaning is *and there*. Because the adverb а там [a tam] comes immediately after a noun that defines a place, the proximity of this noun of place forces the primary meaning of а там [a tam] as an adverb of place to the fore, which makes the reading that K&K had intended (*and then*) come across as *and there* [at the top]. This limits the scope of the possible consequences that K&K's Sam may face as a result of his decision. K&K's Sam is only looking at the near term, while Tolkien's

Sam does not limit his vision of the consequences that may follow his action to those just at the top. *Afterwards* can be at the top or when he has come back down and left the tower altogether. K&K could have avoided this confusion and still matched the slightly colloquial nature of *afterwards* with the dialectical опосля [oposlya].

VAM's rendition of the sentence written in Sam's voice places the accent on Sam's sense of necessity rather than on his *job*. Her Sam says that he has to go all the way to the top first. (надо сначала сходить на самый верх) (VAM R.203) Her version of the sentence in the narrator's voice uses exactly the same formulation. Her narrator says that there was no doubt what Sam had to do. (В том, что надо было делать, не было никаких сомнений) (VAM R.190) This eliminates the parallel between *job* and *duty*, and weakens Sam's character in the process. The motivation of *duty* includes a certain amount of *have to*, but *have to* does not necessarily include a sense of *duty*.

Nemirova has essentially the same formulation as VAM in her rendition of the sentence with *job*. She says that Sam "needs to search here first." (нужно сперва поискать здесь) (N R.179) This makes the scene less dynamic, eliminating the long climb that Sam is committing to with this decision. Her continuation of the sentence is even more prosaic. Her Sam "just could not leave Frodo alone any longer." (только Фродо одного оставлять больше нельзя!) Tolkien's end to this statement is fraught with potential unknown dangers that his Sam is prepared to face in order to save Frodo. Nemirova's Sam could just as well have been making a decision about whether to go to the corner store or not.

Nemirova's version of the sentence with *duty* was given the same treatment. Her Sam "must save Frodo." (должен спасти Фродо) (N R.169) While the root of the word *duty* долг [dolg] is visible in her formulation to the trained linguistic eye, common usage of *must* (должен [dolzhen]) has left it bereft of its sense of duty. There is a sense of obligation, but it is not bound to a sense of honor as *duty* is. Her formulation also lacks Tolkien's marker for the master-servant relationship between Frodo and Sam. Her Sam "must save Frodo," but Tolkien's Sam has a duty to rescue his master. Her rendition of the *duty/job* pair of sentences robs Sam of his faithful dedication to the service of his master, and weakens Sam's character.

Nemirova did, however, get the closing clause of the phrase right. Her Sam must save Frodo "even at the cost of his own life." (хотя бы и ценой собственной жизни) She also had a very elegant, very Tolkienesque embellishment. Tolkien's narrator explains that Sam could not wait to decide. He must act now, because "time was desperately precious." Nemirova's narrator said that "every minute was worth its weight in mithril." (каждая минута на вес мифрила) It is a nice touch, but it does not make up for the failings of the rest of the segment.

K&K have a similar—though less Tolkienesque—formulation of the press of time on Sam to make a decision. Their narrator says: "time was worth its weight in gold." (Время было на вес золота) (K&K R.231) This is a particularly strange thing for Tolkien's narrator to say, given Tolkien's view of gold as the root of all the trouble with the dragon in *The Hobbit*.

G&G have an even weaker formulation of Sam's statement to himself than VAM's and Nemirova's. It has no sense of obligation at all. Their Sam says: "But first let me climb up to the very top." (Но уж пусть я сначала поднимусь на самый верх) (G&G R.190, G&G$_{2002}$919) This eliminates Sam's motivation for his action. Tolkien's Sam is going up the stairs because it is his job (duty). Without this explanation of his motivation, G&G's Sam sounds more like an adventurer than a faithful servant. This is compounded by the fact that G&G also make the same detour in their rendition of the second half of Sam's statement as K&K. Their Sam says: "and there, what happens happens!" (а там - будь что будет!)

G&G's version of the narrator's half of the *job/duty* pair is essentially the same as VAM's and Nemirova's, made even worse by G&G's substitution of *friend* (друг [drug]) for *master*. Their Sam says: "I have to save my friend." (Надо спасти друга) (G&G R.180, G&G$_{2002}$ 911) While the desire to save a friend is a strong motivation that, undoubtedly, is a part of the reasoning behind Sam's decision, it is only a part of the reason that Tolkien gave. Tolkien's Sam was doing his duty. Duty can be to one's friends, but that is not necessarily the case.

G&G's narrator was clearly the understudy to Bobyr's, who was the first to say that Sam had to save "his friend."

> А то, что он должен сделать, Сэм знал совершенно твердо: спасти своего друга или погибнуть, спасая. (B.371, U R.712)
> BT: "And Sam knew absolutely firmly what he must do: save his friend or die saving him.

Sam's conversation with himself was greatly restructured in Bobyr's version, but is nevertheless recognizable from the remaining elements in the story line. Her Sam sees that the orcs are afraid of him and his Sting, and thinks to himself that things will turn out better than he had hoped. It seems to him that Shagrat and Gorbag and their ilk have done all his work for him. Except for that one frightened rat that he heard screaming, there appears not to be a living soul in the place. The realization hits him like a ton of bricks. That scream must have been Frodo. As he starts up the stairs, Bobyr's Sam calls out:

> — Фродо! Фродо! Друг мой! — вскричал Сэм, почти рыдая. — Если вас убили, что мне делать? Ну вот, я пришел, наконец. Я иду прямо наверх, а там — увидим! (B.378, U R.719)
> BT: "Frodo! Frodo! My friend!" called out Sam, almost crying. "If they have killed you, what am I to do? Well, I have finally arrived. I am going straight up, and there we will see [what happens]."

This version eliminates not only Sam's job, but also the dilemma of the decision he has to make. It recasts Sam's character from faithful servant to dedicated friend, and robs the reader of the tension of the choice. It also plays fast and loose with "whatever happens afterwards."

G&G are not alone in painting Sam to look like an adventurer. M&K also skipped the references to Sam's job and duty. M&K's narrator says that Sam "understood what he had to do" (А что ему делать, это он понимал) (M&K R.193), eliminating Sam's duty and substituting cold reason. Sam's job has also been eliminated in the second half of the *job/duty* pair:

> M&K:— Опять небось маху дал, — вздохнул он. — Но будь что будет, сперва доберусь до этой каморки на верхотуре. (M&K R.203)
> BT: "Maybe I've made another blunder," he sighed. "But whatever happens, first I'm going to get to that tiny, little room at the tippy top.

Despite their philosophical detour around *job*, M&K's version is, nevertheless, a masterful stylization of Sam's descriptively colloquial manner of speaking. It has three words that are marked as colloquial variants: *make a blunder* (маху дать), *tiny, little room* (каморка) and *tippy top* (верхотура). This adds a subtle extra layer to Sam's character that most of the other translators do not have. M&K also got the phrasing of "whatever happens afterwards" right.

In his version of Sam's statement about his job, Volkovskij makes a bow to M&K by replicating their formulation of the opening phrase: "Maybe

I am making another blunder." In the closing phrase, however, he joins K&K and G&G in placing the adverb *there* in an ambiguous position, which takes it on a philosophical detour around "whatever happens afterwards."

> «Опять, небось, маху дал, — думал он на бегу. — Ну да ладно, доберусь до верхушки, а там будь что будет». (V R.308)
>
> BT: "Maybe I've made another blunder," he thought on the run. "Well, so what, I'm going to the top, and whatever happens there happens."

His rendition of the narrator's half of the *job/duty* pair also abandons *duty*, taking the same approach as VAM. His narrator said that Sam "had to free his master." (А вызволять хозяина надо) (V R.289)

In Chapter 3 of Book IV, "The Black Gate is Closed," as Sam's hope comes to an end, Tolkien's narrator reaffirms the sense of duty in Sam's job, and his resolve to go on because of it. Sam "had stuck to his master all the way; that was what he had chiefly come for, and he would still stick to him. His master would not go to Mordor alone." (T.310) Tolkien's two repeats of the word *master* within the space of 21 words reinforces their master-servant relationship, but not all the translators managed to replicate Tolkien's repeats, or even the sense of duty in Sam's job.

Yakhnin made no attempt at this philosophical phrase in his retelling. It is, also, no great surprise, that in her condensation, Bobyr' jettisoned both Sam's sense of duty and the cues to the relationship between Frodo and Sam. All that is left is Sam's sense of resolve not to let Frodo go to Mordor alone.

> Фродо хочет уйти в Мордор; но Сэм отнюдь не собирался отпустить его туда одного. (B.187, U T.544)
>
> BT: Frodo wants to go to Mordor; but Sam was definitely not planning to let him go alone.

She recognized Sam's decision to go with Frodo as a key element in the story, but the omission of Sam's motivation flattens the story, and makes it less lifelike.

This segment is one of the many in which G&G's formulation matches Babyr's almost word for word. What was to some extent excusable in a condensation, is less so in a translation. G&G's version read:

> Фродо собирался в Мордор, Сэм отнюдь не собирается отпускать его одного. (G&G T.225, G&G$_{2002}$, 705)
> BT: Frodo was planning to go to Mordor; but Sam is definitely not planning to let him go alone.

The probability is very low that Bobyr' and G&G independently arrived at the same wording for this sentence. Of the 7 other translations, not one other translator used the word *definitely not* (отнюдь) in this segment. It is not called for by the original.

Volkovskij embellished the narration leading up to Sam's decision to go with Frodo in grand style, expanding on Sam's sense of hope—or rather lack thereof—about their adventure. Volkovskij's narrator begins well enough, but continues after Tolkien's had stopped. Tolkien's narrator says: "And after all [Sam] never had any real hope in the affair from the beginning; but being a cheerful Hobbit he had not needed hope, as long as despair could be postponed." (T.310) Volkovskij's rendition of this sentence is reasonably good, but his narrator keeps on going, adding: "up until the last minute, [Sam] had hoped for something, perhaps for a miracle, perhaps just for luck to take a hand." (то ли на чудо, то ли просто на авось) (V T.377)

The kind of luck that Volkovskij's narrator was hoping for is the kind that became a fixture in the Russian mental legacy embodied in the word авоська [avos'ka]. This is a small shopping bag made out of netting so that it is easy to carry around unobtrusively. Soviet stores and shops did not supply their customers with bags for their purchases. The customers had to bring their own. Because of the failure of the centrally planned economy of the Soviet Union to meet the demand for consumer goods, some consumer goods were in short supply. These were known as 'deficit goods.' Shoppers were never sure of getting what they wanted when they went to the stores, so people carried around net shopping bags with them all the time, just on the off-chance that they would find something that they needed to buy while they were out on other business.

An excellent example of this can be seen in the movie *Moscow on the Hudson* with Robin Williams.[7] Williams' character sees a long line, and immediately—without knowing what the line is for—queues up because he knows that whatever deficit product is available, it is worth having. The line is for shoes. When he gets to the front of the line, he asks for two pair, but is told only one pair to a customer. It also turns out that they do not have his size, but he buys a pair anyway. Deficit goods were always good for trading for favors or for other deficit goods. The *avos'ka* and the habit of standing in line first and asking questions later was part of the Soviet way of life.

Volkovskij's embellishment is used as the springboard for Sam's decision to stick with Frodo as he goes into Mordor. This deprives Sam's decision of its motivation and reinforces the role of fate or chance in Volkovskij's version of the tale.

> Последний момент настал, никакого чуда не произошло, но это ничуть не поколебало намерения Сэма держаться с хозяином до конца. Не отпускать же его в Мордор одного. (V T.377-78)
>
> BT: The last minute had arrived, and no miracle had occurred, but that did not in the least shake Sam's intention to stick with his master to the end. Not to let him go to Mordor alone.

Volkovskij did at least manage to include the word *master* in his version.

Nemirova brings Sam's sense of duty to the foreground in her translation, but could not bring herself to repeat *master* twice in the segment.

> Всю дорогу Сэм преданно выполнял свой долг — затем и пошел, чтобы идти до конца. Господин Фродо не пойдет в Мордор один. (N F.253)
>
> BT: The whole way, Sam had faithfully carried out his duty—that is why he had come, to go to the end. Mr. Frodo would not go to Mordor alone.

This is a much stronger statement of purpose than Tolkien's. Her use of *duty* would have been much more in its place in the *job/duty* segment discussed above.

VAM has a similarly strong statement of purpose for Sam, and she did not shrink from Tolkien's repeat of *master* either.

> Сэм был верен хозяину, потому и шел с ним, чтобы не оставлять его одного. Нет, хозяин один в Мордор не пойдет. Сэм его не покинет. (VAM T.277-78)
>
> BT: Sam was faithful to his master. He had gone with him so that he would not be alone. No, his master would not go to Mordor alone. Sam would not desert him.

Gruzberg also had both repeats of *master*, and what would have otherwise been a good rendition of this segment, were it not for a slight detour from singular to plural in the second clause of the first sentence. Instead of saying "what he [Sam] had chiefly come for," Gruzberg's narrator says that was "what they had come for" (Для этого они и пустились в путь). Aleksandrova cleaned up this problem in the CD-ROM edition. Gruzberg's book editor, Zastyrets, just threw the whole phrase out. (G T.304-05)

K&K have the best rendition of this segment, with everything in its place.

> Но Сэм всю дорогу держался рядом с хозяином, он и пошел-то с ним ради этого, и вовсе не собирался оставлять Фродо. Нет! Хозяину не придется идти в Мордор одному. Сэм отправится с ним! (K&K T.339)
>
> BT: But Sam had stayed next to his master the whole way, that was what he had come with him for, and he was not planning to leave Frodo at all. No! His master would not have to go to Mordor alone. Sam was going with him.

As Sam and Frodo draw closer to Mount Doom, Tolkien's attention returns to Sam's job. Even though death appears to be the most likely outcome, duty and honor require that Sam—like Hutchison's batman, Peter McLintock—go on.

> "So that was the job I felt I had to do when I started," thought Sam: "to help Mr. Frodo to the last step and then die with him? Well, if that is the job then I must do it." (R.259)

Tolkien's description of Sam's job here is essentially the same as the job description that Hutchison gives for a batman: "And he would run when his officer went over the top, and fight by his side. When the officer dropped, the batman was beside him."[8]

Volkovskij deftly works *job* (дело [delo]) into his rendition, to produce the most elegant version of this description of Sam's job. Its major failing is that it did not replicate Tolkien's repeat of *job*.

> «Ну что ж, — подумалось Сэму, — что-то такое я чувствовал с самого начала. Взялся за дело, чтоб помогать хозяину, а коли в конце придется умереть вместе — так тому и быть. » (V R.358)
>
> BT: "Well, alright," thought Sam, "I felt something like this from

the very beginning. I took on this job to help the master, and if in the end I have to die together [with him], then that's the way it is."

Bobyr' has a slightly less elegant, though philosophically accurate, rendition of this segment. She combines the feeling of obligation through the use of the word *to have to* (должен [dolzhen]), with a formulation that would be right at home in a military context, like the description of the relationship between an officer and his batman. The mission (задача [zadacha]) of a batman is to serve and protect his charge, and he has to carry it out (выполнить задачу [vypolnit' zadachu]). The effect, however, seems to be lost on those who have not served on active duty in the Armed Forces.

«Так вот как кончится то, что я должен был начать! — подумал он. — Я помогу Фродо дойти до самого конца, а тогда умру с ним вместе? Что ж, если такова моя задача, я должен ее выполнить.» (В.441)
BT: "So this is how the thing I had to start finishes!" he thought. "I help Frodo go to the very end, and then die together with him? Well, if that's my mission, then I have to carry it out."

Umanskij made a slight change in this sentence that retreated from Bobyr's sense of duty and returned to a Russian vision of the role of fate as the prime mover of people's lives. His Sam said:

«Так вот как кончится то, что мне суждено было испытать! — подумал Сэм. — Я помогу Фродо дойти до самого конца, а тогда умру вместе с ним. Что ж, если такова моя задача, я должен ее выполнить.» (U R.782)
BT: " So this is how what I was destined to experience ends!" thought Sam. "I help Frodo go to the very end, and then die together with him. Well, if that's my mission, then I have to carry it out."

This formulation is very wide of the mark. Even the typically fatalistic M&K had a better formulation.

M&K begin the segment nicely, combining *deed* [дело (delo)] with a verb that implies *job* rather than explicitly stating it: *to contract to do something* (подряжаться/подрядиться на что).

— Вот, оказывается, на что я подрядился, — думал Сэм. — Дело-то, стало быть, маленькое, — помочь господину Фродо погибнуть и сгинуть вместе с ним, а что? Так — значит, так. (M&K R.233)

BT: "So this is what it turns out that I signed up for," thought Sam. "It's just a small deed: help Mr. Frodo perish and then die together with him, and what of it? If that's the way it is, that's the way it is."

Gruzberg introduces a sense of obligation, but his version is too terse and not as elegant as M&K's.

— Итак, я должен идти до конца с мастером Фродо и умереть с ним вместе, — подумал Сэм вслух. — Что ж, если это так, я должен сделать это.

BT: "So, I have to go to the end with master Frodo and die together with him," thought Sam out loud. "Alright, if that's it, I have to do it."

JRRT (**Emphasis** added.):

"So **that was the job I felt I had to do when I started**," thought Sam: "to help Mr. Frodo to the last step and then die with him? Well, if that is **the job** then I must do it." (R.259)

Aleksandrova polishes up Gruzberg with a sense of purpose to balance the sense of obligation.

«Стало быть, вот что погнало меня в эти странствия, — подумал Сэм. — Помочь мастеру Фродо дойти до конца и умереть с ним вместе? Что ж, если так, я должен это сделать.»

BT: "So that was what drove me into this journey," thought Sam. "Help Mr. Frodo reach the end [of his quest] and die together with him? "Alright, if that's it, I have to do it."

Zastyrets, Gruzberg's book editor, had his own version of this sentence as well. It falls flat, however, solely on his rendition of *job* as *work* (работа [rabota]), which fails to convey the sense of *duty* inherent in the English word *job*.

«Я чувствовал, когда начал эту работу, — подумал Сэм, — что должен буду помочь мастеру Фродо сделать и этот, последний шаг и умереть вместе с ним. Так я и поступлю, раз по-другому нельзя.» (G R.251)

BT: "I felt, when I started this work," thought Sam, "that I would even have to help master Frodo take this last step and die together with him. Well, that's what I'll do, if there's no other way."

Nemirova has an interesting approach, which captures the sense of obligation very well.

Вот какую обязанность я взвалил на себя, когда напросился в поход. (N R.206)
BT: So this is the obligation I took on, when I got myself into this quest.

This is a suitably powerful statement of purpose. It is unfortunate that Nemirova was unable to replicate it throughout for all Tolkien's uses of *job/duty*.

K&K had an elegant rendition that had a proverbial ring to it. It plays the word *deed* [дело (delo)] off against the verb that is derived from the same root: *to do* (делать).

— Вот, оказывается, к чему я готовился, — подумал Сэм.
— Помогать хозяину до последнего, а потом умереть с ним рядом ... Ну что ж! Дело на то и дело, чтобы его делать.» (K&K R.285)
BT: "So this is what it turns out that I was preparing for," thought Sam. "Help the master up to the last and then die next to him ... "Well, alright! A deed [дело (delo)] is a deed so that it can be done."

Their version, nevertheless, is still missing some of the sense of duty present in the English word *job* in this context that Bobyr', M&K, Gruzberg, Aleksandrova felt that they had to convey with terms and phrases like: "mission," "I have to," "what drove me," what "I signed up for."

The other translators take this segment further afield philosophically. In their samizdat version G&G began this segment with "Well, that's the end of this tale" (Так вот каков конец у этой сказки), echoing the episodes in which Sam compares their quest to a heroic tale (T.407-408, R.281), where G&G used the same word for *tale*. (сказка) (G&G T.312-13, R.243; G&G$_{2002}$ 764-65, 956) It is an interesting touch, much better than the changed print version. Following one's path is a marker for predetermination. G&G should have paid more attention to Bobyr', whose footprints (**emphasis added**) can still be seen in both the samizdat and print versions.

Samizdat:
— Так вот каков конец у этой сказки, — подумал он. — Я помогу Фродо дойти, а потом умру с ним вместе. Что ж, если это — моя дорога, надо ее пройти.

BT: "Well, that's the end of this tale," he thought. "**I help Frodo go to** (the end), **and then die together with him**. Alright, if that's my path, then I have to follow it."

Print: — Значит, обратной дороги не будет, — подумал он. — Ну что ж, примерно так я себе и представил с самого начала: помогу Фродо дойти, а потом умру с ним вместе. Если это моя дорога, надо ее пройти. (G&G R.222, G&G$_{2002}$ 942)

BT: "That means there's no path of return," he thought. "Well, alright, that is about how I had imagined it from the very beginning: **I help Frodo go to** (the end), **and then die together with him**. If that's my path, then I have to follow it."

VAM's rendition was even more decidedly predeterministic.

— Вот, значит, что было мне предназначено с самого начала, — подумал он. — До конца помогать господину Фродо, а потом умереть вместе с ним. Ну что ж, дело есть дело, придется все выполнить. (VAM R.233)

BT: "So that's what was predetermined for me from the very beginning," he thought. "Help Mr. Frodo to the end, and then die together with him. Well, alright, a deed [дело (delo)] is a deed and all of it will have to be done."

Yakhnin shuffles Sam's and the narrator's lines in this segment, highlighting its resonances with the change in the attitude of British soldiers who went off to fight in World War I. At first they were happy to go, but later they realized what they had gotten themselves into. Yakhnin's version of this episode has Sam saying to himself: "Back, you stupid Hobbit, you're not going back." (Ya R.200) Yakhnin's narrator immediately picks up the thread of this thought, and continues:

Как далек был тот день, когда любопытный простак Сэмми с радостью согласился сопровождать хозяина, лишь бы поглядеть на эльфов да мир повидать. Тогда он и представить себе не мог всех опасностей, подстерегавших их на пути. И только теперь до конца осознал, что шли они навстречу неминуемой смерти. (Ya R.200)

BT: How far away was the day, when the curious simpleton Sam had happily agreed to accompany his master, just so he could look at the Elves and see the world. Back then he could not even imagine all the dangers waiting for them along the way. It was only now that he had finally comprehended that they had been heading to meet an inescapable death.

Peter McLintock died at Hutchison's side and is buried in Ration Farm Military Cemetery, la Chappelle-d'Armentières, France. Tolkien gave the story of his batman a happy ending; Sam returned to the Shire to marry his sweetheart, Rose Cotton.

Sam's job was indeed a "punishment," and in more ways than just the privations that he suffered when he accompanied Frodo to Mount Doom and back. To do his job, Sam had to leave Rose Cotton and she was not particularly pleased with him for that. She viewed the year that he was gone with Frodo as "wasted." This, in general, mirrors a feeling about the service of private soldiers (enlisted men) that was widespread in England in the period following World War I.

> "It's Rosie, Rose Cotton," said Sam. "It seems she didn't like my going abroad at all, poor lass; but as I hadn't spoken, she couldn't say so. And I didn't speak, because I had a job to do first. But now I have spoken, and she says: 'Well, you've wasted a year, so why wait longer?' 'Wasted?' I says. 'I wouldn't call it that.' Still I see what she means." (R.376)

In this segment, Tolkien closes the circle on all the repeats of the word *job* throughout the story. The central meaning here is again one of *duty*. Only M&K managed to include that sense here by combining the word *to have to do something* [надо (nado)] with their very serviceable rendition of *job* as *deed* [дело (delo)]. VAM tried to close the circle on *job* the same way that M&K did, but her effort faltered on her rendition of *job*. She translated it as *work* [работа (rabota)], which robs *job* of its sense of duty, even when combined with the sense of obligation from *to have to do something* [надо (nado)]. M&K's version reads:

> — Розочка же, ну Роза Кроттон, — объяснил Сэм. — Ей, бедняжке, оказывается, вовсе не понравилось, что я с вами поехал; ну, я-то с ней тогда еще не разговаривал напрямик, вот она и промолчала. А какие же с ней разговоры, когда сперва надо было, сами знаете, дело сделать. (M&K R.344)

BT: "It's Rosie, well, Rose Mole-town," explained Sam. "It seems that the poor girl did not like my going with you at all, well, I hadn't talked with her straight out then, so she was silent. And what kind of talk could I have had with her when first it was necessary, you know yourself, to do the job [дело (delo)]."

Nemirova makes Tolkien's circumlocution around Sam's proposal of marriage much more understandable to modern readers for whom 'speaking with a girl' is not clearly synonymous with proposing marriage anymore. The first example of this usage in the *OED* is from *Othello* act 1, scene 3. "She thank'd me, And bad me, if I had a Friend that lou'd her, I should but teach him how to tell my Story, And that would wooe her. Vpon this hint I spake." In the Pasternak translation, the last segment of this quote is translated as: "In response to this I also confessed of my love to her" (В ответ на это я тоже ей признался [в любви]).[9] Nemirova used a much better formulation. Her Sam says that they have recently 'cleared up their relationship,' which in Russian is a synonym for a declaration of love/proposal (недавно мы объяснились [в любви]). Nemirova could not, however, bring herself to use the same formulation for "I hadn't spoken" and for "now I have spoken," which does not make her verbose rendition of this segment any the more elegant.

> Дело, сударь, в Розочке. Понимаете, она убивалась, бедняжка, когда я отправился с вами, но смолчала, я тогда и не подозревал, даже и не говорил с ней ни о чем таком. И теперь все откладывал — думал сперва с делами управиться. Ну вот, а недавно мы объяснились. (N R.311)
>
> BT: It's Rosie, sir. You see, she was devastated, the poor thing, when I left with you, but she did not say anything, [and] I did not suspect, had not even talked with her about anything like that. And now, I've been putting it off. I thought first I have to take care of all this business. Well, anyway, we got engaged not long ago.

This completely leaves out the reason that Rosie did not say anything. She did not have a right to, because Sam had not proposed to her yet. If Sam had already proposed to her, given her forthright categorization of the year that he was away with Frodo on the quest to destroy the Ring as "wasted," she would undoubtedly not have hesitated to tell Sam not to go with Frodo.

The sequence of events—who said what to whom when—described in this segment was a big stumbling block for most of the translators. Tolkien's, M&K's and Nemirova's Sams are talking about why they did not propose before they left. All the others are talking about why they did not propose after they came back.

Sam's Job: Frodo's Batman

VAM's version of the sequence of events was that Sam did not understand that Rosie had been suffering during his absence until he got back, but then was not the time to explain things to her, and later he kept quiet because he had all this work to do.

> — Девочка, оказывается, очень переживала, когда мы ушли в Путешествие. Я это понял, когда вернулся. Но тогда, как вы помните, не до объяснений было. Потом я молчал, потому что надо было сначала сделать всю эту работу. (VAM R.345)

BT: "The girl, it turns out, was very distressed when we left on the Journey. I understood that when I got back. But then, as you recall, wasn't the time for explanations. After that I kept quiet, because, to begin with, all this work had to be done."

VAM may have intended to use the same formulation that Nemirova used for *a declaration of love/proposal*, but her execution was poor. She used the plural of the noun behind Nemirova's formulation. In the singular, it would have been correct. In the plural, it means *explanations*, and not *a declaration of love*.

Yakhnin missed the boat to "I had not spoken" entirely. Yakhnin's narrator explains that when Sam got back from their adventure, Rosie had let Sam see that she was displeased. Frodo asks Sam what she was displeased about and Sam says that:

> Роззи попрекала меня тем, что я, не сказавшись, уехал с вами и целый год пропадал невесть где, а она, бедняжка, не имела от меня ни весточки. Уж я ей объяснял, растолковывал, что мы не на прогулку отправились, да разве женщину переговоришь? Одним ее можно успокоить ... (Ya R.314-15)

BT: Rosie reproached me for leaving with you and disappearing who knows where for a whole year without saying anything, and she, the poor thing, didn't hear from me at all. I've been explaining to her, telling her that we did not go off on a picnic, but can you ever talk a woman around [to another way of thinking]? The only thing you can do to calm her down...

"... is to marry her," says Frodo, finishing Sam's sentence for him.

While Tolkien is often criticized for his treatment of female characters, in comparison to Yakhnin's treatment of Rosie, Tolkien almost looks like a feminist.

Gruzberg's version has the same time lapse as the majority of the translators. Gruzberg's Sam is talking about the present and not the past. Gruzberg's Rosie does not like how busy Sam has been cleaning up the Shire. There is no mention of her feelings about Sam going away with Frodo on the quest.

> — Ей не нравятся эти мои разъезды, но она ничего не говорит. А я, пока был занят, тоже молчал, потому что хотел сначала закончить работу. (G R.369)
> BT: "She [Rosie] does not like these travels of mine, but she is not saying anything. And I, while I was busy, kept quiet too, because I wanted to finish work first."

The G&G samizdat version also rearranges the time frame in which the job kept Sam from talking to Rosie's parents and leaves out "but as I hadn't spoken" altogether.

> Samizdat:
> — Похоже ей, бедняжке, не очень-то по нраву был наш отъезд тогда. Ну, а когда мы вернулись, работы невпроворот навалилось, тоже как-то не до этого было.
> BT: "It looks like the poor (girl) was not pleased with our departure then. But when we returned, work piled up so high that you couldn't turn around, and somehow things also never got around to that."

The print version restores "but as I hadn't spoken," but the time lapse remains, and Sam's *job* is still inappropriately rendered as *work*.

> — Похоже, ей, бедняжке, не очень-то по нраву был наш отъезд тогда. Ну я, как собрался, ничего говорить не стал, и она не сказала. А потом я не говорил, потому что работы невпроворот навалилось. (G&G R.334)
> BT: "It looks like the poor (girl) was not pleased with our departure then. But I, though I was planning to, did not say anything, and she didn't say anything. And then I didn't say anything because work piled up so high that you couldn't turn around."
> JRRT: "It seems she didn't like my going abroad at all, poor lass; but as I hadn't spoken, she couldn't say so. And I didn't speak, because I had a job to do first." (R.376)

K&K's rendition seems to have been influenced by G&G because they, too, used "work piled up" as part of their translation of Sam's job, and they have the same time lapse as VAM, Gruzberg and G&G.

> — Бедняжке совсем не по душе пришлось, что я пропадал столько времени. Я с ней сразу не успел поговорить, и она, конечно, тоже смолчала. А потом я опять с ней не поговорил, потому что навалилась работа, и надо было сначала разобраться с делами. (K&K R.420)
>
> BT: "The poor (girl) was not at all happy that I disappeared for such a long time. I did not manage to talk with her right away, and she, of course, kept quiet too. And then I did not talk with her again, because the work piled up, and things had to be sorted out first.

Bobyr' had omitted this passage from her condensation, but Umanskij restored it, unfortunately, following the same detour as all the other translators. His Sam said:

> — В Рози, Рози Коттон, — ответил Сэм. — Кажется, ей вообще не нравились мои отлучки, бедной девочке; но так как я не говорил с ней об этом, она не могла высказать свое мнение. А не говорил я потому, что прежде всего должен был закончить работу. (U R.856)
>
> BT: "It's Rosie, Rosie Cotton," answered Sam. "It seems that she did not like my goings off at all, the poor girl; but since I had not spoken to her about that, she could not express her opinion. And I did not speak, because first of all I had to finish work."

Sam's reason for not proposing to Rosie was not that he had too much work to do. He did not propose because he had a duty to accompany Frodo on Frodo's quest, and he did not want 'to speak' before he went off on an adventure with Frodo from which he might not return. "I didn't speak, because I had a job to do first" refers to the time before their departure, not after. Tolkien, on the other hand, married Edith before he went off to war.

Notes:

1. Quoted in: Humphrey Carpenter. *Tolkien*, NY: Ballantine Books, 1977, p. 91.
2. For a more detailed account of this topic see: Mark T. Hooker, "Frodo's Batman," *Tolkien Studies*, 2003, pp. 127-137.
3. LTC Graham Seton (Hutchison), "Biography of a Batman," *The English Review*, vol. XLIX, August, 1929, pp. 211-222.
4. Hutchison, p. 215.
5. *The Merriam-Webster Dictionary*, New York: Pocket Books, 1974, p. 386.
6. БТСРЯ, стр. 1305.
7. *Moscow on the Hudson*, Columbia Pictures, Directed by Paul Mazursky, Writing credits Paul Mazursky and Leon Capetanos, 1984.
8. Hutchison, p. 220.
9. Вильям Шекспир, *Трагедии • Сонеты*, М: «Художественная литература», 1968, стр. 263. Перевод Б. Пастернак.

Chapter 6

The Temptation of Knowledge and Power
:TOLKIEN:THROUGH:RUSSIAN:EYES:

> So when the woman saw that the tree was good for food, and that it was a delight for the eyes, and that the tree was to be desired to make one wise, she took of its fruit and ate; and she also gave some to her husband, and he ate. Then the eyes of both were opened, and they knew that they were naked, and they sewed fig leaves together and made themselves aprons.
> Genesis 3:6,7

The tale of temptation and betrayal of the Elven-Smiths belongs to the Second Age of Middle-earth. The tale is one of the effects of power, which Tolkien views as "an ominous and sinister word in all the tales, except when applied to the gods." (L.152) Amidst the wasteland of Middle-earth—the result of the battles with the First Enemy—the exiled Elves ignore the stern council that they return to the West. For Tolkien it is a tale of "a sort of second fall or at least 'error' of the Elves," (L.151) in which they "came their nearest to falling to 'magic' and machinery." (L.152) In refusing to return to the West, the Elves "wanted the peace and bliss and perfect memory of 'The West,' and yet to remain on the ordinary earth where their prestige as the highest people, above wild Elves, Dwarves, and Men, was greater than at the bottom of the hierarchy of Valinor." (L.151)

Sauron, too, refuses to return to The West to face the judgement of the gods. Very slowly, following a path paved with good intentions, he gradually becomes the reincarnation of Evil, lusting after absolute power. He plays on the Elves' desire for greatness to convince them that together they can heal the wastelands and "make Western Middle-earth as beautiful as Valinor," which is really "a veiled attack on the gods, an incitement to try and make a separate independent paradise." (L.152) Gil-galad and Elrond rejected his schemes, but the Elves of Eregion fell into his trap. Theirs is the tale that Elrond tells in Chapter 2 of Book II ("The Council of Elrond"). It is a tale:

> of the Elven-Smiths of Eregion and their friendship with Moria, and their eagerness for knowledge, by which Sauron ensnared them. For in that time he was not yet evil to behold, and they received his aid and grew mighty in craft, whereas he learned all their secrets, and betrayed them, and forged secretly in the Mountain of Fire the One Ring to be their master. But Celebrimbor was aware of him, and hid the Three which he had made; and there was war, and the land was laid waste, and the gate of Moria was shut. (F.318)

The key to this passage is the phrase "their [the Elves'] eagerness for knowledge, by which Sauron ensnared them." This phrase ties *knowledge* together with the evil that is Sauron. Without that tie, the base of Tolkien's philosophy of knowledge is weakened. This phrase is well handled by the majority of the translators with variously formulated good renditions that differ more in style than in substance. Bobyr's condensation, unfortunately, does not contain it, or any of the other passages examined in this chapter.

K&K's version of Elrond's tale was that it was "of their eagerness for knowledge, by which Sauron managed to catch them in his nets." (об их страсти к знаниям, через которую Саурон и уловил их в свои сети. (K&K F.363) Gruzberg's rendition was that Elrond told the Council "of their eagerness for knowledge, through which Sauron managed to lure them into a trap" (об их страсти к знаниям, из-за чего Саурон и заманил их в ловушку). Aleksandrova's and Zastyrets' changes to Gruzberg's formulation were purely cosmetic. (G F.322) VAM's Elrond recited a tale "of a thirst for knowledge, through which they wound up in the nets of Sauron." (о жажде знаний, из-за которой они попались в сети Саурона) (VAM F.275) Nemirova mixes Gruzberg and VAM. Her Elrond told a tale of "their thirst for knowledge, which Sauron used to lure them into a trap" (их жажде знаний, которой воспользовался Саурон, чтобы заманить их в ловушку). (N F.283) Gruzberg's version is slightly more colloquial than

K&K's, and VAM's is slightly less literal. All four, nevertheless, convey the thought of the passage well enough.

Volkovskij has a circumstantial tie between Sauron-evil and the Elven-Smiths' eagerness for knowledge. While the phrase "Sauron ensnared them" is missing, his literarily elegant rendition is nonetheless evocative. The guests at Volkovskij's Council of Elrond listened to a tale of:

> о живших в тесной дружбе с морийскими гномами эльфах-кузнецах из Эрегиона, — эльфах, которых погубила неуемная тяга к знанию. В ту пору Саурон еще не стал зримым воплощением зла: прекрасен был его облик и обольстительны речи. Он предложил эльфам свою помощь и вправду научил их многому, но сделал это лишь для того, чтобы вероломно выведать самые сокровенные тайны. Добившись желаемого, Саурон выковал в горниле Огненной горы Кольцо Всевластья, которое должно было дать ему власть над всеми магическими Кольцами эльфов. (V F.333)

BT: the Elven-Smiths of Eregion who lived in close friendship with the Dwarves of Moria, of Elves who were doomed by their uncontrollable craving for knowledge. At that time Sauron had not yet become the visible embodiment of evil: his countenance was fair and his speech seductive. He offered the Elves his help and, in fact, taught them much, but he did this only so that he could traitorously learn their most treasured secrets. Having gained what he desired, in the furnace of the Fiery Mountain Sauron forged the All-powerful Ring, which was supposed to give him power over all the magic Rings of the Elves.

For the Soviet reader, the key word here is вероломно [verolomno], which is normally translated as *traitorously*, or *faithlessly*, but literally means "breaking faith." The use of this word is commonly associated with Nazi Germany's attack on the Soviet Union in June of 1941. Almost every Russian Soviet-era history of World War II includes this word in the lead sentence of its description of the Nazi-German attack. The description of the initial phase of the war in the *Military Encyclopedic Dictionary* begins with it (**emphasis** added). "On 22 June 1941, without a declaration of war, **faithlessly** breaking the non-aggression treaty, fascist-German armies unexpectedly invaded the territory of the USSR." [1] The civilian, though no less strident *Soviet Encyclopedic Dictionary* begins its article on the first phase of the war in the same way, referring to the (**emphasis** added) "**faithless** attack on the USSR by the fascist-German armies during the night of 21-22 June." [2]

For the Soviet reader the use of this word in this context invokes an image as familiar as the "day that will live in infamy" from Roosevelt's speech following the Japanese attack on Pearl Harbor.

For Volkovskij's readers the scene has a sense of déjà vu. The parallels between the Soviets and the Nazis and the Elven-Smiths and Sauron are amazingly striking. As Europe tottered on the brink of war, Stalin and Hitler engaged in a foreign policy game of cooperation and collusion, each seeking to win advantage from the other, very much like Sauron and the Elven-Smiths. In August of 1939, Hitler and Stalin concluded a non-aggression pact[3] that contained secret terms, which effectively divided Eastern Europe between the two. Stalin got part of Poland, and the three Baltic states: Lithuania, Estonia and Latvia. Hitler got the western part of Poland, and the assurance of not having to fight a war on two fronts when he invaded to claim his part of the land-grab. The resulting partition of Poland by Russia and Germany was the *casus belli* for World War II. Less than two years later, Hitler broke the pact, invaded Russia, "and there was war, and the land was laid waste." (F.318)

M&K's formulation not only leaves out Sauron's "betrayal," but also breaks the tie between the Elves' eagerness for knowledge, which Sauron used as bait for his trap, and Sauron's evil nature, because it leaves out the phrase "Sauron ensnared them" and the phrase that associates Sauron and evil. M&K's is a tale:

> о стремлении эльфов Останны к знаниям и о том, как Саурон, прикинувшись другом, предложил им помощь, и они ее приняли, и достигли замечательной искусности в ремеслах (M&K F_{1982}.173, F_{1988}.298)
> BT: of the aspiration of the Elves of Eregion for learning, and about how Sauron, pretending to be a friend, offered them help, and they took it and achieved remarkable mastery in the crafts.
> JRRT (lacunae **highlighted**): of [...] their eagerness for knowledge, **by which Sauron ensnared them. For in that time he was not yet evil to behold,** and they received his aid and grew mighty in craft. (F.318)

M&K's version completely eliminates the implicit association of knowledge and evil that Tolkien's formulation carries.

Yakhnin also abandons Tolkien's association of knowledge and evil. His Elrond tells a different story. In the forgotten reaches of time, the Elves and the Dwarves were staunch friends, who shared their great knowledge and secrets of the crafts. (великие знания и тайны ремесел) It was during that period that they forged the Rings of Happiness. (Кольца Счастья) "But Sauron, the ancient Lord of Mordor, learned the secrets of the Elven-Smiths, and, desiring to rule over all the world, he forged the All-powerful Ring in the Fiery Mountain." (Кольцо Всевластья) (Ya F.187) The evil of his desire to rule the entire world remains, but gone are the betrayal and the stealth with which he carried out his evil deed. Likewise banished to oblivion are Celebrimbor and his role in uncovering the plot. It is Tolkien, done simply as swords and sorcery, without the philosophy.

G&G's formulation has the feeling of Zen formulary about it.

Он начал говорить об эльфийских кузнецах Эрегиона, друживших некогда с гномами Морийского Царства. Эльфы искали все большей и большей мудрости на пути знания, и Саурон подстерег их. [...] Но Саурон, вызнав многие секреты, предал эльфов Эрегиона. (G&G F.289, G&G$_{2002}$.399)

BT: He [Elrond] began to speak of the Elven-Smiths of Eregion, who were once friends with the Dwarves of the Kingdom of Moria. The Elves were searching for more and more wisdom on the path to knowledge and Sauron lay in wait for them. [...] But Sauron, having learned many secrets, betrayed the Elves of Eregion.

This formulation is unsatisfactory because it mixes *wisdom* and *knowledge*. Tolkien always kept the two concepts separate. Wisdom is the province of Gandalf (F.76; R.105), Elrond (F.352; A.420; S.298), Glorfindel (F.299), Aragorn (R.304; R.323) and Arwen Undómiel daughter of Elrond (A.422). The Wise are the Istari and the chief Eldar. (A.456) Saruman, who once was counted among the Wise, but was cast out, is only credited with keeping enough wisdom not to trust orcs. (T.210) *Wisdom* is good and *knowledge*—the province of Saruman—is bad. Mixing them, therefore, is a major deviation from Tolkien's philosophy of knowledge.

The evil potential of knowledge is one of Tolkien's major recurring themes. It is shown most clearly in Tolkien's disregard for the mechanical products of knowledge. This is reflected in Tolkien's description of the tale of the betrayal of the Elven-Smiths, in which he says that they "came their nearest to falling to 'magic' and machinery." (L.152) It can been seen in his criticism of "the abominable chemists and engineers" who have put so much power into the hands of those who would be like Xerxes "that decent folk don't seem to have a chance." He only sees one bright spot "and that is the growing habit of disgruntled men of dynamiting factories and power-stations." (L.64)

The vision of the industrialized Shire under Lotho at the end of *LotR* is Tolkien's idea of what would happen if the knowledge of "the abominable chemists and engineers" was allowed to gain the upper hand. One of "Lotho's" first acts was to tear down the old mill and build a new one "full o' wheels and outlandish contraptions." (R.361) Others followed it, and their only product was hammering, letting out smoke and a stench, and pouring out filth on purpose. They ran 24 hours a day and farmer Cotton opined that "if they want to make the Shire into a desert, they're going the right way about it." (R.361) When the battle of Bywater was over and the intruders chased from the Shire, the Hobbits got rid of the 'new mills' and tore down anything that had been built by 'Sharkey's Men' (R.373), for the Hobbits, like Tolkien, "do not and did not understand or like machines more complicated than a forge-bellows, a water-mill, or handloom." (F.19)

Tolkien's use of the words *metal, wheels, engines* and *machines* is always negative. Treebeard describes Saruman as having "a mind of metal and wheels." (T.96) Isengard is pictured as "smithies and great furnaces. Iron wheels revolved there endlessly, and hammers thudded. At night plumes of vapour steamed from the vents, lit from beneath with red light, or blue, or venomous green." (T.204) At Orthanc, Saruman fought the Ents with what Merry derisively calls "his precious machinery." (T.220) "Suddenly up came fires and foul fumes: the vents and shafts all over the plain began to spout and belch." (T.221)

Beorn, a positive, though enigmatic character, on the other hand, did not care for things made by smith-craft and had few things in his house—save the knives—made of metal at all. (H.127) He is contrasted to the goblins (orcs), which "make clever things." "It is not unlikely," says the narrator, "that they invented some of the machines that have since troubled the world, especially the ingenious devices for killing large numbers of people at once, for wheels and engines and explosions always delighted them." (H.70) Tolkien sees the "special horror of the present world" (L.64) as its globalization. If there are not enough Frodos and disgruntled bombers to fight against knowledge gone awry, "it won't do any good, if it is not universal." (L.64)

For the well-read Soviet reader of samizdat literature, Tolkien's negative image of *metal, wheels, engines* and *machines* will have a certain resonance with the anti-utopia of Evgenyj Zamyatin's novel *We*. It was translated into

English in 1924 and, therefore, predates even *The Hobbit*. Since, however, *We* was also a banned book in the Soviet Union, the number of Soviet readers that would make this association would be rather small, but for those who did make the association, the impact would be considerable. Now that *We* has been published in Russia in the post-Soviet period, the number of readers who make the association will grow.

Zamyatin's hero Д-503—names had been abolished as too individualistic—is a servant of knowledge (знание),[4] a mathematician building the rocket that will take the message of the One Government of the entire planet to other worlds. He lives in a "mechanized, perfect world," [5] "under the beneficent yoke of reason,," [6] where the people work "in a precise, mechanical rhythm," "like the levers of a single large machine." [7] His thoughts "click quietly, with mechanical precision." [8] Even Zamyatin's Big Brother figure, the Benefactor, is portrayed in metallic terms, and the movement of his (its) hand is described as "a slow cast-iron gesture." [9] "Everything new is made of steel: the sun of steel, the trees of steel, the people of steel." [10]

Zamyatin's "ultimate wisdom" (последняя мудрость) is based on the immutable and eternal four rules (правила [pravila]) of arithmetic.[11] As the novel closes, society finally succeeds in "perfecting" mankind by developing a way to purge human beings of their capacity to fantasize. Having had the new operation, the numbers of the One Government will be "perfect," "just like machines," [12] and can enjoy "mathematically infallible happiness." [13] Before he has his operation, however, Д-503 sees them for what they are: "'humans' that's not the word for it: they don't have legs, but some kind of heavy, forged wheels turned by an invisible drive; not humans, but rather some kind of humanoid tractor." [14] Tolkien's negative use of the words *metal, wheels, engines* and *machines* pales by comparison, but nevertheless the philosophy behind them is similar.

In his commentary accompanying the publication of *We* in a collection of anti-utopian novels published in the final days of the Communist era (1989)[15], Aleksej Zverev offers an encapsulation of the perception of the novel by a Russian reader from the Soviet era. The novel was entitled *We*, because "any sort of individuality is excluded in the One Government. The very possibility of becoming 'I' is suppressed; of standing out from the 'we' in some way or another. The only presence is the faceless, enthusiastic crowd, which easily submits to the iron will of the Benefactor. The cherished idea of Stalinism, that people are only 'little screws' in the gigantic mechanism of government, which is controlled by the firm hand of the engineer, has been brought to life by Zamyatin." [16] This commentary shows that, even though the novel was written in 1920, before Lenin's death, Stalin's impact on Soviet society was so great that, for many, Stalin is a fixed reference point against which they define their perception of similar events. For the youngest generation of readers, however, the effect is lessening.

The evil potential of knowledge is also a biblical theme. Hippolytus says that ignorance is a gift of God intended to keep each creature in its natural state, preventing a desire for anything unnatural.[17] This theme comes straight out of Genesis. Adam and Eve were cast out of the Garden of Eden after the serpent tempted Eve to eat the fruit of the tree of knowledge of good and evil. In the Russian Bible *the tree of knowledge of good and evil* is rendered as дерево познания добра и зла [derevo poznaniya dobra i zla]. (Бытие [Genesis] 2:9, 17) Eve saw that the fruit of the tree was not only pleasing to look at and good for food, but was also "desirable for gaining" knowledge [знание (znanie)]. (Бытие [Genesis] 3:6) The word used in both these Bible verses is the same one that most of the translators used as their translation of what the Elves were eager to gain: "knowledge." Bobyr', who did not replicate this segment, and Yakhnin were the exceptions. Yakhnin did not say anything about the Elven-Smiths' *eagerness for knowledge*.

For the Russian reader, the word *knowledge* (знание) will almost certainly trigger the association: *Knowledge is Strength* [Знание — сила], which is the title of a well-established—it has been published since 1926—popular monthly science magazine aimed at young people. This magazine title will be a major element in most Russian readers' understanding of the word *knowledge*, and it will most often be a positive one. This will make it hard for Russian readers to make Tolkien's distinction between *Knowledge* and *Wisdom*.

In Saruman's temptation of Gandalf, knowledge is one of the three goals that could be achieved if they were to join forces.

> We can bide our time, we can keep our thoughts in our hearts, deploring maybe evils done by the way, but approving the high and ultimate purpose: Knowledge, Rule, Order (F.340)

All the other translators—except M&K, Bobyr' and Yakhnin, who glossed it over—used знание [znanie] for *Knowledge* in the passage about Saruman's temptation of Gandalf. Both Bobyr' and Yakhnin ignored this segment. Bobyr' has her narrator summarize the tale in two paragraphs, leaving out the philosophical essence of the episode. (B.59-60) Yakhnin recasts the episode of the Temptation of Gandalf, replacing the offer of *Knowledge, Rule, Order* with a threat. Yakhnin's Saruman tells Gandalf that a New Force has appeared in the world. It is the Great Lord (Великий Властитель [Velikij Vlastitel']), and he cannot be overcome by Men, Elves, Dwarves, "much less the weak Hobbits." In order to save Middle-earth, they have to give him the All-powerful Ring, "otherwise the world will fall into Darkness and not one living creature will survive." (иначе мир погрузится во Тьму и не уцелеет ни одно живое существо) (Ya F.195) This is a much more chilling, direct description of the threat than Tolkien gives the reader at this point.

Yakhnin's Gandalf cuts right to the chase and asks if the Great Lord is Sauron. Saruman acknowledges this to be the case. Gandalf then rejects Saruman's offer by pointing out the illogic of his course of action to save the world. "But he is the Lord of Darkness and the Ruler of Shadow. How do you expect the power of Darkness to save the world from Shadow?" (Ya F.196) Yakhnin's Gandalf follows this with the logical question of whether Saruman has become one of Sauron's henchmen. Yakhnin's narrator provides the answer. Gandalf sees one of the Nine rings upon Saruman's finger. Yakhnin paints an exciting scene, but it lacks the philosophical subtleties of Tolkien's nuanced brush strokes. It is a cheap copy and not the museum-quality reproduction that a good translation should be.

M&K had two different versions of the three goals. Both are major deviations from Tolkien's text. In the first edition (1982), the goals of M&K's Saruman were "Wisdom, the General Welfare and Order." (Мудрость, Всеобщее Благоденствие и Порядок) (M&K, F_{1982}.191) The goals are as admirable as any that could be advanced for society. *Wisdom* is a laudable goal, and a prerequisite for civil society. *The General Welfare* is the basis of the Russian translation of the term *The Welfare State*: государство всеобщего благоденствия (gosudarstvo vseobshchego blagodenstviya). *Order* is a prerequisite for a functioning society. These are not, however, the goals of Tolkien's Saruman. He seeks "Knowledge, Rule and Order." Substituting *Wisdom* for *Knowledge* turns the whole Weltanschauung of the *LotR* on its head. For Tolkien, *Wisdom* is a positive trait, the province of the Istari and Eldar. *Knowledge* is a negative trait, the province of Saruman and Sauron. Eagerness for knowledge was the cause of the fall of the Elven-Smiths and the reason that Adam and Eve were cast out of Paradise. These goals could have been taken directly from Zamyatin's *We*. Zamyatin's *ultimate wisdom* was based on the immutable and eternal four rules of arithmetic (правила арифметики [pravila arifmetiki]). The noun in *the General Welfare* is based on the same root as the word for Zamyatin's Benefactor (Благодетель (Blagodetel']). *Order* is the result of mathematical perfection.

In M&K's second edition (1989) on the eve of the fall of Communism, the three achievements have changed. They are "Omniscience, Despotism and Order" (Всезнание, Самовластие и Порядок). (M&K, F_{1988}.320) This is Saruman's goal of "Knowledge, Rule and Order" taken to its extreme. Here the would-be wielder of the Ring clearly resembles the despotic Stalin, who knew it all and maintained order with an iron hand.

The Russian word Всезнание [Vseznanie] is not the most commonly used translation of *omniscience*. It is not even listed in the most popular desk-top Russian defining dictionary.[18] The more common translation is всеведение [vsevedenie]. Всезнание [Vseznanie] (literally: know-it-all-ness) has fallen into disuse because of the interference with the pejorative word *know-it-all* (Всезнайка [Vseznajka]), which is in the most common desk-top dictionary right where Всезнание [Vseznanie] should be. Any reader who bothers to look up Всезнание [Vseznanie] will immediately be reminded of this meaning, though most will not find it necessary to look it up in order to make the association. For the Soviet reader, in the context of despotism, the meaning of *know-it-all-ism* will come to the fore and together the two words will point disparagingly at Stalin, who was revered as the fount of all knowledge. This feature of Stalin's personality was immortalized in a song by Yuz Aleshkovskij, which began: "Comrade Stalin, you're a great academic (Товарищ Сталин! Вы — большой ученый [Tovarishch Stalin! Vy — bol'shoj uchenyj]). The image is evocative, and the formulation elegant. For the Soviet reader, the evil in M&K's second-edition three goals is ever so much more heinous than Tolkien's; ever so much more Soviet.

In a letter in 1943 to his son Christopher, who had been called up into the Royal Air Force, Tolkien said "the most improper job of any man [...] is bossing other men. Not one in a million is fit for it, and least of all those who seek the opportunity." (L.64) A view similar to Tolkien's condemnation of those who seek to take up the reins of power can be seen in a verse by the popular dissident Russian bard of the Soviet era, A. Galich, quoted in the modern reprint of Zamyatin's *We*.[19] In this verse, Galich warns the reader that there is no need to fear the plague, jail, contagion or hunger. All we have to fear, he says, is the one "Who says I know what must be done!"

The context of the sentence preceding the three goals is also very Soviet, and it is made all the more so by a subtle embellishment added by

M&K (**emphasis** added).

> О наших планах никто не узнает, нам нужно дождаться своего часа, и сначала мы будем даже осуждать жестокие методы Новой Силы, втайне одобряя ее конечную цель (M&K F_{1982}.191; F_{1988}.320)
> BT: No one will know of our plans, we have to bide our time, and in the beginning we will even condemn **the harsh methods of the New Force, secretly** approving of its ultimate goal.
> JRRT: We can bide our time, we can keep our thoughts in our hearts, deploring maybe evils done by the way, but approving the high and ultimate purpose (F.340)

With the addition of a few seemingly simple words, M&K manage to take the Soviet reader back in time to the period of the Russian Revolution and Civil War. Condemning the harsh methods of the New Force while secretly approving of its final goal recalls the polemical exchange between Karl Kautsky and Leon Trotsky in the early 1920s on the means that the new force in Russia—the Bolsheviks—was using to achieve the ultimate goal of Communism. Kautsky was the best-known socialist adversary of the Bolsheviks. He had personally known both Marx and Engels and was their principal literary executor. His influence on the socialist community was worldwide. Trotsky was then still one of the principle leaders of the new Russian government, which was spreading its power with sword raised high.

In the wake of the Russian Revolution there was widespread expectation that a wave of socialism would sweep the world. While the Russians had chosen revolution and terror as their methods, the bulk of the socialist movement in Western Europe wanted to reach its goals through the democratic parliamentary process. Trotsky was defending the new Soviet State's harsh methods against Kautsky's attack.[20] Trotsky rejected Kautsky's arguments with the assertion that "the State terror of a revolutionary class can be condemned 'morally' only by a man who, as a principle rejects (in words) every form of violence whatsoever—consequently, every war and every rising. For this, one has to be merely and simply a hypocritical Quaker."[21] Trotsky was not alone in his attack on Kautsky. Kautsky's international prominence called for bringing all guns to bear on him. One of Lenin's contributions to the fray was a speech at the IV Conference of Provincial Extraordinary Commissions [ЧК (Cheka)] on 6 February 1920 in which he said: "History has shown that it is impossible to achieve victory without revolutionary violence. Without revolutionary violence aimed at the direct enemies of the workers and peasants, it is impossible to break the resistance of these exploiters."[22] Bukharin voiced the opinion that: "Proletarian coercion in all its forms, beginning with shootings ... is a method of making communist man out of the human material of the capitalist epoch."[23] The most insightful distillation of all these arguments, however, is found in the editorial of the first issue of *The Red Sword* (Красный Меч), the organ of the Ukrainian Cheka "For us, the old foundations of morality and humanity, conceived by the bourgeoisie for the oppression and exploitation of the lower classes do not, nor can they exist."[24]

Robert Conquest conservatively estimates that in Lenin's Russia between 1919 and 1923 at least 200,000 people were shot in official executions and that at least another 300,000 died in prisons and the camps of maltreatment, hunger and disease.[25] The methods of the New Force were harsh indeed. When the sailors of Kronstadt rose against the new regime in March 1921, one of the complaints was that the new regime had "brought the workers, instead of freedom, an ever-present fear of being dragged into the torture chambers of the Cheka, which exceeds by many times in its horrors the gendarmerie administration of the Tsarist regime."[26]

Volkovskij echoes M&K's "New Force" with the no less suggestive "new order." (новый порядок [novyj poryadok]) (V F.360) His rendition of the three goals, however, bears a certain resemblance to G&G's.

The ambiguity of Tolkien's formulation of Saruman's three goals was hard for the translators to replicate in Russian. Their versions fell into two primary camps, based on the way that they dealt with the word *rule*. G&G's rendition of *Rule*—with four votes—represents the largest of the two camps. G&G were joined by Nemirova (N F.304) and Aleksandrova. Their version of the three goals is "Knowledge, Power, Order." (Знание, Власть, Порядок) (G&G F.309, G&G$_{2002}$ 416) Volkovskij provided the fourth vote for *Power*. (V F.360) The translation of *Rule* as *Power* focuses clearly on the meaning of *rule* in the Ring rhyme: One Ring to rule them all, where the context of the Ring Rhyme makes *rule* unambiguous. It presents the Russian reader with a maleficent resonance with the statement Tolkien made in a letter that: "'power' is an ominous and sinister word in all the tales, except when applied to the gods." (L.152) In an inducement to Gandalf to join forces, the word *Power* oversteps its mark and is not credible as a temptation. Since Saruman was well-known for the might of his words, they would have most likely been carefully chosen for best effect. *Power* is what he might have thought, but not what he would have said unambiguously. Tolkien's formulation—as can be seen from the split in the translators' renditions of the three goals—is quite suitably ambiguous.

The use of *Power* as the central goal of the three temptations is echoed in the translations of Sauron's name for the Ring: "the Ruling Ring." (F.340) Five of the translators called it the *All-powerful Ring*. (Кольцо Всевластья) (M&K F_{1982}.191, F_{1988}.320, VAM F.81, V F.360, N F.304, Ya F.195) Bobyr', K&K and Aleksandrova had a similar variant: the *Ring of Power*. (Кольцо Власти) (B.60, K&K F.389) This clearly tips the scales in favor of *Power* in Tolkien's balanced understatement about the Ring. In a country where the motto of the Communist Revolution of 1917—*All Power to the Soviets!* (Вся Власть Советамъ!)—was daily fare in the schools until the State that came to power under that slogan collapsed in the early 1990s, the term *All-powerful* has a forceful political ring to it. In Russian, the valence of the word *power* (власть) has lots of ties to the government, and is immediately politicized. The translators who used it were reflecting the Russian mental climate more than they were reflecting Tolkien. Only G&G and Gruzberg had politically neutral variants. G&G called it the *Great Ring*. (Великое Кольцо) (G&G F.310, $G\&G_{2002}$ 416) Gruzberg, faithful to the original as ever, called it the *Ruling Ring* (Правящее Кольцо).

The first two of Volkovskij's three goals are exactly the same as G&G's: "Knowledge, Power (Знание, Власть). His third goal, however, seems to be a throwback to M&K's first-edition list: "Wisdom, General Welfare and Order." (Мудрость, Всеобщее Благоденствие и Порядок) (M&K F_{-1982}.191) Volkovskij's Sauron tempts Gandalf with the possibility of achieving "Common Harmony" (Всеобщий Лад) (V F.360), which is suggestive of Zamyatin's anti-utopia where the numbers of the One Government work "in a precise, mechanical rhythm [...] with mechanical precision [...] just like machines," enjoying "mathematically infallible happiness."

Three of the translators took another tact with the word *rule*. In the context of *rule and order*, *rule* can also call to mind the *rule of law*, as in *law and order*. This usage is quite often found in religious texts—a context in which Tolkien is right at home—where *rule and order* appear together often enough to be considered a set phrase. This phrase can, for example, be found twice in a sermon by John Owen (1616-1683), in which he says: "Keep up church watch with diligence, and by the rule. When I say rule, I mean the life of it. I have no greater jealousy upon my heart, than that God should withdraw himself from his own institutions because of the sins of the people, and leave us only the carcass of outward rule and order. What doth

God give them for? for their own sakes? No; but that they may be clothing for faith and love, meekness of spirit and bowels of compassion, watchfulness and diligence. Take away these, and farewell to all outward rule and order, whatever they are." [27] It is likewise found in an essay by a contemporary of Tolkien's, G.K Chesterton (1874-1936). In his *Orthodoxy*, Chapter VI, "Paradoxes of Christianity," Chesterton says: "[With the coming of Christianity] we must be much more angry with theft than before, and yet much kinder to thieves than before. There was room for wrath and love to run wild. And the more I considered Christianity, the more I found that while it had established a rule and order, the chief aim of that order was to give room for good things to run wild." [28]

In her translation of Chesterton's *Orthodoxy*, N.L. Trauberg dealth with the problems of *rule and order ... order* effectively and efficiently by ignoring *rule* and leaving only *order* behind. Her version read: "And the more I looked at Christianity, the more I could clearly see: it established an order, but that order set all the virtues free." (И чем больше я присматривался к христианству, тем яснее видел: оно установило порядок, но порядок этот выпустил на волю все добродетели.)[29]

K&K, VAM and Gruzberg all approached the enticements that Saruman was offering from this point of view. K&K and VAM translated *Rule* as *Law* (statute) (Закон), as in *rule of law* (власть закона) (literally: power of the law). (K&K F.388, VAM F.296) Gruzberg chose *Law* (system of justice)—право [pravo]—as in *Law and Order* (правопорядок). While a statute is more literally a rule than is Gruzberg's choice, Gruzberg's choice is more appealing philosophically as a system under which to live. That would make it more appealing to Gandalf. The hard rule of law (statute) would be more in keeping with Saruman's liking.

Gruzberg's version is also more appealing linguistically, because it comes closest to replicating the ambiguity and repetition of Tolkien's original, in which the *Rule* of the three temptations ("Knowledge, Rule and Order") is echoed in "One Ring to rule them all," and in "the Ruling Ring." Gruzberg's translation of *Rule*—право [pravo]—is echoed nicely in his incantation: "One Ring to rule them all" (Одно Кольцо, чтобы править [pravit'] всеми ими) (Gruzberg-A), and in his rendition of "the Ruling Ring" (F.340) (Правящее Кольцо [Pravyashchee Kol'tso]). None of the other translators managed to replicate that feat. Later versions of Gruzberg changed the incantation, weakening the connection. In Gruzberg-C, the translation of *Rule* in the incantation is still based on the same root, but with a prefix that changes its meaning: "One Ring to manage them all" [Одно Кольцо, чтобы ими управлять (ypravlyat')].

Umanskij's restoration of this scene offers the reader an insightfully interesting, none-of-the-above rendition of the high and ultimate purpose with which Saruman tempts Gandalf: "Knowledge, Rule and Order." His Saruman tempts Gandalf with Knowledge, Principles and Order (Знание, Принципы, Порядок [Znanie, Printsipy, Poryadok]). (U F.382) In a sense, he sides with K&K, VAM and Gruzberg, in that principles are, in essence, the unwritten law by which an individual lives. As an inducement for Gandalf to join forces with him, it is powerfully seductive. It is not as harsh as the law (either the statute or the system of justice), because principles can be bent. At the same time, it is a very ambiguous term, because principles are so flexibly individual. Saruman's principles are clearly not Gandalf's. It is certainly a better translation of *Rule* than *Power* (власть [vlast']), and it has a certain attractive elegance about it, when compared to the legalistic translations, but Gruzberg's rendition of *Rule* as *Law* (system of justice)— право [pravo]—remains the best of the lot.

Notes:

1. Военный энциклопедический словарь, М: «Военное издательство», 1983, стр. 116.
2. СЭС, стр. 204.а.
3. For more on the Ribbentrop-Molotov Pact, see: George F. Kennan, *Russia and the West under Lenin and Stalin*, Boston: Brown, Little and Company, 1960; and: Richard C. Raack, *Stalin's Drive to the West, 1938-1945: The Origins of the Cold War*, Stanford, CA: Stanford University Press, 1995.
4. Евгений Замятин, *Мы*, в *Антиутопии XX века*, М: изд. «Книжная палата», 1989, стр. 33.
5. Zamyatin, p. 60.
6. Zamyatin, p. 14.
7. Zamyatin, p. 55.
8. Zamyatin, p. 71.
9. Zamyatin, p. 36.
10. Zamyatin, p. 37.
11. Zamyatin, p. 71.
12. Zamyatin, p. 103.
13. Zamyatin, p. 14.
14. Zamyatin, p. 108.

15. Антиутопии XX века, М: изд. «Книжная палата», 1989. Contains: *We*, *Brave New World* and *Animal Farm*.
16. Алексей Зверев, «Зеркала антиутопий», в Антиутопии XX века, М: изд. «Книжная палата», 1989, стр. 341.
17. *The Encyclopedia of Religion*, Mircea Eliade (ed.), New York: MacMillan, 1987, vol. 8, p. 346.
18. Ожегов/Шведова, стр. 104.
19. Quoted in Антиутопии XX века, М: изд. «Книжная палата», 1989, стр. 5.
20. Karl Kautsky, *Terrorism and Communism: A Contribution to the Natural History of Revolution*, translated by W.H. Kerridge, London: The National Labour Press, 1920; reprinted in 1973, Westport, CT: Hyperion Press.
21. Leon Trotsky, *Terror and Communism: A Reply to Karl Kautsky*, Ann Arbor, MI: University of Michigan Press, 1961; reprinted in 1986, Westport, CT: Greenwood Press, pp. 58-59.
22. В.И. Ленин, Полное собрание сочинений, изд. 5-ое, том 40 (декабрь 1919 - апрель 1920), М: Государственное издательство политической литературы, 1963, стр. 117.
23. Quoted in Сергей Петрович Мельгунов, Красный террор в России: 1918-1923, изд. 2-ое дополненное, Берлин, 1924, стр. 55.
24. Quoted in Мельгунов, стр. 70.
25. Robert Conquest, *The Human Cost of Soviet Communism*, Washington: Committee on the Judiciary, US Senate (91st Congress, 2nd Session), 1970, p. 11.
26. "Izvestia of the Provisional Revolutionary Committee of Sailors, Red Army Men and Workers of the Town of Kronstadt," 8 March 1921, Quoted in Conquest, p. 11.
27. "Perilous Times: II Timothy 3:1," http://www.sovereign-grace.com/357.htm.
28. Gilbert K. Chesterton, *Orthodoxy*, London: The Bodley Head, 1957, p. 158. This is the 18th printing. The first printing was in 1908.
29. Gilbert K. Chesterton, Вечный человек (перевод с англ. Н. Трауберг, Л. Сумм), М: Политиздат, 1991, стр. 427.

Chapter 7

One Day in the Life of Frodo Drogovich: Stalin and Yezhov in the Shire
:TOLKIEN:THROUGH:RUSSIAN:EYES:

> [Ivan Denisovich] Shukhov was perfectly content when he fell asleep. [...] A day had gone by unmarred by anything, almost a happy one.
> Aleksandr Solzhenitsyn,
> *One Day in the Life of Ivan Denisovich*

In their first annotation for Chapter 8 of Book 6 ("The Scouring of the Shire"), K&K note that the specialists unanimously agree that this chapter is a parody of socialism in the mold of such anti-utopias as George Orwell's *1984* and *Animal Farm*, and the description of the ant-like civilization in *The Once and Future King* by T. H. White. They also point out Tolkien's well-known, extremely negative opinion of this political system, citing his letter to Christopher (L.64) in November 1943. "Tolkien," they say, "never had any doubts as to the true face of the socialist utopia, which Lotho Sackville-Baggins tries to introduce into the Shire." (K&K R.647)

The parallels between this chapter and Soviet society are readily apparent to any student of Soviet history. That does not, however, include many modern-day Russian readers, who reacted aggressively to suggestions that this chapter was really about Stalin. In the Soviet period, this chapter alone would have been enough to put *LotR* on the censors' list of banned books. It was undoubtedly part of the reason that volume three was not finally officially published until 1992—after the fall of Communism in Russia—ten years after the first official publication of *The Fellowship of the Ring*.

Murav'ev, who translated *The Return of the King* without Kistyakovskij, did not make things any easier for the censors with his rendition of this chapter, which is filled with loaded words from the Soviet era. His rendition of the passage in which the leader of the Shirriffs tells Frodo to come along quietly is overflowing with these words in a heavily stylized parody of the jargon of secret police arrests and the show trials of the mid-1930s.

> Сударь, сударь, одумайтесь. Согласно личному приказу Генералиссимуса вы обязаны немедля и без малейшего сопротивления проследовать под нашим конвоем в Приречье, где будете сданы с рук на руки охранцам. Когда Генералиссимус вынесет приговор по вашему делу, тогда и вам, может быть, дадут слово. И если вы не хотите провести остаток жизни в Исправнорах, то мой вам совет — прикусите языки. (M R. 314-315)
> BT (**Emphasis** added): Sir, sir, bethink yourself. In accordance with the **Generalissimo**'s personal orders you are required, immediately and without the least resistance, to proceed under our **armed escort** to Bywater, where you will be handed over to the **secret police**. When the **Generalissimo** pronounces sentence in your case, then they may give you a chance to speak. And if you do not want to spend the rest of your life in the **Correctional-Labor Burrows**, then my advice to you is: bite your tongues.

Tolkien's version, in comparison, makes nowhere near as forceful an impact on the Soviet reader. It is, as always, the epitome of British understatement.

> There now, Mister, that'll do. It's the Chief's orders that you're to come along quiet. We're going to take you to Bywater and hand you over to the Chief's Men; and when he deals with your case you can have your say. But if you don't want to stay in the Lockholes any longer than you need, I should cut the say short, if I was you. (R.346)

Murav'ev's imitation of a Russian policeman making an arrest is an elegant equal to Tolkien's replication of an English bobby in the performance of his duty. Both are the stuff of stage, screen and literature. The reader could identify the speaker as a policeman simply from the flow of the words, even if the speaker was not identified in the text.

The loaded words in Murav'ev's version, however, give this passage a more sinister, specifically Soviet context. The first loaded word in the passage is *Generalissimo* (Генералиссимус). There was only one Generalissimo in the Soviet Union and that was Stalin. The article in the 1952 edition of *The Great Soviet Encyclopedia* entitled "Generalissimo of the Soviet Union" is 4 columns long and includes a full-page portrait of Stalin.[1] The article leaves no doubt that if you have seen one Soviet Generalissimo, you have seen them all. Almost every Soviet reader would immediately substitute Stalin for *Generalissimo* and the sentence would be perceived as: "In accordance with Stalin's personal order [...]."

Volkovskij took a small step back from the edge of the political cliff that Murav'ev had taken his text up to. He uses the term *Commander-in-chief* (Главнокомандующий [Glavnokomanduyushchij]) (V R.490) where Murav'ev had used *Generalissimo*. During World War II, Stalin was the Supreme Commander-in-chief of all the Commanders-in-chief on the General Staff. This is roughly equivalent to the relationship that exists between the President and the Chiefs of staff in the USA. This gives the text a clearly martial air, as do many of Volkovskij's formulations. Volkovskij's formulation hints at Stalin. Murav'ev's formulation is about as subtle as a brick through a window.

Tolkien's word for this position title was simply *Chief*. The other translators all found suitable, alternate renditions for it. K&K used the most common translation for *Chief*: Начальник [Nachal'nik]. (K&K R.385) While there are some associations with the Soviet period for this word, they are not strong enough to impose a strictly Soviet context on this passage. G&G selected an archaic word for *Leader* (Предводитель [Predvoditel'] G&G R.306, G&G$_{2002}$ 1000), the same one that Bobyr' had used. (B.483) This word is completely free of Soviet baggage for the Soviet reader. Umanskij, who fully restored this chapter in his edition of Bobyr's condensed translation, used the word *Ruler* (Правитель [Pravitel']), which, likewise, has few preexisting associations. (U R.835) VAM gracefully sidestepped the problem with the word Шеф [Shef] (VAM R.315), which has its origins in the French word for *chief*: *chef*. It too is essentially free of any overwhelmingly Soviet context. Gruzberg avoided any possible Soviet contamination altogether by using a word with an entirely foreign valence: *Sheriff* (Шериф). This is not just a transliteration, but a word listed in the *Russian Encyclopedic Dictionary*, which categorizes it as a loan word from English.[2] This keeps Tolkien's tale an English story by an English writer, and does not rearrange the furniture to make it seem more Russian. Aleksandrova changed Gruzberg's *Sheriff* to *Head* (Голова [Golova]), i.e. a person in charge of something. In this meaning, it is a word out of the pre-Soviet past. The dictionary marks this meaning as only being in use prior to the Revolution in 1917.[3] Nemirova decided that the *Chief* should be a *Governor* (Губернатор [Gubernator]), another word with foreign and pre-1917 associations. She did place it in quotes, however, to distance it from its original meaning. (N R.281) Yakhnin has an imaginative title that sounds like it just fell out of one of the Latin annals. His rendition of *Chief* is *His Supremeness the Capitanus Hobbitanus* (его главенство Капитанус Хоббитанус [ego glavenstvo Kapitanus Khobbitanus]). (Ya R.287) With so much clear choice from among a number of more-or-less neutral renditions of *Chief*, Murav'ev's decision to use *Generalissimo* was obviously made for its effect on the Soviet reader.

For those who might have missed the implication of *Generalissimo* as the translation for *Chief*, Murav'ev followed Tolkien's shift to a new sobriquet for *the Chief* a few pages later with another loaded word in the same vein. In the episode that sees the first casualties of the Rebellion fall, the leader of the ruffians who have come to restore order, says: "The Boss is losing his temper." (R.358) Murav'ev renders the word *Boss* with Вождь [Vozhd'] (M R.326), which is the other more commonly recognized sobriquet for Stalin. He was only appointed Generalissimo in 1945. Edvard Radzinsky used *Boss* throughout his book[4] to refer to Stalin. In Russian émigré circles, it was often pointed out with great delight that Вождь [Vozhd'] is the literal Russian translation of *der Führer*, the sobriquet in German for Hitler.

Вождь [Vozhd'] is so loaded in the context of this chapter that none of the other translators dared use it here. VAM rendered *Boss* as Шеф [Shef] (VAM R.327), using the same word she had used for *Chief*, a faux pas that Tolkien would never have approved of. As a philologist, his meticulous attention to word choice meant that if he used two different words, the translation should have two different words as well. K&K's version of *Boss* was also Шеф [Shef] (K&K R.398), which fits well as the second element of their *Chief/Boss* pair: Начальник [Nachal'nik]/Шеф [Shef]. G&G avoided the problem in typical fashion by omitting the phrase with the second sobriquet in it. (G&G R.317, G&G$_{2002}$ 1007) Volkovskij and Yakhnin kept them company. (V R.510, Ya R.298-9) Gruzberg, in keeping with his goal of not russifying the story, used another English loanword; the kind that, when I was learning Russian, all the students—very much with tongue in cheek—used to call 'an old Russian word.' His rendition was Босс [Boss]. It perfectly matches the other half of his *Chief/Boss* pair: Sherif (Шериф). Aleksandrova thought better of this and changed the second element of the pair to *Master* (Хозяин [Khozyain]), the same word that Umanskij had used. (U R.843)

This matches the tone of her pre-Soviet use of *Head*. In that time frame, the Master was the owner of a plantation or estate. Her choice, however, is unfortunate for a number of reasons. In the context of Tolkien, *master* is used to refer to Tom Bombadil and to Frodo in his role as Sam's master. Tolkien would never have approved of a single word doing double duty like this. In the Soviet context, Stalin's close associates referred to him as Хозяин [Khozyain]. That reinserts the kind of political nuance that Gruzberg clearly wished to avoid. Nemirova matched her use of *Governor* with начальство [nachal'stvo], which, while normally a collective noun (*the higher-ups*), is used colloquially in the meaning of *boss*.

The next loaded word in Murav'ev's version of the arrest passage was конвой [konvoj] in the phrase "to proceed under our armed escort" (проследовать под нашим конвоем). While конвой [konvoj] indeed shares the meaning of the English word *convoy*, in the sense of the naval convoys of World War II, "under armed escort" (под конвоем) is the way that prisoners were taken to the Gulag. This phrase stands out in the description of how the NKVD used sleep deprivation as an interrogation tactic in Soviet prisons that was given by Nadezhda Mandel'shtam—the wife of the repressed writer Osip Mandel'shtam—in her memoirs.[5] The dictionary examples for *armed escort* (конвоир) and *to escort under arms* (конвоировать) both have to do with prisoners.[6] The *Military Encyclopedic Dictionary* further specifies that escort duties under arms are performed by special militarized units of the Ministry of the Interior (МВД), the mission of which is to provide armed escort to prisoners of war (военнопленные) as well as to detainees under investigation and on trial or convicts (находящиеся под следствием и судом или осужденные).[7] For the Soviet reader the inclusion of the word *armed escort* (конвой) evokes a much more somber image than does Tolkien's ersatz Bobby asking Frodo to "come along quietly."

The other translators' renditions of the phrase about how they would be taken to Bywater were much more commonplace. Gruzberg's variant was the most literal interpretation of the original, making no effort to emulate the speech style of a Soviet policeman. His policeman told Frodo: "The Sheriff has ordered that you conduct yourself calmly. We will take you to Bywater" (Шериф приказал, чтобы вы вели себя спокойно. Мы отведем вас в Байуотер). Gruzberg's approach keeps it a foreign story, and avoids loading it down with any Soviet psychological baggage that the reader might have. Even his treatment of the place name *Bywater* is a transliteration and not a translation: Байуотер [Bajuoter]. This transliteration captures the sound quality of the name rather than its spelling. Aleksandrova made some stylistic changes and converted Байуотер [Bajuoter] into Приречье [Prirech'e], which won the majority vote for this name among the translators.

K&K's and VAM's fictitious policeman asked Frodo "to follow us" (следовать за нами). (K&K R.385; VAM R.315) Volkovskij's ersatz policeman said that he had been ordered to "deliver" (доставить) Frodo to Bywater "without any excessive fuss" (без лишнего шума). (V R.490) Nemirova's stage policeman said "follow us without resistance" (последовать за нами без сопротивления!).(N R.281) G&G glossed over the whole question of "come along quietly" in typical fashion by leaving it out of their version.

> По приказу Предводителя я должен передать вас его людям в Уводье. (G&G R.306, G&G$_{2002}$ 1000)
> BT: By order of the Leader I am supposed to turn you over to his people in Bywater.
> JRRT (**lacunae** highlighted): It's the Chief's orders **that you're to come along quiet. We're going to take you** to Bywater and hand you over to the Chief's Men [...]

Bobyr' condensed the whole scene out of existence, but Umanskij restored it without any markedly Soviet overtones. His imitation policeman said:

> Есть приказ Правителя, чтобы вы вели себя тихо. Нас послали препроводить вас в Байуотер и передать Людям Правителя. (U R.835)
> BT: The Ruler has ordered that you are to conduct yourselves peacefully. They sent us to escort you to Bywater and turn you over to the Ruler's People.

Yakhnin turns the arresting officers into a bunch of cowed clowns. When Yakhnin's arresting officer has read his official speech, the narrator tells the reader that the officer noticed Frodo reaching for his sword (something very much out of character for Tolkien's Frodo). Yakhnin's sham policeman is immediately taken aback, and begins hemming and hawing that they are only carrying out orders. (Ya R.287) This kind of police force is no threat at all, and Frodo and company have a good laugh at their expense.

The defense of 'I was just carrying out orders' proved unsuccessful at the Nuremberg trials, and instilled a sense of personal responsibility into soldiers and policemen everywhere. Personal responsibility and freedom of choice are at the heart of Tolkien's philosophy, and the response of Yakhnin's arresting officer is a slap in the face for Tolkien's Weltanschauung. Tolkien highlights Bilbo's and Frodo's freedom of choice in "The Quest of Erebor," where he has Frodo say that either he or Bilbo might have refused to do what they did, and that Gandalf "could not compel" them. He was not even permitted to try to do so. (AH_{2002}.370)

While Gandalf was not permitted to compel them, the forces of Darkness has no such limitation. Tolkien recognizes that in his justification for the participation of Robin Smallburrow in the activities of the Sherriffs. Robin's participation is coerced. If any of the Hobbits stand up for their rights in recognition of their personal responsibility, they are dragged off to jail by the Chief's Men or beaten. (R.347) The philosophical gap between the excuse given by Yakhnin's arresting officer and the justification given for Robin Smallburrow is as wide as the Grand Canyon. Yakhnin omitted Smallburrow's justification, which in the political climate of the USSR would have had an explosive impact on Soviet readers, because Robin's situation would have been uncomfortably familiar to them. Yakhnin's excuse would have caused the Soviet censor little concern, because it pointed clearly at the Nazis as the prototype for the bad guys, and not at the Soviets. Though his retelling was published in the post-Soviet period, in some ways Yakhnin's version is nevertheless very Soviet indeed.

The answer to the question of whom Frodo and company would be turned over to in Bywater was the third loaded word in Murav'ev's version of this passage. According to Murav'ev, Bywater was where they would be turned over to the охранцы [okhrantsy] (M R.314), a reference to the Tsarist secret police, the Okhranka. For the Soviet reader, the jump from one brand of secret police—Tsarist or not—to another—the NKVD, KGB—would be almost instinctive. In Tolkien's original, Frodo and company were to be turned over to "the Chief's Men." (R.346) Needless to say, the other translators had much more neutral renditions of "the Chief's Men." With this third loaded keyword, Murav'ev set the stage for the "show trial" to follow. For the Soviet reader of Murav'ev's version, it is clear that Frodo and company are being arrested on the Generalissimo's (read: Stalin's) orders, and will be taken under armed guard to Bywater, where they will be handed over to the okhrantsy (read: NKVD - predecessor to the KGB) for the pre-trial extraction of confessions that can be used at the show trial to follow.

The fact that Murav'ev had a show trial in mind is clear from his description of the trial. At the trial in Murav'ev's version, Frodo will not be given a chance to speak in his own defense until after sentence has been pronounced. In his book on the Show Trials, Joel Carmichael says "in the great bulk of cases there was never any question of a defense at all."[8]

> Когда Генералиссимус вынесет приговор по вашему делу, тогда и вам, может быть, дадут слово. (M R.314-315)
> BT: When the Generalissimo pronounces sentence in your case, then they may give you a chance to speak.

Murav'ev's version is exactly what Nadezhda Mandel'shtam talked about in her memoirs.[9] The verdict was predetermined, she said. Many trials followed prepared scripts which included a predetermined verdict.[10] The trial in Tolkien's version, on the other hand, is a reflection of the English court system. The accused can speak in his own defense during the proceedings. "[W]hen he [the Chief] deals with your case you can have your say," advises Tolkien's arresting officer. (R.346) Nevertheless, a guilty verdict seems assured in Tolkien's version as well, judging from the advice of the Shirriff-Leader: "But if you don't want to stay in the Lockholes any longer than you need, I should cut the say short, if I was you." (R.346)

The length of the sentence and the place that it will be served are, of course, both touchstones of Soviet reality in Murav'ev's version. In their rendition, the *Lockholes* became the "Correctional-Labor Burrows" (Исправноры), a made-up word composed of the abbreviation for correctional-labor: исправ [isprav]. Using the abbreviated instead of the full form of the word gives the *Correctional-Labor Burrows* (Исправноры) a wonderfully malevolent taste of bureaucratic alphabet soup, which is a very subtle, but deftly added touch in defining the character of the leader of the Shirriffs. In its full form—исправительно-трудовой [ispravitel'no-trudovoj]—the adjective is only used as a part of the official names of prisons. The only example in the Russian defining dictionary is "Correctional-Labor Camp" (исправительно-трудовая колония),[11] an island in the Gulag archipelago.

The length of the prison sentence that Frodo faces in Tolkien's version is indeterminate: "not any longer than you need." It nonetheless suggests an eventual release from prison. Tolkien hints that it might be as little as a year in the episode that sees the first casualties of the Rebellion fall, when he has the leader of the ruffians who have come to restore order, say: "Or we'll take fifty of you to the Lockholes for a year." (R.358) Murav'ev's Shirriff-Leader is much more specific and much more Soviet in his advice about how long Frodo might go to the Correctional-Labor Burrows: "the rest of your life" (остаток жизни). (M R.315) In Murav'ev's version of the threat to put fifty Hobbits in the Lockholes for a year, "for a year" disappeared and the Hobbits turned into "hostages" (заложники): "or we'll immediately take fifty hostages to the Correctional-Labor Burrows." (а то заберем сразу полсотни заложников в Исправноры) (M R.326)

Murav'ev's slight change again takes the Soviet reader back to the period of the Russian Revolution and Civil War. Hostage taking was a common method of repression in the young Soviet State. Sergej Mel'gunov devotes a whole chapter to it in his book *The Red Terror*.[12] The chapter chronicles case after case in which hostages were shot by the Soviets as a reprisal: 500 shot in Saint Petersburg, 400 shot in Kronshtadt, more than 300 shot in Moscow, 59 in Pyatigorsk, and so on.

Yakhnin avoided this problem by leaving this segment out. (Ya R.298-99) All the other translators, in various formulations, were true to Tolkien's original vision.

Tolkien specifies a year in the Lockholes, but in the Soviet Union, for many, being sentenced to the camps was tantamount to a sentence of death. Robert Conquest estimates that not more than 10% of those in the camps during the Great Terror survived.[13] In an effort to mask the scope of the executions, rather than announce that an individual had been shot, the Soviets euphemistically said that the accused had been sentenced to "10 years without the right of correspondence."[14] Those people never made it to the camps.

Little more than a page after the passage in which Frodo and company are arrested, Tolkien has Shirriff Smallburrow explain to Sam why the Hobbits are not doing more to oppose the Chief and his policies. Tolkien's text is an understated indictment of the police state. Murav'ev's version continues to drop heavily weighted words, suggestive of the period of Stalinist terror on the Soviet reader.

> Повсюду эти Большие начальники, громилы Генералиссимуса. Чуть кто из нас заартачится — его сразу волокут в Исправноры. Первого взяли старину Пончика, Вила Туполапа, голову нашего, а за ним уж и не сочтешь, тем более с конца сентября сажают пачками. Теперь еще и бьют смертным боем. (M R.316)
> BT: These Big bosses, thugs of the Generalissimo's, are everywhere. One of us only has to begin to dissent, and they drag him off to the Correctional-Labor Burrows straight away. The first one they took was old Doughnut, Will Bluntpaw, our mayor, after him there's no counting them, especially since the end of September they've been

jailing them in droves. Now they are even beating them with deadly blows.

JRRT: But it's these Men, Sam, the Chief's Men. He sends them round everywhere, and if any of us small folk stand up for our rights, they drag him off to the Lockholes. They took old Flourdumpling, old Will Whitfoot the Mayor, first and they've taken a lot more. Lately it's been getting worse. Often they beat 'em now. (R.347)

While Tolkien only said (**emphasis** added): "**Lately** it's been getting worse. Often they beat 'em **now**" (R.347), Murav'ev added a time specification for when the Chief's men began beating the prisoners in the Lockholes: "the end of September" (с конца сентября). This embellishment immediately attracts the attention of those reading the Russian and the English texts in parallel. When "the end of September" is viewed in the context of "the Big bosses (Большие начальники), the thugs (громилы) of the Generalissimo" (i.e., Stalin's men), "jailing them in droves" (сажают пачками) together with the additional embellishment of "beating them with deadly blows" (бьют смертным боем), the Soviet reader is prompted to recall that Yezhov[15] was appointed People's Commissar in charge of the People's Commissariat for Internal Affairs (NKVD) on the authority of a telegram from Stalin to the Politburo dated 25 September 1936.[16] The date was widely known from Khrushchev's "Secret Speech" at the XX Party Congress in 1956, when he began the process of destalinization.

Murav'ev's embellishment of the passage, specifying when things changed in the Lockholes, fits neatly into Tolkien's chronology. The time frame is Tolkien's, but Tolkien does not tell the reader when Sharky came to the Shire until much later in the story, in the conversation between Merry and farmer Cotton. (R.361) Murav'ev's move of the information about the date of Sharky's arrival forward in the text makes Saruman into Yezhov. The attributes all fit. The period that Yezhov headed the NKVD (1936-1938) was the high tide of Stalinist terror and is named after him. It is known as the Ежовщина [Yezhovshchina].

Commissar in charge of the NKVD is a position that was considered one of the "Big bosses" in Stalin's Soviet Union, and Yezhov's appointment was accompanied by the unrestricted right for the NKVD to use any means, including beatings and torture, in investigations of "enemies of the people."[17] Hand-written comments like "beat again and again!" were made by Politburo members in the margins of NKVD lists of individuals under 'investigation.'[18]

Nadezhda Mandel'shtam comments on the difference in the types of people working as NKVD interrogators before and after 1937.[19] Before 1937, the interrogators were well-read and intelligent, ideologically motivated; the avant-garde of the "new people," convinced that what they were doing was helping to build the new Soviet State. After 1937, they were replaced by a new type of interrogator of a completely different physical type, who had no ideological motivation, new or otherwise. The methods changed, too. Before 1937, the NKVD had been proud of its psychological methods of torture. After 1937, they began to use primitive, physical methods like beatings.[20] They were only concerned with meeting their quota of confessions. In a word: thugs.

During the *Yezhovshchina*, people were almost literally jailed in droves. The number of political arrests in 1937 was ten times the number in 1936.[21] Robert Conquest estimates the number of arrests between 1937 and 1938 at between 7 and 8 million.[22] That is 4.5 to 5% of the population.[23] The Party cadre, however, were especially hard hit. Of the 1,966 delegates to the XVII Party Congress in 1934, 1,108—56%—were arrested as "enemies of the people." [24]

Stalin invented the term "enemy of the people" (враг народа),[25] and it is inseparably entwined with the period of Stalinist terror. Murav'ev even managed to work in a hint of this term in his rendition of the conversation between Farmer Cotton and Frodo about the situation in the Shire. In Tolkien's version, Farmer Cotton says: "if anyone got 'uppish' as they [the powers that be] called it, they [the ones who got 'uppish'] followed Will," the Mayor, to the Lockholes. (R.360) Murav'ev's Farmer Cotton says: "if anyone, as they put it, 'exhibited hostility' [literally: enemy-ness], he quickly ended up where Will Bluntpaw was." (если же кто, говоря по-ихнему, «проявлял враждебность», тот живо оказывался, где и Вил Туполап) (М R.329) In the context of political repression, Murav'ev's wink will be as good as a nod to the Soviet reader.

Umanskij was the only other translator to keep Murav'ev company in politicizing this line. His version of *'uppish'* was "to stand up for out rights." (вступаться за наши права) (U R.836) The other translators—less Yakhnin and Bobyr' who omitted this line—all had much less pointed versions of *'uppish.'* Gruzberg's rendition had the best feel about it because the verb he chose contained an element that means "high." His version reads: "became 'haughty'" (literally: high-measured) (становился «высокомерным»). Aleksandrova did not like that and changed it to "started sticking their nose out" (задирать нос). Nemirova's formulation was a close second. It reads: "And those who dared to be impertinent" (А кто осмеливался дерзить). (N R.295) G&G had a serviceable rendition, which read: "began to think too much of himself." (начинал «воображать о себе») (G&G R.319, G&G$_{2002}$ 1009) K&K hedged their bets by using two colloquial verbs to better define the concept of 'uppishness' to the Russian reader. Their version reads: "began 'to get too proud' or 'to stick out'" (начал [...] «заноситься» или «высовываться»). (K&K R.401) Volkovskij was quite reserved in his formulation. He said: "spoke up" (голос подать). (V R.493) VAM was the closest to Murav'ev with her "exhibited 'disobedience'." (проявлял [...] «непослушание») (VAM R.329) None of them, however, comes close to the impact of Murav'ev's "exhibited hostility" («проявлял враждебность») on the Soviet reader.

In general, the other translators all kept more to Tolkien's general understated condemnation of the police state, rather than trying to make it more specifically Soviet. There were, however, a number of interesting interpretations of "the Chief's Men," which is paired with "us small folk" (R.347) to create an us-them opposition, echoing the opposition of "large stupid folk like you and me" (H.16) and "the Halflings." (R.510) Umanskij's rendition of the opposition is the best. It faces "people" (люди) off against "us, the small folk" (нас, малый народ). (U R.836) Gruzberg had a wonderfully evocative rendition that set "people" (люди) against "us small Hobbits" (нас, маленьких хоббитов). Aleksandrova spoils the effect by changing Gruzberg's *small Hobbits* to *plain Hobbits* (простые [prostye]). K&K's version—"the Big (folk)" (Большие) vs. "a Hobbit" (хоббит) (K&K R.386)—is less successful because it gives up both the words *us* and *small* and uses a singular instead of a plural in the second half. VAM has two versions of the opposition. In the first edition it is: *behemoths* (громадины) and *not-tall-lings* (невысоклики). (VAM R$_{1991}$.316) In her second edition (2003), she changed both elements of the opposition so that it became: *huge-lings* (огромины) and a more literal *halflings* (полуростики). (VAM R$_{2003}$.1157) The second version has a much better ring to it. G&G skirt the problem of creating an opposition by making the second half of it general instead of specific. Their rendition is (**emphasis** added):

[...] вся беда в Людях, в Людях Предводителя. Они всюду шныряют, и чуть только кто-нибудь против, сразу хватают. (G&G R.307)
BT: the whole problem is with the **People**, the Leader's **People**. They

are darting around everywhere, and just as soon as **someone** is against, they grab [them] immediately.

Volkovskij and Nemirova take the same tact as G&G for the second half of the pair. Volkovskij's rendition of the first half, however, was quite good. He resurrected an archaic word and redefined it with an apposition: "people, the Commander-in-chief's big'uns" (в людях, в большунах Главнокомандующего). (V R.493) Nemirova used the same word that VAM used in her first-edition (1991) version: *behemoths* (громадины). (N R.283)

Gruzberg's typically accurate rendition is marred by a shift in the last sentence of the passage. He concludes with: "They [the Chief's Men] often beat us up" (Они нас часто избивают), while Tolkien said: "Often they beat 'em [the prisoners] now." (R.347) Gruzberg's slip of the typewriter shifts the physical terror of beatings from the prisoners to the general population, which is a major shift toward the extreme in the policy range of the police state of the Shire in the year 3019 (S.R. 1419). Volkovskij joins him in making the same assumption. "If things ain't their way, they beat immediately." (Как что не по ихнему, сразу бьют) (V R.493) Aleksandrova put Gruzberg's text back into Tolkien's perspective.

There is some context that could support Gruzberg's view of the general populace as the target of the beatings later in the chapter, in the episode in which Merry confronts the ruffians in Bywater. The leader of the ruffians foolishly decides to try to fight his way out of the trap and yells to his men to attack the Hobbits. 'At 'em, lads!' he cried. 'Let 'em have it!' (R.358)

Volkovskij's version—as well as most of his dialog in this chapter—is full of slang that would feel at home in an infantry army barracks. His leader of the ruffians says:

— За мной, ребята! — скомандовал он. — Вмажем мелюзге по соплям! (V R.511)

BT: "Follow me, guys!" he commanded. "We'll bust the little creeps to snot!"

"Follow me!" is the motto of the infantry and is a line spoken on stage and screen as the troops go over the top to attack the enemy. The addition of "he commanded" cements its place in military jargon, and the following slang phrase adds an excellent touch of local color. Unfortunately, his Hobbits sound only slightly better.

All the other translators—except G&G, Umanskij and Yakhnin—use "Beat them" (Бей их) either for "At 'em" or for "Let 'em have it" in the ruffian's lines. (M R.327; K&K R.399; VAM R.328; N R.294; Ya R.299) Murav'ev uses it for both phrases and embellishes the repeat so that it reads:

— Бей их, ребята! — крикнул он. — Бей насмерть! (M R.327)
BT: "Beat them, guys!," he yelled. "Beat [them] to death!"

This embellishment cleverly reinforces the context of the Yezhovshchina of the late 1930s, very much in the same way that Tolkien himself carefully layered his information with studied repeats to give his images more depth. While it is a good imitation of Tolkien's style, the message is Murav'ev's, and it is delivered much more directly than Tolkien's euphemistic "At 'em!" and "Let 'em have it!". VAM's version was very close to Murav'ev's, but with a slightly less lethal outcome. Her rendition reads:

— Бей их, ребята! — зарычал он. — Никого не щадить!
(VAM R.328)
BT: "Beat them, guys!," he roared. "Don't spare anyone!"

Yezhov's NKVD did not spare anyone. It simply ran out of room in the prisons and the camps to process all the detainees. Nemirova followed VAM's lead. Her chief ruffian said: "Beat [them], show no pity!" (Бей, не жалей!). (N R.294)

Tolkien's version of events in the police state of the Shire in the year 3019 (S.R. 1419) reflects an apologist view of Stalin that was held by many both in the West and in the Soviet Union. In a conversation between Frodo and Pippin, Frodo defends Lotho—Murav'ev's *Generalissimo* (Генералиссимус) and Вождь [Vozhd']—because:

> Lotho never meant things to come to this pass. He has been a wicked fool, but he's caught now. The ruffians are on top, gathering, robbing and bullying, and running or ruining things as they like, in his name. And not in his name even for much longer. He's a prisoner in Bag End now, I expect, and very frightened. We ought to try and rescue him. (R.352)

In the Soviet Union it was widely believed that Stalin was the prisoner of the system that he had created. Ilya Ehrenburg, a well-known Soviet writer, said: "We thought (probably because we wanted to think so) that Stalin did not know about the senseless reprisals against the Communists and the Soviet intellectuals. [...] Yes, not only I, but very many others thought that the evil came from the small man they called 'the Stalinist People's Commissar.'" [26] This belief was so widely held that Khrushchev felt compelled to address it in his "Secret Speech" in 1956. "No, it would be naive to think that this was done by Yezhov alone. It is completely clear that Stalin decided in these matters, and that without his orders and approval, Yezhov could not have done this." [27]

Murav'ev's rather literal rendition of this passage stands out against the background of the widespread creative license he took with the translation of other parts of this chapter. The accuracy of his translation of this segment, when he did not hesitate to make changes to the original at other places in this chapter, shows that he recognized Tolkien's description of the apologist theory of Stalinism as an essential part of the history of the Soviet Union that he was writing with his changes and embellishments to the chapter, and considered it accurate enough to leave it unaltered. His earlier changes to the text show that he would not have hesitated to adapt it to his own ends, if he had felt it necessary.

> Лотто не только не виновник, он даже не зачинщик всего этого безобразия. Ну, дурак он, конечно, злобный дурак, в том его и беда. А подручные взяли верх: они и отбирают, и грабят, и бесчинствуют его именем. Он заключенный, узник в Торбе-на-Круче. И наверно, перепуган до смерти. Хорошо бы его все-таки вызволить. (M R.321)
>
> BT: Lotho is not only not the culprit, he is not even the instigator of this whole mess. Well, he is a fool, of course, a wicked fool, and that is his trouble. It's the subordinates who have taken over: they are confiscating, stealing and committing excesses in his name. He is a prisoner, a captive in Bag End. And probably scared to death. It would be good to set him free all the same.

By this point in the story, the Soviet reader of Murav'ev's version of the chapter is reading *Lotho* as Stalin and *subordinates* as Yezhov and company. The main difference between Murav'ev's version and Tolkien's original is the omission of the phrase: "And not in his name even for much longer." While this is a repeat of earlier references to removing Lotho, there is no reason to remove it from the passage. Repeats are an integral part of

Tolkien's style, adding depth to the story. The suppression of a repeat only serves to make the story shallower.

Frodo, however, is not able to rescue Lotho because Wormtongue—Saruman's henchman—had already killed him, and, Tolkien hints, eaten him. Again Murav'ev follows Tolkien closely. His version reads:

> Саруман: Это он, Гниль, прикончил вашего Генералиссимуса, вашего разлюбезненького Вождя. Что, Гниль, неправда? Правда! Заколол его, я так думаю, во сне. А потом закопал, хотя вряд ли: Гниль у нас всегда такой голодненький. (M R.338-339)
>
> BT: Saruman: It was Worm who finished off your Generalissimo, your dear little Вождь [Vozhd']. Isn't that right, Worm? Yes! Stabbed him in his sleep, I believe. And then buried him, although probably not; our Worm is always so hungry.

With the exception of the titles (Chief/Boss:Generalissimo/Вождь [Vozhd']), the differences with Tolkien's original are little more than stylistic.

> Saruman: Worm killed your Chief, poor little fellow, your nice little Boss. Didn't you, Worm? Stabbed him in his sleep, I believe. Buried him, I hope; though Worm has been very hungry lately. [...] (R.370)

In real life, the story played out another way in the Soviet Union. Yezhov, like Mandel'shtam's pre-1937 interrogator, fell victim to the system he had perfected. Stalin had Yezhov removed on 8 December 1938. Yezhov was only finally shot on 4 February 1940. Stalin's death on 5 March 1953, however, is as much, if not more, of a riddle wrapped in a mystery inside an enigma as any that Churchill[28] had to deal with. There are numerous contradictory versions of the story of his death. The key, unresolved question is, as Victor Alexandrov put it: "Had Stalin been allowed to die, or had there been, as widespread rumor had it, joint action against him by his successors?" [29] Stalin's son was sure that his father had been murdered.[30] In his book, *The Riddle of Stalin's Death*,[31] Avtorkhanov contends that Beriya killed Stalin and was then removed himself later in 1953.

Notes:

1. Большая советская энциклопедия, 1952, т. 10, "Генералиссимус Советского Союза", стр. 401-403.
2. СЭС, 1990, стр. 1532.
3. БТСРЯ, стр. 214.б.
4. Edvard Radzinsky, *Stalin*, (translated from Russian by H. T. Willetts), London, Sceptre, 1996.
5. Н.Я. Мандельштам, Воспоминания: книга первая (4-е издание), Paris, YMCA Press, 1982, стр. 80. Published in English as: *Hope Against Hope: a Memoir*, translated by Max Hayward, New York: Modern Library, 1999.
6. Ожегов/Шведова, 4-е издание, 1997, стр. 289; БТСРЯ, стр. 457.в-8.а.
7. Военный энциклопедический словарь, М: Военное издательство, 1983, стр. 349-50.
8. Joel Carmichael, *Stalin's Masterpiece: The 'Show Trials' and Purges of the Thirties — The Consolidation of the Bolshevik Dictatorship*, New York, St. Martin's Press, 1976, p. 149.
9. Мандельштам, стр. 83.
10. Alexandr N. Jakowlew, "Blutige Vergangenheit," in *Jahrbuch für historische Kommunismusforschung* 1993, Akademie Verlag, Berlin, 1993, p. 233.
11. Ожегов/Шведова, стр. 254.
12. Сергей Петрович Мельгунов, Красный террор в России: 1918-1923, изд. 2-ое дополненное, Берлин, 1924, стр. 37-55.
13. Robert Conquest, *The Great Terror: A Reassessment*, Oxford, Oxford University Press, 1990, p. 485.
14. Conquest, p. 486.
15. In some sources the name Ежов is transliterated as Ezhov.
16. Речь Хрущева на закрытом заседании XX съезда КПСС (24-25 февраля 1956 г.), Мюнхен: изд. «Голос народа», 1956, стр. 18.
17. Хрущев, стр. 27.
18. Jakowlew, p. 234.
19. Мандельштам, «Христофорич», стр. 84-94.
20. Мандельштам, стр. 80.
21. Хрущев, стр. 20.
22. Conquest, p. 485.
23. The population at that time was 156 million.
24. Хрущев, стр. 16.
25. Хрущев, стр. 9.
26. И. Эренбург, «Люди, годы, жизнь», Новый мир, № 5, 1962, стр. 152.
27. Хрущев, стр. 26.

28. Winston Churchill, Radio talk, 1 October 1939, quoted in *Into the Battle* (1941), p. 131.
29. Victor Alexandrov, *The Kremlin: Nerve-Centre of Russian History*, New York: St. Martin's Press, 1963, p. 326.
30. Абдурахман Авторханов, Загадка смерти Сталина: заговор Берии, Франкфурт/М: Посев, 1979, стр. 214.
31. Абдурахман Авторханов, Загадка смерти Сталина: заговор Берии, Франкфурт/М: Посев, 1979.

Chapter 8

What's in a Name?
:TOLKIEN:THROUGH:RUSSIAN:EYES:

> What's in a name? That which we call a rose by any other name would smell as sweet.
> William Shakespeare,
> *Romeo and Juliet,* Act II, Scene 2.

Baggins. *Baggins* is one of the names that Tolkien intended to be translated. His "Notes on Nomenclature" [1] say that the translated name should contain an element meaning *sack* or *bag*. "Nomenclature" also points to two other names that should contain the same element so that the three names together can be played off one against the other: **Bag End** (Bilbo's house) and **Sackville-Baggins** (Bilbo's ne'er-do-well relations).

As he did with all the names, Gruzberg left the names in their original form and transliterated them: Бильбо Бэггинс [Bilbo Baggins], Бэг-Энд [Bag End] and Сэквил-Бэггинс [Sackvil-Baggins]. While there are those Russian readers who find this approach unsatisfactory, it is readily defensible when applied throughout as Gruzberg did. It adds a certain feeling of exoticness to the story for the Russian reader. Leaving the names in transliteration keeps it a very English story.

In a letter to Rayner Unwin, Tolkien said:

> "*In principle* I object as strongly as is possible to the 'translation' of the *nomenclature* at all (even by a competent person). I wonder why a translator should think himself called on or entitled to do any such thing. That this is an 'imaginary' world does not give him any right to remodel it according to his fancy, even if he could in a few months create a new coherent structure which it took me years to work out. [...] After all the book is English, and by an Englishman, and presumably

even those who wish its narrative and dialogue turned into an idiom that they understand, will not ask of a translator that he should deliberately attempt to destroy the local colour." (L.249-50)

Baggins (Бэггинс) is used by a number of the other translators as well. Rakhmanova, Umanskij, K&K Yakhnin and Cherkhanova (the adaptation of *The Hobbit* for English-learners) all use it. Bobyr' uses it in *The Hobbit*, but omits Bilbo's last name in *LotR*. It is the version used in the Suslin Hobbit knock-offs, and the comic-book editions of *The Hobbit*. It is likewise used in the Russian subtitles to Peter Jackson's three Tolkien movies.

Even though K&K transliterated *Baggins* and *Sackville-Baggins*, they translated *Bag End*. In their annotation for *Baggins*, they explain the name *Baggins*—not as a simple derivative of the name of Bilbo's estate, *Bag End*, which they translated as Котомка [Kotomka: backpack]—but rather as a reference to a custom in rural England, the four-o'clock tea, known as *baggins*, which was taken between the traditional English lunch and the conventional five-o'clock tea. (Km H.312-13)

The other form of *Baggins* that is widely recognized in Russia is Торбинс [Torbins]. This is the form of the name used in the first officially published Russian edition of the *LotR* by M&K. It was used by a number of other translators as well. G&G used it in their samizdat *LotR*. Both VAM and Nemirova (both originally samizdat) used it as well. Kaminskaya and Anonymous used it in their *Hobbit*s. It is also used in Gruzberg-B. It can be found in the Korolev *Tolkien Encyclopedia*, and in the Rolf English edition of *LotR* with Russian notes.

Kistyakovskij's name is built on the basis of the word торба [torba], which is, however, not one of the more common Russian words for *bag*. It is not even listed as a suggested translation in the two-volume *New English-Russian Dictionary*.[2] The suggested translations there are мешок [meshok], сума [suma] and сумка [sumka]. Торба [torba] has a certain foreign air about it. Most Russian speakers incorrectly assume that торба [torba] is a Ukrainian or Polish loan word. A quick glance in a Russian-Polish and a Russian-Ukrainian dictionary says why. The suggested translations for сума [suma] and сумка [sumka] are: Polish:[3] torba and torba, torebka; Ukrainian: [4] торба [torba] and сумка [sumka], торбинка [torbinka]. In reality, however, торба [torba] was originally a Turkish word, and it was indeed in use in Russian in the nineteenth century. (Dal' IV.418)

In their samizdat version, which was intended to fill in the gap left when the publication of M&K's official first volume of the trilogy was not followed by the publication of the next two, G&G primarily used Kistyakovskij's names. In their printed version, however, G&G built their version of Bilbo's last name on the commonly used word сумка [sumka], which means *bag*, as in lady's handbag. The ending that they used, however, was not *-ins* but *-nix*, and *Baggins* became Сумникс [Sumniks]. Together with *Baggins*, the names *Bolger* and *Boffin* also got the new ending.

Bolger ($G\&G_p$) - Пузикс [Puziks]: [puzo] = belly, compare: наесться от пуза [naest'sya ot puza] = *eat as much as you want*. Freddy Bolger's nickname is "Fatty."

Bolger (M&K and $G\&G_s$) - Боббер [Bobber]: бобр [bobr] = beaver, бобёр [bober] = beaver pelt,

Boffin ($G\&G_p$)[5] - Умникс [Umniks]: ум [um] = brain, умный [umnyj] = smart.[6]

Boffin (M&K) - Булкинс [Bulkins]: булка [bulka] = dinner roll.

The ending *-ins* was not, however, eliminated from all G&G's names.

Holman ($G\&G_p$) - Хаткинс [Khatkins]: хатка [khatka] = a little peasant's hut.

Holman ($M\&K_2$)[7] - Норн [Norn]: норный [nornyj, adj.] = hole dwelling.

Hornblower ($G\&G_p$)[8] - Дудкинс [Dudkins]: дудка [dudka] = pipe, fife.

Hornblower (M&K) - Дудстон [Dudston]: дудка [dudka] = pipe, fife.

Sandyman ($G\&G_p$) - Песошкинс [Pesoshkins]: песок [pesok] = sand.

Sandyman (M&K and $G\&G_s$) - Пескунс [Peskuns]: песок [pesok] = sand.

Smallburrow ($G\&G_{both}$) - Норкинс [Norkins]: норка [norka] = a small burrow.

Smallburrow (M&K)[9] - Норочкинс [Norochkins]: норочка [norochka] = small burrow.

When it finally dawned on me that G&G's version of Bilbo's last name was spelled *Sumniks* instead of *Sumkins*, the first thing I thought of was that the ending *-nix* is reminiscent of the names used in the comic book series *Asterix*, written by Goscinny and drawn by Uderzo, in which many of the characters' names end in *-ix*, for example: Asterix, Obelix, Getafix, Vitalstatistix and Cacofonix. In Russian, Asterix is spelled Астерикс [Asteriks]. The series was first translated into Russian in 1994, while G&G

first appeared in print in 1991, so G&G most likely had something else in mind when they picked this ending. As *Asterix* becomes more widely read among Russian Tolkien fans, the parallels between the two names will inevitably be drawn. The *Asterix* series tells the story of a small village of indomitable Gauls holding out against the Roman invasions in 50 B.C. This image is a nice fit for the indomitable Frodo Bag-nix (Сумникс [Sumniks]) holding out against the spreading shadow of Mordor in the Third Age of Middle-earth.

Kistyakovskij's translation of *Bag End* as Торба-на-Круче [Torba-na-Kruche] does not convey the sense that Tolkien wanted *Bag End* to have, which was more or less that of a calque from the French *cul-de-sac* [literally: the end of a sack/bag], which is in widespread use in English. Торба-на-Круче [Torba-na-Kruche] is literally: bag on a steep slope. This plays more as a description of Bilbo's home—a bag (hole) dug into the side of the hill—than as a description of the lane that led to the farm where Tolkien's Aunt Jane lived in Dormston in Worcestershire. The lane led to the farm and no further, and the local people sometimes called it 'Bag End'.[10]

In Russian, *cul-de-sac* is translated as тупик [tupik] or глухой переулок [glukhoj pereulok, literally: a deaf lane]. It would have been hard to do something with that and achieve the alliteration that *Baggins* and *Bag End* have.

When dealing with *Bag End*, M&K, Nemirova and G&G could not seem to make up their minds. Both have two versions of the name for *Bag End*. Kistyakovskij's (Nemirova's) long name (Торба-на-Круче [Torba-na-Kruche]) alternates with its shortened form (Торба [Torba]) almost indiscriminately. In the printed version of G&G, Засумки [Zasumki] and Сумкина горка [Sumkina gorka] alternate with one another in the same manner. G&G's dual name for a single location is more confusing than Kistyakovskij's long and shortened forms of a single name. Condensing long forms into short ones is common in all languages, and is readily understood by the reader. Though the swap of Засумки [Zasumki] and Сумкина горка [Sumkina gorka] is in keeping with Tolkien's practice of providing variants of toponyms, Tolkien's variants were in other languages. G&G's are both in Common Speech.

Засумки [Zasumki] is made up of the preposition *behind* or *beyond*—за [za]—plus the word for *bag* сумка [sumka]. G&G use the name in the plural, which is quite common in Russian toponyms. In this form, Засумки [Zasumki] can be interpreted to mean the place beyond the bag. Сумкина горка [Sumkina gorka] is just the combination of the archaic adjective form of the word сумка [sumka] with the word for *little hill*: горка [gorka]. Both of these combine very nicely with their rendition of *Baggins* as Сумникс [Sumniks] so that it is clear that Bilbo's name and the name of his home have something to do with one another.

For the most part, VAM followed Kistyakovskij's lead for the names in the first version of her translation. *Bilbo Baggins* was Бильбо Торбинс [Bilbo Torbins] and *Bag End* was Торба-на-Круче [Torba-na-Kruche], but the *Sackville-Bagginses* were the Сумкин-Торбинсы [Sumkin-Torbinsy], which is not nearly as funny as the M&K and G&G parodies, but it is what Tolkien wanted: two essentially synonymous elements with the meaning of *sack* and *bag*. As such it is quite successful.

In her revised edition, VAM leaves Bilbo's name unchanged as Бильбо Торбинс [Bilbo Torbins], but *Bag End* became Торба-в-Холме [Torba-v-Kholme: literally *Bag in a Hill*]. The change from Круча [Krucha] to the more commonly used translation of *hill*—Холм [Kholm]—makes the name of Bilbo's home seem somewhat more prosaic and homey, which is more in keeping with the idea of Aunt Jane's house.

Kistyakovskij's translation of *Sackville-Baggins* is most imaginative. Tolkien had wanted this name to have two different elements, each with the meaning of *sack* or *bag* that would make up the two halves of a hyphenated name. Hyphenated names normally imply that the bearer of the name is from an old—and snobbish—aristocratic family. To make his hyphenated name sound even more pretentious, Tolkien gave it a French (Norman) air, by adding the suffix *-ville* to the word used for the first part of the name—the part that carried the meaning *sack*. For this part of the name Kistyakovskij chose the word кошель [koshel'], an archaic word, the meaning of which is *money bag* (purse). To give it the required French air, Kistyakovskij simply placed the French feminine definite article *la* in front of it. The combination Лякошель-Торбинс [Lyakoshel'-Torbins] has a quite comic air. It literally would be read as *La bag money-Baggins*.

Nemirova went Kistyakovskij one better. She changed the first part of his hyphenated name to Кошелье- [Koshel'e-], to rhyme with the Russian spelling of Richelieu (Ришелье [Rishel'e]), famous to Russian readers from his role in *The Three Musketeers*. It is an effectively elegant change that carries essentially the same meaning as Kistyakovskij's, but with more subtlety.

G&G's parody of Tolkien's ne'er-do-well hyphenated name has almost slapstick impact: Дерикуль [Derikul']. This name is made up of two words that can be read as an imperative sentence. The first word is the imperative form of the verb драть [drat'], which means to *rip off*. It is used to express taking unfair advantage of someone, i.e. ripping them off, and is used in fixed expressions like, драть втридорога [drat' vtridoroga: *to take triple the price*] and драть с живого и мёртвого [drat' s zhivogo i mertvogo: *to take advantage of both the living and the dead*]. The second part of this imperative sentence is the word куль [kul'], which means *sack*, as in flour sack. Together they could essentially be understood as *Rip-off the bag*, which is very much in character for the Sackville-Bagginses.

Yakhnin's version of *Sackville-Baggins* lacks even the subtleties of G&G's slapstick rendition. His is an "in your face" name, intended to appeal to his young audience. It is built on the Russian verb *to steal* (грабить [grabit']), which he combines with the typically Hobbitish ending -*ins*. The effect of his Грабинс-Бэггинс [Grabins-Behggins] on the Russian reader is something like Thievins-Baggins. Any hint of Norman pretentiousness is lost in Yakhnin's directness.

Volkovskij also translates the three names, but with an archaic word so obscure that it sent Russian Tolkienists everywhere off in search of Dal'—the classic dictionary of nineteenth century Russian—to look up its meaning. But in vain. Since this word is not a part of everyone's active vocabulary, it was easy for Volkovskij to redefine its meaning to suit the context of the story. He offers his own modified definition of it in the text. He called it a "back bag," which is not what it says in Dal'. In actuality, Volkovskij was merely resurrecting the sound envelope and the word-formation pattern, not the word itself. He skillfully enhances his linguistic illusion, by establishing the stylistic markers of this "renewal-logism" with a pair of embellishments to the "Prologue." Having performed this trick of linguistic legerdemain, he then built his triad of names on it.

The first embellishment is to the last paragraph of "On Finding the Ring." It establishes бебень [beben'] as an "old Hobbit" word and defines it as заплечная котомка [zaplechnaya kotomka (literally: back bag)], using the same word that K&K had used in their name. (Embellishments **emphasized.**)

> Bilbo returned to his **estate, which is called Beben' (an interesting, obviously old Hobbit word — since time immemorial this has been the word used for a back bag)**, in the fifty-second year of his

life, 22 June 1342 S.R., and from that point nothing notable occurred in the Shire until in 1401 he prepared to celebrate his hundred-and-eleventh birthday. It is here that our history begins. (V F.32)

JRRT: He returned to his home at Bag End on June the 22nd in his fifty-second year (S.R. 1342), and nothing very notable occurred in the Shire until Mr. Baggins began preparations for the celebration of his hundred-and-eleventh birthday (S.R. 1401). At this point this History begins. (P.35-36)

Volkovskij continues establishing the pedigree for the word бебень [beben'] in his embellishment to the "Note on the Shire Records," in which Tolkien lists Meriadoc's publications. One of these is called *Old Words and Names in the Shire*. In the original, the book shows Meriadoc's "special interest in discovering the kinship with the language of the Rohirrim of such "shire-words" as *mathom* and old elements in place names." (P.39) In Volkovskij's version, the book examined the derivation of ancient words like «мутень» [muten'] and «бебень» [beben'], which he set off in inverted commas. This squarely places Volkovskij's name for *Bag End*, and, by implication, his name for *Baggins* in the category of "shire-words" like *mathom* (V F.34), which Tolkien had explained several pages earlier. (P.25) The word-formation pattern that Volkovskij is using is no longer productive and has a definite archaic feel to it, which enhances the impression that Volkovskij's names ending in -ень [-en'] are indeed old words.

Volkovskij has lots of names with the same ending to increase the feeling of depth for his linguistic illusion that бебень [beben'] and мутень [muten'] are old "shire-words." His names for the Stoors and Fallohides both end in -ень [-en'] in the singular: Схватень [Skhvaten'] and Скрытень [Skryten'], as does his version of the nickname for Hamfast Gamgee: Gaffer (Старбень [Starben']). The effect is especially well highlighted when Бебень [Beben'] and Старбень [Starben'] appear immediately next to one another in the text. (F.47, V F.42) The first part of the nickname Gaffer, Стар [Star], is readily recognizable as the root of the adjective for *old*: старый [staryj]. This hints that the names can be analyzed linguistically, and the meaning of мутень [muten'] suddenly becomes clear to the general reader, who has had neither the inclination, nor the opportunity to look in Dal'. It is derived from the adjective мутный [mutnyj], which means *unclear*, *confused*, *vague*.

The derived meaning of мутень [muten'] is a much better fit for the context than the one resurrected from Dal'. In Dal', this word means a person, who is a trouble-maker, while, in Tolkien, it is a thing. This just reinforces the conclusion that Volkovskij was resurrecting the sound envelope and the word-formation pattern, not the word itself.

He further polishes this sense of exotic familiarity in his version of the full name of *Bag End*, Бебень-на-Бугре [Beben'-na-Bugre], literally *Back Bag on the Knoll*, which rolls *the Hill* and *Bag End* into one like Kistyakovskij, Nemirova and VAM did with their Торба-на-Круче [Torba-na-Kruche] (Kistyakovskij, Nemirova) and Торба-в-Холме [Torba-v-Kholme] (VAM). Seeing Бебень [Beben'] used in combination with normal words in this fashion will give the reader another commonplace reference point to help Бебень [Beben'] seem more familiar.

Having established a base with Бебень [Beben'], Volkovskij deftly follows through with Беббинс [Bebbins] for Baggins. The linguistic relationship is relatively obvious to the non-linguist and there is no interference from words in widespread modern use. None begin with беб [beb]. The double "BB" makes it look much more foreign and is in keeping with Tolkien's doubling the letter "G" in *Baggins*. His rendition of *Sackville-Baggins* is reminiscent of G&G's *Grab-the-bag-and-run* Bagginses (Дерикуль-Сумникс [Derikul'-Sumniks]), and is perhaps somewhat more successful in the attempt. The first part of Volkovskij's name is Хапни [Khapni], which is the imperative of the colloquial verb хапнуть [khapnut']: *to steal, to rip off*. When combined with Беббинс [Bebbins] it suggests a meaning for the name of *steal-the-back bag*, or *steal Бебень [Beben'], Bag End*, which is just what the Хапни-Беббинсы [Khapni-Bebbinses] tried to do.

Cotton. Tolkien explains that this name is a place name in origin, and should be translated as a combination of the elements: *cottage + town*. He expressly said that it was not to be understood as the textile cotton, even though that is the most commonly used meaning of the word today. This, however, is almost exactly how G&G translated the name in the samizdat edition of their text. They treated it like it was one of the botanical names of Bree. Their translation, Хлопчатник [Khlopchatnik], is the Russian word for the cotton plant (Gossypium). In the printed version G&G changed the name to Недосёлок [Nedoselok], which is based on a root used in a number of words for various kinds of villages: settlement (посёлок [poselok]), new settlement (новосёлок [novoselok], new settlement made by people who left a larger settlement (выселок [vyselok] and отсёлок [otselok]). The prefixes от- [ot-] and вы- [vy-] mean *away from* and *out of.* The prefix [nedo-] means *not quite*, as in 'not quite a settlement.'

While G&G used Kistyakovskij's names in most places in their samizdat edition of *LotR*, they could not do so here. The name *Cotton* only appears in volume III. At the time that G&G were preparing their translation for samizdat publication, only volume I of the abridged M&K translation was in print. G&G, therefore, had no way of knowing how Kistyakovskij had handled the name *Cotton* and struck out on their own.

Nemirova was in the same boat as G&G, and her version of *Cotton* was not much better than theirs. She named Cotton Шерстон [Sherston], combining the word for *wool* шерсть [sherst'] with Tolkien's original ending *-ton*. The ending *-ton* is not productive in Russian toponymy and is only seen in loan words like бетон [concrete] and жетон [token]. What Nemirova has, therefore, done is to combine a Russian word with a foreign ending, producing some bilingual alphabet soup, which is never very palatable to monolingual readers.

Murav'ev—Kistyakovskij had died before the third volume was completed—rendered *Cotton* as Кроттон [Krotton], which is based on the Russian word *mole*: крот [krot], and makes farmer Cotton seem like he would be more at home in *The Wind in the Willows*. *Krotton* is the version that Korolev used in his Tolkien Encyclopedia. (Kr E.146)

Gruzberg, of course, and Bobyr'/Umanskij both transliterated Cotton as Коттон [Kotton].

Volkovskij gave farmer Cotton one of his "old shirish" names: Сдружень [Sdruzhen']. It is based on the verb *to unite in friendship* (сдружить [sdruzhit']), which gives farmer Cotton the air of a peacemaker.

Yakhnin gave the names short shrift, and farmer Cotton was lucky to get one. Many of Tolkien's named bit players lost their names in the Yakhnin retelling. Cotton's part in the tale was simply too large to let him come on stage without a name, so Yakhnin turned his title into a name. He called him Огородник [Ogorodnik], a type of small-scale farmer.

VAM used the ending -инс [-ins] for her version of the name *Cotton*. She called him Норкинс [Norkins]. The ending -инс [-ins] has come to be thought of as typical of Hobbit names in Russia. It can be seen in the work of a number of the translators in a number of names that had other endings in the original. For example:

Boffin (M&K) - Булкинс [Bulkins]: булка [bulka] = dinner roll.

Boffin (Nemirova) - Мудренс [Mudrens]: мудрый [mudryj] = intelligent.

Brockhouse (VAM) - Барсучинс [Barsuchins]: барсук [barsuk] = badger.

Chubbs (subtitles) - Пышкинс [Pyshkins]: пышка [pyshka] = doughnut, a chubby baby.

Flourdumpling[11] (G&G$_s$) - Булкинс [Bulkins]: булка [bulka] = dinner roll.

Grubb (subtitles) - Хрюшкинс [Khryushkins]: хрюшка [khryushka] = pig.

Grubb, Grubb and **Burrows** (*The Hobbit*, Anonymous) - Коппинс, Коппинс и Норытвинс [Koppins, Koppins, i Norytvins]: копать [kopat'] = to dig and нора + рыть [nora + ryt'] = burrow + to dig.

Holman (G&G) - Хаткинс [Khatkins]: хата [khata] = a hut, a cabin.

Sackville-Baggins (Yakhnin) - Грабинс-Бэггинс [Grabins-Behggins]: грабить [grabit'] = to steal.

Smallburrow (Volkovskij) - Горушкинс [Gorushkins]: горушка [gorushka] = small mountain [гора (gora)].

Smallburrow (Nemirova) - Ямкинс [Yamkins]: яма [yama] = pit.

Underhill (K&K) - Подхолминс [Podkholmins]: под [pod] = under, and холм [kholm] = hill.

VAM's version of *Cotton* (Норкинс [Norkins]) is based on the Russian noun нора [nora], which means a *burrow*. Using this root could have been a problem for her translation of the name *Smallburrow*, but she solved that problem by using the same root for her version of *Smallburrow* that she used for the names of two of the members of the firm of attorneys who were selling Bilbo's estate when he got back from his adventure: Messrs. Grubb, Grubb and Burrows. (H.284) Her firm of attorneys was called Ройл, Ройл и Закопанс [Rojl, Rojl i Zakopans]. While the underlying formation of the last of the three names is clear—a combination of the almost obligatory *-ns* ending for Hobbit names added to the root of the Russian verb *to dig*: закопать [zakopat']—the underlying structure of the names *Grubb and Grubb* uses neither an ending obviously borrowed from Tolkien, nor one that is productive in Russian. Her name for *Grubb* is based on the Russian verb *to burrow* (рыть [ryt']), the root for which is рой [roj], as can be seen in the first person singular: рою [royu]. The ending -л [-l] is not productive with verb stems ending in -й [-j] in Russian. The ending -ло [-lo], however, is productive with this root ending. It can be used to form nouns like стойло [stojlo]—*a stall*—the place where horses or cattle stand, derived from the verb стоять > стою [stoyat' > stoyu: to stand > I stand]. Using that noun as an analogy, a ройло [rojlo] would be a place where Hobbits burrow.

VAM could have made a very successful name out of that. Dal' lists a related word with the meaning of *plowed field*: ролья [rol'ya], which would also have made an interesting Hobbit name. (Dal' IV.103) Her name for *Smallburrow* is Мелкорой [Melkoroj], literally: *shallow burrower*. Her use of рой [roj] as the final element in the name is not without precedent, but the precedent is hardly a commonplace word and this type of construction is no longer productive in Russian. It is a word that only a dictionary diver could love. Modern desk-top defining dictionaries carry no listing for this word. It is пескорой [peskoroj], which is attested in the standard dictionary of nineteenth century Russian (Dal' III.104) as a *sand eel* (Ammodytes, Greek for *sand dweller*). It is also attested in the Ushakov academic dictionary from the 1930s as a *sand wasp* (order Hymenoptera).[12]

K&K's version of *Cotton* also uses the ending *-ins* taken from the Bilbo's surname. Their version of *Cotton* is Хижинс [Khizhins]. It is derived from the word хижина [khizhina], which means *shack* or *hut*. It is the word used in the standard translation of *Uncle Tom's Cabin* (Хижина дяди Тома [Khizhina dyadi Toma)]. This is a much poorer abode than the *cottage* that Tolkien envisioned. They would have done much better to use the name that G&G used for *Holman* - Хаткинс [Khatkins]: хатка [khatka] = a hut, a cabin.

Crickhollow was Frodo's destination when he left Hobbiton at the start of his quest. Tolkien's instruction in "Nomenclature" was that the name is made up of two elements. The first element—*crick*—is an obsolete element that is to be retained in the target language. The second element—*hollow*—is meant to be recognizable, and should be translated. Gruzberg and Umanskij true to form, transliterated it: Крикхоллоу [Krikkhollou].

Bobyr' ignored this name, as did G&G in their samizdat edition.

Volkovskij translated it as *Dry Gulch* (Сухой Овражек [Sukhoj Ovrazhek]), which sounds more at home in a Western than in the Shire. In their print edition, G&G tried to follow Tolkien's advice, and made up a name that retained *crick* to be combined with a translation of *hollow*. They truncated *crick* to кри- [kri-] and chopped off the first letter of the Russian word for *hollow* (овражек > вражек [ovrazhek > vrazhek]). The result was Крикражки [Krivrazhki], with a plural ending, which is typical of Russian place names. Because of their adaptation of the elements that made up the name, this version falls short of the mark and takes on a different meaning. Instead of *Crickhollow*, it suggests the combination of the Russian words for *crooked*—as in dishonest—(кривой [krivoj]) and *little enemies*—a disdainful diminutive—(вражки [vrazhki]).

The majority vote for *hollow* among the translators went to балка [balka]. For Kistyakovskij, *Crickhollow* became another member of his family of 'rabbit' names. (q.v. **Fallohide**) He rendered it as *Rabbit Hollow* (Кроличья Балка [Krolich'ya Balka]). VAM had an imaginative, very usable rendition based on балка [balka] that matched Tolkien's instructions almost exactly. She created a Russian sounding adjective out of *crick* by adding an ending that is usually used to make adjectives out of the names of types of animals, the same ending that can be seen in Kistyakovskij's *Rabbit Hollow*. This is a soft ending, which causes the final 'K' sound in *crick* to change to a Russian Ч [Ch]. When her new adjective is combined with the word for *hollow* that got the majority vote, it produces the eminently readable Кричья Балка [Krich'ya Balka]. Exactly what Tolkien had ordered. Unfortunately, most monolingual Russian readers see an existing Russian root in her creation. The Russian noun *yell* is крик [krik]. On the other hand, to a multilingual reader like the author, who can see what VAM was trying—albeit not too successfully—to do, it is an elegant way of making Tolkien's immutable first element in the name fit into the scheme of Russian orthography.

K&K also decided to keep *crick* as Tolkien had suggested. In an attempt to avoid the inevitable association with the Russian word *yell* (крик [krik]), they created an archaic style adjective with a double letter 'KK,' which clearly marks it as a foreign word, because double letters—other than those at root boundaries like 'SS' and 'NN'—are very uncommon in Russian. The end result is quite readable: Криккова [Krikkova], though a number of Russian readers continue to be troubled by interference from the Russian noun *yell*. K&K's choice of the second part of the name, was undoubtedly in response to the need to differentiate the *hollow* in *Crickhollow* from the *dingle* in *Derndingle* (q.v.), where they had already used балка [balka] for *dingle*. The result is a quite serviceable Криккова Лощинка [Krikkova Loshchinka].

Nemirova translated *Crickhollow* as *River Hollow* (Ручейная Балка [Ruchejnaya Balka]), apparently interpreting *crick* as the variant of *creek* to be found in certain dialects of English, exemplified by the expression "The good Lord willin', and the crick don't rise." Yakhnin also had trouble interpreting *crick*. He turned it into *Cricket Hollow* (Сверчковая Лощина [Sverchkovaya Loshchina]), following his English-Russian dictionary rather than looking in a toponymic dictionary to find the real meaning of *crick*.

K&K had an endnote to explain the etymology of *crick*. It gives the original spelling of *Crickhollow* and points to the place name *Crickhowel* as an example of *crick* used in a toponym. (K&K F.630, H.337) Their etymology of *crick*, however, is open to interpretation. K&K said that *crick* is related to Tolkien's *Carrock*, based on the Welsh word *carreg*, which means *craig* in English.

Crickhowel is the anglicized form of the Welsh place name Crucywel, normally interpreted to mean Hywel's cairn. The John Jones *Welsh Place Names*[13] says that the Hywel referenced in the name was a prince of Glamorgan, who marked the boundaries to his land with cairns (heaps of stones). A reflection of this meaning can be found in Gaelic and Irish in *crioch* (*criche* in the genitive), which means *boundary, limit, frontier*. In modern Welsh *crug* (pronounced [krik]) still means *hillock, heap, cairn*.

The first meaning of *crug* in the Great Welsh-English dictionary is encountered much more often in place names. It is hill, hillock. This meaning is found in place names like Cricklas [green hill], Yr Wyddgrug [the conspicuous hill] (with lenition of the 'C' to 'G' as is common in Welsh compound names), better known by its Norman translation, Mold (short for *Mont haut*), Cricieth [the hill of the captives], and in the tautology Creech Hill: *cruc* (Old Welsh) + *hill* (English). Tolkien would have undoubtedly been aware of this meaning as well, but he did not give a meaning for *crick* in "Nomenclature." He only indicated that it was an obsolete element. Given Tolkien's love of linguistic jests, it is not unreasonable to assume that he saw a pun behind *Crickhowel* turned *Crickhollow*, and did not want to "spoil the joke," as Bilbo put it. The combination of *crug* (Welsh: *hill*) and *hollow* (English: *depression*) is a bilingual oxymoron.

Derndingle. Tolkien recommended translating the elements of the Common Speech name for the meeting place of the Ents. He glossed the first element, *dern*, as an obsolete word meaning *secret* or *hidden*. The second element, *dingle*, means a *deep (tree-shadowed) dell*. He felt that the translated name should likewise be built from obsolete, poetic or dialectical elements.

G&G did not attempt to deal with *Derndingle* in any of their versions, and omitted it together with *Entmoot* (q.v.), as did Bobyr'. Umanskij restored the chapter on Treebeard, but *Derndingle* was misspelled in the process. It became *Derdingle* (Дердингл [Derdingl]).

Gruzberg transliterated the name as Дерндингл [Derndingl]. Given that for most English-speaking readers, who have not read Tolkien's "Nomenclature," *Derndingle* is just so much alphabet soup, Gruzberg's transliteration has much the same flavor as the original. Gruzberg's lack of access to Tolkien's "Nomenclature" is evident, however, in his gloss for *Derndingle*, in which he calls it a "grassy hollow" (травяная лощина). Zastyrets, Gruzberg's book editor, took that footnote out. (G. T.95)

Murav'ev used a common element for the first part of his name: тайно [tajno], which means *secret*. For the second element, he used the same word as he did for the second element in *Rivendell*: дол [dol], an archaic word for *valley*, etymologically related to the word *dell*. This results in a name that is much more transparent to the Russian reader than *Derndingle* is to the English-speaking reader. This removes some of the secrecy that surrounded the meeting place of the Ents in Tolkien's version, and makes it just a little less mysterious, but it is, nevertheless, a good rendition, more or less complying with Tolkien's instructions, only missing the mark with regard to the stylistic register for the part with the meaning of *secret*.

K&K also chose to use a common element for the first part of the name, but not one that had the meaning that Tolkien used. Instead of being *secret*, their dell is *enchanted* (заколдованная [zakoldovannaya]). This is a step further away from Tolkien's intent, giving the Ents a touch more magic than they have in the original. For the second part of the name, they used a the element: балка [balka], which means *a hollow*. The overall result, however, has a nice feel to it. A hint at the relationship of the VAM and the K&K versions can be seen in VAM's rendition of *Derndingle* as Заколдованный Овраг [Zakoldovannyj Ovrag]. They were the only translators to use *enchanted* (заколдованный [zakoldovannyj]) instead of *secret* for *dern*. VAM's choice of овраг [gully], however, is more mundane than балка [a hollow], which makes her version a little less magical than K&K's.

Nemirova had a "none of the above" rendition of *Derndingle*. She turned it into Запретное Урочище [Zapretnoe Urochishche]. In the context of a high-level meeting of Ents, Nemirova's name calls to mind the term (запретная зона [zapretnaya zona]), which literally means *forbidden zone*. The first word is the same and the second word (urochishche) defines 'zones' of land with different topographical features from the surrounding territory, like a dry spot in a swamp or a clearing in a forest. In more colloquial English, her name would better be translated as *restricted area*. Restricted areas house secret government and military installations, where the public is not permitted. In the Soviet period, when Nemirova was doing her translation, many of these did not even have names as far as the outside world was concerned. They were simply post office box (почтовый ящик [pochtovyj yashchik]) numbers, places that did not show up on any map. It is an interesting image, but a little too Soviet to have a long shelf life.

Volkovskij took a wrong turn at the two-volume English-Russian dictionary[14] and turned *Derndingle* into a "Patch Hollow" [Латаная Лощина (Latanaya Loshchina)]. The English-Russian dictionary[15] lists *dern* not as *hidden, secret*, but as a derivative of *darn*. This is the alternate pronunciation of *darn* (a mild curse), which is something Jed Clampett might say. The page where *darn* is located lists two homonyms: 1) *to mend*, as in to darn socks and 2) a euphemism for *damn*. Since the article for *dern* did not specify which of the two *darn*s it referred to, Volkovskij selected the first word in the example given for *darn* with the meaning of *to mend*, which is *to patch and darn* (латать и штопать [latat' i shtopat']). The image is intriguing, but it is more at home in the Oz books with the Patch-work Girl of Oz, than in Tolkien as the secret gathering place of the Ents. Volkovskij clearly did not read Tolkien's "Nomenclature."

Yakhnin shows his roots as a children's storyteller with his name for *Derndingle*. He sets up the *secret* element in the name with a description of the place where the Ents meet as "the most secret place, where no outsider has ever set foot." (Ya T.62) He then gives this place a name with an alliterative pun that would delight any young audience. He calls it Бор-Бормотун [Bor-Bormotun]. The first word (bor) is a pine forest, usually on a hill. The second word in his compound (бормотун [bormotun]) is a slang word for someone who mumbles, which is what Treebeard sounds like he is doing when he speaks Entish. Yakhnin clearly enjoys this kind of word play, because he creates a whole string of similar puns as part of his description of Fangorn forest. There, among other things, one can find чащи молчащие [chashchi molchashchie] and гущи гудящие [gushchi gudyashchie]. The two alliterations play on synonyms for *thicket*. One is silent, the other is noisy. The closest English approximation is 'mute butte' and 'cricket thicket'.

Durin. The name of the royal house of the Dwarves was not included in Tolkien's "Nomenclature," which means that he intended for it to be transliterated instead of translated. This presents a particular problem for Russian translators, because, if it is transliterated, the name will suffer from interference with an existing Russian word, дурень [duren'], which means *fool* or *simpleton*, which, in the nineteenth century, was spelled дуринъ [durin"] (Dal' I.502), letter for letter the same as Tolkien's name. Дурень [Duren'] is the word that Nemirova uses for *fool* in the dialogue between the two powers inside Frodo's head in the Chapter "The Breaking of the Fellowship," where the one voice cries: "Take it off! Fool, take it off!" (F.519; N F.469)

While this kind of interference is completely unacceptable as an association for such a royal name as Durin, Дурин [Durin] was, nevertheless, the rendition used in the subtitles, and in Umanskij's rendition of *The Hobbit* and *LotR*. It should be noted, however, that the subtitlers are somewhat constrained by the fact that the audience can hear how the name is pronounced in English, and cannot, therefore, stray too far afield.

Rakhmanova and Gruzberg both skillfully circumvented the problem by transliterating the name as Дьюрин [D'yurin] (Rakhmanova) and as Дюрин [Dyurin] (Gruzberg). This is a sufficiently un-Russian letter/sound combination to avoid the confusion with дуринь [durin']. This is the same approach as is used for the spelling of the name of the author of *The Three Musketeers*, Alexander Dumas (1802-1870), which, if spelled with the letter 'U' [У], would coincide with the Russian word for *Congress* (Дума [Duma]). In Russian his name is written Дюма [Dyuma]. In French the final 'S' in his name is not pronounced. This approach is, in fact, used for all French names beginning with 'Du-,' like Duval (Дюваль [Dyuval]), Dubois (Дюбуа [Dyubua]), Dupont (Дюпон [Dyupon]) and Dunkerque (Дюнкерк [Dyunkerk]).

K&K, Kaminskaya and Perumov follow Rakhmanova's lead, while Bobyr'/Batalina understandably uses Gruzberg's approach in *The Hobbit*. Bobyr' avoided the name altogether in *LotR*. All the rest of the translators rendered the name as Дарин [Darin], which—if it awakens any association at all for the Russian reader—makes the name sound like a derivative of the Russian word for *gift* (дар [dar]). Дарины [dariny, pl.] is an old Russian betrothal custom in which the bride and the groom exchange traditional gifts. She gives him the yarns and cloths and embroidery that she has made and he gives her a special head dress. (Dal' I.415)

In their extensive endnote on the Dwarves' names, K&K point out that the names of Tolkien's Dwarves are taken from the *Elder Edda* from the *Voluspa* [The Wise Woman's Prophecy], which they quote, using the A. Korsun Russian translation. Their note is essentially a recap of Jim Allan's analysis of Dwarf names in *An Introduction to Elvish*.[16]

The same problem of interference from дуринъ [durin"] also affected Tolkien's new name for the sword that was broken once it had been reforged: *Anduril*. The majority of the translators simply dropped the letter 'U' from the name to make it *Andril*. This produces a very readable Russian name and removes the primary problem with Tolkien's original name, the Russian root дур [dur], which is at the base of a number of words such as *foolishness* (дурь [dur']), *fool* (дурак [durak]), *dope* (in the sense of *a narcotic*: дурман [durman]), and *loony bin* (дурдом [durdom]). K&K used the approach that the majority of the translators applied to *Durin*, and made the name of the sword *Andaril*. Because *Anduril* is a Quenya name, removing or changing a letter in it complicates the task of those Russian Tolkienists who want to study Elvish. Gruzberg and Umanskij left the name as it was, spelling it Андуриль [Anduril']. Bobyr' omitted the name, just leaving its translation. (B.68, U F.397)

Entmoot. Tolkien has no specific recommendation in "Nomenclature" for *Entmoot*, a gathering of Ents. (T.103) He recommends that *Ent* be retained alone and in compounds. Gruzberg, true to form, transliterated *Entmoot* as Энтмут [Ehntmut], as did Umanskij. Tolkien was obviously playing on the obsolete meaning of the word *moot* (*meeting, assembly*). The word *moot* can also be seen with this meaning spelled as *mote*, in words like *burgh-mote*, *folk-mote* (also spelled *folkmoot*), *hall-mote*, *hundred-mote*. This root still survives in modern Dutch with the meaning of *to meet*. In the sentence 'I met John,' the Dutch word for *met* is *ontmoet*, which is pronounced [ont-moot].

In Anglo-Saxon and late-medieval England, a moot was the meeting place for courts and other governmental bodies, within such administrative districts as a *hundred*, a *wapentake*, or a *shire*. It is undoubtedly the continuation of the *Witenagemot*,[17] the assembly of the *witan* [the wise]. In the "Erybyggja Saga" [The Story of the Ere-Dwellers], an Icelandic (Old Norse) Saga from around the middle of the thirteenth century, King Harald summoned an eight-folks' mote in Thrandheim to have Biorn Ketilson declared an outlaw. This moot was a gathering of the eight folks (adminstrative districts) of the "province" of Thrandheim, who held their folk-mote at Eyrathing.

Moots were held at well-known sites which might be marked by a conspicuous natural feature such as a hill or tree or by a manmade feature such as an earthen mound or standing stone. Moot sites can be found throughout England, Scotland, Ireland and Wales. For some sites, the memory of the function of Moot Hill has remained alive into modern times. Scotland was united by Kenneth MacAplin who defeated the Picts in 838 A.D., and placed The Stone of Destiny on the Moot Hill at Scone. The Kings of Scotland (including Macbeth and Robert the Bruce) were crowned there until Edward I moved the Coronation Stone to Westminster in 1296. The Moot Hill near Ellon, a town north of Aberdeen, which was the main settlement of the Pictish province of Buchan before 400 B.C., is where the Celtic Mormaers, and then the Norman (Comyn) Earls of Buchan, held court and dispensed justice. Moot Hill in the market town of Driffield was the site of an early parliament.

While initially moots were situated in the open countryside, they eventually moved indoors. The name *moot hall* has outlived its use as a council chamber and is now only a historical, architectural artifact in English towns where the structure has survived.

Nemirova translates *Entmoot* with the term from Russian history the function of which equates to that of the English *moot*. She equates *moot* with вече [veche]. Russian readers will immediately recognize *veche* from school. The veche in Russia dates from the tenth to the fifteenth century. Like the moot, the veche was an open-air gathering. The most famous is the Novgorod [New Town] veche. It had the power to elect the city's primary civil and military officials, the посадник [posadnik] and the тысяцкий [tysyatskij]. Novgorod is one of Russia's oldest cities, first being mentioned in 859. The veche survived in Novgorod until 1478, when Ivan III conquered the city and dissolved it. The same fate fell to the veche in Pskov in 1510. Nemirova's choice of *veche* for *moot* is a very good match, suffering only in that she does not combine it with *Ent*. She wins the prize for historical correctness. Kistyakovskij gets the prize for inventiveness.

Kistyakovskij has a very elegant translation of *moot*. Most of the translators followed Tolkien's recommendation and transliterated *Ent*. Kistyakovskij, however, renders *Ent* as *Ont*, based on the Sindarin word for *Ent*, *Onod*, instead of the Rohirrimic word used in *LotR*, which is derived from an Old English word for *Giant* used in *Beowulf*. To this he adds an archaic root meaning *to talk* or *to speak* (молвить [molvit'] Dal' II.340) and finishes it off with a noun ending, creating the quite evocative word, Онтомолвище [Ontomolvishche], which can be interpreted to mean *a talking of Ents*. This clearly plays to one of the definitions for *moot* in the *OED*: "Argument; discussion; disputation; talking." Kistyakovskij's invention is the hands down winner for its imaginativeness. Volkovskij slightly changes Kistyakovskij's creation, replacing *Ont* with *Ent* to produce Энтомолвище [Ehntomolvishche].

G&G omit *Entmoot* and *Derndingle* (q.v.), and condense the segment in which they appear so that only Treebeard's gloss of *Entmoot* survives. Bobyr' left these two out as well. G&G's version of Treebeard's gloss is: сбор Энтов [sbor Entov]. Сбор [sbor] is a contemporary word that is often associated with the recall of military reservists for training. It can also have the meaning of meeting, but less often so. Either of the meanings could be supported by this context, but since the chapter closes with the Ents marching off to wage war on Isengard, the military context will come to the fore.

K&K also passed on trying to create a new word for *Entmoot* and used Treebeard's gloss instead. While G&G use a modern form of the Russian word for gathering (сбор [sbor]) for their rendition of the *moot*, K&K use an archaic version of the same word: собор [sobor]. (K&K T.107) During the Soviet period, the word собор [sobor] was considered politically incorrect. In the meaning of *a meeting* it was used for gatherings of the pre-Revolutionary ruling classes or of church groups. It even has an alternate meaning of *cathedral*. These associations made it a sort of taboo word in polite Soviet society. In its primary meaning of *meeting* or *gathering* it was replaced by the word собрание [sobranie]. In the immediate post-Soviet period, the use of собор [sobor] gives K&K's name an interestingly positive tone, as old, pre-Soviet values, including religion, regain their prior prominence.

VAM, too, skips creating a new word for *Entmoot*, using an archaic word for *assembly* instead: сход [skhod]. This was an assembly of a more recent vintage than вече [veche]. The сход [skhod] was still in current use in the late nineteenth and early twentieth centuries. It is associated with farming communities and collective farms, which gives it a slight rustic tint that is not entirely out of place in Tolkien's Legendarium. It competes well with вече [veche], but the functions of the вече [veche] are a better match for *moot*.

Yakhnin likewise skirted the problem of dreaming up a new word for *Entmoot*, and used yet another expression for *gathering*. He said "we will all get together in a group (Соберемся скопом [Soberemsya skopom]). (Ya T.62) This is a very colloquial expression and lacks any hint of history or tradition, which would probably have been lost on Yakhnin's intended young audience in any event. An event described in this manner would probably have ended in a drunken brawl, which is hardly a suitable outcome for a gathering of Ents.

Kistyakovskij, Gruzberg, Nemirova and Volkovskij all nicely calque Treebeard's gloss of *Entmoot*—gathering of Ents—with the modern собрание энтов [sobranie ehntov]. Собрание [sobranie] is the noun from the verb *to gather* (собирать/собрать [sobirat'/sobrat']). Энтов [Ehntov] is the genitive plural of *Ent*.

Tolkien used the word *moot* in his description of Shire politics as well. There, Tolkien refers to the Thain as the master of the Shire-moot. (F.30) Ideally, the translation of *Shire-moot* should match the translation of *Entmoot*. Four of the translators used some variant of сход [skhod], which VAM had used for *moot* in her rendition of *Entmoot*. Unfortunately, VAM was not one of them. Her rendition of *Shire-moot* was based on the same word that G&G had used when talking about *Entmoot*: Сбор [Sbor]. She prettied it up with an adjective string that could have come right off the pages of a Soviet newspaper. Her name for the *Shire-moot* was *The Great All-Hobbit Assembly* (Великий Всехоббитский Сбор [Velikij Vsekhobbitskij Sbor]). The prefix *All-* was used to describe the great Socialist Soviet People's Congresses like the Всероссийский Съезд Советов [Vserossijskij S"ezd Sovetov], which was the name of the ruling body of the Russian Soviet Federal Socialist Republic (RSFSR) from 1918-1925 and the Всесоюзная Коммунистическая Партия (большевиков) [Vsesoyuznaya Kommunisticheskaya Partiya (bol'shevikov)], which was the name of the Communist Party of the Soviet Union (CPSU) from 1925-1952. The Socialist-Soviet allusion carried by this version of the name will be a turn-off to most Russian readers, and Tolkien would have undoubtedly been none too pleased with it himself.

The only two translators to match the elements in *Entmoot* and *Shire-moot* were Gruzberg and Nemirova. They both repeated the element собрание [sobranie]. Gruzberg said that the *Shire-moot* was the *gathering of the Shire* (собрание Шира [sobranie Shira]), echoing his rendition of Treebeard's gloss of *Entmoot*, собрание энтов [sobranie ehntov]. Nemirova made it the *Hobbit gathering* (Хоббитское собрание [khobbitskoe sobranie]), and then added a belt to her suspenders translation, like she had done with

Entmoot, by calling it the Вече [Veche]. Consistency of terms is very important when translating Tolkien, and Gruzberg and Nemirova were both obviously aware of this.

Most of the translators who included *Thain*—Bobyr' and Yakhnin left it out—simply transliterated it as Тан [Tan] (there is no 'Th' sound in Russian). This is the same rendition as is used in the Pasternak Russian translation[18] of *Macbeth* for the title *Thane*, a land-holding noble in the King's service. Macbeth became the Thane of Cawdor in Shakespeare's play. This spelling represents the Scottish usage of the title. The *OED* hypothosizes that, if the Old English word with the same meaning (*thegn*) had remained actively used into modern times, normal orthographic changes would have resulted in Tolkien's spelling of **thain*. Some historians now use *thegn* to distinguish Anglo-Saxon thanes from Scottish thanes.

The root in **thain* can be seen in the modern English words *captain* and *chieftain*, both meaning *headman*. These words are a combination of the Latin word for *head*, *caput* (*capitis* in the genitive), and the French *chef* [chief] with the element *thain*. Compare the German word for *captain*, *Hauptmann*, which is literally *headman*.

Kistyakovskij did something to rescue *Thain* from the bowl of alphabet soup that the transliteration floats in for most Russian readers. He turned it into Хоббитан [Khobbitan], which rhymes with the Russian word for the rank of *captain* (капитан [kapitan]). It is an elegant reconstruction of the linguistic process that produced *captain*, but with a Tolkienesque first element. This is the same approach that VAM used very successfully for her version of *The Shire*: Hobbitshire. (q.v.)

Umanskij was the only one to translate *Thain*. He used the word *Ruler* (Правитель [Pravitel']. U F.201, R.842) The translation is transparent to the modern reader, but it lacks the subtlety and depth of Tolkien's archeologism. Worse yet, Umanskij tries to make *Ruler* do double duty as both *Thain* and *The Chief*. (U R.836) This shows an inexcusably poor grasp of Tolkien's finely nuanced vocabulary and word choice.

Nemirova could have parlayed her success with *veche* into a double win, if she had continued along the same historical, functional line and made *Thain* — посадник [Posadnik]. The functions of both were essentially the same.

Fallohide. Tolkien notes that this name is one of special difficulty, because of the first element, *fallow*, which he uses with the archaic meaning of *yellow* or *pale*. He suggests that the translator concentrate on the sense of *fallow* first and not be concerned if an archaic form cannot be found. Only K&K manage to combine both *pale* and *hide* in their rendition of the name, producing Белоскоры [Beloskory (pl.)]. While бело [belo] is a common element for *pale*, скор [skor] is an archaic element for *hide*. It only still shows up in the words for *egg shell*: скорлупа [skorlupa] and *furrier*: скорняк [skornyak]. The modern word *hide* is шкура [shkura]. For a bilingual reader with knowledge of Tolkien's instructions in "Nomenclature," this a very successful solution to this difficult problem. Some native speakers, however, tend to miss the point, and associate скор [skor] with the word for *speedy* (скорый [skoryj]), which means that they perceive the *Fallohides* to mean "White Speedies."

G&G take another tact altogether. They turn the Fallohides into the "Forest (Hobbits)" (Лесовики [Lesoviki (pl.)]), in which лес [les] means *forest* and -овик [-ovik] is a noun suffix for persons having something to do with the adjectival root to which it is attached. This is obviously taken from Tolkien's description of the Fallohides in the prologue: "They were lovers of trees and of woodlands." (F.22) The change of the attribute used to identify them from an indication of their skin color to an indication of what they were fond of could be viewed as a concession to contemporary political correctness, but it is no more appropriate than any other political distortion introduced into the text.

Kistyakovskij, uncharacteristically, only used one of the two elements in his rendition. His name is Беляки [Belyaki (pl.)]. It is based on a productive suffix for adjectives that creates nouns for persons or things that have the characteristic of the adjective. His Fallohides, are, therefore, *the ones who are white*.

His choice for this name was governed, however, by other considerations. In the introduction to the second, unabridged edition of the first volume of the set, refuting all Tolkien's protestations to the contrary (L.158n; L.406-7), Murav'ev provides an etymology of the word *Hobbit* as: "ho(mo) [Latin for man] + (ra)bbit." (M&K$_{1988}$, F.20) Kistyakovskij was following Murav'ev's etymology instead of Tolkien's, when he made up his names. His names for the three strains of Hobbits can all be associated with rabbits:

Fallohides   Беляки [Belyaki]: This name is the Russian word for *white hare*;

Stoors   Струсы [Strusy]: This name is derived from the verb *to cower* струсить [strusit'], a characteristic so typical for a hare that it is part of the Latin name for hares (*Lepus Timidus*), as well as the descriptor for the hare in Fangorn's list of Living Creatures (T.84); and

Harfoots   Лапитупы [Lapitupy]: This name means *blunt paw*. It is derived from лапа [lapa] - paw, and тупой [tupoj] - an adjective, meaning *blunt*. Lapitup is the name of a character in a novella by Yurij Olesha (1899-1960) entitled Три толстяка [The Three Fat Men],[19] in which Olesha uses animals to describe the characters. The Director limped like a wounded crow, the Spaniard looked like a rat, standing on its hind legs.[20] Lapitup was the circus strongman and, when he did his act, his "muscles moved under his skin, exactly like rabbits that had been swallowed by a boa constrictor." [21]

The story is an allegory of the Revolution of 1917, written as a fairy tale for children, in which the three Fat Men play the role of the bourgeoisie. Lapitup is one of the supporters of the three Fat Men, having sold out to them for gold,[22] which, in the light of K&K's description of Bilbo as "he is a typical, modern, rural 'bourgeois'" (K&K H.313), makes Lapitup an interesting character model for the Harfoots. On the other hand, given Tolkien's attitude towards gold (q.v.), Tolkien would certainly not have approved of the comparison.

The Three Fat Men was written in 1924, but not published until 1928. It was the first Revolutionary fairy tale in Soviet literature. Critical reception was varied, but A.V. Lunacharsky (1875-1933), the leading Soviet literary critic of the time, viewed it as an indication of the acceptance of the Revolution by the artistic intelligentsia. It was made into a play, an opera, a ballet, a movie and was dramatized on the radio. For the older generation of Soviet readers, the name would have been familiar. Younger Russian readers, however, have no associations with the name *Lapitup*.

Kistyakovskij's accent on the "(ra)bbit" in *Hobbit* does not stop there. Based on the words for *rabbit* (кролик [krolik]) and for *hare* (зайчик [zajchik]) he builds a whole family of "(ra)bbit" names. *Bandobras Took* becomes Брандобрас Крол [Bandobras Krol]; *Tookland*, Укролье [Ukrol'e], literally *Rabbit-land*; and *Tuckborough*, Укрольные Низины [Ukrol'nye Niziny], literally *the Rabbit-land Lowlands*. *Crickhollow*, where Frodo moved before going on his quest, becomes Кроличья Балка [Krolich'ya Balka], literally *Rabbit Hollow*.

Buckland becomes Заячьи Холмы [Zayach'i Kholmy], literally *Hare Hills*; *Buckelbury* is Зайгород [Zajgorod], literally *Hare-town*; and the *Brandybucks* are Брендизайки [Brendizajki], read as the *Brandy-hares*. The accent on "(ra)bbit" is even further strengthened by the use of the Russian word for *burrow* нора [nora] for the "holes in the ground" in which Hobbits live. *Hobbiton* is Норгорд [Norgord] and *Smallburrow* is Норочкинс [Norochkins]. To put more icing on the cake, *Longbottom*, the source of the best tobacco in the Shire, is rendered as Длинохвостье [Dlinokhvost'e], literally *Longtail-land*. *Longtail* is the name of the rabbit hero in the Russian fairy tale about the rabbit who was not afraid of anything.

This presents a completely different picture of the Hobbits for the Russian reader than the one that Tolkien paints for the English-speaking reader. In his letter to Roger Lancelyn Green, Tolkien stated that "the only E. word that influenced the invention [of the name Hobbit] was 'hole'; ... the trolls' use of *rabbit* was merely an obvious insult, of no more etymological significance than Thorin's insult to Bilbo 'descendent of rats!'" (L.406) Tolkien would doubtless not have been pleased with Murav'ev's etymology or Kistyakovskij's family of "(ra)bbit" names. Nevertheless, Kistyakovskij's Hobbit names are a linguistic tour de force, reflecting his skill and imagination.

The Gruzberg-A and -B version of *Fallohide* both use a derivative of an existing adjective meaning *Pale Face*: Светлоликий [Svetlolikij]. They simply dropped part of the adjective ending to produce: Светлолики [Svetloliki]. This is comprised of the elements светло [svetlo], which means *light* or *pale* and лик [lik], which is an archaic word for *face*. In Gruzberg-B, the unknown editors used the same names for the three strains of Hobbits as are used in the A version, however, the first time that the names are introduced, each of them is followed by Kistyakovskij's name for that strain in parentheses [eg.: Светлолики (Беляки)], so that readers already familiar with those names can follow the story. In Gruzberg-C, the version obtained directly from the author and not modified by all and sundry while being readied for posting on the web, *Fallohide* is transliterated in good Gruzberg fashion (Феллоухайды [Felloukhajdy, pl.]), as are *Harfoots* (Харфуты [Kharfuty, pl.]), *Stoors* (Стуры [Stury, pl.]). The CD-ROM and the print version followed suit. Umanskij used the same transliteration for *Harfoots* and *Stoors*, but spelled *Fallohide* as if it were pronounced *Falloheed: (Фэллоухиды [Fehllokhidy, pl.]).

VAM's rendition of *Fallohide* is Светлинги [Svetlingi (pl.)]. The first element is Russian: the same element as is used in the Gruzberg-A version:

светло [svetlo]. The second element (-линг [-ling]) is not productive in Russian and is probably taken from the name given to Hobbits by men, *Halflings*, and from the analogous *Easterlings*, which VAM rendered very adeptly as полуростки [polurostki] and востокане [vostokane]. The result is a hybrid, which is neither Russian nor Tolkien, and only intriguing to the bilingual reader. Her renditions of the names of the other two strains of Hobbits show different approaches. The *Stoors* are the Сторы [Story (pl.)], a transliteration with a long 'O' sound instead of an 'OO' sound, and the *Harfoots* are the Мохноноги [Mokhnonogi], literally the *Shaggy Feet*.

Nemirova turns *Fallohides* into the *Brown Heads* (Буроголовые [Burogolovye]). Her name is a combination of a color for hair (бурый [buryj]) and the adjective for *head*, and keys on Tolkien's description of Hobbits' hair as "commonly brown" (P.20), which was a characteristic of all Hobbits, not just the Fallohides. Her version of *Harfoots* Шерстоноги [Sherstonogi (pl.)], on the other hand, is very readable. It means *wooly footed*. Her renditions of *Stoors* is Стурсы [Stursy (pl.)], a transliteration that includes the English plural ending -s, and follows it with a Russian plural ending -ы [-y]. Both VAM and Gruzberg dropped the English plural ending before adding the Russian one. For the Russian reader it is just so much alphabet soup in any event, and the extra 's' will not be of any consequence, but it is disturbing for the bilingual reader. More disturbing is the fact that she mixed translation and transliteration in her approach to the three names. They should either all be translated or all be transliterated. A combination of the two approaches is unsatisfactory.

Volkovskij's version of *Fallohide* is also a descriptive translation, made to look, in the singular, like an old Shirish word ending in -ень [-en']. It is based on the root скрыть [skryt'], which means *to hide* or *to conceal*. His name (Скрытни [Skrytni, pl.]) could best be translated as *the hidden ones*. This interpretation is supported by Volkovskij's final sentence in the paragraph describing the Fallohides, which bears but faint resemblance to what Tolkien was talking about.

> Копни поглубже родословную любого видного семейства и наверняка наткнешься на скрытня: Туки ведь от них пошли, да и хозяева Баковин тоже. (V P.17)
>
> BT: Dig deeper into the family tree of any prominent family and you will probably bump into a "hidden one": The Tooks came from them as well as the Masters of Buckland.
>
> JRRT: Even in Bilbo's time the strong Fallohidish strain could still be

noted among the greater families, such as the Tooks and the Masters of Buckland. (F.22)

If one has to dig deeper into a family tree to find a Fallohidish strain, then it must have been hidden. In Tolkien's version, no effort was needed to note it among the greater families of the Shire. Volkovskij apparently made a translation mistake, and adjusted the text to make his interpretation fit. He was confused by the homonyms *hide* as in *to conceal*, and *hide* as in *the skin of an animal*.

His versions of the names *Harfoot* and *Stoor* are equally unusual. His Harfoots became the Расторопы [Rastoropy, pl.]. This name is derived from the adjective расторопный [rastoropnyj] which means *quick, prompt, efficient*. It makes the Harfoots sound like businessmen, or Practical Pig, of *Three Little Pigs* fame, instead of like "the most normal and representative variety of Hobbit." (F.22)

Volkovskij's version of *Stoors* is Схватни [Skhvatni, pl.]. This name does not comfortably fit the word-formation pattern used in his other 'old Hobbit' names. His other names are substantivized adjectives. Dal' substantiates an appropriate adjective form, but the meaning that it gives is a string of archaic words describing the narrow point of an object, as in *waist*. (Dal' IV.369) This meaning hardly seems appropriate for the Stoors, whose name suggests the Dutch word *stoer*, meaning *brave*, unless Volkovskij was looking for a translation of *tuck* (compare Tuckborough) in its meaning of the flat fold normally sewn into a woman's dress to make it narrower at the waist, which, given his treatment of *Fallohides*, is not impossible. Attributing other meanings of the root given in Dal' to Volkovskij's name lends it a meaning of *grasp, seize*, which makes the Stoors either very smart, because they are able to grasp the meaning of things, or very grasping. *Grasping* would seem to point to the Sackville-Bagginses, who were not overly typical Hobbits. Another possibility is based on the word схватка [skhvatka], which means a *fight*. This would make the Stoors a quarrelsome lot, somewhat suggestive of the stereotypical Irishman of literary fame. Think of the extended fight scene in *A Quiet Man* with John Wayne and Maureen O'Hara.[23]

The way that VAM condensed the old Shirish names for the days of the week from their long, archaic forms to their modern, enigmatic forms suggest another approach to reading the meaning in Volkovskij's rendition of *Stoors*.

Tolkien explains that the days of the week in Shirish were named after, 1) the Stars, 2) the Sun, 3) the Moon, 4) the Two Trees, 5) the Heavens, 6) the Sea and 7) the Valar or powers in that order. "[T]he meanings of their translated names were soon forgotten, or no longer attended to, and the forms were much reduced, especially in everyday pronunciation." (A.484) He then gives both the archaic full form and the shortened form used at the time of the War of the Ring. VAM's excellent reproduction of these pairs shows the modern forms all ending in -ень [-en'], and the archaic forms in день [den'], which means *day*: In their modern forms, some of VAM's names for the days of the week are equally as enigmatic as Бебень [Beben'].

Modern	Archaic	Meaning
1) звездень [zvezden']	звездодень [zvezdoden']	звезда [zvezda] = star,
2) солдень [solden']	солнцедень [solntseden']	солнце [solntse] = sun,
3) лунень [lunen']	лунодень [lunoden']	луна [luna] = moon,
4) древень [dreven']	древодень [drevoden']	дерево [derevo] = tree,[24]
5) небень [neben']	небодень [neboden']	небо [nebo] = heaven,
6) морень [moren']	моредень [moreden']	море [more] = sea,
7) высень [vysen']	высокдень [vysokden']	высокий [vysokij] = high (adj.).[25]

(Following the Russian custom, none of them were capitalized.)

Approaching Volkovskij's name as having been formed through this pattern of condensation results in a verbose form of the name that would have been Схвати день! [Svkhati den']. This is the translation of the proverbial Latin admonition *Carpe Diem!*, that is used by some English-Russian translators, who lack a strong enough classical background to know that *Carpe Diem!* is normally translated into Russian as Лови день! [Lovi den'!], and translate the English translation of the proverb (Seize the day!) somewhat literally. *Seize the day!* is an interesting philosophy for the Hobbits who were less shy of men, having lived long by the banks of the River Anduin, until they followed the Harfoots west, settling between Tharbad and the borders of Dunland, before moving north again. (F.22)

Both Bobyr' and Yakhnin passed on the opportunity to show what they could do with the names of the three strains of Hobbits, and omitted them.

Frogmorton. Tolkien's instructions to translators indicate that *Frogmorton* should be translated as a combination of the elements: *frog + moor + town*. There are four occurrences of *Frogmorton* in *LotR*: three in Chapter VIII of Book 6 ("The Scouring of the Shire"), and one in Appendix B ("The Tale of Years"). Volkovskij declined all three of the opportunities that Tolkien gave him to show off his skill as a wordsmith. The Appendices in the set containing the Volkovskij translation were done by Korolev, who left out the date entry for Frodo's arrest in Frogmorton.

Gruzberg's and Umanskij's transliteration was Фрогмортон [Frogmorton]. Nemirova uses this version on her map, but, in the text, she uses *Frog Meadow* (Лягушачий Луг [Lyagushachij Lug]), building on the same linguistic foundation as Murav'ev, who did volume III without Kistyakovskij. (N R.281)

Murav'ev uses an existing word—(Лягушатник [Lyagushatnik])— that has three possible meanings: 1) an aquarium for frogs in a science classroom, 2) a kiddie (shallow) swimming pool, and 3) a body of water that has a lot of frogs in it. It is built on the Russian root for *frog* (лягушка [lyagushka]). To make his name sound like a place name, Murav'ev makes it plural, which is a common feature of Russian toponymy. His Лягушатники [Lyagushatniki] is the best of the adapted versions.

Frogmorton is only in volume III, and, at the time that they were working on their samizdat follow-up to the abridged M&K volume I, G&G could not have seen what Murav'ev made of *Frogmorton*, nevertheless, they used Лягушатники [Lyagushatniki] in the samizdat version of their translation, too. In the printed version, however, they changed it to Дрягва [Dryagva]. This is a dialectical word for *bog*, *quagmire*, *swamp*. It is less satisfactory than Murav'ev's because its meaning will not be transparent to the majority of readers who do not take the trouble to look it up in a specialized dictionary. G&G's unique usage of Дрягва [Dryagva] as the translation for *Frogmorton* is one of the things that makes it possible to clearly identify the Appendices in the 1993 set of *The Hobbit*, *LotR* and *The Silmarillion* by "Olimp" Publishers (p. 77), which did not attribute any of the translations it contained. The Appendices were done by G&G. *The Hobbit* was the Rakhmanova translation. *LotR* was done by M&K, and *The Silmarillion* was done by Estel, whose version is the one most often printed. The original (1992) M&K, which was republished in the "Olimp" set, did not contain the Appendices.

Yakhnin uses an obsolete adjective form of *frog* and combines it with the word for *mill-pond* to form Лягушкина Запруда [Lyagushkina Zapruda: Frog Pond]. It is an elegant construction that feels right at home in the text. It is an imaginative invention that competes well with Murav'ev's.

VAM built her name on the word for *toad* (жаба [zhaba]). At first glance, the linguistic model behind her name seems a bit strange for Russian. It uses -с [-s] as an ending, which is not productive in Russian. Her name is Жабс [Zhabs]. The model becomes clear, however, when viewed against the backdrop of Soviet literature. It is a type of construction for talking names that is reminiscent of the names that Nikolaj Nosov used in his well-known children's book *Dunno on the Moon*.[26] When Dunno[27] goes to the moon, he meets Mr. Спрутс [Spruts], derived from the word for *octopus* (спрут [sprut]), Mr. Клопс [Klops], derived from the word for *bug* (клоп [klop]), Mr. Тупс [Tups], derived from the word for *dumb* (тупой [tupoj]), and Mr. Крабс [Krabs], which is derived from the word for *crab*. The fact that all of these characters are Soviet parodies of the enemies of the working class, the bourgeoisie, prompts some readers to recall the pre-Revolutionary use of an enclytic -с [-s] as form of (dis)respect used when addressing one's betters, similar to saying 'sir' at the end of every sentence. In the Soviet period, when Nosov wrote his book, the use of this form of address was especially sarcastic and pejorative.

In the context of Tolkien, Nosov's names have an extra appeal for a researcher familiar with them, because Dunno and his friends are called коротышки [korotyshki, pl.], which is the diminutive of the same word that Bobyr'/Umanskij used for *Hobbits*, making them somewhat smaller than Hobbits. Bobyr'/Umanskij call the Hobbits коротыши [korotyshi, pl.]. It is related to the Russian word for *short* (короткий [korotkij]), and might best be translated as *shortnik*.

> <...> за быстрым, прозрачным Брендивейном, живут среди зеленых холмов Шира Коротыши. (В.5)
> BT: [...] across the swift, clear Brandywine, among the green hills of the Shire, live the Shortniks.

> — Теперь же, теперь же, мой дорогой коротыш! — сказал Гандальф. (U F.216)
> BT: "Right away, right away, my dear Shortnik!" said Gandalf.
> JRRT: "Now, now my dear Hobbit!" said Gandalf. (F.60)

As if that were not enough, *Dunno on the Moon* also has two characters with names that sound strangely Hobbitish: Скрягинс [Skryagins] and Гадкинз [Gadkinz]. The first one is based on the word for *skinflint* (скряга [skryaga]), and the second is based on the word for *lowdown skunk* (гад [gad]). Both are, needless to say, negative characters. Skryagins is a factory owner. Gadkinz is a newspaper magnate. To really put the Hobbit icing on the cake, Nosov remarks on Dunno's predilection for bright-colored clothes, like a blue hat, yellow trousers, an orange shirt, and a green tie. Though it is highly improbably that either Tolkien or Nosov had ever heard of each other, Tolkien's description of the Hobbits' sartorial preferences sounds very similar. He said that Hobbits "dressed in bright colors, being notably fond of yellow and green." (F.20)

It is easy, therefore, to see why VAM would find this an attractive word formation model. In an unauthorized continuation of the story—*The New Adventures of Dunno: On the Moon Again*,[28] the Russian writer Boris Karlov introduces Mr. Жабс [Zhabs], validating the model that Nosov and VAM used to build their names. Taken to its improbable extreme, using the political implications of Nosov's name formation model, Жабс [Zhabs] could be read as the ancestral estate of a bourgeois landowner, Toad Hall, the home of Mr. Toad from *The Wind in the Willows*.

K&K build their name on the sound that frogs make (квак [kvak]), rather than on the word for *frog*. Unfortunately, they do not translate the other two elements, which produces another hybrid, half-translated, half-transliterated name: Квакмортон [Kvakmorton]. Neither, uncharacteristically, do they have an endnote to explain the meaning of the name. Without a contextual prompt or an endnote to make the reader think of frogs in connection with квак [kvak], the first part of the name will be just so much more foreign alphabet soup. Mix-and-match names like this only confuse the monolingual reader, who will be inclined to read the first part of the name as the transliteration of a foreign word, which, in this case, is quite possible. K&K's name is the transliteration that would have resulted if Tolkien's name had been *Quackmorton. (Compare: quarter | квартал [kvartal].) In English, *quack* is the sound that ducks make, so the hypothetical *Quackmorton would have been a town on the moor where there are a lot of ducks quacking. *Quackmorton could likewise be seen as a town on the moor where you would not want to seek medical assistance. A *quack* is, after all, also an incompetent medical doctor. K&K's name would have worked with an endnote, but a joke that needs an explanation is not funny.

Gamgee. In "Nomenclature," Tolkien said that this was an uncommon English surname for which he did not know the derivation. His instructions were to treat the name as meaningless and to transliterate it. When transliterating English names, the Russians usually do not seek a letter-for-letter equivalence in the Cyrillic alphabet, but try to approximate the sound of the name instead. In "Nomenclature," Tolkien essentially quotes from the *OED* article on *Gamgee*, which explains that gamgee tissue was invented by Dr. Sampson Gamgee (1828-1886). The pronunciation given by the *OED* is [Gam-jee] with the first 'G' pronounced as in *gap*, and the second pronounced as in *ginger*.

The phonetic approach applied to the Russian spelling of *Gamgee* produced some interesting results. Gruzberg, Umanskij, G&G, VAM and subtitles spelled the name Гэмджи [Gehmdzhi]. Bobyr' had an essentially identical spelling that used an "A" as the first vowel. This is the *OED* pronunciation.

K&K and the unknown editors of Gruzberg-A spell *Gamgee* as Гэмги [Gehmgi]. This assumes that the name is pronounced [Gam-gee] with both 'G's pronounced hard, as in *gap*. Nemirova had a none-of-the-above solution that turned the name into Джемджи [Dzhemdzhi]. This assumes that the name is pronounced [Jam-jee], with both 'G's pronounced as in *ginger*. Upon hearing this pronounciation, David Doughan immediately saw through to the possible new meaning that it gives to *Gamgee*: someone with "an excessive love of preserves, which is surely a Hobbitish trait."

Though Tolkien's recommendation in "Nomenclature" was to treat *Gamgee* as meaningless and simply to transliterate it, Kistyakovskij gave Sam a meaningful surname based on the word скромный [skromnyj], which means *modest* or *humble*. The description is a good one, but it is an oversimplification of Sam's character that draws conclusions for the reader, rather than letting the reader develop his or her own conclusions about Sam's character as Tolkien intended. Sam is a much more complex character than just Frodo's 'humble' servant. This version of the name was repeated in Gruzberg-B. He calls him Сэм Скромби [Sehm Skrombi].

Volkovskij also translated *Gamgee*. In his version, Sam's last name is Гужни [Guzhni]. This is another of Volkovskij's old Shirish names ending in -ень [-en'] (q.v. **Baggins**), which have a fugitive 'E' in the genitive, changing the ending from -ень [-en'] to -ни [-ni]. His name is formed from the word гуж [guzh], which is a part of a harness. Horse-drawn conveyances having fallen out of favor, гуж [guzh] survives in modern Russian in the expression взялся за гуж, не говори, что не дюж, which roughly translates to *once you have put on the harness, don't say that you aren't up to the job*. In that context, Volkovskij's name is an interesting commentary on Sam's steadfastness. There are times when it seems to wane, as in the scene in Chapter 3 of Book VI ("Mount Doom"). Sam's mental state reaches the low point of their quest, but hardly has Sam vocalized his despair in the face of impending doom, than the narrator (Tolkien) gives him a vision of new hope. (R.259) Sam was up to the job he had taken on when he put on the *harness* (гуж [guzh]) of accompanying Frodo on his quest, and Volkovskij's translation of his name highlights that.

Yakhnin's version of *Gamgee* displays an erudite splendor that may escape some of his readers. His rendition of *Gamgee* is Плутоу [Plutou]. This combines a Russian root with an ending that marks his name as foreign. Russian names do not end in -оу. That combination is only possible in the transliteration of foreign names. If such a name really existed in English, it would be spelled *Plutow. (Compare Gruzberg's rendition of Crickhollow: Крикхоллоу [Krikkhollou].)

The name is, nevertheless, a "speaking" name. It is a play on the Russian term плутоватый слуга [plutovatyj sluga, literally: roguish servant]. In the jargon of the theater, this is the *zanni*, the archetypical valet-buffoon of the travelling commedia dell'arte troupes of Europe that catered to audiences made up of common people, playing in town squares during fairs. The performances were improvised rather than scripted, and the humor was direct, bawdy and coarse. The scenarios were populist, rather than elitist, and the zanni—the servant—was generally the sympathetic character, not the master. The goal of the zanni was to avoid being beaten and to outwit their masters, a scenario that spoke readily to the commedia's audience. The plot of these set pieces usually revolves around a pair of young lovers (sometimes even two), who are being kept apart by the zanni's master. The zanni agrees to help the lovers, and after seemingly making a mess of the whole affair, emerges triumphant in the end. The English word *zany* is a close linguistic relative of the word *zanni*. Zanni itself is derived from a dialectal nickname for Giovanni, reflecting the Italian roots of commedia dell'arte, which flourished from the sixteenth to the eighteenth centuries. Toward the later part of this period, zanni plots from the commedia dell'arte were scripted and moved into "legitimate" theater, resulting in such classic stage plays as: *Il Servitore di Due Padroni*, [A Servant of Two Masters] (1745) by Carlo Goldoni (1707-1793), *Crispin, rival de son maître*, [Crispin, The Rival of his Master] (1707) by Alain René Le Sage (1668- 1747), and *Les Fourberies de Scapin* [Scapino's Rogueries] (1671) by Molière (1622-1673), which in Russian is titled Плутни Скапена [Plutni Skapena].

This gives Sam a wholly different role to play in the story, but given Yakhnin's other major distortions to the story, like having the Elves make all the rings, another change, more or less, is hardly significant.

Goldberry. Tolkien included *Goldberry* in his list of translatable names. G&G turned it into Златеника [Zlatenika], which is made up of the archaic word for *gold* (злато [zlato]) and an ending -ника [-nika], which occurs in the names of several berries, such as *strawberry*: (wild) земляника [zemlyanika], *strawberry* (cultivated) клубника [klubnika]; *whortleberry* черника [chernika] and *foxberry* брусника [brusnika]. This name is the most imaginative of all the variants that the translators produced. Aleksandrova obviously agreed with this evaluation of G&G's name, because she used it, too. G&G's rendition succeeds in capturing both elements in the name, whereas most other translators' names only capture one.

K&K also built their name on the archaic word for *gold* (злато [zlato]), but they added the ending -вика [-vika] instead. This is the ending of the Russian word for *blackberries* (ежевика [ezhevika]). On the one hand, K&K's construction is less successful than G&G's, because the ending -вика [-vika] is less productive than the ending -ника [-nika].[29] On the other hand, it does make K&K's *Goldberry* a rarer sort of berry than G&G's.

Kistyakovskij uses an existing word Золотинка [Zolotinka], which means *gold nugget*. This is a subtle change that takes Goldberry out of the world of living plants and makes her more a part of Arda itself—a mineral. VAM, Nemirova, Volkovskij and the unknown editors of Gruzberg-B also use Kistyakovskij's name. Gruzberg's own rendition was, as usual, a transliteration: Голдбери [Goldberi]. Umanskij's was almost the same, except that it used a double 'RR': Голдберри [Goldberri].

Volkovskij adds an interesting touch to Goldberry's formal name. Tolkien has her introduce herself to Frodo as "Goldberry, daughter of the River." (F.172) In Volkovskij's version she introduces herself as Золотинка, дочь Водяницы [Zolotinka, doch' Vodyanitsy]. (V F.178) Водяница [vodyanitsa] is the archaic word for a class of water spirits that is commonly known in modern Russia only as a русалка [rusalka] (feminine water spirit). In the past, though, there was a difference between the two. Rusalkas are considered нежить [nezhit'], the general name for evil spirits of nature. They are pictured as beautiful, pale women with long green hair, which illustrators inevitably show them combing. They sing enchanting songs to lure their victims into the water where they will be drowned. It was believed that they were the spirits of babies who died before being baptized and of young women who had drowned themselves because of a disappointment in love.

A водяница [vodyanitsa], however, was not considered нежить [nezhit']. She was the spirit of someone who had drowned after having been baptized. (Dal' I.219) For those few who know the difference today, Goldberry is, therefore, a positive figure. For those who do not know the difference, she is simply the daughter of a rusalka, a normally evil spirit. This makes Volkovskij's embellishment much less successful than Kistyakovskij's.

Kistyakovskij made her the daughter of the river emperor (речная царевна [rechnaya tsarevna]) (M&K F_{1982}.89, F_{1988}.166), which evokes an image of fairy tale beauty and splendor, avoiding the associations with rusalkas and нежить [nezhit']. It is much more explicit than simply capitalizing *River* as Tolkien did, but, perhaps, right on the mark for a less attentive audience, indifferent to the significance of capital letters. All the other translators, except Yakhnin, used a much more literal Дочь Реки [Doch' Reki]: Daughter of the River.

Yakhnin joined Kistyakovskij in making her the daughter of the river emperor (царевна речная [tsarevna rechnaya]), reversing the word order to give her title a more fairy-tale-like ring. (Ya F.91) On the other hand, his rendition of her name is much too prosaic. He called her Златовласка [Zlatovlaska]. This is built on the same archaic word for *gold* that G&G and K&K used. It is paired with a second archaic element that has nothing to do with *berries*. The second element means *hair*, and just to make sure that his readers do not miss the implication of the name 'hidden' behind the archaic elements, Yakhnin introduces her with a description one line earlier, using the modern words for *golden haired*: с золотыми волосами [s zolotymi volosami]. The change is subtle, but Goldberry definitely loses by it.

Hobbiton. In his "Nomenclature," Tolkien said that the name *Hobbiton* was to contain the element *Hobbit* and an element meaning *village*. As *Hobbit* is хоббит [hobbit] in Russian, except in Bobyr'/Umanskij, all the *LotR* translators—less Kistyakovskij, VAM and Yakhnin—simply chose to transliterate *Hobbiton* as well. Even though they transliterated the name, in their endnote, K&K provided a gloss for it, explaining that *-ton* is a common element in British toponymy, and a contraction of the word *town*.

Kistyakovskij invented a picturesque name that plays on historical Russian toponymy and on the opening line of *The Hobbit*: "In a hole in the ground there lived a Hobbit." He took the Russian word used for *hole in the ground* in the Rakhmanova translation—нора [nora]: *burrow* (R H.5)—and combined it with an archaic element meaning town: -горд [–gord]. This element is distantly related to the second element in the name *Midgard* of the Norse myths. It shows up in contemporary Russian place names as -город [–gorod] or -град [–grad]. For example: Nizhnij Novgorod, Leningrad. His rendition of *Hobbiton* is Норгорд [Norgord], which literally means *Burrow-city*. This is perhaps a bit grand for what Tolkien had intended as a country town, but then again, so was Kistyakovskij's name for *The Shire*: *Hobbitania*. (q.v.)

VAM took a very unusual approach. She transliterated *Hobbiton* as if it were spelled *Hobbittown: Хоббиттаун [Hobbittaun]. That is, of course, what Tolkien meant, and VAM's spelling will be clear to the monolingual Russian reader, who will recognize it as a part of such widely known foreign place names as Jamestown (Джеймстаун [Dzhejmstaun]), Georgetown (Джорджтаун [Dzhordzhtaun]) and Cape Town (Кейптаун [Kejptaun]). This gives Hobbiton an air of a world-class city. Her translation is, perhaps, slightly more imposing than it needs to be, but it shows the same incisive kind of linguistic wit as her translation of *the Shire*: Hobbitshire (q.v.), and Kistyakovskij's translation of *Thain*: Hobbittan. (q.v. **Entmoot**) She wisely took the step—common in Russian texts dealing with foreign place names—of preceding the name with the Russian word for *town* (городок [gorodok]) in the opening paragraph of Chapter 1 of volume I. This makes things much clearer to the reader, which is one of the key characteristics of VAM's translation. Yakhnin followed her lead.

In *The Hobbit*, the name *Hobbiton* appears in the announcement of the sale at auction of "the effects of the late Bilbo Baggins Esquire, of Bag-End, Underhill, Hobbiton." (H.284) Rakhmanova essentially transliterated the whole thing, with the exception of *Underhill*, which she translated: Бильбо Бэггинс, эсквайр, из Бэг-Энда Под Холмом, графство Хоббитон [Bilbo Baggins, ehskvajr, of Bag End Under the Hill, county of Hobbiton]. (R H.251) She, like VAM, preceded *Hobbiton* with a word indicating to the Russian reader that this was a foreign geographical name. She, however, said that it was a county (графство [grafstvo]). This confuses *Hobbiton* with *the Shire*, and Kaminskaya and Korolev both followed her lead.

The Kaminskaya translation of Bilbo's name and address on the notice of auction followed Kistyakovskij's lead, but with a bow to VAM, and a nod to Rakhmanova. Her version said: Бильбо Торбинс, эсквайр, проживавший по адресу Торба-в-Холме, Хоббитания [Bil'bo Torbins, ehskvajr, living at Bag-in-the-Hill, Hobbitaniya (the Shire)]. (Ksk H.132) Just like Rakhmanova, she confuses *Hobbiton* with *the Shire*, but she uses Kistyakovksij's translation of *the Shire* (Хоббитания [Khobbitaniya]) instead of Rakhmanova's графство Хоббитон [grafstvo Khobbiton]). Just like VAM, she changed Kistyakovskij's Торба-на-Круче [Torba-na-Kruche] to Торба-в-Холме [Torba-v-Kholme]. (q.v. **Baggins**) The embellishment of the address with проживавший по адресу [living at] gives the address a nice touch of official Soviet jargon.

Korolev likewise followed Kistyakovskij's lead for the names in Bilbo's address, but with a bow to Kaminskaya. Just like Kaminskaya he turned *Hobbiton* into the Shire (Хоббитания [Khobbitaniya]). His address was also much too terse, leaving out all the fancy parts of Tolkien's formulation and restructuring the phrase into smaller bit-sized chunks. His announcement was for the sale at auction of "the things of Mr. Bilbo Torbins. The auction will take place at Bag-on-a-Steep-Slope, Hobbitaniya." (Kor H.343) The other disappointment here is the use of the Russian word for *Mister* (господин [gospodin]) instead of *Esquire* (эсквайр [ehskvajr]). While, at first glance, ehskvajr may look like just so much Russian alphabet soup, the word эсквайр [ehskvajr] is listed in Russian dictionaries with the meaning of an honorific title peculiar to Great Britain.[30] Even though it may not be a part of every Russian's active vocabulary, there is no ready Russian equivalent that would be more recognizable. To give Korolev his due, however, господин [gospodin] is more widely recognized and it also is marked as an honorific for a foreigner. Following the Revolution in 1917, the use of господин [gospodin] was discouraged when referring to citizens of the Soviet Union and came to be used only when referring to foreigners. In polite Soviet company, Soviet citizens were addressed with their first name and patronymic (i.e. father's first name plus a suffix that means *son/daughter of*). If he had been a truly Russian Hobbit, in polite company, Bilbo would have been addressed not as Mister Baggins, but as Bil'bo Bungovich [Бильбо Бунгович (Bilbo son of Bungo)], and the announcement of the auction would have been for the sale of the effects of the late Bilbo Bungovich Baggins, of Bag End, Underhill, Hobbiton.

Yakhnin has a very terse rendition of the announcement of the sale "at auction of the property of the late Bilbo Baggins, owner of the Estate 'Under Hill' in the town of Hobbitown." (Ya H.357) The deletions that Yakhnin makes to compact the announcement are more than compensated for by the change that he makes to the names of the attorneys running the auction: Grubb, Grubb and Burrowes. In Yakhnin's version, the first name in the list is Sackville-Baggins. The inclusion of the Sackville-Bagginses in the list is grotesquely funny. It is as if Yakhnin had read the biography of their namesake, Sir Richard Sackville (1516-1566), who was in fact a lawyer. He was so (in)famous for the fortune that he amassed over his lifetime that he was known by his contemporaries as "fill-sack," rather than "Sack-ville."

Isengard. This is the Rohan name for the fortress, based on Noldorin.[31] It was known as Angrenost, *angren = iron, ost = fortress*. Since it is a Rohan name, its elements are based on Old English. Tolkien's recommendation was to leave this name untranslated, because the elements which made it up were so old that their original meaning had become obscured. He reasoned that *isen* is an old variant of the English word for *iron*, and would still be recognized as holding the meaning of *iron* in the Germanic languages, thus making the meaning transparent to the reader. Russian, however, is a Slavic language, and the word for *iron* is железо [zhelezo]. This means that the Russian reader will see no association between the element *isen* and its archaic meaning of *iron*. In all the Russian versions, except Kistyakovskij's and G&G's samizdat version, *Isengard* was transliterated.

Perumov and all the other translators—except Volkovskij—transliterated it with the Russian letter И [I], which is pronounced like the English sound 'EE' in the word *steel* (Исенгард [Isengard]). When he read his own works, Tolkien pronounced the letter 'I' in Isengard like the 'I' in *iron*, which gives it the same sound as the modern German word for *iron*: *Eisen*. To achieve the same sound in Russian, which is normally the goal in transliterating foreign names into Russian, the 'I' in Isengard should have been transliterated as Ай [Aj]. It is a small, subtle change, but it hides the meaning of *iron* in the first element of the name for those Russians, who do speak German. Volkovskij got it right in his version: Айсенгард [Ajsengard]. Korolev used the same form in his Tolkien Encyclopedia.

In the second unabridged edition of the M&K translation of volume I (1988), *Isengard* is transliterated, but in the first abridged edition (1982) and the G&G samizdat follow-on to it, *Isengard* was rendered as Скальбург [Skal'burg]. (M&K$_{1982}$, F.189, F.193) Kistyakovskij's approach to this name, as well as to others, was to create a name based on Tolkien's description rather than to translate or to transliterate Tolkien's name. On the same page that the name *Skal'burg* first appears, Isengard is described as "a circle of sheer rocks that enclose a valley as with a wall, and in the midst of that valley is a tower of stone called Orthanc." (F.338) Kistyakovskij uses the word скала [skala]—*rock face* or *cliff*—in his translation of this description.

The ending -бург [-burg] will be easily recognized by Russian readers as the German word for castle. It has its own entry in the Russian encyclopedic dictionary.[32] This ending can be found in a number of Russian place names like Saint Petersburg, Ekaterinburg and Shlissel'burg, all of which were changed after the Soviets took power. Saint Petersburg became Leningrad, Ekaterinburg became Sverdlovsk and Shlissel'burg became Petrokrepost', the last change taking place during World War II. For many Russians of Kistyakovskij's and Murav'ev's generation, World War II only ended last week and the association tied to the ending -бург [-burg] will evoke a strong negative image of a hostile stronghold to be conquered. Kistyakovskij's Скальбург [Skal'burg] can, therefore, be interpreted to mean "a hostile castle located on a cliff." For the Soviet reader, this is a much more effective name than Isengard, which does not carry any psychological baggage with it to evoke an image in the Russian reader's mind. For the post-Soviet generation of readers, the impact of *-burg* has been largely erased. Following the collapse of Communism, the old names were restored.

The reason that the name was probably changed in the second edition was that Tolkien has other names that end in *-burg*. Mundburg (Minas Tirith) and Hornburg are castles that belong to the "good guys," and, given Tolkien's finely nuanced nomenclature, the names of castles that belonged to the "bad guys" could not possibly have the same ending. These names do not show up, however, until volume II, which means that there would not have been any interference between *Skalburg* and *Mundburg* or *Hornburg* until volume II was published, and that was 7 years after the abridged volume I.

The translation of *Isengard* as *Skal'burg* was obviously not firmly fixed in Kistyakovskij's mind, so the change from *Skal'burg* back to the transliteration of *Isengard* should not have come as too great a surprise.

Between the two instances of the use of *Skal'burg* cited above, the name can be found written as Скальград [Skal'grad]. (M&K$_{1982}$, F.192) This is the same ending that could be found in Stalingrad and Leningrad. Perhaps Kistyakovskij (and Murav'ev) had considered making a veiled political allusion to Stalingrad with *Skal'grad*, but he (or the censor) had not been thorough enough when cleaning up the text. The political motivation to do something like that was certainly present. (q.v. **One Day in the Life of Frodo Drogovich**) The context would have supported it. No younger generation Russian will believe it.

Lithe. Tolkien glosses "the former" and "the later Lithe" as the Old English words for the months June and July. Since Hobbit calendar names were not intended to be part of the Common Speech, but holdovers from the Hobbits' language before migration, Tolkien felt that they should not be translated.

Bobyr', G&G and Yakhnin avoided the problem of this name by omitting *Lithe* altogether. Gruzberg followed Tolkien's advice and transliterated the name on a letter-for-letter basis: Лите [Lite], pronounced [leet-yeh]. (There is no 'TH' sound in Russian.) K&K and VAM aimed at a sound transliteration and produced Лит [Lit], pronounced [lee-t]. The *OED* notes that *lithe* is pronounced to rhyme with *blithe* and *scythe*. K&K also included an endnote to explain where *Lithe* came from, essentially quoting from Tolkien's "Nomenclature," and pointing out that *Lithe* has nothing to do with the summer solstice. (K&K F.606) Umanskij's solution was to omit the name *Lithe*, and to say that the elections for Mayor were held "not long before the summer solstice." (незадолго до Дня летнего солнцестояния [nezadolgo do Dnya letnego solntsestoyaniya]) (U F.201)

Nemirova transliterates the sound of *Lithe* correctly as Лайт [Lajt], which rhymes with *light*. It is unfortunate, however, that 'T' is as close as Russians can get to 'Th', because without the ability to convey the distinctive difference of these two sounds (T/Th), Nemirova's transliteration is the same as the transliteration of *lite*, a concept that is on its way to becoming a household word in Russian, as the new market economy floods the country with *lite* softdrinks and *lite* cigarettes and *lite* versions of software, all of which are spelled лайт [lajt] in Russian. For the New Russians who read Nemirova's translation, Tolkien's *Lithe* has become a holiday lite, which, given the Hobbits' propensity for food, drink and pipe-weed, seems somewhat out of character. To give Nemirova her due, however, when she was working on her translation in the Soviet Union, during the first samizdat "translation boom" of the early 1980s, there was no interference with her transliteration. Лайт [Lajt] products only reached the Russian market after the Soviet Union collapsed. This also means that Gruzberg, VAM and K&K were not avoiding the interference of *lite* product names, but were simply unsure of how *lithe* was pronounced.

Aleksandrova avoided *the Lithe* and made it *the Turning-day* [Поворотный день (Povorotnyj den')] at midsummer. This does make it clearer to the reader, but, in the process it, unfortunately, diminishes the magic of Tolkien's spell that is built up out of all the names that generated stories in Tolkien's mind.[33]

Kistyakovskij, as if he had read Tolkien's gloss in "Nomenclature," created an appropriate translation of *Lithe* from the old Slavic word for *July*. The root for this word can still be seen in modern Polish, Belorussian and Ukrainian names for *July*: lipiec,ліпень [lipen'] and липень [lipen']. Kistyakovskij added a prefix meaning *near* or *attached to* (при- [pri-]), and made it plural (many Russian holiday names are plural) to produce a word which suggests a meaning of *a holiday attached to July* (прилипки [prilipki, pl.]). This is a very inventive creation that is every bit as obscure to the modern Russian reader as *Lithe* is to the modern English reader. It preserves Tolkien's relationship between *Lithe* and the old name of the month of July. A very good feat of linguistic legerdemain.

Volkovskij also has an interesting piece of linguistic sleight of hand, but, like the sorcerer's apprentice, the spell gets out of hand. His name for *Lithe* begins with the word: хмелина [khmelina], which is a vine of the hops-plant (хмель [khmel'], Latin: Humulus lupulus). (Dal' IV.554) He makes this plural хмелины [khmeliny], which makes it sound like the existing names of celebrations, many of which are religious, and disappeared when the Communists came to power and instituted state atheism. For example: a wake in memory of the dead (проводины [provodiny]), a period of forty days of mourning and prayers for the dead (сороковины [sorokoviny]), nameday of the saint after whom someone is named (именины [imeniny]), Пчельники [pchel'niki], which is a celebration of bees (пчела [pchela]: bee) and honey on July second.[34]

Hops are used to brew beer. (Dal' III.116) Up into the nineteenth century in Russia beer brewing was a festive occasion in which the whole community took part. This was known as a *beer holiday* (пивной праздник [pivnoj prazdnik]). (Dal' III.116) The brewing of the beer was traditionally accompanied by a song[35] to the harvest god, Ладо [Lado],[36] and the main *beer holiday* was the one to celebrate the arrival of Lado on the eve of Saint John the Baptist's Day (June 24),[37] because at Russian latitudes, the first harvest coincides with the solstice, which occurs at this time.[38] Even though хмелины [khmeliny] is an invented name, its implication is clear enough. This is just an attempt to make an end-run around Tolkien's complaint about the Swedish translation.

A description of one from Tereshchenko's *The Way of Life of the Russian People* gives an idea of what went on at a Russian beer brewing festival.

> It is a genuine Russian good time, when they brew beer. When they do, it does not make for cheerfulness just within the family circle, but throughout the neighborhood. People everywhere say: "Where they're brewing beer, there's a good time." [...] Who does not like to have a little fun! And who, if not a Russian, enjoys one's self wholeheartedly! A break from rural life begins with a favorite pastime: brewing beer. [...] It happens that in some places they do drink too much and that even the girls wake up the next morning with a headache.[39]

Specifically referring to a description of a celebration on 24 June in sixteenth century Pskov, Tereshchenko adds:

> [They] celebrated Kupalo day with no less debauchery: they gathered herbs in the fields and in oak forests according to superstitious rites; at night they made merry, beating on drums, playing on horns and fiddles; young women and maidens danced and embraced with boys, forgetting shame and chastity.[40]

Zabylin adds another element to the celebration with his description of what went on at a fair. "This celebration was accompanied by games and dancing, eating and drinking, and especially by fist fights."[41]

Undoubtedly a fun time was had by all, but this is a far cry from what is suggested by Tolkien's "Free Fair on the White Downs at the Lithe." (F.31)

Lune [Lhûne]. Tolkien annotated *Lune* as a Hobbit borrowing of the Elven word *lhûne*, which, therefore, should not be translated, but transliterated. He especially did not want it translated in the sense of *lunar*, but that was what Umanskij, VAM, Nemirova, Kistyakovskij, Volkovskij, Perumov and the editors of Gruzberg-A did. While the translation in Gruzberg-A reads: *the Mountains of the Moon* (Горы Луны [Gory Luny]), all the rest say: *the Lunar Mountains* (Лунные горы [Lunnye gory)].

G&G resolved the problem by translating the meaning of *lhûne*. It means *blue*. In Sindarin, *the Mountains of Lune* are called *Ered Luin*: the Blue Mountains. G&G's name, therefore, became Синие Горы [Sinie Gory] throughout. This is also the name on K&K's map. Yakhnin avoids the name in his text, but on his map, he uses the same approach as G&G. He just uses another adjective for *blue*. He calls *the Mountains of Lune* Голубые Горы [Golubye Gory].

This is the same name that Korolev lists *the Mountains of Lune* under in his Tolkien Encyclopedia. He glosses the name in English and in Sindarin, and offers the "Westron" translation of горы Лун [gory Lun]. This is less than satisfactory, because the average Russian reader will interpret this to mean *the Mountains of the Moons*. Лун [lun] is the genitive plural of the Russian word for *moon*. The effect of multiple moons is to move Tolkien off world into the realm of science fiction. On her map, Nemirova uses the same name as Yakhnin and Korolev, and under it, she includes the name *Ered Luin* in parentheses.

Only Gruzberg and K&K followed Tolkien's advice to transliterate the name. In Gruzberg-C, the final version supplied by the author and not taken from the Internet, it was *The Lune Mountains* (Горы Луне [Gory Lune]). (Gr F.21) In Russian, however, луне [lune] coincides with the spelling of the locative and the dative singular of the Russian word for *moon* (луна [luna]). The Russian reader will be confused by this as were the editors of Gruzberg-A, who changed it so that it would make sense for them. Gruzberg could better have replaced the locative/dative ending -e [-e] with the letter -э [-eh], which would be immediately recognized as the ending of an indeclinable foreign word.

K&K had the best solution for this thorny problem. They transliterated it as Льюнские горы [L'yunskie gory], giving it a Russian adjectival ending. This transliteration is such an un-Russian combination of letters and sounds that the Russian reader will see no connection with the moon (луна [luna]) whatsoever. This is similar to Gruzberg's and Rakhmanova's solution for a transliteration of Durin. (q.v.)

Michel Delving. *Michel Delving* was not included in Tolkien's guide to translators, which meant that he did not intend it to be translated. VAM, K&K, Umanskij, Perumov and Gruzberg (Aleksandrova) followed Tolkien's lack of advice and transliterated the name. The differences in their transliterations center on the pronunciation of the 'I' and the 'CH' in *Michel*. Gruzberg transliterated the name as Майкл-Дельвинг [Maikl-Del'ving], which would be pronounced [Mike-l] with a long 'I'. Aleksandrova, VAM, Umanskij, Perumov and K&K transliterated it as Мичел [Michel], where 'CH' is a single letter in Russian with the sound of 'CH' in the English word *church*, and 'I' is pronounced 'EE.' Even though they transliterated the name, in their endnote K&K provided a gloss for it, pointing to Old English, where *Michel* means *great* and offering two approximate translations: *The Great Quarries* (Большие Карьеры [Bol'shie Kar'ery]) or *The Big Burrows* (Большие Норы [Bol'shie Nory]). (K&K F.604)

Michel usually shows up on the map of England in place-name pairs, where one of the place names is *Michel* (also *Great*) and the other is *Little*. Tolkien was clearly playing on this meaning, because his map of the Shire (F.40) has arrows pointing to both Michel and Little Delving. K&K's map (K&K F. back inside cover) shows Малый Делвинг [Malyj Delving]. Nemirova's map (N R. back inside cover) shows the way to Великие Норы [Velikie Nory: *The Great Burrows*], which is the name that she also uses in the text.

G&G transliterated *Michel*, but translated *Delving*. In their transliteration, they followed Gruzberg's example and rendered the 'CH' as 'K'. Their translation of *Delving* was based on the Russian word for *digging*: рыть [ryt']. They gave it a plural ending -ы [-y], which is a common feature of Russian place names. Their name was: Микорыты [Mikoryty]. G&G's map (G&G F.28), however, points the way to Малоройка [Malorojka], breaking the *Michel-Little Delving* pair, by not using the same base name in both, not to mention not using a translated adjective in both. Their version of *Little Delving* is made up of the elements мало [malo: small] and рой [roj], the first person singular of рыть [ryt': *to dig*] is рою [royu]. The ending [-ka] is used to form substantives from verbs. To make their *Michel-Little* pair match, they would have had to have named *Michel Delving* Великоройка [Velikorojka]. While their treatment of *Michel Delving* is nowhere near as satisfactory as Kistyakovskij's, their *Little Delving* could have competed with it satisfactorily.

Kistyakovskij concentrated his attention on the meaning of the verb *to delve*, in Old English *delfan*: *to dig the ground with a spade*. He used the same form of the verb that G&G used for their translation of *Little Delving* (рой [roj]). He combined this with an ending that is common in Russian place names: -ск [-sk]. This ending appears in such place names as Arkhangelsk, Chelyabinsk and Norilsk. The first element in his name comes from the word *ground*: земля [zemlya]. Together, these two elements produce a place name, which can be interpreted to mean *ground dig town*: Землеройск [Zemlerojsk], an elegant and imaginative solution that is readily transparent to the Russian reader. It, unfortunately, gives up on the problem of creating a *Michel-Little* pair, but that was not a major problem, as there was no map in M&K, and *Little Delving* is only on the map.

Volkovskij, like Kistyakovskij, focused on *Delving*, but added a little something extra to *Michel*. The basis of his name is a now archaic German loanword for the profession of digger [грабарь (grabar')]. (Dal' I.388) In German, *graben* means *to dig*. He added an ending that creates nouns for the places where a profession is practiced like *carpentry shop* [столярня (stolyarnya)], which is where a carpenter (столяр [stolyar]) works, and *bakery* [пекарня (pekarnya)], which is where a baker [пекарь (pekar)] works. Both these words are precisely paralleled in German. A German carpenter (Tischler) works in a *carpentry shop* (Tischlerei) and a German baker (Bäcker) works in a *bakery* (Bäckerei).

His use of an archaic word as the base for the name is a good match for Tolkien's use of *delve*, which the widely available desk-top edition of the *Oxford American Dictionary* defines as *to search deeply for information*.[42] For the modern reader who does not take the time to look in a more extensive dictionary, the name will be just as obscure as Tolkien's is to the less inquisitive English-speaking reader, but it will have a tantalizingly common ending to make it seem as if it should be familiar.

Volkovskij put some icing on the cake by turning "the chief township of the Shire" (F.26) into стольная Грабарня [stol'naya Grabarnya]. (V F.21) This gives his text the feeling that it has just stepped out of the Russian sagas (былины [byliny]), where стольный [stol'nyj] is the adjective for *throne*. In the sagas, the great heroes Il'ya Muromets and Dobrynya Nikitich ride to Kiev, *the town of the throne* [стольный Киев-град (stol'nyj Kiev-grad)].[43] Prince Vladimir, whose name means *ruler of the world*, is called *Vladimir of throned Kiev* [Владимир стольно-киевский (Vladimir stol'no-kievskij)].[44] This is far too grand, and much too Russian a sobriquet for

Michel Delving, which Tolkien purposely did not call the capital of the Shire, playing down the idea of an administrative hierarchy: "The Shire at this time hardly had any 'government'. [...] The only real official in the Shire at this date was the Mayor of Michel Delving (or of the Shire)." (F.30-31)

In his Tolkien Encyclopedia, Korolev followed Volkovskij's lead for the root of his name for *Michel Delving*, but gave it a different ending. He called it Грабарище [Grabarishche], applying an ending that is used to make words for things that are "big". This is the same ending that Volkovskij used to describe the strides taken by the giant tree-men seen on the North Moors, шажище [shazhishche]. It is an inventive choice but it falls flat because of the foreign root to which it is attached.

Bobyr' and Yakhnin avoided the problem of Michel Delving by leaving out the name altogether.

Mirkwood. Tolkien glosses *Mirkwood* as a name borrowed from ancient Germanic geography and legend. His recommendation is to translate it by sense, using poetic or antique elements where possible.

There was more unanimity about the choice of the Russian word for the second element than for the first. The choice was between either the suffix -лесье [-les'e], which means *woods*, and the word лес [les], which means *forest*. The difference between the two is that лес [les] can stand alone, but -лесье [-les'e] always has to be combined with a truncated qualifier in a single word.

K&K, Volkovskij, Perumov and the editors of Gruzberg-A and the editors of the Egmont *Hobbit* use an existing word—чернолесье [chernoles'e]—which means *deciduous forest*. Using an existing word in Tolkien's new context diminishes Tolkien's new image, because the existing word imposes its familiar images on the reader first. Bobyr'/Umanskij *LotR* tried to avoid this problem by creating the unusual combination of Чернолес [Chernoles], which has a certain charm to it. Rakhmanova, Sedov, Utilova and Yakhnin got away from the problem of interference from an existing word, by combining the full adjective for *black*—черный [chernyj]—with лес [les]. This makes the name Черный Лес [Chernyj Les] just different enough from the existing word for *deciduous forest* that the meaning of the adjective can take over and make it a *black forest* instead of a deciduous one. Their choice of *black* as the adjective to modify *forest* in this name is quite appropriate. *Black* is the adjective used by Tolkien elsewhere to describe the forces of evil. Compare: *Black Country* (Mordor), *Black Gate* (Moranon), *Black Riders* (Nazgul), *Black Land* (Mordor) and *the Black One* (Sauron).

To give K&K, Volkovskij and the editors of Gruzberg-A their due, the first element of чернолесье [chernoles'e] also means *black*. In addition, in its primary meaning of *deciduous forest*, чернолесье [chernoles'e] is an appropriate translation for the name that the Elves gave Mirkwood after their victory in the North: *Eryn Lasgalen*, the Wood of Greenleaves. (R.468)

Interestingly enough, the first element in Tolkien's made-up name of *Lasgalen* even bears a certain linguistic relation to the Russian word for *forest* (лес [les]). Tolkien's name hints at a recasting of elements taken from Welsh, where *glas* has the meaning of *green* in Welsh toponyms and *dalen* means *leaf*. The word *glas* can be seen spelled *las* in Welsh placenames like *Rhiwlas* [green slope]. It is spelled *las*, because Welsh words that begin with "G" lose their initial "G" in compounds and after articles. The Russian word for *forest* strongly suggests a relationship to the Welsh *(g)las* [green] because forests are green and because лес [les] has the same consonant envelope as the Welsh *(g)las* [green]. Vowels are the least stable part of any word, and in Polish the word for *forest* still is *las*. The coincidence of both the consonant envelope and semantic valence suggests that the words were once related.

Kistyakovskij avoids any chance of interference from the word for *deciduous forest* by creating a new name: Лихолесье [Likholes'e]. His first element—лихо [likho]—is an archaic word meaning *evil*, and the name of an ogre-like character from Russian folklore. This gives the woods a much more explicitly sinister feeling in Russian than *mirk* does in English, providing it with some of the sense of the alternate name for *Mirkwood*, "forest of great fear" (Taur e-Ndaedelos). (R.515) Like *mirk*, лихо [likho] is a word from the old sagas and fairy tales. All in all, an elegant, evocative name.

In the third volume, one of the ones that Murav'ev did without Kistyakovskij, Murav'ev likewise resorts to a forest name right out of the old sagas and fairy tales. In Chapter 9 of Book V, Legolas pledges that he will fight such battles as yet need to be fought in the name of the folk of the Great Wood. (R.188) This was the name of Mirkwood before the shadow of Dol Guldur fell upon it. Murav'ev gives it the name of the deep, dark wood of Russian folklore and legend: дремучий лес [dremuchij les]. (M R.170) Literally, its name means sleeping forest, but the fairy tales and legends of this sleeping forest fill it with all sorts of scary things to frighten travelers and challenge heroes. This name has exactly the right feeling for Tolkien's

Mirkwood, and would have been a viable alternative to Kistyakovskij's Лихолесье [Likholes'e], but feels out of place as the name of the forest for which Legolas is prepared to fight.

Kistyakovskij's name is used in the Nemirova *LotR*, and in the Korolev, Kaminskaya and Anonymous translations of *The Hobbit*. It is also found in Gruzberg-B, where, the first time it appears, it is followed by a note in parentheses that says, "(less often Чернолесье [Chernoles'e])." In Gruzberg-C, the final version supplied by the author and not taken from the Internet, and in the Gruzberg *Hobbit*, *Mirkwood* is transliterated as *forest Merkvud* (лес Мерквуд [les Merkvud]). In its first appearance in the CD-ROM version of the "Prolog," the name is given a short definition: *the Forest of Gloom* (Лес Мрака [Les Mraka]). That embellishment is missing in Gruzberg-C and -E (the print version). (G F.21)

While Volkovskij did not follow Kistyakovskij's lead for *Mirkwood*, he did dig up an interesting word based on лихо [likho]. Лихолетье [likholet'e] was his word for the "*tweens*, as the Hobbits called the irresponsible twenties between childhood and coming of age at thirty-three." (P.44) Literally it means *the evil years*, an apt enough description of many a teenager. None of the other translators had an image that was anywhere near as picturesque.

In her first edition of *The Hobbit* and *LotR*, VAM used Kistyakovskij's Лихолесье [Likholes'e]. For her second edition, she created her own unique name for *Mirkwood*. Her second-edition name is based on the adjective темный [dark], which she employs as an alternative adjective for the forces of evil in much the same way Tolkien does. Compare: *the Black Country* (R.302) with *the Dark Country* (T.273), both referring to Mordor; and *the Dark Lord* (F.81) with *your Black Master* (R.64), both referring to Sauron. Her version of *Mirkwood* is Темнолесье [Temnoles'e], which avoids the interference of the existing word чернолесье [deciduous forest], and gives Mirkwood an appropriately maleficent air in the context of Tolkien.

G&G took an entirely different approach in the printed version of their translation. They based their name on the adjective for the Russian adjective for *twilight* (сумеречный [sumerechnyj]), adding the toponymic ending -ье [-'e]. Initially this would seem a good choice because of its association with the twilight of the Gods from Northern mythology. Their name, unfortunately, has no linguistic markers to show that it is the name of a forest. It suffers from interference with names describing places, based on their location relative to a river, for example:

заречье [zarech'e] = land across the river,
поречье [porech'e] = land along the river,
староречье [starorech'e] = old river bed,
междуречье [mezhdurech'e] = land between two rivers,
приречье [prirech'e] = land by a river.

The last of these is Kistyakovskij's translation of the name *Bywater*, seconded by VAM, K&K and Aleksandrova. It is a good solution, because Bywater is a town located by the river Water. The interference with these existing words makes the reader's initial impression of Сумеречье [Sumerech'e] one of an area near a twilight river rather than of a forest covered in twilight.

For those with a knowledge of ancient history, there is another source of interference. It is the collection of city states known as Sumer that emerged in what is now southern Iraq about 4000 B.C.. Sumer occupied the flood plain of the lower reaches of the Tigris and Euphrates Rivers, which in Russian is described as the 'land of the two rivers': двуречье [dvurech'e].[45] *Sumer* is spelled Сумер [Sumer] in Russian, and the combination of Сумер [Sumer] and речье [rech'e] suggests another name for the Sumarian land of the two rivers.

The unknown translator of the segment from *The Hobbit* in Англия [Angliya] magazine used the noun лес [les] like Rakhmanova, but combined it with the adjective глухой [glukhoj], which means *dense, overgrown forest*. The combination глухой лес [glukhoj les] is the first example given in the modern desk-top defining dictionary for this meaning of глухой [glukhoj].[46] He or she would have been better off to use the word глушняк [glushnyak], which means *impassable, ancient, primordial forest*, (Dal' I.359) a very good match for Tolkien's "the great mountainous forest regions that anciently formed a barrier to the south of the lands of the Germanic expansion." (L.369)

The Bobyr' (Batalina) *Hobbit* uses Чёрный Лес [Black Forest] in the map on the flyleaf, but in the text *Mirkwood* is called the *Forest of outer darkness* (Кромешный лес [Kromeshnyj les]). This plays on the associations of evil of Biblical proportions tied to the adjective кромешный [kromeshnyj], which is used in the terms *absolute hell* (ад кромешный [ad kromeshnyj]) and *the outer darkness* (тьма кромешная (t'ma kromeshnaya)]. Кромешный [kromeshnyj] is an Old Church Slavonic word meaning *extreme, outmost*, which is derived from the word крома [kroma], meaning *edge*. *Absolute hell* (ад кромешный) is used as a synonym for *Sodom and Gomorrah*, the extremes of chaos and disorder. *The outer darkness* (Тьма кромешная) is a synonym for *Hell* in the sense of Matthew 8:12.[47]

> А сыны царства извержены будут во тьму внешнюю: там будет плач и скрежет зубов.
> BT: And the sons of the kingdom will be cast out into the outer darkness: there will be wailing and the gnashing of teeth.

The use of кромешный [kromeshnyj] produces a feeling of dread and evil more at home in *The Silmarillion* than in *LotR*.

Mount Doom. Tolkien's instructions for this name were to translate *doom* in the sense of *doomsday*, because of Mount Doom's association with the prophecies foretelling of the doom that would mark the end of the Third Age, when Isildur's Bane was found again. He notes that the word *doom* originally meant *judgement* (both formal and legal or personal), but that, because of its special use in *doomsday*, it is now commonly understood to carry a sense "of death, finality or fate (impending or foretold)."

Fate was key in all the translations of *Mount Doom*. The Galperin English-Russian dictionary offers two translations for *fate*: судьба [sud'ba] and рок [rok].[48] There is a subtle difference in the two. The standard Russian desk-top defining dictionary defines судьба [sud'ba: *fate*] as *the confluence of events beyond the control of the individual*.[49] It defines рок [rok: *doom*] as *an unfavorable судьба* [sud'ba].[50] Of the two, рок [rok] is the one that is the closest to the meaning that Tolkien wanted to convey. Meeting one's doom is never a favorable outcome, while meeting one's fate may or may not be favorable.

K&K and Gruzberg used the Russian word судьба [sud'ba]: Гора Судьбы [Mountain of Fate]. This approach could have been successful, if they had not used the word судьба [sud'ba] in other contexts as well. In Chapter 1 of volume II, for example, Gandalf and Frodo are discussing Frodo's escape from the Black Riders, and Gandalf tells him "Yes, fortune or fate have helped you, not to mention courage." (F.293) Both Gruzberg and K&K quite competently translate *fortune or fate* as счастье или судьба [schast'e ili sud'ba]. While *doomsday* in Russia is день страшного суда [den' strashnogo suda], the use of судьба [sud'ba] as the translation of *fate* here, and in other places in the text, makes it impossible for судьба [sud'ba] to double as the translation of *doom*. Tolkien was very particular about his word choice, and would never have approved of the same word being used for both *fate* and *doom*.

Kistyakovskij, VAM, G&G, Volkovskij and Nemirova all used the Russian word рок [rok] in their names for *Mount Doom*. Kistyakovskij, VAM, Volkovskij and Nemirova used *Doom Mountain* (Роковая гора [Rokovaya gora]). Nemirova's map shows Mount Doom as Orodruin, and then under that in parentheses, it is labeled Роковая гора [Rokovaya Gora] (N F. front inside cover). This is also her chapter title for Chapter 3 of Book VI, "Mount Doom."

G&G alternated between *Doom Mountain* (Роковая гора [Rokovaya gora]) and *Mountain of Doom* (Гора рока [Gora roka]). Their chapter title, however, is *Fiery Mountain* (Огненная Гора [Ognennaya Gora]) in both their samizdat and print versions. This is the literal translation of *Orodruin*. (R.515) Yakhnin also uses *Fiery Mountain* both on his map and in his text. In the samizdat version of Chapter 1 of Book VI, where Tolkien's Sam enters Mordor and sees "Orodruin, the Mountain of Fire" (R.214), G&G's Sam sees "Orodruin, the Mountain of Terror" (Ородруин, Гора Ужаса [Orodruin, Gora Uzhasa]), which is the name used by Bobyr/Umanskij (B.56, 373, 440, U F.370, R.714, R.782), offering another indication of the relationship between the Bobyr' and G&G texts. While *Mountain of Terror* is a good description, that is really the name of the Ered Gorgoroth, the Mountains of Terror in Doriath, which are more at home in *The Silmarillion*. The name *Mountains of Terror* only appears twice in *LotR*. (F.260; T.422) G&G corrected this line in the print version. (G&G R.181)

To be truly successful, the translation of *Mount Doom* has to match the translation of the *Crack(s) of Doom*, the great volcanic rift, in the depths of which burned the only fire that could unmake the Ring. (F.94, R.274-76) The translators who had chosen судьба [sud'ba: *fate*] and рок [rok: *doom*] for their rendition of *Mount Doom*, almost without exception, stayed the course with their interpretations of the *Crack(s) of Doom*. Kistyakovskij, VAM, G&G, Volkovskij and Nemirova all used either the Russian word роковой [rokovoj (adjective)] or the word рок [rok (noun)] in their names for the *Crack(s) of Doom*. K&K and Gruzberg both stuck to their choice of судьба [sud'ba: *fate*] as the translation of *doom*. Umanskij kept them company. Nemirova was the odd woman out. She provided the reader with three choices. In volume I, the *Crack of Doom* became the *Fateful Crack* (Роковая Щель [Rokovaya Shchel']) (N F.79, 80, 84, 472), repeating her choice for the word *doom* in her chapter title. In volume II, it became the *Deadly abyss*

(Гибельная пропасть [Gibel'naya propast']) (N T.354), offering the reader a more concrete view of the doom that awaits Frodo and Sam there. In volume III, it changed again to become the *Deadly Crack*. (Гибельная Щель [Gibel'naya Shchel']) (N R.212, 220, 224) Mix-and-match renditions of a name for which Tolkien only gave one version are less than successful and confusing to the reader. Nemirova would have done much better to stick to her first choice throughout.

Oliphaunt. Tolkien intended this to be a "rusticism" for the word *elephant*. It was to be slightly deformed on the premise that the names of foreign animals, seldom or never seen, should sound somewhat strange as well. He was disappointed that the Dutch translator used *olifant*, which is the modern Dutch word for *elephant*, because it lost the archaic coloration that he wanted this name to have. Kistyakovskij and Volkovskij use олифант [olifant], and Gruzberg uses олифонт [olifont], but the contemporary Russian word for *elephant* is слон [slon]. Nemirova and Yakhnin followed along with олифант [olifant]. For the Russian reader any version of *oliphaunt* is a very unusual word indeed. None of the variations used by the translators are to be found in any of the widely-used dictionaries, and for most Russian readers, *oliphaunt* will never be more than an alphabet-soup word, without a hint of слон [slon: elephant] in it. G&G use елефант [elefant], and the editors of Gruzberg-A used элефант [ehlefant], which is an obvious transliteration of the word *elephant*. K&K and VAM use олифан [olifan], which K&K gloss in their endnote not only as the Old English word for *elephant*, but also as the name of Roland's horn in the old French saga *Song of Roland*. (K&K T.524)

Púkel-men. Tolkien points to the origin of this name in the word *puck*—a mischievous sprite in the folklore of England, Wales, Ireland, Norway and Iceland. In Old English it was known as a *pûca*. Harvey the six-foot-tall, invisible rabbit in the movie (Universal, 1950) of the same name, starring Jimmy Stewart, was a puca.

In Welsh there are two related words for *puca*: *pwcca* and *bwcca*. They are essentially the same spirit, the P > B shift being well documented in the Celtic languages. One of the key characteristics of the bwcca is that it makes knocking noises. In the Cornish tin mines, before their name was anglicized to *knockers*, it was the bwccas who warned the miners of impending cave-ins and led them to rich veins of ore by making knocking noises. Making scary noises in the dark is so common a characteristic of mischievous spirits that it is even part of the Dutch word for *poltergeist, klopgeest*. In Dutch *kloppen* is the verb for *to knock* or *to make a bumping noise*. The word *poltergeist*, which came to English from German, also originally meant 'a things that go bump in the night' spirit. In German *poltern* means *to knock, to rattle, to thump*. These are the spirits that gave rise to the well-known supplication from an old Cornish litany for deliverance from what must have been a common fear of the time: "From ghoulies and ghosties and long-legged beasties, and things that go bump in the night, Good Lord, deliver us!" The linguistic relationship between the Welsh *pwcca/bwcca* and the Russian word пукать [pukat'] is evident in the meaning that the Russian word had in the nineteenth century. This word used to mean *to knock* or *to make a bumping noise*. (Dal' III.537) Today is has been reduced in stature to the impolite word for flatulence, leaving the scary stuff to the word пугало [pugalo].

Tolkien also observed that derivatives of *puck* were often applied to those who were ugly or misshapen, much as were the Púkel-men themselves. He left it to the translator to decide whether to keep *Púkel* or to translate it.

Bobyr'/Umanskij omitted the segment with this name in it.

In their endnote, K&K explain the name, glossing *Púkel-men* as *people-goblins* (люди-гоблины [lyudi-gobliny]), noting the name's etymology and pointing to Shakespeare's Puck in *A Midsummer-night's Dream* and Kipling's Puck of *Puck of Pook's Hill* as examples of pûcas in English literature. (K&K R.605) In the text, however, K&K dig into their knowledge of folklore for their rendition of this name, and use the archaic word шишига [shishiga].

At the beginning of the seventeenth century in Russia, шиш [shish] was the name applied to hoboes and outlaws. By the nineteenth century, шиш [shish] and all its variants—шишига [shishiga], шишко [shishko], шишкун [shishkun], шишок [shishok]—were generalized to include all kinds of lesser evil spirits that inhabited woods, waters, grain sheds and bath houses. When a pillar of dust that had been raised by a whirlwind walked down the street in those times, people would say that a шишига [shishiga] was getting married. Шишига [Shishiga] is a good match for *Púkel-men*, not only for its folklore match, but also because, just like *puck*, it was sometimes applied to small, unsightly people.

Gruzberg had a more straightforward approach. He transliterated *Púkel* on a letter-for-letter basis and translated *men*: Пукель-люди [Pukel'-lyudi]. Aleksandrova, unfortunately, took off the "-men" and left the Russian reader with just so much alphabet soup, and the automatic gloss function for the English text contains no definition for *Púkel-men*.

Kistyakovskij and VAM also transliterated *Púkel*, but on the basis of its sound. VAM transliterated it as пуколы [pukoly, the ending -y is a Russian plural]. For the modern Russian reader, if it suggests anything, пуколы [pukoly] is most likely to recall the modern meaning of the Russian verb пукать [pukat'], *to fart*, which is undoubtedly why Kistyakovskij doubled the "K" in his version—Пукколы [Pukkoly]—to make it sound foreign, and keep the reader from looking for a Russian root in the name. Double letters are very rare in Russian. In his Tolkien Encyclopedia, Korolev sticks with Kistyakovskij.

Gruzberg avoids the problem of interference with пукать [pukat'], because by the point that the name appears in the story his reader already knows that Gruzberg transliterates all the names and the reader is not looking for correlates in Russian.

Volkovskij follows Kistyakovskij's lead, but adds an appositive to further define who the Pukkoly are. He calls them the "Pukels-People with a paunch" (Пукколы-Пузаны [Pukkoly-Puzany]). (V R.98) At their next appearance he makes the *Púkel-men* "graven images" (истуканы [istukany]) (V R.99), and at their third, and final appearance, reduces them to the "stone people with a paunch" (каменные пузаны [kamennye puzany]). (V R.170) This strips them of their former glory and makes them much more powerless and mournful than Tolkien had painted them.

Nemirova tries her hand at a translation of the name, but her effort takes a wrong turn. She calls them the *Pop-Eyes* (Пучеглазы [Pucheglazy]). (N R.58) Tolkien's description of the Púkel-men's eyes is that they were dark holes that stared sadly at the passersby. (R.80) The holes of their eyes were the only features left on the statues, the rest having been worn away. Nemirova gets that part of the description right, which creates a logical mismatch: statues with all their features worn away could not have protruding eyes.

In their samizdat version, G&G avoid the problem of *Púkel-men*, by omitting the name altogether. The Púkel-men were reinstated in G&G's print version, but in a much simplified form as "idols" (идолы [idoly]), and missing much of their poignancy. Compare G&G's version to Tolkien's:

G&G: Всадники не обращали на идолов внимания, а Мерри разглядывал скорбные силуэты статуй с любопытством и почти с жалостью. (G&G R.61/830)

BT: The riders paid no attention to the idols, but Merry kept looking at the mournful silhouettes of the statues with curiosity and almost with pity.

JRRT: The Riders hardly glanced at them. The Púkel-men they called them, and heeded them little: no power or terror was left in them; but Merry gazed at them with wonder and a feeling almost of pity, as they loomed up mournfully in the dusk. (R.80)

Yaknin has a similar approach. He describes the Púkel-men first as "sitting figures" (сидящие фигуры [sidyashchie figury]), and then as "stone statues" (каменные изваяния [kamennye izvayaniya], and for the third time as "graven images" (истуканы [istukany]). (Ya R.54-55) Yakhnin, too, rearranges the text, robbing it of its poignancy, shifting Merry's interest to the history of the builders of the road that they were traversing.

Всадники не обращали внимания на безобидных истуканов, которые, по преданию, колдовской силы не имели. Но Мерри разглядывал их с интересом, прикидывая, из какой же седой древности дошли эти посланцы далеких предков. (Ya R.55)

BT: The riders did not pay any attention to the harmless graven images, which, according to legend, had no magical powers. But Merry examined them with interest, trying to imagine the grey antiquity from which these ambassadors of the ancient ancestors came.

Yakhnin's skill as a storyteller is obvious in the way that he paints the scene for the reader, but his rendition makes it equally obvious that this is not a translation.

Radagast. Tolkien provided no instructions for this name in his "Nomenclature," which meant that he thought that it should be transliterated. Not surprisingly, all of the translators (both of *The Hobbit* and *LotR*) did just that. Radegast (Радегаст) is, after all, the name of a deity right out of Russian mythology. Only the unknown translator of the segment of *The Hobbit* that appeared in the magazine Англия [Angliya] transliterated the name as Rehdegast (Рэдегаст), a sound transliteration. All the rest recognized the name for what it was and spelled it Radagast (Радагаст). This is not

Tolkien's only borrowing from the Slavic realm. Tolkien's name *Boromir* is also Slavic in origin. (q.v. **Shadowfax**)

Radegast was a member of the pantheon of Slavic deities that in some ways resembles Tolkien's pantheon from *The Silmarillion*. Just as the Ainur are the offspring of the thought of Eru, the One, who in Arda is called Ilúvatar (S.15), the Сварожичи [Svarozhichi (-ич [-ich] = son of, -и [-i] = plural)] were the children of the One god Сварогъ [Svarog" (рог [rog] = horn, compare cornucopia)]. The other Сварожичи [Svarozhichi] included: Дажьбог [Dazh'bog], the sun; Перун [Perun], the god of thunder and lightning; and Велес [Veles], the god of the animals, who took on the form of a bear, and is, therefore, somewhat suggestive of Beorn.

The name *Radegast* suggests the meaning of *welcome guest* (рад [rad] = happy, гость [gost'] = guest), yet Radegast was depicted as armed from head to toe. In his right hand he held a shield decorated with the head of an ox: the symbol of stubborn bravery. In his left hand he held a double-headed battle ax. A statue to him showed him mounted on a white horse, and the best horses were always kept in his temple. His worshipers and priests believed that the god would ride one of the horses at night while about his errands, and whichever horse appeared to be the most tired when they entered the temple in the morning was assumed to be the one that the god had chosen to ride that night. The animal that had been favored by the deity was garlanded with flowers and treated to the best food and water.

Radegast's helmet was topped by the figure of a cockerel with its wings spread. The Slavs considered the cockerel to be the embodiment of fire, and as such the cockerel was considered the best sacrifice to appease the supreme deity Сварогъ [Svarog"], the creator of fire and the father of the sun. It was a folk belief that cock crow at dawn marked the end of the rein of the evil forces of darkness that held sway over the world between sunset and sunrise. The cockerel on Radegast's helmet was to warn the forces of evil that their time was at an end, and to cast fear into their hearts.

In *LotR*, Tolkien uses cock crow in exactly this way in Book I, Chapter 11 ("A Knife in the Dark"). The Black Riders of Mordor prowl about in the dark of night looking for Frodo, breaking into the house at Crickhollow and ransacking the room that Frodo had booked at the inn in Bree. At first the cock crows "far away" as the black figures go about their business in "the cold hour before dawn." (F.238) Shortly thereafter, the cock crows "lustily in the inn-yard," as Frodo awakens from a troubled dream. (F.240) The Black Riders are gone.

Tolkien had already described the power of the rising sun over the forces of evil that roam about in the darkness in the episode with the Trolls in *The Hobbit*. (H.51-52) When the sun came up and found the trolls above ground, they turned to stone.

Tolkien repeats the image of cock crow at the coming of dawn again in Book V, Chapter 4 ("The Siege of Gondor"). This time the cock's crow is echoed far away by the "great horns of the North wildly blowing. Rohan had come at last" (R.126) to break the siege. The cockerel on Radegast's helmet was meant to conjure up a similar image in the minds of those who saw it.

Mountains, settlements, castles and rivers were named after Radegast.[51] The leader of the second wave of barbarians to invade the Roman homeland in the twilight of the Empire in 405 A.D. was named Radegast. His force numbered almost one-third million and was the largest single attacking force in recorded (Roman) history up until that time. While some of his force had iron weapons, others were armed with stone-tipped spears. Despite their numbers, they were no match for the well-armed, well-organized legions that came out to meet them and were quickly dispatched.[52]

Rivendell. Tolkien explains this name as the Common Speech translation of *Imladris(t)*, where *imlad* means *valley* or *dell*, and *ris* (clearly related to the German word *Riß*) means *cleave* or *split*. He left it to the translator's discretion as to whether the name should be transliterated or translated. If it was translated, he noted, the first element—*riven*— should not be interpreted as *river*, which was the case in the Swedish translation.

Kistyakovskij follows Tolkien's instructions to the letter with an archaic Russian word meaning *dell* or *valley* (раздол [razdol]). It is made up of the elements раз [raz], meaning *to divide* or *to split*, and дол [dol], which is related to the English word *dell*. The archaic character of the word fits in well with Tolkien's style. The classic Russian defining dictionary of the nineteenth century explains it as "a plain in a dell in the mountains." (Dal' IV.27) Kaminskaya, Kamenkovich (*The Hobbit*), Nemirova (*LotR*) and Korolev (Encyclopedia) followed Kistyakovskij's lead and also used Раздол [Razdol] for *Rivendell*.

While Раздол [Razdol] does not suffer from interference with the word *river* which was a concern for Tolkien in English—the Russian word for *river* is река [reka]—it does suffer from another kind of interference. Раздол [razdol] also has the meaning of *freedom, liberty*. (Dal' IV.27) This meaning can still be found today in the modern, standard desk-top Russian defining dictionary under the heading раздолье [razdol'e].[58] In the Soviet Union, where reading between the lines was the national sport of the intellectual reading public, this is a particularly loaded concept to attach to the location of the Last Homely House east of the Sea (F.296), the last refuge of the company before heading East to Mordor on their quest. Given Kistyakovskij's linguistic acuity, the double meaning was undoubtedly not accidental.

Volkovskij follows Kistyakovskij's lead, in looking to archaic terms for his rendition of *Rivendell*. He chose another archaic Russian word for *dell* or *valley* (Разлог [Razlog]). In the classic Russian defining dictionary of the nineteenth century разлог [razlog] is defined as: "a deep and straight раздол [razdol] in the mountains, cutting across the ridge." (Dal' II.262) Volkovskij's choice avoids any potential interference that the name Раздол [Razdol] has with the modern word раздолье [razdol'e] (freedom, liberty), and will likewise force readers who want to know its archaic meaning to go dictionary diving. Kistyakovskij's name remains the better of the two as is shown by the number of other translators who also chose to use Раздол [Razdol] for their rendition of *Rivendell*.

VAM and a number of the other translators chose to transliterate *Rivendell*. VAM's version uses sound as the basis for the transliteration, Райвендел [Rajvendel], which would be pronounced with a long 'I,' as in *rivalry*. Rakhmanova (*The Hobbit*), Gruzberg, Bobyr'/Umanskij, K&K, Perumov and the subtitles transliterated *Rivendell* on a letter-for-letter basis, Ривенделл [Rivendell], which would be pronounced with a long 'EE,' as if spelled *Reevendell. K&K, of course, provided a gloss for the meaning of the name in an endnote. (K&K H.326)

The editors of Gruzberg-A were not careful when they tried to replace the original transliteration with Kistyakovskij's translation, which led to Раздол [Razdol] and Ривенделл [Rivendell] being used throughout, seemingly interchangeably, which fits so well with Tolkien's style of multiple names for places in various languages that it is only noticeable as a mistake upon a very close reading of the original and the translation in parallel.

In their printed version, G&G use Дольн [Dol'n]. The root of this word is immediately clear to the contemporary reader as the one in the Russian word *valley* (долина [dolina]). Its unusual form gives it a feeling of familiar exoticness, but Kistyakovskij's version remains far more elegant.

Yakhnin played odd-man-out with *Rivendell*. His translation is Эльфорт [Ehl'fort]. This rendition is a combination of *elf* + *fort*. Both are loanwords in Russian, and each has its own dictionary article. This interpretation is supported by Yakhnin's answer to Frodo's question of where he is when he awakes in Rivendell. Tolkien's Gandalf tells Frodo that he is in "the House of Elrond." (F.289) Yakhnin's Gandalf tells Frodo that he is "in Elrond's castle" (в замке Элронда [v zamke Ehlronda]). (Ya T.168) While a castle can be an impressive architectural triumph like Neuschwanstein, in the context of Эльфорт [Ehl'fort: elven fort], the reader is prompted to think in military lines, which takes away from the homeliness and grandeur of the Last Homely House east of the Sea. This military interpretation is contradicted later in the chapter by Yakhnin's elegantly embellished translation of Tolkien's description of the porch in Elrond's garden high above the river, which could well have been based on Neuschwanstein (JRRT F.298; Ya, T.171), but the military interpretation is the first impression of readers who see the name out of context.

Rohan. *Rohan* is not mentioned in Tolkien's "Nomenclature," which means that he did not intend it to be translated. Most of the translators followed that advice, and *Rohan* and the *Rohirrim* become Рохан and рохирримы with a Russian plural ending -ы [-y] on top of Tolkien's plural ending -*rim*, which—Tolkien's intentions to the contrary (L.178)—resembles a plural ending in Hebrew. In Hebrew 'soos' (Samech-Vav-Samech) is the singular of *horse*, and 'soosim' (Samech-Vav-Samech-Yud-Mem sofit) is the plural.

Yakhnin resuscitates an obsolete word for his rendition of *Rohan*. He calls it Коника [Konika]. The classic dictionary of nineteenth century Russian defines коника [konika] as the *mugwort plant* (Latin: *Artemisia vulgaris*). (Dal' II.156) As far as modern, urban native speakers are concerned, Yakhnin could just as well have made the name up. Very few can be found who would recognize коника [konika] as a plant. More troublesome for Yakhnin's name is the interference that it gets from the name of the Japanese firm Konica, which has achieved considerable name recognition in Russia. In Russian, Konica is spelled Коника [Konika]. For adult, modern, urban Russian readers, Yakhnin's name suggests that the descendants of the Riders of Rohan now live in Japan and have founded an international corporation that is a well-known provider of imaging solutions.

The saving grace of Yakhnin's name is that the intended audience for his retelling is children. Children will be less likely to have the same association that adults do with the name, and will be more likely to see Коника [Konika] as a country name based on the Russian word for *horse* (конь [kon']). There are a number of foreign toponyms that have the same ending, such as *Corsica*: Корсика [Korsika], *Costa Rica*: Коста-Рика [Kosta-Rika], *Thessalonika*: Фессалоника [Fessalonika] and *Tanganyika*: Танганьика [Tangan'ika].

In Kistyakovskij's good, imaginative rendition, *Rohan* became Ристания [Ristaniya]. The ending -ия [-iya] is easily recognizable as the name of a country. It is to be found in the Russian names for *Germany*: Германия [Germaniya], *Spain*: Испания [Ispaniya], *England*: Англия [Angliya], *Italy*: Италия [Italiya], *Austria*: Австрия [Avstriya], etc. It is the same ending that he used in his name for the *Shire*: Хоббитания [Khobbitaniya]. The first part of Ристания [Ristaniya] is derived from the archaic Russian word for *gymkhana*: ристанье [ristan'e], in which the well-read Russian reader will easily see the association with horses and an equestrian people.

Nemirova followed Kistyakovskij's lead, and used *Ristaniya* in her text, but her map shows Рохан [Rokhan] with (Ristaniya) underneath it in parentheses. G&G only used *Ristaniya* in their samizdat text. In the print version of their text, they changed to Рохан [Rokhan].

Strangely, though, Kistyakovskij does not use *Ristaniya* throughout the text. He uses it interchangeably with another form that he introduces in an embellishment to the text as the Gondorian name for *Ristaniya*: Мустангрим [Mustangrim].

> Саруман живет далеко на юге, в крепости Скальбург к северу от Ристании, которую гондорцы называют Мустангримом. (M&K F_{1982}.189, F_{1988}.318[59])
>
> BT: Saruman lives far to the south, in the fortress of Skal'burg to the north of Rohan, which the Gondorians call Mustang-rim.
>
> JRRT: That is far south in Isengard, in the end of the Misty Mountains, not far from the Gap of Rohan. (F.338)

This name is based on the word мустанг [mustang], which gives it a decidedly American tint. The definition of мустанг [mustang] in the standard Russian desk-top defining dictionary[60] reads:

> МУСТА'НГ, Одичавшая домашняя лошадь североамериканских прерий.
>
> BT: MUSTA'NG, A wild, previously domesticated horse of the North American prairies.

Tolkien, indeed, does have two names for *Rohan* and the *Rohirrim*. In the language of the Rohirrim, their land is *the Mark of the Riders* and they call themselves the *Eorlingas*, after the first king of the Mark, Eorl. In Gondor, the land is called *Rohan* and its people the *Rohirrim*. (A.430) M&K did not do the Appendices, and the embellishment to the description of the location of Isengard could simply be viewed as a condensation of the Appendices into the text. M&K use their Eorlingian (Ристания [Ristaniya] and Ристанийцы [Ristanijtsy]) and Gondorian names (Мустангрим [Mustangrim] and Мустангримцы [Mustangrimtsy]) interchangeably throughout the text. Tolkien only uses *Eorlingas* in the text when the speaker is Eorlingian.

Murav'vev's choice of which to use in the translation of the title of Chapter V of Book V ("The Ride of the Rohirrim") is an interesting one. His title for that chapter is "The March of the Mustang-rim-ians" (Поход Мустангримцев [Pokhod Mustangrimtsev]). (M&K R.111) The decided American tint that the word *mustang* (мустанг [mustang]) adds to the name Мустангримцы [Mustangrimtsy] is almost like casting the U.S. Cavalry to play the role wearing their own uniforms.

Sandyman. Tolkien gave no instructions for this name in "Nomenclature." No explanation was intended to mean that the translator should transliterate the name rather than translate it. That is exactly what K&K (Сэндиман [Sehndiman]) and Gruzberg (Сэндимен [Sehndimen]) and Umanskij (Сэндимэн [Sehndimehn]) did.

The other translators, however, decided to translate the name by sense. There was no problem of avoiding interference from the name *the Sandman*, which is a stumbling block for some American readers. None of the Russian translators took that detour. In Russian children's folklore children are visited at bedtime by Дрёма [Drëma], whose name has nothing at all to do with sand. Дрёма [Drëma] is pictured either as a kind old woman with soft hands or as one of the little people with a soothing voice. When it gets dark, Дрёма [Drema] squeezes in through the cracks in the window or the door and closes the children's eyes, tucks them in and gently strokes their heads. The name Дрёма [Drema] is linguistically related to the verb *to doze, to slumber* (дремать [dremat']). This is the same root as is used in the name of the dark and mysterious forest found in many Russian fairy tales: the Sleeping Forest (дремучий лес [dremuchyj les]). (q.v. **Mirkwood**)

For the British reader, the most-likely possible interference is from the name *Sandeman*. The House of Sandeman has been a purveyor of fine Port wines and Sherry for over 200 years. None of the translators produced a rendition that included an allusion to this potential wrong turn either.

Kistyakovskij pulled off another feat of linguistic legerdemain with his name Пескунс [Peskuns]. It rolls the words for *sand* (песок [pesok]) and *skunk* (скунс [skuns]) into one. It gives the miller an offensive air right from the start. Ending in *-ns*, it sounds right at home with all the Russian Hobbit names that end in -нс [-ns], an ending has come to be thought of as typical of Hobbit names in Russia.

Banks (M&K) - Норкинс [Norkins]: нора [nora] = burrow.
Brandibuck (Ya) - Крольчинс [Krol'chins]: крольчиха [krol'chikha] = female rabbit.
Brockhouse (V) - Барсучинс [Barsuchins]: барсук [barsuk] = badger.
Cotton (VAM) - Норкинс [Norkins]: нора [nora] = burrow.
Cotton (K&K) - Хижинс [Khizhins]: хижина [khizhina] = shack or hut.
Goodchild (VAM) - Деткинс [Detkins]: дети [deti (pl.)] = children.
Hornblower (G&G, subtitles) - Дудкинс [Dudkins]: дудка [dudka] = pipe, fife.
Rushlight (V) - Камышкинс [Kamyshkins]: камыш [kamysh] = reed, rush.
Smallburrow (M&K) - Норочкинс [Norochkins]: норочка [norochka] = small burrow.
Underhill (K&K) - Подхолминс [Podkholmins]: под [pod] = under, холм [kholm] = hill.

VAM used the same name as Kistyakovskij in her first edition (1991). As in most other cases, G&G used Kistyakovskij's name in their samizdat version, too. In their print version, however, their name is based on a diminutive form of the word for *sand*, песочек [pesochek], which also has a fugitive letter in the oblique cases: i.e. the genitive case is песочка [pesochka]. Their name is Песошкинс [Pesoshkins]. The substitution of the letter Ш [sh] for the expected letter Ч [ch] in the diminutive gives the name a rustic, unlettered air, without, however, disturbing the reader's association with the word *sand*.

For his version of the name *Sandyman* Volkovskij resuscitates an archaic word envelope (охряк [okhryak]). This word was originally associated with ochre, and while some shades of this color are suggestive of the color of sand, that could hardly seem a good fit for a speaking name that should mean *sand*. Russian readers (and a prominent Russian-language search engine) are quick to point out that охряк [okhryak] contains the word хряк [khryak], which originally meant *pig*. (Dal' IV.657) Today this is a slang word that means *a rich, dishonorable person*,[61] which is not a bad description of Ted Sandyman in his ultimate role as a friend of Saruman's. (R.366, 361)

Nemirova produced a hybrid, half-translated, half-transliterated name. She translated *sand* (песок [pesok]) and kept *man*, which resulted in Пескоман [Peskoman]. As is the case with most such attempts, the result was unsatisfactory. The problem with this Russian-English hybrid is that is looks like a class of existing Russian words, which, unfortunately, are based on the Greek word for *mania*; for example, англоман [angloman: Anglophile], библиоман [biblioman: bibliophile], клептоман [kleptoman: kleptomaniac], наркоман [narkoman: drug addict], пироман [piroman: pyromaniac]. The implication of Nemirova's name is, therefore, *sand-maniac, a person who has an obsession with sand.

In a version of her translation that she graciously made available to the author as a computer file, VAM has another elegant version of the name *Sandyman* (Песчаник [Peschanik]). This is an existing word that means *sandstone* or *ground squirel* (Suslik Fulvus), or *sanderling* (any of a number of birds of the genus Calidris), or a *Brown Hare* (Lepus Capensis), or a fish in the family Salmonidae, Coregonus Maraena. The ending used in this word is very productive, and there are often several simultaneously active homonyms based on it, as is the case with this word. One of the uses of this ending is to turn adjectives into the names of professions. For example, a butcher is a мясник [myasnik]: мясной [myasnoj] = meat (adj.), and roll baker is а булочник [bulochnik]: булочный [bulochnyj] = roll (adj.). Her *Sandyman* would, therefore, be a sand merchant. In her revised edition (2003), she changed the name to Песокс [Pesoks], using the same word formation model that she used for *Frogmorton*. (q.v.): an enclytic -с [-s] is added to the word *sand* (песок [pesok]). This gives the name a very negative charge, very much appropriate to the character it belongs to, and an excellent competitor for Kistyakovskij's evocative name.

The Scarlet Book of Westmarch. The title of the work that Tolkien 'translated' (A.513) into *The Hobbit* and *LotR* echoes the naming of books for the color of their cover, that is a common feature of ancient manuscripts. There is, for example, *The Red Book of Hergest* [Welsh: Llyfr Coch

Hergest]—one of the most important Welsh medieval manuscripts—which was written circa 1375-1425. It is housed in the Bodleian Library, Oxford (MS Jesus College MS CXI). *The White Book of Rhydderch* [Welsh: Llyfr Gwyn Rhydderch], including a copy of "Culhwch and Olwen"—one of the earliest-known (circa 1100) Arthurian romances—was penned sometime between 1300 and 1325. It is sheltered at the National Library of Wales (Peniarth MS 4 and 5). *The Black Book of Carmarthen* [Welsh: Llyfr Du Caerfyrddin], which contains the "Merlin" poems, was scribed at the Priory of St. John at Carmarthen some time around 1250. It too resides at the National Library of Wales (MS Peniarth 1).

The 'black' books of Russian lore were anything but a source of chivalrous and religious poetry as was *The Black Book of Carmarthen*. The black books of Russian folklore were full of incantations and charms, spells and enchantments. Their owners were considered the practitioners of the evil arts, who were burned at the stake along with their books. The association of the color black with books of bewitchment and evil enchantments was so strong in Russian that the word чернокнижие [chernoknizhie, literally: black bookishness] became the Russian equivalent to the English *black magic*. This is the word that K&K and VAM use to translate *evil arts* in Chapter V of Book IV ("The Window on the West"). (T.363)

The color black is indicative of the deity behind the power of these books. The color of the devil in Russian folklore is black. This belief is so strongly held that one of the Russian euphemisms for the devil is черный [chernyj, literally: the black one].[53] The pre-Christian duality of the opposing forces of Good and Evil among the Slavs was Белобог и Чернобог [Chernobog i Belobog, literally: White God and Black God].[54] In modern times, this folk image was the cause of any number of incidents involving students from Africa who came to study in Moscow.

Translating the title of *The Red Book of Westmarch* presents a certain problem for Russian translators, because of the associations that the color red carried in Soviet Russia. Красный (krasnyj [red]) is the color of the Revolution; of the Communist Party. The article on красный [red] in the *Defining Dictionary of the Language of the Soviet Period*[55] is two pages long. Red October [the Revolution of 1917], Red Square [site of the mausoleum where Lenin and Stalin lay in rest on public view], the Red Army [name for the Soviet Army from 1918 to 1946], *Red Star* [the official newspaper of the Red Army], the Red Fleet [name of the Soviet Navy from 1918 to 1937], are just but a few of the many 'Soviet' uses of the word *red* that were long in daily use that would make it hard for the Russian reader to see the word *red* without at least some of these associations creeping into the reader's perception of it.

As if that was not enough, the name of endangered species list is also the *Red Book* (Красная книга [Krasnaya kniga]). The list contains almost 250 species and subspecies, including 34 insects.

The majority vote among the translators was for *The Scarlet Book* (Алая Книга [Alaya Kniga]). VAM, Umanskij and Gruzberg—joined by Perumov—were the only dissenters. They all chose to stick with the most direct translation—*The Red Book* (Красная Книга [Krasnaya Kniga])—despite the possible associations with things Soviet. While changing *The Red Book* into *The Scarlet Book* breaks the association with things Soviet for the Russian reader, it also breaks the reader's association with *The Red Book of Hergest*, which the recently reprinted (1990), pre-Soviet (1891) Brokhauz and Efron *Encyclopedic Dictionary* [56] presents as Красная Книга [Krasnaya Kniga]. While at first glance that may not seem like a serious problem, there is more significance to it than meets the eye. The second part of Tolkien's title is the key.

Tolkien's instructions to translators for *Westmarch*—the area in the Shire in which *The Red Book* was found—said that the name should be translated and that the meaning that he intended for *march* was 'borderland'. The word *march* in the meaning of 'borderland' comes from the Anglo-Saxon word *mearc*, which means boundary. This root is also reflected in such place names as Denmark, Steyrmark and Riddermark and in the title Marquis, the ruler of a mark.

The most obvious topographic corollary to Tolkien's Westmarch in the Shire are the Welsh Marches[57] in England, which have long been a border region. When the Romans tried to conquer Wales (48 A.D. - 84 A.D.), the Welsh Marches formed the northwest border of the Roman Empire. In the late eighth century, king Offa of Mercia (757-796) built a great dyke [earthen wall] in the Welsh Marches approximately twenty feet high. It extended over 100 miles from the mouth of the river Dee to the mouth of the river Wye. During the Norman period, the Welsh Marches formed a buffer zone between England and Wales that had political and legal autonomy, but was under Norman control. From the English point of view, the Welsh Marches marked the western border of England. In other words, the Welsh Marches were also the Westmarch.

In naming the manuscript from which *The Hobbit* and *LotR* were 'translated' *The Red Book of Westmarch*, Tolkien planted an Easter-egg allusion for the well-read reader to discover. Hergest is located in the Welsh Marches. *The Red Book of Hergest*, which Lady Charlotte Guest translated into the *Mabinogion*, therefore, could also be called *The Red Book of Westmarch*, after the area—rather than the exact place—in which it was found. Tolkien could not have not been aware of the parallels.

There were a number of different renditions of *Westmarch*. Only Yakhnin and Bobyr' ignored the challenge of this name. Russian historiography uses the word марка [marka] for both the *Marches* of England and the *Marks* —borderlands—of the continent. Gruzberg, Nemirova and Volkovskij were the only translators to take full advantage of the word марка [marka] for the *Mark* of the Rohirrim. Nemirova even used Маркграф [Markgraf], as Éomer's title. (N T.26) Their success with the *Mark of Rohan* meant, therefore, that they were forced to seek another word for the *Westmarch* of the Shire. Both Gruzberg's and Umanskij's version of *Westmarch* has a modern, very straightforward flavor to it: Западные Границы [Western Borders]. Both Nemirova and Volkovskij, however, took their cue for *Westmarch* from M&K.

M&K's first-edition rendition of *Westmarch* was Западный Край [Zapadnyj Kraj: Western Country]. In the context of Tolkien, this has a certain hint of Westernesse about it, pointing more to a location outside the Shire than within it, and it is quite understandable that M&K changed their minds between the first (1982) and second (1988) editions of volume I. This, however, is the version that Nemirova used. This choice underscores the samizdat origin of her translation in the vacuum between the publication of M&K's first abridged volume and the resumption of publication with the unabridged volume I six years later.

Nemirova was not, however, oblivious to the problems with this name. Her solution was part of her "belt and suspenders" approach to the names. Her double name for *The Shire* combined Kistyakovskij's imaginative Хоббитания [Khobbitaniya] with the prosaic Край [Kraj: a Country]. (N F.10) Within that context, her title of *The Red Book of Westmarch* reads 'The Scarlet Book of the Western Shire" (N F.5, F.9, F.17), which, while not overly imaginative, is certainly readable.

In their second edition, M&K keyed on the word for *bounds* or *boundary* that is in more common usage today. Their second-edition *Westmarch* became Западные Пределы [Zapadnye Predely: Western Boundaries].

(M&K₁₉₈₈, P.31) This is the version that Volkovskij used. (V P.13) M&K repeat the same term that they used for *Westmarch* in their rendition of the territory that is Éomer's charge: the East-mark. (T.47) In their rendition, the territory under Éomer's charge is also called the Западные Пределы [Zapadnye Predely: Western Boundaries] (M&K T.38), changing *east* into *west*. Tolkien would never have approved of two identical toponyms, one in the Shire and one in Rohan, let alone the reversal of the East-mark's location.

While Volkovskij followed right along behind M&K in the translation of *The Red Book of Westmarch*, his version of Éomer's charge—the East-mark (T.47)—was based on a common word for *border*, which shows up in the Russian term for *overseas* (за рубежом [za rubezhom]). He called *The East-mark* Восточное порубежье [Vostochnoe porubezh'e: the Eastern borderlands]. (V T. 46) Though this is a competent, transparent translation, Volkovskij would have been better off to use the word марка [marka] for *mark* throughout, instead of playing mix and match with Tolkien's carefully chosen nomenclature.

While ignoring the East-mark, Yakhnin gives Éomer a promotion. Instead of being one of the military leaders of the four marks, Yakhnin's Éomer was "the chief guard of the lord of the Horsemen, the great Theodin." (Ya T.22) Making him the chief guard eliminates the need to say anything about the East-mark. He was in charge of everything.

While K&K used circumlocutions at every occurrence of the *Mark* of the Rohirrim, they chose a very good Russian word for *March* that is found in many of the definitions of марка [marka]. It does not have quite the same archaic feeling about it as *March* does in English, but it is nevertheless a good fit. They called the *Westmarch* Западная Окраина [Zapadnaya Okraina: West March]. (K&K P.17) It is linguistically related to the name of the Ukraine. This word would have made an excellent pair with марка [marka] to replicate Tolkien's *March/Mark*.

While Nemirova's translation of *The Red Book of Westmarch* was *The Scarlet Book of the Western Shire*, when it came to the term *Wardens of the Westmarch* in "Note on the Shire Records" (P.37), she used another translation of *Westmarch*. Her translation for this was Хранители Западной Закраины [Khraniteli Zapadnoj Zakrainy]. (N P.24) This word, while related linguistically to *Okraina*, is not a geographic term. It means *edge*, as in the edge of a cloud, the edge of a roof or the edge of table. This makes it much less satisfactory than K&K's choice.

G&G had a similarly poor approach to *Westmarch*. They used a word that appears in the dictionary definitions of *Zakraina*. This word is used in even more technical texts, such as aircraft specifications, where it describes the leading edge of a wing. They turned *Westmarch* into Западный Кром [Zapadnyj Krom: the Western Edge]. (G&G P.9) While they circumlocuted their way around most uses of the *Mark* of the Rohirrim, they did find a translation for the territory that is Éomer's charge: the East-mark. (T.47) They called it Восточные Пределы [Vostochnye Predely: Eastern Boundaries] (G&G T.32), the rendition that M&K should have had.

VAM had a good alternate with a more modern flavor to it: Западное Приграничье [Zapadnoe Prigranich'e: the Western Borderlands]. (VAM F_{2003}.221) Her version of the *Mark* of the Rohirrim was Рубежный Край [Border Country]. (VAM T_{2003}.606)This is also a good rendition, because, under the influence of the adjective *border*, the meaning of край as *edge* or *border* comes to the fore. In this meaning, край is, in essence, the calque of the Anglo-Saxon word *mearc*. It is a second-best choice to K&K's *Okraina*.

Shadowfax. Tolkien glosses this name as that of a horse having a "shadow-grey mane (and coat)." It is a Rohan name, and the language of Rohan was based on Old English. Had the name existed in Old English, it would have been spelled **Sceadu-faex*. Tolkien recommends that the name be transliterated, using the simplified form of *Scadufax*, which is exactly what K&K did, with an endnote to explain the name, of course. (K&K F.393, F.680)

Yakhnin circumlocuted his way around the name throughout the text and Shadowfax had his role cut short. In Yakhnin's version, when Gwaihir rescues Gandalf from Orthanc, he does not take him to Edoras as is the case in the original (F.343), but to the northern edge of Mirkwood. From there Yakhnin's Gandalf has to make his way on foot through the forest to the camp of the Wood-elves, arriving just as his strength was giving out. (Ya F.199)

Tolkien had felt that it might be possible to translate the name in the Germanic languages using related elements, but the analogous Russian elements do not look anything at all like *Shadowfax*. *Shadow* in Russian is тень [ten'], and *fax* in the meaning of *mane* is грива [griva]; *coat* would be масть [mast']. Nevertheless, all the other translators gave it a try. The classic nineteenth century defining dictionary (Dal' I.156) lists an example that could have worked well as the model for the translation for *Shadowfax*:

белогривая лошадь [belogrivaya loshad'], *a white maned horse*, but none of the translators used that for *Shadowfax*. This was, however, the preferred model for the translations of the name of Théoden's horse Snowmane. Kistyakovskij called him Белогрив [Belogriv]. The other translators who did something with *Snowmane*, all played some variation on the theme of Снежногривый [Snezhnogrivyj]. It would have been equally easy to create a combination of грива [griva] and *gray*. This was the approach taken in Russian to translate the names Skinfaxi ("Shining-maned"), the horse whose mane lights up the day as he pulls Dagur's chariot across the sky, and Hrimfaxi ("Frost-maned"), the horse that pulls Nott across the sky, leaving dew behind. In the translations by Steblin-Kamenskij and Smirnitskaya they are called Ясная Грива [Yasnaya Griva] and Инеистая Грива [Ineistaya Griva], literally *Bright Mane* and *Dew Mane*.[62]

VAM's name is Серосвет [Serosvet], *Gray-colored*. It is immediately transparent to the reader as a color, but quite prosaic in comparison to some of the other versions.

In the first edition of the M&K translation, Kistyakovskij used Беллазор [Bellazor] for *Shadowfax*. (M&K F_{1982}.194) Because it has a double 'LL' it suggests foreign loan words like *belladona* (белладонна [belladonna]), *belles lettres* (беллетристика [belletristika]) and бельэтаж [bel'ehtazh: the dress circle at a theater], in which the root *bell-* means *beautiful*. (Dal' I.81) The second part of the name is зор [zor], which means *view* in such words as *review* (обзор [obzor]), *inspector* (ревизор [revizor]) from the French *reviewer* and *range of interests* (кругозор [krugozor]) literally *rounded outlook*. This combination is strongly suggestive of a calque of the French *Belle vue* (Fairview). This name was hardly one of Kistyakovskij's best efforts.

In their samizdat version, which was produced as a follow-on to the first M&K version, when it became apparent that the rest of the M&K translation of the trilogy would be a long time in coming, G&G used Kistyakovskij's names, including Беллазор [Bellazor]. In their print version, G&G use the word сполох [spolokh], which in the plural сполохи [spolokhi] means *flash of lightning* or *northern lights*. In the singular, however, it is an archaic word for *alarm*, as in *sound the alarm*, which better matches Gandalf's Rohan nickname *Stormcrow* than it does a grey-coated steed.

In the second edition, Kistyakovskij changed the name to Светозар [Svetozar], which means *radiance*. (M&K F_{1988}.324) This name is the poetic sobriquet for the god of creation of the pagan Slavs: Сварогъ [Svarog"],[63] who created light in the darkness. Светозар [Svetozar] is perhaps a bit grand as a name for *Shadowfax*, but the number of Russian readers who will be well-read enough in Slavic folklore to make the connection is small. Those who consult the classic defining dictionary of the nineteenth century (Dal' IV.159) will find светозарный [svetozarnyj] listed as an adjective used with the sun in the expression: светозарное солнце [svetozarnoe solntse], *radiant sun.* Volkovskij joined Kistyakovskij and used Светозар [Svetozar] as the name for *Shadowfax.*

Nemirova's name is *Warrior against the Shadow* (Тенебор [Tenebor]), as if *fax* were an old form of *warrior.* Her name is built on the elements for *shadow* (тень [ten']) and for *fighter* (борец [borets]). This name gives up both the color that Tolkien wanted Shadowfax to have and the reflection of the speed with which Shadowfax ran, an element that a number of the other translators successfully played on. When quizzed about which character the name *Tenebor* should apply to, one Russian respondent thought that it would be Boromir. The logic of his conclusion is undeniably good. Boromir fought to the last against the forces of darkness, and his name contains the Old Slavic element for *warrior* or *fighter.*

Tolkien adapted the Old Slavic name *Borimir* [literally: *Warrior for Peace*] into *Boromir,* just like he adapted the name of the Old Slavic deity *Radegast* into *Radagast* (q.v.). The first element in Боримир [Borimir] is found in the words for *battle* (борьба [bor'ba]) and for *warrior* (борец [borets]). The second element is the word for *peace* (мир [mir]). This meaning, which is transparent to the Russian reader, but hidden to the English reader, gives the Russian reader a different impression of Boromir from the start. The combination of his Slavic name and his character traits make it seem to the Russian reader that Boromir just stepped off the pages of one of the Russian sagas (былины [byliny]), and earns him a certain amount of sympathy.

Shadowfax was the one name that Gruzberg permitted himself the liberty of changing to a speaking name. His name is Обгоняющий Тень [Obgonyayushchij Ten'], which means *Outrunning its Shadow*, as if *fax* meant *fast* instead of *mane* (and *coat).* The image is quite appropriate, given Gandalf's description: "swift as the flowing wind." (F.344)

Shadowfax is also one of the names that Bobyr' tackled. Her version of this name—also used by Umanskij—is Быстрокрыл [Bystrokryl] (B.483, U T.524) meaning *Fleet-winged,* which Shadowfax certainly is. This name prompts the reader to think of Pegasus, which may have been what Tolkien had in mind, but did not say. It competes very well with Gruzberg's name, but loses out because of its existing associations. Despite its mistranslation,

Gruzberg's name remains the winner, because of the evocativeness of its image, and because it kept one element of the original name.

Shire. Tolkien's recommendation for the translation of *Shire* was to use an archaic word with the meaning *district*. The editors of Gruzberg-A used the word Удел [Udel], which fits Tolkien's instructions perfectly. Удел [Udel] was used in Russia in feudal times to designate a separately administered district of the kingdom. Volkovskij, subsequently, also adopted Удел [Udel] for his rendition of the Shire. Kistyakovskij, Korolev, Nemirova and VAM decided instead, with good effect, that this was the translation of *farthing*.

K&K dug up and redefined an archaic word (заселье [zasel'e]), which is absent in modern defining dictionaries. The word they used is based on the verb *to settle, to colonize* заселять [zaselyat'], focusing on the fact that the Hobbits moved to the Shire from across the mountains, (F.23-24) and that the Bree-Hobbits called the people of the Shire "colonists." (F.29) The ending -ье [-'e] is widely used to designate place names as can be seen in a number of the translators' works:

Brandy Hall (G&G) - Брендинорье [Brendinor'e]: literally Brandy-hole-place.
Bridgefields (VAM, K&K) - Замостье [Zamost'e]: literally Beyond-the-bridge-land.
Bywater (G&G) - Уводье [Uvod'e]: literally By-water-place.
Bywater (V) - Заручье [Zaruch'e]: literally Across-the-creek-place.
Green Hill Country (Alexandrova) - Зеленохолмье [Zelenokholm'e]: literally Green-hill-land.
Tookland (M&K) - Укролье [Ukrol'e]: literally Rabbit-land.

K&K's name (заселье [zasel'e]) remains, however, less elegant than Удел [Udel].

G&G, Bobyr'/Umanskij, Gruzberg-C and the subtitles simply transliterated *Shire*, as Шир [Shir], which is pronounced like the word *shear* to match the pronunciation of *shire* in names such as Oxfordshire, Cheshire and Devonshire, which are spelled Оксфордшир, Чешир and Девоншир in Russian. In their endnote, explaining the word *Shire* and why they chose to render it as Заселье [Zasel'e] (K&K F.596), K&K quite correctly point out that when it stands alone, *Shire* is pronounced Шайр [Shajr], with a long 'I,' as in *hire* or *tire*. VAM avoided this trap in her version by creating her own compound place name *ending in -shire*, Хоббитшир [Hobbitshire], which captures the feeling of British toponymy that is somehow missing in a Russian text, where Шир [Shir] stands alone.

The ever inventive Kistyakovskij created a name on an entirely different pattern. He turned the *Shire* from a district into a whole country, by combining the word *Hobbit* with the ending -ания [-aniya], which can be recognized in various Russian names for countries, as in Germany (Германия [Germaniya]), Spain (Испания [Ispaniya]), and Great Britain (Великобритания [Velikobritaniya]). This ending is also commonly found in English names for geographic entities such as Lithuania, Tasmania, Pennsylvania. Kistyakovskij's new country, Хоббитания [Khobbitaniya], is easily transparent to the Russian reader, but it does feel a bit grandiose for what should have been a simple district in rural England.

This may be somewhat explained by the description of the size of the Shire in the first edition of the M&K translation. According to M&K in this edition, the Shire is 100 leagues from east to west and 150 leagues from north to south. (M&K F_{1982}.7) In their second edition, the Shire shrunk back to Tolkien's 40 by 50 leagues. (JRRT F.24; M&K F_{1988}.36) Tolkien had also shrunk the Shire, but his change was nowhere nearly as large as the change that M&K made. In Tolkien's first edition (1954), the Shire was 50 leagues east to west by nearly 50 north to south. (F_{1954}.15) With the fourth edition (1965), it changed to 40 by 50, omitting the "nearly." (F.24)

Though the name *Shire* does not appear in *The Hobbit*, Kamenkovich, nevertheless, embellished her text with it, using Kistyakovskij's name for the *Shire*, *Hobbitania*, in the comparison of the Tooks and the Bagginses in the first chapter. (Km H.9; JRRT H.16)

In her introduction, Nemirova says that offering alternatives to those of Kistyakovskij's names like *Hobbitania* would be like trying to give Don Quixote or Paris another name. She hedges her bets with a "belt-and-suspenders" approach to the names, and ends up with two names for the *Shire*. Her map shows the location of Hobbitania, but in her "Prologue," the Hobbits are "residents of the Край [Kraj] or Hobbitaniya." (N P.10) The Russian word *kraj* is an administrative district, and, in older texts, it means a *country*. *Hobbitania* then plays mix and match with *The Kraj* throughout Nemirova's text. This approach is not entirely out of place given Tolkien's inclination to gloss names in different languages, but it is, nevertheless, an embellishment to the text. *Kraj* by itself would have been reasonably successful, but it cannot compete with the likes of *Hobbitania* (Kistyakovskij) and *Hobbitshire* (VAM).

Reinforcing Nemirova's point about the immutability of Kistyakovskij's *Hobbitania* as a name for the *Shire*, Kaminskaya, Korolev, Perumov and Yakhnin use it as well. (q.v. **Hobbiton**)

Town Hole is Tolkien's wonderful Hobbit pun for *Town Hall*. It appears in the anecdote that Pippin told at the Prancing Pony about how Will Whitfoot got his nickname. (F.214) Because Tolkien's pun is a play on the similarity of the sound envelopes of *hole* and *hall*, it would appear almost impossible to translate. In Russian, *town hall* is one word (ратуша [ratusha]), not two, and this word does not look anything like the Russian word for the *hole* in the ground (нора [nora]), which is the key to the pun from the opening line of *The Hobbit*.

Bobyr'/Umanskij and Yakhnin left it out altogether. G&G reduce the anecdote to "a tale of the collapsing roof in Michel Delving," that Frodo knew by heart. Tolkien's pun and the story of how Will Whitfoot got his nickname are lost by the wayside. (G&G F. 186) Volkovskij also avoids specifying which roof fell in, but at least he got the anecdote across. (V F.218) VAM and Nemirova give up the pun, but give their readers an elegant sentence that gets the anecdote right, and says that it was the roof of the Town Hall. (N F.187) The ever verbosely correct K&K say that the roof of the City Hall hole (нора Городской Управы [nora Gorodskoj Upravy]) fell in. (K&K F.244) Gruzberg calls the *Town Hole* the "Hole Taun" (Нора Таун [Nora Taun]), serving up some incomprehensible alphabet soup to his readers of the same flavor as VAM's and Yakhnin's rendition of *Hobbiton*. (q.v.) (G. F.215)

In M&K's first, abridged edition (1982), they left out the whole anecdote, but in the second edition (1988), they brought it back in style, and located it in the Ратушная Нора [Ratushnaya Nora], literally, *The Town-Hall Hole*. (M&K F_{1988}.200) This was a valiant effort at Tolkien's pun in Russian, but it was not really a pun. At best, it is an elegant calque.

Aleksandrova gets the prize for originality. Her version of *Town Hole* combines the Russian words for *town hall* and *hole* where they overlap—the end of the word for *hole* (нора [nora]) and the beginning of the word for *town hall* (ратуша [ratusha])—to form Норратуша [Norratusha]. It does what Tolkien's name does. It makes the reader stop for a minute to think about the name before the meaning sinks in.

Treebeard. Tolkien glosses this name as a translation of the Sindarin name *Fangorn*, in which *fang* means *beard* and *orn* means *tree*. He wanted it to be translated by sense. Gruzberg, G&G and K&K did exactly that. Gruzberg used archaic elements for his name, while G&G and K&K mixed a modern element with an archaic one.

In Gruzberg-A and -B, Treebeard is called Древобрад [Drevobrad]. Because both elements are archaic, the name is less transparent for the modern Russian reader. In Gruzberg-C, the name was changed to Древобородый [Drevoborodyj], on the analogy of a number of existing Russian adjectives like redbeard (рыжебородый [ryzheborodyj]), and blackbeard (чернобородый [chernoborodyj]) of literary fame, based on the modern word *beard* (борода [boroda]), that G&G and K&K had used from the start. K&K, Perumov and G&G$_p$ called *Treebeard* Древобород [Drevoborod]. Древобрад [Drevobrad] had a much greater sense of wonder about it. It is too bad that Gruzberg changed it. Volkovskij, fortunately, preserved Древобрад [Drevobrad] in his translation.

The same linguistic process that took the name from Древобрад [Drevobrad] to Древобород [Drevoborod] can be seen at work in both the elements of this name. The old form брада [brada] was replaced by a newer form борода [boroda], as the liquid 'R' filled itself out with a vowel on either side. This is exactly the same thing that happened to град [grad] (q.v. **Hobbiton**), when it turned into город [gorod]: *town*.

The modern Russian word for *tree* (дерево [derevo]) used to be древо [drevo]. This form is still preserved in modern Russian in the word for *lumber* or *timber* (древесина [drevesina]). The same root is also found in the Russian word for *ancient* древний [drevnij].

The use of the same root in the Russian words for *tree* and for *ancient* points clearly to a primeval concept of tree that matches Tolkien's. Fangorn, whose name contains—all his anthropomorphic attributes to the contrary—the element *orn* (*tree*), is called "Eldest" by Celeborn. Tolkien underscores the ancient origin of the treeherds, and by implication their flocks, in the rhyme that lists the Living Creatures recited by Fangorn, where the Ents are called "the earthborn, old as mountains." (T.84) He returns to their antiquity and adds a glimpse of their power in his description of the Old Forest, which "was indeed ancient, a survivor of vast forgotten woods; and in it there lived yet, ageing no quicker than the hills, the fathers of the fathers of trees, remembering times when they were lords." (F.181)

In the Roman descriptions of the German lands, the Hercynian Forest sounds like those vast forgotten woods of which the Old Forest was but a remnant. The Hercynian Forest was nine-days journey in breadth and stretched from the banks of the Rhine to the remote regions of the Dacians. So vast was it that even Germans, who had traveled through it for sixty days, were unable to reach or even hear news of the place that it began.[64]

The root of the Russian word for *tree* древо [drevo] is really a Proto-Indo-European word, which shows up in Gaelic as *dervo-* and in Welsh as *derwen* (oak tree). In Old Indian compounds it appears as **daru-*, **dru-*. which is a part of the name *the Druadan forest*. The inhabitants of this forest were the Woses, a name that Tolkien glosses in his notes on nomenclature as *old men of the woods*. The name of their forest, therefore, is essentially just a repeat of their name (*dru-* = *forest* and *adan* = *man*): forest-man.

This root is also a part of the etymology of *Druid*. The standard etymology explains **dru-* as meaning *tree* and *-id* as coming from *-wid*, which carries the meaning of *knowledge*. The ending *-wid* is still active in Russian today with this meaning in the form -вед [-ved]. It is used in words like языковед [yazykoved]: linguist and медведь [medved'], the descriptive name for bear that was used to avoid its taboo name, which was believed to invoke the bear's spirit if it was said aloud. Медведь [medved'] literally means *honey knower*. (Compare the English word: *mead*, a fermented drink made from honey.) On the analogy of медведь [medved'], **druwid* would mean *tree knower*.

In ancient times, trees were important for other things than they are now. Marriages were performed and courts of law were held under linden trees. The birth of the son of a king was celebrated with the planting of a linden tree. Not only the Celts, but also the Russians believed in sacred forests and worshiped trees. The oak was sacred to Перун [Perun], the god of thunder and lightning, because lightning struck oak trees more often than others.

VAM also used the element древ [drev] in her name, but did not bother to translate the second element: *beard*. She rendered the name as Древесник [Drevesnik]. Words that end in -ник [-nik] are formed from adjectives to make nouns that have the characteristic of the adjective. VAM is playing on the adjective for *wood* or *timber*, древесный [drevesnyj], rather than on the one for *ancient* (древний [drevnij]). That gives Treebeard a heavy, wooden character, rather than the character of a bearded sage.

Umanskij's name also makes a play on this adjective. He calls *Treebeard* 'Wooden-bearded' (Древеснобородый [Drevesnoborodyj]), which is much more clumsy than VAM's quite readable invention.

Nemirova has a similar approach. She uses the same adjective form, but without the suffix. Her rendition of *Treebeard* is Древес [Dreves]. It is more elegant than VAM's because it hints at a more ancient form, since less complex forms (her two-syllable noun) normally precede more complex forms derived from them, like VAM's and Umanskij's three-syllable adjective. VAM's construction points to the adjective preceding the name. Nemirova's chapter title is "The Old Ent" (Старый Энт [Staryj Ehnt]). It shifts the accent slightly from Treebeard's appearance and his genus to his age, but with negligible philosophical impact.

Kistyakovskij, like VAM, did not translate the second element for *beard*. He, however, took the other extreme in meaning for the root древ [drev]. He accents Treebeard's antiquity almost to the exclusion of Treebeard's 'tree-ishness.' His name is Древень [Dreven']. It is built with the same archaic suffix (-ень [-en']) that he used in his name for *Quickbeam*: Скоростень [Skorosten'].⁶⁵ This is the same suffix that Volkovskij later used to create his family of old Shirish words like бебень [beben'] and мутень [muten']. (q.v. **Baggins**) Kistyakovskij's name could be understood to mean 𝔄𝔫𝔠𝔦𝔢𝔫𝔱𝔫𝔢𝔰𝔰, written in Gothic letters because of the feeling that the suffix gives it.

The editors of Gruzberg-A and -B, did not use Kistyakovskij's name, because *Treebeard* only appears in the second volume of the set and they had no way of knowing what Kistyakovskij did with the name at the time that they were preparing their editions. They left Gruzberg's original name—Древобрад [Drevobrad]—in place in both versions.

G&G were faced with the same dilemma as the unknown editors of Gruzberg-A and -B. *Treebeard* only appears in the second volume of the three and they had no way of knowing what Kistyakovskij did with the name. They apparently were not pleased with the Common Speech name for *Fangorn, Treebeard.* Their chapter title is "Fangorn," and that is the name used for the Ent every place except one. When he introduces himself to the Hobbits, he says: "Fangorn is my name according to some, Drevoborod others make it. Fangorn will do." (G&G$_p$ T.60) This is the exact opposite of Tolkien's introduction, which ends with "Treebeard will do." (T.84) After the introduction Tolkien refers to him as *Treebeard*, while G&G continue to refer to him as *Fangorn*.

Yakhnin has a hybrid, none-of-the-above approach. His name is Трибор [Tribor]. For the bilingual reader, it is the transliteration of *tree* (три [tri]) combined with the Russian word for *pine forest*: бор [bor]. For the monolingual Russian reader, his attempt at linguistic legerdemain falls flat. This reader will see the first element as the Russian word *three* (три [tri]), and will initially assume—because of the context of the chapter opening—that the second element is the word for *pine forest*. At this point the name will be perceived as meaning something like 'three forests.' As the story progresses, however, the other possible meaning that бор [bor] can have in names will come to the fore. Given some of Yakhnin's other name puns, this ambiguity is most likely intentional.

When the Ents go off to destroy Isengard, the reader will lead towards interpreting бор [bor] as *warrior*. This is the meaning that Russians first see in *Boromir*, assuming that it is composed of бор [bor: warrior], plus the element мир [mir: peace]. Boromir, should, therefore, mean 'Warrior for Peace.' (q.v. **Shadowfax**) Yakhnin's pun-name, in essence, becomes 'three-forest/warrior.' Like all hybrid names, it is less than successful.

Yakhnin does, however, manage to preserve the elements *tree* and *beard* in his description of Tribor. He describes Tribor's beard as having "a touch of green" (с прозеленью борода [s prozelen'yu boroda] Ya T.50), and calls him a "bearded giant" ([borodatyj gigant] Ya, T.50) and а бородач [borodach] (Ya T.52), which means *someone with a beard*. The element *tree* finds its home in Yakhnin's name for *Ent*, which is древ [drev], drawing on the archaic root that Gruzberg used. The excellent descriptions, though, do not make up for the failure of his name.

Variags. Tolkien makes no comment on this name in "Nomenclature," and with good reason. It appears only twice in the text, in the Chapter "The Battle of The Pelennor Fields," and is hardly more than an extra brush stroke in the background of Tolkien's epic canvas. A number of the Russian translators, however, clearly recognized the problem that this name presents in writing for a Russian audience, and took pains to avoid it. Tolkien's name is essentially the transliteration of the Russian word for the Varangians: варяги [variagi (pl.), using the Library of Congress transliteration system with which Tolkien would have been familiar]. For the Russian reader, the equation of the Varangians with the Variags is equally as serious as Perumov's complaint (q.v. **History**) about the Haradrim fighting under a red banner, and would have been but yet another reason for the Soviet censors to ban Tolkien in the USSR.

Nemirova changed one of the two references to Variags to *Southerners* (южане [yuzhane]) and changed the other to *barbarians* (варвары [varvary]). (N R.115, 116) Bobyr'/Umanskij and G&G have the knights of Dol Amroth chasing only trolls and orcs, omitting the Variags. (B.395, U R.734; G&G R.122) Bobyr'/Umanskij and the samizdat G&G omit the other reference. In their print version, G&G change the spelling of Variags to break any connection with the existing term from Russian historiography. G&G's Variags were the варайги [varajgi] from Khand. (G&G R.120) VAM makes a more drastic spelling change to produce варакхи [varakkhi]. (VAM R133, 135)

Volkovskij offered the Wargs an expanded role in his version of Tolkien's tale. In the segment where the tide of battle has shifted, and the knights of Dol Amroth are driving the enemy before them, Tolkien lists the enemy as: troll-men, Variags and orcs. (R.150) Volkovskij's list is "half-trolls, wargs (варги [vargi]) and orcs." (V R.200) It is an interesting change (or typographical error) that offers Volkovskij's readers a slightly different view of the battle, and reduces the Variags' participation in the battle by half.

Volkovskij did not, however, entirely wipe the Variags from the face of Middle-earth. Tolkien included the Variags in another list of the forces of evil two pages earlier. There the Variags of Khand are listed among the Easterlings, the Southrons and black men like half-trolls from far Harad. (R.148) In this list, Volkovskij renders *Variags* as варьяги [var'yagi (pl.)]. Volkovskij's addition of an extra letter to his name will not perceptibly slow the reader down in making the logical leap from Volkovskij's rendition of the name to the Varangians of Russian history. In her revised edition (2003), however, VAM decided to keep Volkovskij company. (VAM R_{2003}.1006, 1007)

Murav'ev makes a subtle, but effective spelling shift to create the дикари-воряги [dikari-voryagy (pl.)]. (M R.131, 132) The shift from 'A' to 'O' in the first syllable of the name prompts the reader to think of thieves (вор/ворюга [vor: thief/voryuga: really big thief]) first, and only later, if at all, of the Varangians. The combination of воряги [voryagi] with дикари [dikari (pl.): wild men] to make a compound noun also draws the reader's attention away from the варяги [varyagi] of Russian history. Their name would be read as 'the wild-men-thieves', which conveys a very evocative image. This is the best of the efforts to sidestep the problem of Tolkien's name for the Russian audience.

K&K used a letter-for-letter transliteration of Tolkien's name (вариаги [variagi (pl.)]; K&K R159, 161), and, of course, qualified it with an endnote. In their endnote (K&K R612), K&K gloss *Variags* as варяги [varyagi: the Varangians] and offer the meaning of "northern mercenaries," Scandinavians in the service of the Byzantine Emperor. Aleksandrova, the final editor of Gruzberg-D, used a similar circumlocution in her version of the lists. She called the *Variags* the "brutal Northerners" (жестокие северяне [zhestokie severyane]).

Aleksandrova's change shows rather clearly how she perceived the name *Variags*. The identification of the *Variags* as 'Northerners' is not found in the text or on Tolkien's map. (F.16-17) In the text, the implication is that they came from the south. On his map, Tolkien places Khand south-east of Mordor. Aleksandrova's identification of the Variags as 'Northerners', is, therefore, a result of her perception of the meaning of the name rather than an interpretation of the text. It was this perception of the name that made the other translators attempt to recast the name in a less recognizable form, like they did for Durin (q.v.).

Gruzberg, who had the best reaction to *Durin*—a name with an unsuitable connotation in Russian—took no steps here to avoid confusion between the *Variags* and the варяги [varyagi (pl.)] of Russian history. In his text, the *Variags* were the варяги [varyagi]. Gruzberg's print editor, Zastyrets, however, chose a less confrontational path. In his version, the *Variags* are the Вэрьяги [Vehr'yagi], essentially following Volkovskij's lead, with, perhaps, a little more success. (G R.140, 142)

Even K&K took care to tread lightly on this issue. Their endnote cautiously avoids the other half of the association with the name. The article in the *Soviet Encyclopedic Dictionary* (1990) confirms K&K's identification of the Varangians as Scandinavian mercenaries, and even adds that the Old Russian name for the Baltic Sea was the Варяжское море [Varyazhskoe more: The Varangian Sea], clearly confirming their area of origin. What K&K had left out, however, was that the Varangians were also the semi-legendary princes Ryurik, Sineus and Truvor, a detail that plays prominently in the Encyclopedic Dictionary article. According to Russian legend, Ryurik and his brothers were invited to come and rule Novgorod by the people of the city. Ryurik[66] was the founder of the dynasty of Russian princes known as the Ryurikoviches, who ruled from the ninth to the sixteenth century.

When Ryurik came to Novgorod, he brought his Germanic title of *Konung* with him. In the course of time it was russified into князь [knyaz'].

This title is commonly translated as *prince*, but its linguistic relatives in a number of other languages all mean *king*. In Swedish there is *konung*, in Norwegian and Danish, *konge*, in German, *König*, in Dutch, *koning*, in English, *king*, and in Finnish, *kuningas*. This root can also be seen in the Polish, książę, and in the Czech, kníže. The change from *konung* to князь [knyaz'] is a result of the same linguistic process that caused Vaeringjar (pl.) to change to варяги [varyagi]. The same shift can also be seen in the Old Russian word for money, пенязь [penyaz'] (Dal' III.30, 549), which is related to the German Pfennig, the English penny, the Norwegian and Danish penge, the Swedish pengar, the Polish pieniądz, and the Czech peníz.

Murav'ev resurrected the original form of Ryurik's title (Конунг [Konung]) in his rendition of the title for the King of the Mark of Rohan. His choice is linguistically correct, because it better reflects the Anglo-Saxon origins of the King of the Mark of Rohan than does the modern Russian word for *king* (король [korol']), which is derived from Charlemagne (742-814), known in Latin as *Carolus Magnus*, and in Russian as Карл Великий [Karl Velikij]. The modern Hungarian, Czech and Polish words for *king* came from the same place: król (Polish), král (Czech), kiraly (Hungarian).

Wargs, hounds of Sauron, an evil breed of demonic wolves. Tolkien provided no instructions for this name in his "Nomenclature," which meant that he felt the name should be retained as is. In old Prussian, *wargs* means *evil*. *Wearg* was one of the epithets in Old English for *wolf*, but Tolkien obviously felt that this usage was too far removed from the present-day reader to be recognized.

Tolkien's name is also found in the Norse sagas in the term *vargr i veum* [a wolf in the sanctuary]. This is the name that was applied to someone who had committed a murder in a holy place. The application of this name to someone was legal pronouncement. The person so named was deemed outside the law, which meant that anyone could take his life without guilt or censure, in the same way that, according to old German law, wolves could be hunted and killed freely, even in forests where other hunting was considered poaching, and was punishable.

Derivatives of the root on which Tolkien's name is based are still in use in the modern Slavic languages. In Polish this root is found as wróg [enemy]. In Ukrainian, it is ворог [vorog: enemy]. In modern Czech, *vrah* means *murderer*. In contemporary Russian, враг [vrag] means *enemy*, but historically it used to also mean *the devil*. In his book[67] on the forces of evil, Sergej Maksimov (1831-1901) includes враг [vrag] in his list of names for the devil along with ворог [vorog], лихой [likhoj] (See Kistyakovskij's name for **Mirkwood**) and черный [chernyj: black] (q.v. **The Scarlet Book of Westmarch** and **Shadowfax**). In this context, враг [vrag] is a good match for Tolkien's *the Enemy*, as in "some spoke in whispers of the Enemy and of the Land of Mordor." (F.72) This is the word that all the translators—except Bobyr' and Yakhnin, who omitted the sentence—used for *the Enemy*.

In Gandalf's list of living servants of the Dark Lord of Mordor (F.293), the relationship between wargs and werewolves is presented as the same as that between orcs and trolls. This list places the words *warg* and *werewolf* in the same sentence, and all the translators—except VAM and Nemirova—transliterated *wargs* as варги [vargi (pl.)], giving it a Russian plural ending. Nemirova's transliteration was уорги [uorgi (pl.)], using the transliteration that can be found for an initial 'W' in names like *Will*, which Nemirova transliterated as Уилл [Uill]. (N F.187) It makes her name stand out and puts it in a class with a number of names of other unpleasant things that begin with 'U' in Russian, like упырь [upyr': *vampire*], as умерший [umershij: *the deceased*] and умирашка [umirashka: *corpse*], and VAM's and Kistyakovskij's names for *Barrow-wight* Умертвие [Umertvie: Kistyakovskij], умерлия [umerliya: VAM]. It also breaks any connection with the existing Russian word for *enemy*, and makes her name every bit as unusual as Tolkien's is for the English reader.

VAM's choice was ворог [vorog]. In modern Russian, the use of this word carries a stylistic marking. The modern desk-top dictionaries mark it as high style or poetic, and define it as meaning враг [vrag: *enemy*]. The approximate English pair for враг/ворог is *enemy/foe*. Since VAM's name already has an existing meaning, it is less suitable than Tolkien's, which, for the casual reader, has no meaning other than that created by Tolkien.

In the sentence that contains both *warg* and *werewolf*, the vote was split for the Russian rendition of *werewolf*. Half the votes went to оборотень [oboroten']. Half (M&K, G&G, Nemirova and Volkovskij) went to волколак [volkolak]. Yakhnin abstained. The difference between the two words is slight and the definition of each in the dictionary includes the other. Волколак [volkolak] is specifically a werewolf; the first part of the word (волк [volk]) means *wolf*. Оборотень [oboroten'] is a more general classification, not specifying what kind of animal the person turns into. It fits best with Tolkien's description of Beorn: "a skin changer", who is sometimes a huge black bear and sometimes a great strong, black-haired man with huge arms and a great beard. (H.118)

In the segment in *The Hobbit* about Beorn, half the translators (VAM, Km, Korolev and Anonymous) used оборотень [oboroten']. The other half (Rakhmanova, Gruzberg, Bobyr', Yakhnin and Kaminskaya) skillfully avoided using it. The word carries too many ready associations with it. Tolkien's circumlocution makes the description work much better.

In the scene in which the company is attacked by "a great host of wargs," (F.389-91), Tolkien alternates the words *wolf* and *warg*. M&K were troubled by the ambiguity, and changed the *wargs* to *werewolves* (волколаки [volkolaki]). They also standardized Tolkien's alternation of *wolf* and *warg* to *werewolves* (волколаки [volkolaki]). They set the stage for this with a deft embellishment to Aragorn's and Boromir's exchange of proverbs. (F.389) It resolves the difference between *skin changer* (оборотень [oboroten']) and *werewolf* (волколак [volkolak]), by combining *wolf* and *shape shifter* with a hyphen, which is a common method of forming new words in Russian (волки-оборотни [volki-oborotni]). M&K's embellishment marks the point, after which all the *wolves* and *wargs* in M&K's text change to *werewolves* (волколаки [volkolaki]). (M&K F.368) M&K were resolute in their intention to standardize on one term instead of alternating *wolves*, *werewolves* and *wargs*. In their translation of the description of the lands defended by the Beornings, where Tolkien had said: "neither orc nor wolf dared to go" (F.301), M&K changed the *wolves* to *werewolves* (волколаки [volkolak]) there as well. (M&K F_{1982}.162; M&K F_{1988}.281) All the other translators left the *wolves*, where Tolkien had put them.

Yakhnin had a construction similar to M&K's combination of *wolf* and *shape shifter*. He replaced the commonly used word for *wolf* (волк [volk]) with влак [vlak], to produce влаки-оборотни [vlaki-oborotni (pl.)]. *Vlak is a hypothetical ancient form of волк [volk] with the vowel on the other side of the liquid 'L,' based on the example of the vowel changes around the liquid 'R' in the root of the word *garden*, which is reflected in its various forms in Leningrad, Isengard and город [gorod: *city*]. Yakhnin's linguistic sleight of hand will be lost on those of his readers who are not classical linguists, and will really fall flat for those with a knowledge of Czech, Slovak or Bulgarian, where *vlak* means *railroad train*. For those readers the company is being attacked by a snarling pack of *shape-shifting trains, which raises the question of why they did not see their tracks beforehand.

And the Winner is ...

The question that is invariably the most asked about the Russian translations of *LotR* is "which is the best?". The answer to this question is very subjective, because, as the saying goes: *Beauty is in the eye of the beholder*. The table below attempts to quantify the process, but it nevertheless remains a subjective assessment, based on the author's personal linguistic appraisal, as described in the preceding narrative. There are other drawbacks to the chart as well. It addresses the success of the translation of the names separately from the quality of the translation of the text, and it assumes that the names should be translated, something that Tolkien was not entirely sure could be done. The author shares his skepticism.

In terms of the overall success in dealing with the names, Gruzberg's decision to transliterate almost all the names seems the best one, though many a Russian reader will take umbrage at this suggestion. It leaves Tolkien's linguistic realm in its original state, and makes it possible for interested readers to delve deeper into it, if they desire. It is essentially impossible to replicate all of Tolkien's linguistic jests, and any attempt inevitably falls short in one way or another. The summary of the table results only serves to point this out. Even the translator with the most successful names, Kistyakovskij, captured little more than 50% of the available points.

As Tolkien said in a letter, (L.249-50) there is no reason to think that his names can be translated, just because they are made up. *Stratford-on-Avon*, *Dover* and *Oxford* are all also speaking names, but no translator would dare to literally translate their meanings of "the place that the Roman road crosses the river," "Water" and "the place that the ox crossed (the river)". Separated from their commonly accepted form, the names would no longer communicate their place in the world to the reader, and the reader would become completely lost. The same happens when the interwoven scheme of Tolkien's names fails to take into account all the interconnections, either through oversight or because the requisite linguistic connections are not possible in the target language.

Though translation of the names is to be discouraged, the Russian renditions of Tolkien's names are both imaginative and inventive, and can be appreciated in relative isolation from the rest of the text. The table below points to the best renditions of 32 of Tolkien's names. (Ties were possible, so the total number of points does not equal 32. Where more than one translator used the same form, the first one to use it got the point.) The clear winner is Kistyakovskij with 17 points. His translations of the names are uniquely resourceful. He is followed by K&K with 5 points. Gruzberg and Nemirova trail with 4 points each. Bobyr' has 3 points. VAM and Yakhnin have 2 each. All the rest of the translators have 1 point each.

Name	Best Translation	Translator
Baggins	Торбинс [Torbins]	Kistyakovskij
Cotton	Коттон [Kotton]	Bobyr'
Crickhollow	Кричья Балка [Krich'ya Balka]	VAM
	Криккова Лощина [Krikkova Loshchina]	K&K
Derndingle	Тайнодол [Tajnodol]	Kistyakovskij
Durin	Дюрин [Dyurin]	Gruzberg
	Дьюрин [D'yurin]	Bobyr'
Entmoot	Онтомолвище [Ontomolvishche]	Kistyakovskij
	вече [veche]	Nemirova
Fallohide	Белоскоры [Beloskory (pl.)]	K&K
Frogmorton	Лягушатники [Lyagushatniki]	Kistyakovskij
	Лягушкина Запруда [Lyagushkina Zapruda]	Yakhnin
Gamgee	Гэмджи [Gehmdzhi]	Bobyr'
	Плутоу [Plutou][68]	Yakhnin
Goldberry	Златеника [Zlatenika]	G&G
Hobbiton	Норгорд [Norgord]	Kistyakovskij
Isengard	Айсенгард [Ajsengard]	Volkovskij
Lithe	прилипки [prilipki, pl.]	Kistyakovskij
Lune	Льюнские горы [L'yunskie gory]	K&K
Michel Delving	Великие Норы [Velikie Nory]	Nemirova
Mirkwood	Лихолесье [Likholes'e]	Kistyakovskij
Mount Doom	Роковая гора [Rokovaya gora]	Kistyakovskij
Oliphaunt	олифант [olifant]	Kistyakovskij
Púkel-men	Шишига [shishiga]	K&K
Radagast	no contest	
Red Book	Красная Книга [Krasnaya Kniga]	Gruzberg
	Западной Окраины [Zapadnoj Okrainy]	K&K
Rivendell	Раздол [Razdol]	Kistyakovskij

Rohan	Ристания [Ristaniya]	Kistyakovskij
	Мустангрим [Mustangrim]	Kistyakovskij
Sackville-Baggins	Лякошель-Торбинс [Lyakoshel'-Torbins]	Kistyakovskij
	Кошелье -Торбинс [Koshel'e-Torbins]	Nemirova
Sandyman	Пескунс [Peskuns]	Kistyakovskij
Shadowfax	Обгоняющий Тень [Obgonyayushchij Ten']	Gruzberg
Shire	Хоббитшир [Hobbitshire]	VAM
	Хоббитания [Khobbitaniya]	Kistyakovskij
Thain	Хоббитан [Khobbitan]	Kistyakovskij
Town Hole	Норратуша [Norratusha]	Aleksandrova
Treebeard	Древобрад [Drevobrad]	Gruzberg-A
Variags	воряги [voryagi]	Kistyakovskij
Wargs	уорги [uorgi (pl.)]	Nemirova

Notes:

1. *A Tolkien Compass*, Jared Lobdell (ed.), New York: Ballantine Books, 1975, pp.168-216.
2. *New English-Russian Dictionary*, J.R. Galperin (ed.), M: Soviet Encyclopedia, 1972.
3. Podręczny słownik Rosyjsko-Polski, J. H. Dworecki (red.), Warszawa: Wiedza Powszechna, 1963.
4. Русско-Украинский словарь, М. Я. Калинович (ред.), Киев: изд. Академии Наук Украинской ССР, 1962.
5. This name only appears in *The Fellowship of the Ring* and was, therefore not included in G&G$_s$.
6. The *New English-Russian Dictionary* defines *boffin* as a scientist, special consultant. (p. 173) This colloquial usage was popular in Britain during World War II as a description of the eggheads who helped win the war.
7. This name only appears in *The Fellowship of the Ring* and was, therefore not included in G&G$_s$, nor was it included in M&K$_1$.
8. Omitted in G&G$_s$.
9. Only in *The Return of the King*, and, therefore, not in M&K$_1$.
10. Carpenter, Humphrey, *Tolkien*, New York: Ballantine Books, 1977, pp. 120, 197.
11. Will Whitfoot, the Mayor.
12. Толковый словарь русского языка, под ред. Ушакова. М: Государственное издательство иностранных и национальных словарей, 1939, стр. 239.
13. *Welsh Place Names*, Cardiff: John Jones Publishing, 1996.
14. Гальперин, 341.а.
15. Гальперин, 366.а.
16. *An Introduction to Elvish*, Jim Allan (compiler and editor), Frome, Somerset: Bran's Head Books, 1978, pp. 220-226.
17. Also substantiated as *Weidenagamoot*.
18. Вильям Шекспир. Трагедии • Сонеты, М: «Художественная литература», 1968.
19. Юрий Олеша. Повести и рассказы, М: изд. «Художественная литература», 1965, стр. 121-238.
20. Olesha, p. 168.
21. Olesha, p. 164.
22. Olesha, p. 164.
23. *The Quiet Man* (1952). Directed by John Ford, Writing credits Frank S. Nugent, Maurice Walsh (story).
24. For a more extensive explanation of the etymology of the word for *tree* and its relationship to the word *Druid*, see the article on Treebeard.

25. Highday/Highdei in Shirish. (A.484)
26. Носов, Николай Николаевич. Незнайка на луне, М: Детская литература, 1965. This novella is not available in translation, but the first book of the series, of which *Dunno on the Moon* is the third and last, is available: *The Adventures of Dunno and his Friends*, M: Progress Publishers, 1980. Illustrations by A. Laptev. Translated by Margaret Wettlin.
27. For those who missed the point, the Russian name literally means 'one who does not know.'
28. Карлов, Борис. Новые приключения Незнайки. Снова на луне, М: Азбука, 1999. This book has since been pulled from distribution in a copyright dispute. The cover art can still be seen at <http://bkarlov.narod.ru/neznayka.htm>.
29. Обратный словарь русского языка, М: «Советская энциклопедия», 1974, стр. 34-35.
30. СЭС, стр. 1579.
31. HoMe, vol. 5, p. 386, p. 423.
32. СЭС, стр. 178.
33. Carpenter, 1977, p.193.
34. Рожнова., Полина. Радоница: русский народный календарь, М: «Дружба народов», 1997, стр. 88.
35. А.Б. Терещенко. Быт русского народа, т. 4 и 5, М: «Русская книга», 1999, печатается по оригиналу 1847-1848 годов, стр. 195.
36. Терещенко, стр. 250.
   Josef Ružička. Slovanská Mythologie, Praha: Nakladatel Alois Wiesner, 1924, p. 74.
   Русский народъ: его обычаи, обряды, преданія, суеверія и поэзія, М. Забылин (собр.), Москва: М. Березина, 1880, репринтное воспроизведение, М: совместное Советско-канадское предприятие «Книга Принтшоп», 1990, стр. 67.
37. Ružička, p. 117. Терещенко, стр. 256.
38. И. Панкеев. Русские праздники, М: Яуза, 1998, стр. 241.
39. Терещенко, стр. 194, 195.
40. Терещенко, стр. 257.
41. Забылин, стр. 83.
42. OAD, New York: Avon Books, 1980, p. 226.
43. Былины. М: Детская литература, 1969, стр. 32, 138.
44. Былины, стр. 18, 97, 145, 219.
45. <http://edic.ru/history/art/art_2197.html>.
46. Ожегов/Шведова, стр. 133.
47. Н. Николаюк, Библейское слово в нашей речи, СПб.: ООО «Светлячок», 1998, pp. 17 and 404-5.
48. Galperin, p. 496.
49. Ожегов/Шведова, стр. 778.

50. Ожегов/Шведова, стр. 683.
51. Ružička, p. 146.
52. R.A. Lafferty. *The Fall of Rome*, New York: Doubleday, 1971, pp. 221-28. Радагаст is spelled *Radagais* in this source.
53. Энциклопедический словарь: Славянская мифология, М: Эллис Лак, 1995, стр. 391.
54. Ibid., стр. 43.
55. В.М. Мокиенко, Т.Г. Никитина. Толковый словарь языка Совдепии, СП-б: Фолио-Пресс, 1998, стр. 290-292.
56. Энциклопедический словарь, Брокгаузъ (Лейпцигъ) и Ефронъ (С.-Петербургъ), 1891, т. 9, стр. 432. Reprinted by Терра, Ярославль, 1990.
57. Trevor Rowley, *The Landscape of the Welsh Marches*, M. Joseph, London, 1986.
58. Ожегов /Шведова. 1997, стр. 646.
59. In the 1988 edition, *Skal'burg* was replaced by *Isengrad*. Otherwise, the quotes are identical.
60. Ожегов /Шведова. 1997, стр. 371.
61. Никитина, Т.Г.. Как говорит молодежь: Словарь молодежного сленга. По материалам 70-90-х годов. (2-е изд.), СПб: Фолио-Пресс, 1998, p. 503.
62. <http://edinorog13.narod.ru/mythology/skand3.html>, <http://trutvangar.narod.ru/topor/sage/podval/41.html>.
63. И.И. Тёрохъ. Карпаты и славяне: предание, Нью Іоркъ: издание Общества ревнителей русской старины, 1941, стр. 5, 150.
64. Julius Caesar. *The Gallic War*, VI. 25.
65. Kistyakovskij's name is built on the root word for *speed*: скорость [skorost']. Скоростень [Skorosten'] could be understood to mean 𝕾𝖕𝖊𝖊𝖉𝖞.
66. Also spelled *Riurik* and *Riurikoviches* in some sources.
67. Максимов, Сергей. Нечистая сила, М: «Русский Духовный Центр», 1993. Reprint of the 1903 edition.
68. The door prize for originality.

FROM THE LIBRARIES
AT UNDERTOWERS
AT THE GREAT SMIALS AND
AT BRANDY HALL

Bibliography of Translations

The Lord of the Rings

Bobyr', Zinaida Anatol'evna (retold by). *Povest' o Kol'tse*. Her abridged and adapted retelling of *The Lord of the Rings* circulated in samizdat beginning in the mid-1960s. A version of her translation edited by Semen Ya. Umanskij and dated 1975-1978 was found in the private library of Evgeniya Smagina, who graciously made it available to the author.

———. *Povest' o Kol'tse*. M: SP Interprint, 1990.

———. *Vlastelin Kolets*. M: Molodaya Gvardiya, 1991. Printed in a two-volume set with her translation of *The Hobbit*.

Grigor'eva, Natalya, and Vladimir Grushetskij (trans.). *Vlastelin Kolets*. Verse translated by I. Grinshpun. In the 1980s, their translation of *The Two Towers* and *The Return of the King* circulated widely in samizdat, often in combination with the Gruzberg translation of *The Fellowship of the Ring*. The samizdat version (G&G$_s$) was considerably revised before going into print.

———. *Vlastelin Kolets*. St. Petersburg: Severo-Zapad, 1991. One-volume edition.

———. *Bratstvo Kol'tsa*. St. Petersburg: Severo-Zapad, 1992. Vol. I of the six-volume Centenary edition of Tolkien's collected works. (G&G$_p$)

———. *Dve Kreposti*. St. Petersburg: Severo-Zapad, 1992. Vol. II of the six-volume Centenary edition of Tolkien's collected works.

———. *Vozvrashchenie Korolya*. St. Petersburg: Severo-Zapad, 1992. Vol. III of the six-volume Centenary edition of Tolkien's collected works.

———. *Vlastelin Kolets*. M: TO Izdatel', 1993. Two-volume set.

———. *Vlastelin Kolets*. St. Petersburg: Terra/Azbuka, 1996. One-volume edition.

———. *Bratstvo Kol'tsa*. St. Petersburg: Azbuka, 2000.

———. *Dve Kreposti*. St. Petersburg: Azbuka, 2000.

———. *Vozvrashchenie Korolya*. St. Petersburg: Azbuka, 2000.

———. *Vlastelin Kolets*. St. Petersburg: Azbuka, 2000. One-volume edition.

———. *Vlastelin Kolets*. St. Petersburg: Azbuka, 2002, 2003. One-volume edition, with the Rakhmanova translation of *The Hobbit*.

Gruzberg, Aleksandr Abramovich (trans.). *Vlastelin kolets.* The first Russian full samizdat translation (ca. 1976). Verse translated by Yu. Batalina (née Gruzberg, his daughter). It was available on the Internet in two versions, A and B. The A version is characterized by having almost all the names in transliteration. The B version uses the names from M&K, and was most often combined with volumes II and III of the G&G samizdat translation to form a complete three-volume set. B versions with all three volumes in the Gruzberg translation were less common, but not rare. Gruzberg has requested that all versions of his translation be pulled from the Internet, but copies can still be found here and there. Gruzberg provided the author of this work with a file of his translation. This version has been designated Gruzberg-C. It is considered the authoritative version of Gruzberg's vision of the translation. Gruzberg's translation was subsequently published in two further versions with identifiable editorial changes to the text.

——. *Vlastelin Kolets.* M: IDDK, 2000, 2001. This is the CD-ROM with both *The Hobbit* and *The Lord of the Rings,* in both Russian and English. It was edited by E.Yu. Aleksandrova. This version is designated Gruzberg-D.

——. *Vlastelin Kolets.* Ekaterinburg: U-Faktoriya, 2002. This is the print version in three volumes. It was edited by Arkadij Zastyrets. This version is designated Gruzberg-E.

——. *Vlastelin Kolets.* Ekaterinburg: U-Faktoriya, 2003. This is a re-print of Gruzberg-E in one volume.

Kamenkovich, Mariya (née Trofimchik) and Valerij Karrik (pseudonym: real name Kamenkovich)(trans.). *Sodruzhestvo Kol'tsa.* Prose translation and annotations by M. Kamenkovich and V. Karrik. Verse translated by M. Kamenkovich and Sergej Stepanov. Afterword by M. Kamenkovich. St. Petersburg: Terra/Azbuka, 1994. Fully annotated.

——. *Dve Bashni.* St. Petersburg: Terra/Azbuka, 1994.

——. *Vozvrashchenie Korolya.* St. Petersburg: Terra/Azbuka, 1995.

——. *Vlastelin Kolets: Kniga I: Sodruzhestvo Kol'tsa.* St. Petersburg: Azbuka, 1999.

——. *Vlastelin Kolets: Kniga II: Dve Bashni.* St. Petersburg: Azbuka, 1999.

——. *Vlastelin Kolets: Kniga III: Vozvrashchenie Korolya.* St. Petersburg: Azbuka, 1999.

——. *Vlastelin Kolets: Kniga I: Sodruzhestvo Kol'tsa.* St. Petersburg: Amfora, 2000.

——. *Vlastelin Kolets: Kniga II: Dve Bashni.* St. Petersburg: Amfora, 2000.

——. *Vlastelin Kolets: Kniga III: Vozvrashchenie Korolya.* St. Petersburg: Amfora, 2000.

——. *Vlastelin Kolets.* St. Petersburg: Amfora, 2001. One-volume edition.

——. *Vlastelin Kolets: Kniga I: Sodruzhestvo Kol'tsa.* St. Petersburg: Amfora,

2002. Cover art is from the movie. Issued as a set with *The Hobbit*.
———. *Vlastelin Kolets: Kniga II: Dve Bashni*. St. Petersburg: Amfora, 2002.
———. *Vlastelin Kolets: Kniga III: Vozvrashchenie Korolya*. St. Petersburg: Amfora, 2002.
———. *Vlastelin Kolets*. St. Petersburg: Amfora, 2002. One-volume edition.
Matorina, Valeriya Aleksandrovna (trans.). *Sodruzhestvo Kol'tsa*. Khabarovsk: Amur, 1991.
———. *Dve Tverdyni*. Khabarovsk: Amur, 1991.
———. *Vozvrashchenie Korolya*. Khabarovsk: Amur, 1991.
———. *Khobbit, ili Tuda i Obratno. Vlastelin Kolets*. M: EKSMO-Press, 2003. Published in a single volume with *The Hobbit*.
Murav'ev, Vladimir, and Andrej Kistyakovskij (trans.). *Khraniteli*. Abridged translation. M: Detskaya Literatura, 1982. (M&K$_1$) Verse and all the names translated by A. Kistyakovskij. Kistyakovskij died in 1987, before all three volumes could be completed.
———. *Khraniteli*. Unabridged translation. Prologue and translation of first book by Murav'ev. M: Raduga, 1988, 1990, 1991. (M&K$_2$)
———. *Dve Tverdyni*. M: Raduga, 1990
———. *Khraniteli*. Ioshkar-ola: Marijskoe Knizhnoe Izdatel'stvo, 1992.
———. *Dve Tverdyni*. Novosibirsk: Knizhnoe Izdatel'stvo, 1992.
———. *Vozvrashen'e Gosudarya*. M: Raduga, 1992.
———. *Vozvrashen'e Gosudarya*. Novosibirsk: Knizhnoe Izdatel'stvo, 1993.
———. *Prilozheniya / Khraniteli*. Baku: Olimp, 1993.
———. *Dve Tverdyni / Vozvrashchenie Gosudarya*. Baku: Olimp, 1993.
———. *Khraniteli*. Tula: Filin, 1994. Vol. II of a four-volume set. Vol. I is the Rakhmanova translation of *The Hobbit*.
———. *Dve Tverdyni*. Tula: Filin, 1994. Vol. III of a four-volume set.
———. *Vozvrashchenie Gosudarya*. Tula: Filin, 1994. Vol. IV of a four-volume set.
———. *Khraniteli*. M: EKSMO-Press/Yauza, 1998. Illustrated by Leo Khao.
———. *Dve Tverdyni*. M: EKSMO-Press/Yauza, 1998.
———. *Vozvrashchenie Gosudarya*. M: EKSMO-Press/Yauza, 1998.
———. *Khraniteli*. M: Rosman-Press, 2000.
———. *Dve Tverdyni*. M: Rosman-Press, 2000.
———. *Vozvrashchenie Gosudarya*. M: Rosman-Press, 2000.
———. *Vlastelin Kolets*. M: EKSMO-Press/Yauza, 2001, 2003. One-volume edition.
———. *Vlastelin Kolets*. M: Rosman-Press, 2002. One-volume edition.
Nemirova, Alina V. (trans.). *Khraniteli Kol'tsa*. M: AST, Khar'kov: Folio, 2002.
———. *Dve Tverdyni*. M: AST, Khar'kov: Folio, 2002.

———. *Vozvrashchenie Korolya.* M: AST, Khar'kov: Folio, 2002. Issued as part of a set with the Korolev translation of *The Hobbit*, and the Estel' (Chertkova) translation of *The Silmarillion*.

———. *Polnaya istoriya Sredizem'ya.* M: AST, 2003. A one-volume edition with the Korolev translation of *The Hobbit*, and the Estel' (Chertkova) translation of *The Silmarillion*.

Subtitles. *The Fellowship of the Ring*, New Line Cinema, 2002. The translation team consisted of: Ail, Аликс, Archi, BellaT, Fridmanka, grampasso, ivanko, little Mu, Mrs. Underhill, Natalie, Sare, TheHutt, Vasya Gondorsky. They were aided by a discussion group consisting of: Iolly, 10th nazgul, =Назгул=, Анхен, almost_happy, Astra, BAndViG, Berta, Chameleon, Cet, Dudette, Eujenia, Finord, freshy, Gaerie, hinotf, Hoffmann, Holly, Inga, Janus, Katherine Kinn, kryaba, Laimar, Lindalae, Masha Klim, Maeglin, Mechanic, Nata, PeterGreat, Пластун, RedFox, Rika, romx, Ryo, shred, shs, Sniff, Tick, Тсарь, Twilight, Varrah,|VentiL, Water Lily, Zandr. Fragments of the text—including the Incantation of the One Ring (Kistyakovskij)—were taken from the M&K translation. The translation of the beer song was by TheHutt. The translation of the poem Gandalf's Fireworks (I. Grinshpun) was taken from the G&G. The subtitle files were downloaded from the web at <http://www.thehutt.de/fotr_see_subs.zip>.

Volkovskij, Vitalij (trans.). Verse translated by V. Vosedoj. *Druzhestvo Kol'tsa.* M: AST, St. Petersburg: Terra Fantastica, 2000. Part of a five-volume set, including the Estel' (Chertkova) translation of *The Silmarillion* and the Korolev translation of *The Hobbit*. Cover art by Greg and Tim Hildebrandt.

———. *Dve Tverdyni.* M: AST, St. Petersburg: Terra Fantastica, 2000.

———. *Vozvrashchenie Gosudarya.* M: AST, St. Petersburg: Terra Fantastica, 2000.

Yakhnin, Leonid L. (retold by). *Khraniteli.* M: Armada/Al'fa-kniga, 1999. Illustrated by N. Kundukhov. Cover art by T.N. Khromova.

———. *Dve Bashni.* M: Armada/Al'fa-kniga, 1999.

———. *Vozvrashchenie Korolya.* M: Armada/Al'fa-kniga, 1999.

———. *Khraniteli.* M: Armada/Al'fa-kniga, 2001.

———. *Dve Bashni.* M: Armada/Al'fa-kniga, 2001.

———. *Vozvrashchenie Korolya.* M: Armada/Al'fa-kniga, 2001.

The Hobbit

Anonymous. "Nebyvaloe Pristanishche" ["Strange Lodgings"] in *Angliya: Ezhekvartal'nyj zhurnal o segodnyashnej zhizni v Velkobritanii* [England: Quarterly Journal of Life Today in Great Britain], No. 2 (issue 30), 1969, pp. 30-40. The only Russian translation published during the author's life.

Anonymous. This is a computer file that was available on these servers: <ftp://sympad.moldnet.md/pub/etext1/tran/ru/fiction/jrrt/index.htm>, <ftp://ftp.nit.spb.su/etext/translate/tolkien.j.r.r/>, <http://nmsf.sscc.ru/Scripts/cp2koi.pl/lib/books/russian/036/> and <http://kniga2001.narod.ru/tolkien/02books/files/hobb2.zip>.

Bobyr', Zinaida Anatol'evna (trans.). *Khobbit, ili Tuda i Obratno*. M: Molodaya Gvardiya, 1991. Illustrated by M.I. Sivenkova. (Version A) Part of a two-volume set with her translation of *The Lord of the Rings*.

———. *Khobbit, ili Tuda i Obratno*. Perm': Knizhnyj Mir, 1994. Edited by Yu. Batalina (Gruzberg's daughter). Illustrated by A. Filippov and A. Bytmanov. Copyright date: 1992. (Version B)

Gruzberg, Aleksandr Abramovich (trans.). *Khobbit, ili Tuda i Obratno* in *Vlastelin Kolets* (E. Aleksandrova ed.). M: IDDK, 2000, 2001. This is a CD-ROM with both *The Lord of the Rings* and *The Hobbit* on it.

———. *Khobbit, ili Tuda i Obratno* (E.V. Chernyak ed.). Ekaterinburg: Litur, 2001. Illustrated by E. Nitylkina.

Kamenkovich, Mariya (née Trofimchik), and Sergej Stepanov (trans.). *Khobbit, ili Tuda i Obratno*. St. Petersburg: Terra/Azbuka, 1995, 1999.

———. *Khobbit, ili Tuda i Obratno*. St. Petersburg: Amfora, 2000.

———. *Khobbit, ili Tuda i Obratno* in *Tom Bombadil i Drugie Istorii* [Tom Bombadil and Other Stories], St. Petersburg: Azbuka, 2000, 2001.

———. *Khobbit, ili Tuda i Obratno*. St. Petersburg: Amfora, 2002. Cover art is from the Movie. Issued as a set with *The Lord of the Rings*.

Kaminskaya, Lyudmila (trans.). *Khobbit, ili Tuda i Obratno*. M: Inter V.M., 1993. This is the translation of the comic-book edition of: J.R.R. Tolkien. *The Hobbit: or There and Back Again* Adapted by Charles Dixon with Sean Deming, illustrated by David Wenzel, Forrestville, CA/New York: Eclipse Books, New York: Ballantine Books, 1990.

Korolev, Kirill (trans.). Verse translated by Vladimir Tikhomirov. *Khobbit, ili Tuda i Obratno*. M: AST, St. Petersburg: Terra Fantastica, 2000, 2001. Cover art by Greg and Tim Hildebrandt. Part of a five-volume set, including the Estel' (Chertkova) translation of *The Silmarillion* and the Volkovskij translation of *The Lord of the Rings*.

———. *Khobbit, ili Tuda i Obratno*. M: AST/Astrel, 2000. Illustrated by I. Olejnikov.

———. *Khobbit, ili Tuda i Obratno*. M: EKSMO-Press, St. Petersburg: Terra Fantastica, 2002. Also contains a number of Tolkien's minor works.

———. *Khobbit, ili Tuda i obratno: Izbrannye proizvedeniya* [The Hobbit, or There and Back Again: Selected Works], M: EKSMO-Press, Saint Petersburg: Terra Fantastica, 2002.

———. *Khobbit, ili Tuda i Obratno*. M: AST, 2002, 2003.

———. *Khobbit, ili Tuda i Obratno*. M: AST, 2002. Issued as part of a set with the Nemirova translation of *The Lord of the Rings*, and the Estel' (Chertkova) translation of *The Silmarillion*.

———. *Polnaya istoriya Sredizem'ya*. M: AST, 2003. A one-volume edition with the Nemirova translation of *The Lord of the Rings*, and the Estel' (Chertkova) translation of *The Silmarillion*.

Matorina, Valeriya Aleksandrovna (trans.). *Khobbit, ili Tuda i Obratno*. Khabarovsk: Amur, 1990.

———. *Khobbit, ili Tuda i Obratno*. Zaporozh'e: Interbuk-Khortitsa, 1994.

———. *Khobbit, ili Tuda i Obratno*. M: EKSMO-Press, 2000. Corrected edition. Cover art by Durell [sic] Sweet. Illustrated by I. Pankov.

———. *Khobbit, ili Tuda i Obratno*. M: EKSMO-Press, 2002. Also contains a number of Tolkien's minor works, including the Stepashkina translation of "Leaf by Niggle."

———. *Khobbit, ili Tuda i Obratno. Vlastelin Kolets*. M: EKSMO-Press, 2003. Published in a single volume with *The Lord of the Rings*.

Rakhmanova, Nataliya L. (trans.). *Khobbit, ili Tuda i Obratno*. Leningrad: Detskaya Literatura, 1976. Illustrated by M. Belomlinskij.

———. *Khobbit, ili Tuda i Obratno*. Leningrad: Detskaya Literatura, 1989, 1991. Revised edition.

———. *Khobbit, ili Tuda i Obratno*. Novosibirsk: Knizhnoe Izdatel'stvo, 1989, 1992.

———. *Khobbit, ili Tuda i Obratno*, in *Zabytyj den' rozhdeniya: Skazki anglijskikh pisatelej* [The Forgotten Birthday: Fairy Tales by English Authors]. M: Pravda, 1990.

———. *Khobbit, ili Tuda i Obratno*. Magadan: Knizhnoe izdatel'stvo, 1991.

———. *Khobbit, ili Tuda i Obratno*, in *List Raboty Melkina i drugie volshebnye skazki*. M: RIF, 1991.

———. *Khobbit, ili Tuda i Obratno*. St. Petersburg: Severo-Zapad, 1991.

———. *Khobbit, ili Tuda i Obratno*. St. Petersburg: Detskaya Literatura, 1992.

———. *Khobbit, ili Tuda i Obratno*. Minsk: Vyshejshaya Shkola, 1992.

———. *Khobbit, ili Tuda i Obratno*. St. Petersburg: Severo-Zapad, 1993. Vol. IV of the six-volume Centenary edition of Tolkien's collected works.

———. *Khobbit, ili Tuda i Obratno*. Baku: Kontsern "Olimp", 1993.

———. *Khobbit, ili Tuda i Obratno*. Tula: Filin, 1994. Vol. I of a four-volume set.

Volumes II - IV are the Murav'ev and Kistyakovskij translation of *The Lord of the Rings*.

———. *Khobbit, ili Tuda i Obratno*. Minsk: Kavaler, 1996. Illustrated by N. Bajrachnyj.

———. *Khobbit, ili Tuda i Obratno* in *Shkol'naya Roman-Gazeta*, No. 10, 1996, pp. 2-40 and 57-92.

———. *Khobbit, ili Tuda i Obratno* in *Perevodnaya Slovesnost': Fata-Morgana i Ostrov Sal'tkroka*. M: Drofa, 1996. Grade-school reader.

———. *Khobbit, ili Tuda i Obratno*. St. Petersburg, Lenizdat, 1996. In a single volume with Ursula K. Le Guin's *A Wizard of Earthsea*.

———. *Khobbit, ili Tuda i Obratno* in *Skazki Veka* [Fairy Tales of the Century]. M: Polifakt, 1999.

———. *Khobbit, ili Tuda i Obratno*. St. Petersburg: Azbuka, 1999. Illustrated by M. Belomlinskij.

———. *Khobbit, ili Tuda i Obratno* in *Priklyucheniya Toma Bombadila i drugie istorii* [The Adventures of Tom Bombadil and other stories]. St. Petersburg: Azbuka, 2000. Cover art by Denis Gordeev.

———. *Khobbit, ili Tuda i Obratno*. St. Petersburg: Azbuka/Oniks 21 Vek, 2001. Illustrated by M. Belomlinskij.

———. *Khobbit, ili Tuda i Obratno*. St. Petersburg: Azbuka, 2002, 2003. Part of a one-volume edition also containing the Grigor'eva and Grushetskij translation of *The Lord of the Rings*.

———. *Khobbit, ili Tuda i Obratno*. St. Petersburg: Azbuka-klassika, 2002.

Sedov, S. (retold by). *Khobbit*. M: Belyj Gorod, 1999, 2001. Comic book. Illustrated by E. Uzdennikov.

Umanskij, Semen Ya.. This version survived as a manuscript dated 1975-1978 in the personal library of Evgeniya Smagina, who graciously made a copy available to the author in 2003. The bound typescript likewise contained Umanskij's revisions of the Bobyr'translation of *LotR*, which made it, at first, seem to be a revision of Bobyr's translation. The Umanskij version of *The Hobbit*, however, shows no resemblance to the Bobyr' version published in 1992 by Knizhnyj Mir Publishers in Perm'.

Utilova, N. (retold by). *Khobbit*. M: Avlad, 1992. Hard cover comic book. Illustrated by: R. Ramazanov, A. Shevtsov, R. Azizov.

Yakhnin, Leonid L. (retold by). *Khobbit, ili Tuda i Obratno*. M: Armada/Al'fa-kniga, 1999, 2001. A book-length retelling for children.

———. *Khobbit, ili Tuda i Obratno*. M: OOO "Ras-Min" (MediaKniga), 2002. Audio-book in MP3 format on CD-ROM.

———. *Khobbit, ili Tuda i Obratno*. M: Olma-Press Obrazovanie, 2003.

Yakovlev, Lev (ed.). *Khobbit*. M: Egmont - Rossiya, 2001. Comic book. Illustrated by Elena Volod'kina.

Hobbit Knock-offs

Suslin, Dmitrij Yu.. *Khobbit i Gehndal'f* [The Hobbit and Gandalf], M: Al'fa-kniga, 2000.

———. *Khobbit i Glaz Drakona* [The Hobbit and the Eye of the Dragon], M: Al'fa-kniga, 2000. For a review, see: Mark T. Hooker, "The Suslin *Hobbit* Knock-offs," *Beyond Bree*, March 2002, p. 7.

———. *Khobbit i Saruman* [The Hobbit and Saruman], M: Al'fa-kniga, 2000, 2002.

———. *Khobbit i Gorlum* [The Hobbit and Gollum], M: Al'fa-kniga, 2001.

———. *Khobbit i Gehndal'f* [The Hobbit and Gandalf], M: Al'fa-kniga, 2001. Includes both *Khobbit i Glaz Drakona* and *Khobbit i Gehndal'f*.

———. *Khobbit i Gorlum* [The Hobbit and Gollum], M: Al'fa-kniga, 2001.

———. *Khobbit i Koltso Vsevlast'ya* [The Hobbit and the All-powerful Ring], M: Al'fa-kniga, 2003.

Proskurin, Vadim. *Khobbit, kotoryj slishkom mnogo znal* [The Hobbit Who Knew too Much], M: Al'fa-kniga, 2002.

———. Khobbit, kotoryj poznal istiny [The Hobbit Who Learned the Truth], M: Al'fa-kniga, 2003.

These books form the core of Mr. Hooker's next Tolkien in Russia project.

Index

abridgement   11, 17-19, 20, 22, 25, 27, 52, 64, 77, 89, 100, 104, 111, 124, 155, 156, 167, 170, 187, 190, 206, 221

Adam and Eve	176-177
adaptation of imported of ideas	25, 40
admonition of language arts teachers (see also repeats)	105
adverb *there*	151, 153-155
Agreement (part of Tolkien's structure)	104, 111-115
Alekhin	22
Aleksandrova	28
Alice in Wonderland	32
All Power to the Soviets! (Communist slogan)	181
All-powerful Ring	171, 173, 181
allegory	27
alphabet soup	192, 211, 216, 223, 227, 232, 238, 255, 274
alternative guide to morality	32
Alternativists	34
America	42, 58, 60
'an ill wind ...' (proverb)	91-92
ancient	275
Anduril	219
Angliya (British Cold-War magazine)	17, 51
anti-utopia	174-175, 181, 185
Aphilosophicals	34
apolitical	28
approaches to the study of Tolkien's texts	44
Aragorn	42
Arbat Trilogy (Rybakov's books)	48
Arda out in the Sticks (Russian web site)	31
Armenian translation of *The Hobbit*	68
Asterix (Comic-book character)	205-206
Atheism	37
Atheists	41
attention to word choice, meticulous	188, 223, 252
auction of Bilbo's possessions	237-239

Bag End	203-204, 206-210
Baggins	203-204, 206-207, 285
baggins (four-o'clock tea)	204
Baltic Sea	280
Bandobras Took	225
Banks	263
banned book	15, 175, 185
Barrow-wight	282
Batalina	19, 51
batman (a soldier servant)	145-146, 149-150, 158-159, 163
beatification of J.R.R. Tolkien	38
beer brewing festival	242-243
Belomlinskij (illustrator)	68-69
benefit (translation of *worth*)	98
Beorn	85, 89-90, 174, 283
Beowulf	130-131, 220
Berlin, the capture of by Soviet troops	27
best fairy tales of the twentieth century	51
best translation	32, 284
betrayal of the Elven-Smiths	169-173
beyond all hope (a religious definition)	141
Big Brother	175
Bil'bo Bungovich	238
Bilbo Baggins	86-90, 103-104, 107-108, 112, 115, 117
Biography of a Batman	149
black, the color	66-67, 247, 249, 265, 282
Blair, Tony	29
Bobyr' (translator)	17-18, 20, 22-23, 25, 27, 32, 53, 92, 135, 285
Bobyr'/G&G	147, 153, 155, 161, 187
Bobyr's translation of *The Hobbit*	51
Boffin	205, 212
boffin	287
Bolger	205
Bolshevik	30, 179
boom	20-24, 33, 35
first	20-24, 33
second	24
publishing	17, 24, 32
"read Tolkien in the original"	24
translation	21, 23, 33, 35
Boromir	271, 278

Boss (nickname)	188
Brandibuck	226, 263
Brandy Hall	272
brass ring	74-75
Braude (translator from Swedish)	71
Brezhnev	23, 82, 84
Bridgefields	272
British Labor Movement	28
British understatement	38, 86, 96, 181, 186
understated condemnation of the police state	196
British working-class culture	28
Brockhouse	212, 263
Buckelbury	226
Buckland	226
bwcca (Welsh word; see also puca)	253
Bywater	189, 250, 272
collective, the	32
camps (the GULAG)	180, 198
canonical texts	45
canonical-historiographic approach	45
Capitanus Hobbitanus	188
carefully layered structure	198
Carpe Diem!	229
Catherine II	25, 140
Catholic	38
Catechism	141-142
religious concepts	44
Catholicism	34, 37-39
Celts	276
censors	16, 23, 55, 61, 64, 68, 71, 81-82, 135
centrally planned economy	156
Chaadaev	25, 47, 139-140, 143
Chertkova (translator)	22
Chesterton (an Inklling)	182
Chief (nickname)	187
Christ	39
Christ's Transfiguration on Mount Tabor	141-142
Christian hope	137
Christian writer	140
Christian-like doctrine of Tolkienism	37

Christianity	34, 39, 41, 123, 139-140
Christianized mythology	41
Christians	34, 41
Chubbs	212
Chukovskij (Russian author)	83
Church of Byzantium	140
Church of Rome	140
circumlocution	105, 127, 138, 164, 268, 269, 280, 283
Civil War (the Russian)	179, 193
cock crow at dawn	257
Cold War	17, 21, 29, 51, 55, 58, 60-63, 100
collapse of Communism	17, 23, 31-32
comic-book editions	52
commedia dell'arte	234
Common Harmony	181
Communism	60, 140
Communism, fall of	29, 185
Communist ideology	43
Communist State	30
computers	19, 23
Comsomol (Communist youth organization)	32
consumer goods	156
Conquest (Soviet analyst)	180, 193, 195
copying machines	19
Coronation Stone (Scottish history)	220
Correctional-Labor Burrows	186, 192-193
Cotton (Tolkien's name, not the fabric)	210-212, 263, 285
courage	112, 251
CPSU (Communist Party of the Soviet Union)	222
Crack(s) of Doom	252
Cricket Hollow	215
Crickhollow	213-215, 225, 234, 285
Crickhowel	215
crisis period in late-stage Communism	43
Crucywel (Welsh place name)	215
"cult book," why *The Lord of the Rings* became a	36
cultural gap, bridging the	53
Cyrillic letters	140
daughter of the river emperor	236
days of the week in Shirish	229

decision to give up the Ring	103, 109-110, 114-115, 117
deficit goods	156-157
deletions	239
Derndingle	214-217, 221, 285
desire	128
despair	128, 130, 133-135, 142, 156
dictionary diving	208, 213, 259
Diderot	25, 140
dissident	19
diversity of Russian Tolkienism	43
doom	252
doom and gloom	131, 140, 142
Dostoevskij (Russian author)	26
double letters	210, 235, 255
Doughan	45, 233
dragon-lore	79
dragon-spell	84
dragon-talk	80, 82, 84
dragons	72, 75, 80, 99
Druadan forest	276
Druid	276
duality of mythology	42
duality of the individual	44
Dumas (French author)	218
Dunno on the Moon (Nosov's book)	231-232
Durin	27, 218, 244, 280, 285
Dutch translation	253
duty	150-155, 157-161, 163, 167
Dwarf	57
East, The	55, 60-61, 63-67
East-mark	268-269
Easterlings	227
Eastern Orthodox Church	139
eavesdropping	148-149
Eddas	79, 137, 219
editions of *The Hobbit*	53-54, 56
Edwardian society	37
Ehrenburg (Soviet author)	198
Elder Edda	79, 137, 219
elephant	253

Elven-Smiths of Eregion	170-173
Elvenking	90, 92
embellishment	18, 25, 56, 76-77, 85, 111, 121, 125-126, 129, 134, 137, 153, 156-157, 178, 194, 198-199, 208-209, 236, 238, 249, 260-262, 273, 283
enchanted	216
ending -ton	211
ending -ания [-aniya],	273
ending -бург [-burg]	240
ending -вед [-ved]	276
ending -вика [-vika]	235
ending -ень [-en']	209, 227, 233, 229, 277
ending -ия [-iya]	261
ending -инс [-ins]	211, 213
ending -лесье [-les'e]	247
ending -ник [-nik]	264
ending -ника [-nika]	235
ending -нс [-ns]	263
ending -ье [-'e]	249, 272
ending -ы [-y] (Russian plural)	260, 227, 282
'enemy of the people' (Stalinist characterization)	195
Engels (Marxist philosopher)	131
English story by an English writer	187
English definition of a gentleman	112
English literary tradition	44
English-language books, dificulty in obtaining	19, 30
English-language editions by Russian publishers	24
English society of the 1930s, ferment in	39
enjoy	75, 77
Entmoot	216, 219, 221-223, 285
epic cycles of Northern and Western Europe	44
Erestor	128, 131, 133
esquire	238
evil	16-17, 27, 43, 60, 92, 99, 126, 131, 169, 171-174, 176, 178-179, 199, 236, 248, 250-251, 257-258, 265, 279, 281-282
challenge of evil	17
gold, the root of all evil	78, 85, 124
"Evil Empire" speech (Reagan's)	21
evil potential of knowledge	173
executions	180, 193

Faerie	57-59
Fafnir (the dragon)	79
Fahrenheit 451	20
faithful servant	153-154
Fallohide	224-227, 285
false hope	21, 128-130, 133-136
fandom	33
Fangorn	277
fatalism	124, 130, 139-140, 157, 159, 251
feet	52-53
Fenrir	97, 99
Finrod	41
first name and patronymic	238
first official publication	185
five-year plans	105
Flourdumpling	212
folly	21, 128-133, 135-136, 142
"forbidden-fruit" books, demand for	32
foretelling	123-129, 251
former Soviet Union	42
freedom of choice	108, 110-112, 154, 90-191
freedom of speech and the press	20, 32
friends (Sam and Frodo's relationship)	153-154
friends (Bilbo and Gandalf's relationship)	115
Frodo	42
Frodo's quest	123
Frogmorton	230-231, 264, 285
G&G (translators)	24, 28, 30, 32-33, 120, 122, 167, 205, 230
G&G/Bobyr' (translators; relationship between)	147, 153, 155, 161, 187
Gaffer	209
Galadriel	26, 85, 92-94, 123-124
Galich (Russian bard)	178
Gamgee	233-234, 285
Gandalf	103-104, 107-108, 112, 127-131
General Welfare	177, 181
Generalissimo	186-188, 191, 193-194, 198
Germanic title of *Konung*	280-281
Gimli	85, 92-94, 123-124
Glavlit (Soviet censorship organization)	23
Gnomes	56

goblets	90
God	55, 68, 70-71, 141
empty euphemisms for	55, 68, 70-71
of the Bible	141
Tolkien and Lewis on	38-39
Goethe (German author)	137
gold	84-86, 88, 90, 92, 94-99, 124, 153
as the root of all evil	78, 85, 124
Goldberry	235-236, 285
her formal name (daughter of the River)	235
Goodchild	263
grassy hollow	216
Great All-Hobbit Assembly	222
Great Terror	193
Great Wood	248
Green Hill Country	272
Grigor'eva (see also G&G)	22
Grubb	212
Grushetskij (see also G&G)	22
Gruzberg (translator)	18-19, 22, 24, 28, 51, 53, 120, 122, 222, 284-285
CD-ROM	24
Gulag	189, 192
GUOT (Soviet censorship organization)	23
Halflings	196, 227
hall (halls of waiting)	85, 89, 95-97, 99
Toad Hall	232
Brandy Hall	272
Town Hall (see also Town Hole)	274
Hamfast Gamgee	209
Harfoots	225-228, 229
Hercynian Forest	276
hide-and-seek with the censors (see also censorship)	83
High Elves of the West	56-57, 59, 92
hippies	43
system hippies	35
Hippolytus	176
Hitler	172, 188
hoard of treasure	87
Hobbit (Russian translation for)	236
etymology of	224, 226

The Hobbit, editions of	67, 72, 94
"Hobbit Games" (Russian role-playing games)	36, 41
Hobbitania	237-238 273
Hobbiton	226, 236-237, 275, 285
Hobbitshire	223, 237, 273
Hobbittan	237
Hobbittown	237
Holman	205, 212-213
honor	108, 115, 158
hope	17, 21, 34, 123-128, 130, 133, 135-136, 138-139, 141-142, 156
Hornblower	205, 263
Hornburg	240
hostages	193
Hrimfaxi	270
Hutchison (World War I author)	149, 158, 163
hybrid name	227, 232, 264, 278
ideological vacuum	31
Iliad	137
Imladris(t)	258
imperialist aggressors	60
imported ideas	25, 37
individual	32, 37
individuality	175
industrialized Shire	174
intelligentsia	32
interference	96, 125, 1778, 210, 214, 218, 240, 242, 247-250, 255, 258-260, 262-263
International Labor Movement	29
interrogator	200
iron	239
Isengard	239-240, 261, 283, 285
Isherwood (British author)	37
Jackson's movie version of *The Lord of the Rings*	33
jargon of the Cold War	55
job	150-152, 154, 158-161, 163, 166-167
Johnstone (literary analyst)	37, 39
joke	117-121
'just carrying out orders'	190

K&K (translators)	28, 122, 125, 167, 224, 232, 285
Kamenkovich (translator; see also K&K)	24-26
Kaminskaya (translator)	52
Karl Kautsky (Marxist philosopher)	179
Karrik (translator; sell also K&K)	24
KGB	19, 191
Khrushchev	17, 23, 81, 82-84, 194, 199
king of the Wood-elves	91
Kirillov (translator)	34
Kistyakovskij (translator; see also M&K)	20, 23, 33, 186, 220, 223, 226, 230, 273, 284-285, 293
accent on the "(ra)bbit" in Hobbit (see also *Hobbit*)	225-226
Klimov (samizdat publisher)	19
klopgeest	254
knockers	254
knowledge	170-178, 180-183
eagerness for	177
Knowledge is Strength (Russian magazine title)	176
knowledge of English	33
Konica	260
Korolev (translator)	50, 74
Korolev (Encyclopedia)	11
lack of literariness	116
lack of personal control over events	29
lacunae	50, 66, 76, 88-89, 100, 119-120, 172, 190, 274
Lado (god of the pagan Slavs)	243
Last Homely House, the	96
Latin annals	188
Latin letters	140
law	181-183
layered evolutionary structure	103, 110, 112, 114-115
Lenin	30, 176, 179, 265
Lenin's Russia	180
Leningrad	241, 283
Lewis, C.S.	38, 40
on JRRT	16
lhûne	243
liberalism	30
liminal sociocultural phenomenon	43
liquid 'R' (linguistic term)	275, 283

lite	241
Lithe	241-242, 285
Little Delving	245
loanword	30, 259
English	188
German	246
Lockholes	192
Longbottom	226
Lord of the Rings breakfast cereal	45
Lord of the Rings copies stolen from libraries	21
Lotho	174, 198-199
Lune	243, 285
M&K (translators)	21, 26, 30, 32, 36, 124, 127, 131-132, 139, 142
magic	43
Magic kingdom	59
Mandel'shtam (wife of Russian author)	189, 192, 195
map, Belomlinskij	67-69
march (borderland; see also merc)	266-267
Mark of Rohan	267, 269, 281
Market Capitalism	39, 140
market-driven publishing	23
marriage, proposal of	164, 167
Marx	179
Marxism	25, 37-39, 99, 131
Marxist revolution	25
Master (nickname for Stalin)	188
master-servant relationship	146-147, 151-152, 155, 157-158
mathematically infallible happiness (Zamyatin)	175
mathom	209
Matorina (translator; see also VAM)	22
mearc (boarderland; see also march)	266, 269
mechanical products of knowledge	173
mechanized and standardized 'post-war' society	37
Melgounov (commentator on Soviet Russia)	28
Melkorianism	42
Menshevik	30
metal, wheels, engines and machines	174-175
Michel Delving	245, 247, 285
Midgard	237
Ministry of the Interior (the police)	189

Mirkwood	247-249, 282, 285
mithril	153
mix-and-match names	232, 253, 268, 273
moot	219-220, 222
Mount Doom	251, 285
Mountain of Terror	252
Mountains of the Moons	244
movie, opinion poll on the translation of	33
movie fever	24
movie subtitles	33, 294
Mundburg	240
Murav'ev (translator; see also M&K)	20, 23, 28, 30, 32-33, 186, 192, 230
mustache (Stalin trademark)	83
mustang	261
mythological consciousness	41
mythological legacy of England	31
Mythomania Tolkienensis	34, 36, 45
names can be translated?	284
names, derivational studies of Tolkien's	72
names, immutability of Kistyakovskij's names	274
Nazis	171, 191
necessity	137
Nemirova (translator)	22, 24, 122, 220, 222, 285
neo-paganism	40, 44
neo-religiosity	44
New Age hybrid of Rasputin and a Hobbit.	35
New Force	177, 179-180
new leader of the orcs	91
nezhit' (Russian name for evil spirits of nature)	236
Nienna (Tolkienesque Russian author)	29, 34
Niennism	29-30, 39
NKVD (see also KGB)	189, 191, 194-195, 198
Noldor	57
Nordic Sagas	34
Northern theory of Courage	34, 41, 130, 137-139
Northerners	34
Nosov (Russian author)	231-232, 264
"Notes on Nomenclature"	203
Novgorod	220, 280
Nuremberg Trials	190

ode "To a Girl, Buying The Lord of the Rings at a Book Stand"	35-36
Old Forest	275
old Shirish names for the days of the week	228
old Shirish words	209, 211, 277
Olesha (Russian author)	225
Oliphaunt	253, 285
omitted words	53, 59-60, 88, 90, 93, 135, 147, 155, 167, 191, 195, 199, 204, 216, 219, 229, 254, 282
"On Fairy-Stories"	36-37, 42-43
opposition to Soviet ideology	42
optimism	16
orcs	174
Order	176-178, 180-183
overwhelming personality	80, 82
Paganism	140-141
Russians	276
European pagan mythology	41
sacred forests	276
Paris Commune	28-29
Patch Hollow	217
perception of Tolkien (Russian)	26
Perestroika	22-23, 32
personal responsibility	190-191
Perumov (Tolkienesque Russian author)	26-29, 34, 278
Perun (god of the pagan Slavs)	141, 257, 276
pessimism	16
Peter McLintock (a real batman)	149, 158, 163
philosophical comments by Tolkien	76, 84, 90
philosophical debate in search of "the truth"	35
philosophical divergences	112, 133
philosophical fault line	128-129, 140
philosophical issues of translating Tolkien's work	52
philosophical vacuum	31
photo-negative theology	38
Pinocchio	25, 31
pirated editions	32
plan	103-112, 115
whole plan	110
planned-economy publishing	20
Plutow	234

police state of the Shire	198
police state, indictment of the	193
Polish translation	15, 22, 72
Politburo	194
political arrests	195
political beliefs	39
political change in the Soviet Union	23
political climate of the 1980s	32
political climate of the USSR	191
political implications of the word *plan*	106
political interpretation of Tolkien's original texts	28
political joke	58
political nuance	189
political subtext	62
political uses of *The Lord of the Rings*	20
poltergeist	254
Popov (Russian Tolkienist)	31-32, 34, 58
post-Communist generation	55
post-Communist Russia	43
post-Soviet editions	55
post-Soviet period	191
post-Soviet Russian reader	81
power	85, 169, 178, 180-181
precious goblets	89
predestination	129, 139
predetermination	129, 131, 135, 161-162
Presto Publishers (*The Hobbit* in English)	24
princes Ryurik, Sineus and Truvor	280
principles	183
prison sentence, length of	192
prisons	180, 198
"Professor Tolkien and his Heritage" (conference title)	29, 40
promise	104, 108, 111-115
pseudo-historical chronicles	40
Pskov	220
public school, the worlds of, and the Icelandic sagas	37-38
publication dates	15-18, 20-24, 30, 32, 50-51, 82
publishing industry under State control	50
puca | pûca | puck | pwcca (Welsh word)	253
Puck	254
Púkel-men	253-255, 285

punishment, Sam's	148-149, 163
puns and riddles	38
Pushkin (Rusian author)	31
Quackmorton	232
quasi-historical chronicles	44
quasi-historical past	40
questioning of Tolkien's system of values	42
Quickbeam	277
Rabbit Hollow	225
rabbit names for Hobbits (see also Kistyakovskij)	214, 224-225
Radagast	256, 258, 271, 285
Ragnarok	34, 95, 99, 100, 131
Rakhmanova	50-51, 55-56, 65, 71, 77, 82-84, 89, 100
"read-Tolkien-in-the-original" boom	24
reading between the lines	9, 55, 62, 259
Reagan (U.S. President)	21
real names, power of	79
realism, literary (see also Socialist realism)	17
recognition of necessity	131
red banner	27-29, 278
Red Banner, Order of the	27
red flag	27-29
Red Terror, the	28, 193
red, the color	265
Red Book (see also "The Red Book")	27, 264, 266-268, 285
redemption of the Dwarves	85, 94, 124
rejection of modern mechanized civilization	37-38
rejection of aristocratism	26
relationship between Frodo and Sam (see also friends)	26, 146
religion	39, 41
religious content of Tolkien's works	41
religious non-Christians	41
repeats as an integral part of Tolkien's style	105, 109, 111, 155, 158, 198-200
restricted areas	217
Ring, the	104, 107-110, 114-115, 121
Ring of Darkness	26
Ring Rhyme, the	180, 183
Rings of Happiness	173
Rivendell	258-259, 285

River Hollow	215
Rohan	260, 262, 286
role playing Tolkien's works	44
role-playing games	43
Rose Cotton	163-167
Rule	176, 178, 180-183
Ruling Ring, the	181
Rushlight	263
Russia in the post-Soviet period of the 1990s	39
Russia, state of thinking in modern	34
Russian	
adaptation of Tolkien's works and philosophy	31
concept of "The Church"	42
intellectuals	35
mental climate	25, 181
mental legacy	156
mentality	28-29
Ministry of the Interior [the police]	43
nihilists	29
philosophical discussion	129
sagas	246
search for something to believe in	40
society	43
soldiers storming Berlin	26
spelling of Tolkien's name	73
Russian Revolution	30, 179, 193
Russian Tolkienism	33, 40, 42
is anti-establishmentarian	42
first wave of	30
second wave of	32
Rybakov (Russian author)	48
Ryurikoviches	280
Sackville, Sir Richard (1516-1566)	239
Sackville-Baggins	203-204, 207-208, 210, 212, 228, 239, 286
sacred forests	276
sacred texts	40-42
Saint John of Oxford?	38
Saint John the Baptist's Day (June 24)	243
Sam in Yakhnin's version	235

samizdat   15, 17-19, 22-25, 30, 49, 81, 166, 204, 211, 230, 239-240, 242, 261, 263, 267, 270
   continuations 30
   appearance of an author in 19
   reading 20
   the ideas in 20
   written out entirely by hand 19
sand-maniac 264
Sandeman, the House of 263
Sandman, the 262
Sandyman 205, 262-264, 286
Saruman 177, 180, 183
Saruman's temptation of Gandalf 176
Sauron 170-173, 177
Scadufax 269
scale, a little loose (on Smaug) 78, 79
scarlet standard (see also Red Flag) 28
school-yard bravado 112
science fiction 17
Second Age of Middle-earth 169
Secondary World 37, 43-44
   creation of 36, 40
secret police 186, 191
Secret Speech, Khrushchev's, in 1956 199
Sedov (comic book editor) 52
semantic lapses 136
sense of honor 152
senseless reprisals 199
sentence of death 193
sentenced to the camps 193
servant 146-147
Shadowfax 269-271
shape-shifting trains 283
Sharky (nickname) 194
Sherif 188
Sheriff 186-187
Shire 272-273, 286
   size of the 273
Shire-moot 222
show trial 191
Sigurd 79

Silver Crown of the Lords of Westernesse	18, 25
Skal'burg	240, 261
Skibniewska (Polish translator)	22
Skinfaxi	270
slang	197
Sleeping Forest	248, 262
Smallburrow	205, 212-213, 226, 263
Smaug	72-74, 79-83, 85
smith-craft	174
smoke	72
Snowmane	270
social climate in which Tolkien wrote	22
social climate of England in the 1930s	37
social transition	23
socialist realism	16
socialist utopia	185
soldier-servant (see also batman)	145
Soviet	
censor (see also censorship)	60
Communism	41
heaven, cliché for	60
heritage	26
history	185
inferiority complex	56
jargon	60
moral code	32
period	42
psychological baggage	189
reader	84
reading climate	65
social experiment	39
society	185
Soviet Union	55, 156, 171
Soviet Union collapsed	37
Soviet way of life	157
Soviet-era Russian readers	83
speaking names	263, 271, 284
spiritual values to fill the vacuum	37
squire	146
Stalin	80-84, 172, 175-176, 178, 185, 187-189, 191, 194-195, 198-200, 241, 265
apologist view of	198

destalinization	17, 84
Stalingrad	241
Stalinist terror	193, 195
State terror	179
state-controlled publishing industry	17-18, 23, 51
Sterling (science-fiction author)	35
Stoors	225-228
Strugatskij (Russian author)	46
stylization of Sam's manner of speaking	154
stylized parody of the jargon of secret police arrests	186
subtitles	33
Sumer	250
summer solstice	241
suspension of disbelief	38
Swedish translation	243, 258
swords and sorcery	132
taboo name	27, 218, 221, 276, 278
teenagers	33
temptation	169
Temptation of Gandalf	177
terror, revolutionary	179
physical terror	197
'Th' sound in Russian	223, 241
Thain (see also Hobbittan)	223, 286
The Annotated Hobbit	53
"The Big Bad Cockroach"	83
The Black Book of Arda (Nienna's book)	29-30, 34
"The Monsters and The Critics"	130
The New Adventures of Dunno (Karlov's book)	232
"The Quest of Erebor"	191
"The Red Book of Hergest"	264, 267
"The Red Book of Westmarch"	27, 265-268
"The Red Flag"	28
The Riddle of Stalin's Death (Avtorkhanov's book)	200
"The Scarlet Book of Westmarch"	264-267
"The Scouring of the Shire"	185
"the thaw" in Soviet literature	17
The Three Fat Men (Olesha's novella)	225
The Wind in the Willows	211, 232
Thorin Oakenshield	85, 94-95

thunder and lightning in the mountains at night	61-65
thunder-battle	64-65
titles, number stocked in bookstore	24
Tolkianity	34, 38, 45
Tolkien, Christopher	45
Tolkien, Edith	167
Tolkien - read "out of context"	31
Tolkien fans	33
Tolkien scholars	33
Tolkien Text Translation Group (TTT)	25
Tolkien, the "visionary"	35
Tolkien's books impression of	29
Tolkien's mythology	41
Tolkien's own biography	31
Tolkien's philosophy	123
Tolkien's political views	16
Tolkien's pre-Christian world	41
Tolkien's world and his text are not synonymous	40
Tolkien, perception of	26
Tolkienesque poems, parodies and stories	26, 35
Tolkienia	45
Tolkienian Church	42
Tolkienian reality	44
Tolkienian reality is broader than the text	40, 45
Tolkienism	29-30, 33, 41, 43-45
Tolkienism as a religion	43
Tolkienism as it exists in Moscow	43
Tolkienism in Russia	31, 34, 42
Tolkienism is anti-authoritarian	43
Tolkienism is really a misnomer	33
Tolkienist temple	45
Tolkienists	44
who have not read Tolkien	40, 42
tolkinutye	34, 36, 45
Tolstoy (Russian author)	48
Tolstoyanism	48
Tookland	225, 272
toponymy	209, 210, 266
British	237, 245, 272-273
Russian	211, 214, 230, 237, 240, 245-246, 272
Welsh	215, 248

touched in the head by Tolkien (tolkinutye)	34, 36, 45
Town Hole	274, 286
Transfiguration	142
transitional period: 19th to 20th century	23
translation as a method of self-expression	25
translation boom	21, 23, 33, 35
translation of the movie	33
translation of the nomenclature (see also names)	203, 284
translations, numerous competing	24-25, 45
transliterating English names	233
transliteration	189, 239, 282
Trauberg	20, 108, 182
treatment of female characters	165
tree	276, 278
tree of knowledge	176
Treebeard	275, 277, 286
trial	192
show trials	186, 191-192, 201n
Nuremberg Trials	190
Trotsky (Soviet politician)	179
TTT (Tolkien Text Translation Group)	25
Tuckborough	225
tweens	249
twentieth-century society	29
typewriters	19
typographical error	63
U.S. Cavalry	262
Umanskij (translator)	18, 22, 27, 51, 53, 82, 113, 122, 223
underground movement	36
Underhill	212, 263
understatement (see also British understatement)	38
uppish	195
usefulness	98-99
Utilova (translator)	52, 100
Valar	42
Valhalla	95, 97, 99
VAM (translator)	22, 24, 28, 32, 91, 122, 216, 223, 229, 232, 237, 272, 285
Varangians	278-280
Variags	278-280, 286

veche (Russian governing body)	220
Victorian era	22-23
Volkovskij (translator)	24, 28, 139, 187, 197, 208-210, 227-229, 239
Wardens of the Westmarch	268
Wargs	279, 281-283, 286
We (Zamyatin's book)	174-175, 177
Welsh-Russian linguistic relationship	248
Welsh Marches (see also march)	266
werewolf	282
West, The	55, 59-61, 63-65, 68
child of the kindly	60
Westmarch	266-268
wheels	175
willpower	112
wisdom	21, 130, 134, 173, 175-177, 181
ultimate	177
true	129-130
Witenagemot	219
wolf	283
Wood-elves	57, 59-60, 74, 91
World War I	37, 145, 148-149, 151, 162-163, 167
World War II	26-29, 132, 145, 171-172, 187
worth	98
Woses	276
Wright brothers	58
xUSSR	23
Yakhnin (translator)	24, 33, 133, 172, 177, 191, 217, 234-235, 256, 285
Yakovlev	52, 73
Yezhov	194-195, 198-200
yoke of reason	175
Zabelina	22
Zamyatin (Russian author)	174-177, 181
zanni	234

About The Author

Mark T. Hooker is a visiting scholar at Indiana University's Russian and East European Institute (REEI). Retired, he conducts research for publication. His articles on Tolkien have been published in English in *Beyond Bree* and *Tolkien Studies*, in Dutch in *Lembas* (the journal of the Dutch Tolkien Society) and in Russian in *Palantir* (the journal of the St. Petersburg Tolkien Society. He is the author of *The Military Uses of Literature* (Praeger, 1996), *Implied, but not **Stated*** (distributed by Slavica, 1999) and *The History of Holland* (Greenwood, 1999). He recently presented a paper on the Harry Potter vs. Tanya Grotter controversy at the first international Harry Potter Conference, Nimbus-2003. He is a graduate of the Russian Advanced Course at DLIWC.

: ХОББИТ : ВЛАСТЕЛИНЪ : КОЛЕЦЪ :
: БЕГГИНСЪ : ТОРБИНС : СУМНИКС :
: ХОББИТШИР : ХОББИТАНИЯ : ШИР :
: ЕДИНОЕ : КОЛЬЦО : ВСЕВЛАСТЬЯ :
: CAN : YOU : NOT : READ : THE : LINES :
: ABOVE? : THEY : ARE : IN : RUSSIAN :

About Walking Tree Publishers

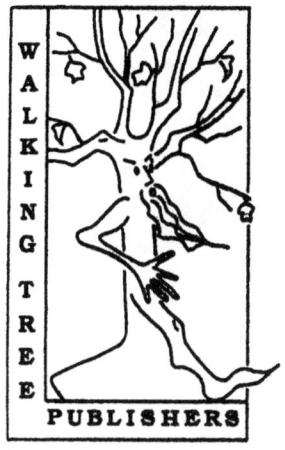

Walking Tree Publishers was founded in 1997 as a forum for publication of material (books, videos, CDs, etc.) related to Tolkien and Middle-earth studies. Manuscripts and project proposals can be submitted to the board of editors (please include an SAE):

Walking Tree Publishers
CH-3052 Zollikofen
Switzerland
e-mail: walkingtree@go.to
http://go.to/walkingtree

Publications:
Cormarë Series
News from the Shire and Beyond. Studies on Tolkien.
  Edited by Peter Buchs and Thomas Honegger.
  Zurich and Berne 1997. (Cormarë Series 1) (currently out of print).
Root and Branch. Approaches towards Understanding Tolkien.
  Edited by Thomas Honegger. Zurich and Berne 1999. (Cormarë Series 2)
Richard Sturch. *Four Christian Fantasists. A Study of the Fantastic Writings of George MacDonald, Charles Williams, C. S. Lewis and J.R.R. Tolkien.*
  Zurich and Berne 2001. (Cormarë Series 3)
Tolkien in Translation.
  Edited by Thomas Honegger. Zurich and Berne 2003. (Cormarë Series 4)
Mark T. Hooker. *Tolkien Through Russian Eyes.* Zurich and Berne 2003. (Cormarë Series 5)

Forthcoming:
Translating Tolkien.
  Edited by Thomas Honegger. Zurich and Berne 2004. (Cormarë Series 6)

Tales of Yore Series
Kay Woollard. *The Terror of Tatty Walk. A Frightener*.
  CD and Booklet. Zurich and Berne 2000.
Kay Woollard. *Wilmot's Strange Stone*.
  CDs and Booklet. Zurich and Berne 2001.

www.ingramcontent.com/pod-product-compliance
Lightning Source LLC
Chambersburg PA
CBHW070721160426
43192CB00009B/1272